Al
Merry Christmas '85

Randy & Diane

Those Bittersweet Schooldays

THE LITTLE WHITE SCHOOLHOUSE

Volume III

Those Bittersweet Schooldays

John C. Charyk

Western Producer Prairie Books
Saskatoon, Saskatchewan

COPYRIGHT©1977 JOHN C. CHARYK
WESTERN PRODUCER PRAIRIE BOOKS
Saskatoon, Saskatchewan

All rights reserved. No part of this publication may be reproduced, stored in a retrieval system, or transmitted, in any form or by any means, electronic, mechanical, photocopying, recording or otherwise, without the prior permission of the publisher.

Canadian Cataloguing in Publication Data

Charyk, John C., 1908-
    The little white schoolhouse

    Includes indexes.
    Contents: v. 1. The little white
schoolhouse. - v. 2. Pulse of the community. - v. 3. Those bittersweet schooldays.
    ISBN 0-919306-08-X (v. 1)
    ISBN 0-919306-87-X (v. 3)

    1. Rural schools - Prairie Provinces.
I. Title. II. Title: Pulse of the community. III. Title: Those bittersweet
schooldays.
LB1568.C2C46   372.9'712   C70-2407 rev.2

Cover painting by Don Frache

Printed in Canada by
MODERN PRESS
1
Saskatoon, Saskatchewan

TO

My Mother and Father, Anna and John Charyk,

and

to all those pioneers across Canada who, in one way or another, contributed their precious time and energy towards making the rural schools of our land a truly proud moment in the growth of a great Canadian nation.

*The roots of education are bitter,
but the fruit is sweet.*

— ARISTOTLE

Contents

Preface

Yes, here is another book about the one-room country schoolhouse. It is a companion volume to *The Little White Schoolhouse* and *Pulse of the Community,* and follows the same pattern of narrating. A goodly number of people encouraged me to continue my efforts towards recording the history of the rural school so it pleases me to be able to say, "Here is volume three of *The Little White Schoolhouse!*" However, this was not the only reason for writing the book, for I had educational and historical commitments to fulfill.

When Alfred Lord Tennyson put the words, "I am a part of all that I have met," in the mouth of Ulysses, he expressed an appropriate definition of learning. Education is not limited to what is ordinarily taught in the classrooms, but includes every aspect of living. There are no neutral moments in education. What you are today is the result of all you saw, heard, felt and did yesterday. Changes in the learner's behavior, for good or bad, take place continually, and ensue from the nature of his environment and the manner in which he relates to it.

The part of education that goes on in school is organized, structured and assisted; hence, it is more effective and efficient than any random activity in the world at large. There is no way that the natural curiosity of a child will prompt him to seek out the knowledge, the information, the discipline and the skills which he requires. In addition, it is in the school environment that each student develops to his maximum potential as a contributing and participating member of society, rather than a selfish individual pressing his own interests, and achieving his own goals. The aim of education is to pass on inherited wisdom and this can only be achieved in schools that have been organized for this purpose.

Education, with its organized and unorganized aspects, is influenced by a variety of societal, economic, political, scientific and spiritual changes that are taking place continually. Therefore, the purpose of this book is to show how a number of such factors affected the education of the rural child in the first half of the twentieth century. It must be noted that an account or an evaluation of a system of education in any particular period of time cannot be truly given unless the conditions that formed the setting within which it operated are also included.

I wish to express my thanks and appreciation to the hundreds of people across Canada who in one way or another supplied me with pertinent historical information. Such first-hand knowledge enabled me to bring *Those Bittersweet Schooldays* into fruition. The various archives I visited in Western Canada were most cooperative and helpful in providing me with any historical material they possessed on the topic of rural education. In addition, much valuable information was gleaned from the hundreds of local history books appearing on the market in increasing numbers. Such books are proving their worth to many history research workers and I am sure, judging from my own experience with these publications, they will become even more important in future years.

All the people and organizations referred to above can rest assured that they have had an integral part in making it possible for me to write *Those Bitterwsweet Schooldays*. For this I am grateful to them all.

1

Farming Was a Way of Life

The rural scene of today is so vastly different to that of a few decades ago, that harkening back to any period prior to World War II is to enter into another world. The changes have been many, but whether all of these have been for the best is a matter of opinion. Somewhere along the way many worthwhile things have been lost. Some of the innovations haven't been for the best as time has shown. Education is one such loser.

During the heyday of the one-room country school, the way of life of that period produced boys and girls that were the best and largest pool of capable and successful citizens from which the nation had to draw. Rural life established a sense of values and obligations which made for success in whatever fields the youngsters entered. A veteran officer of World War II avers that the best soldiers the armed services had were those with farm backgrounds. Farm youth proved equally efficient in industry.

Farming was, in a very real sense, a way of life in that era. But as time went on, farming gravitated towards a way of earning a living, and finally became a straight dollars-and-cents proposition. Such changes in attitudes brought corresponding modifications in the goals towards which education was morally bound to strive. No one needs to be reminded of the results.

Schools must keep two basic considerations in mind if they are to function effectively in society. First, education must recognize and accept the inherent nature of man; second, education must satisfy the fundamental demands of the social order of the day. Everything the students become depends on all they did, saw, heard and felt during the time of their youth on the farm. Hence, to understand these intrinsic and stimulating factors of rural education, it is necessary to familiarize oneself with farm life as it existed in Western Canada between the two world wars.

The pattern of development of the agricultural areas of Western Canada varied somewhat and proceeded at different rates in the prairie areas, the park lands, the bush country, the coastal environs, the mountainous sections and the forested regions. Yet, paradoxically, farm life in one region did not differ appreciably from that which existed in any other part.

A quarter-section of land was the economic unit which began agricultural Western Canada in its truest sense. It was home and livelihood for the majority of the prairie farmers. Farming then was an out-and-out cooperative effort. The father was the owner-manager-employee of the farm, but the mother was no less important in a commercial and provisional way. Furthermore, the children were partners in the enterprise and just as essential to its successful operation as the adults. Through the varied and intensive training and experience provided by the farming activities the youngsters became self-reliant and capable.

Farm life, as the boys and girls knew it, revolved about animals and plants. The horse was the basic unit of power with the tractor gradually taking over.

Where the horses provided the power, the size of a farm was determined by the capacity for work of a six-horse team. Consequently a half-section was the ideal size. It afforded ample pasture and hay for the cows and the horses and included about as much cropland as one man could cultivate with any type of horse-drawn vehicle.

Working a six-horse outfit was not easy. The farmer was up early in the morning to feed, water and harness the horses before breakfast and out in the field by seven o'clock at the latest. Horses moved at a rate of two miles per hour, so it was an average day's work to seed twenty-five acres with a twelve-foot, twenty-four-run drill, or to plough five acres with a fourteen-inch gang plow. The outfit was brought in at noon to feed and rest the horses, as well as to enable the farmer to have his own dinner. Then it was back out to the field, sometimes a mile away. When it was time to stop for the day, the man and horses had put in a ten-hour day. It was probably longer for the teamster, as he still had to attend to the horses after the day's work in the field was done.

The type of work on the farm varied with the seasons. The first job, just before the spring work got underway, was to clean the grain by putting it through the manually-operated fanning mill, or haul it to the elevator in town, where it was cleaned speedily by power machinery. Next, feed for the work horses had to be readied. This required crushing enough chop and filling the barn loft with the best hay of the previous year's crop. When time permitted, the sets of harnesses were checked and any necessary repairs made. If the work horses had been running loose all winter they were brought in and a feeding and retraining program was initiated to prepare them for the hard work ahead.

Once the spring work got underway, it kept rolling along until all the grain was seeded. This was followed closely by summerfallowing and fencing, two demanding tasks that continued all summer until interrupted by the haying season. So during the long, hot, dry days, the mower, the hay rake or buck pole, pitchforks and hay racks would take over from the discs and the post-hole auger.

Haying was probably the best season of the agricultural year. It wasn't an easy task. The hours were long, the sun hot (or there was no haying), and the work strenuous. Still, this was the time of year most enjoyed by the farmers. There isn't anything associated with farming more than the fascinating aroma of newly-cut or curing hay. Whether it was put up in windrows or in stacks, the mowed grass was soft, springy and pleasant to walk upon. Besides, it contained a sweetness which all hands seemed to discover sooner or later, inducing each one of them to go around with a piece of grass dangling from the corner of his mouth. Riding a mower or rake also gave a young fellow some time and solitude in which to meditate and self-evaluate. There was also the unselfish satisfaction in knowing that because of their hard work food was being garnered for the livestock for the approaching winter.

In the meantime, if the farmer wasn't crowded for time, he took another swing at the summerfallow, transforming it from the telltale green to the desirable velvety black.

The fields of ripening grain were a constant reminder to the farmer that he had better put the binder in shape. This was a major undertaking each year and always took more time than anticipated, probably not for the actual time spent in repairing it, but for the hours lost in seeing how badly some of the parts had worn. Sooner or later, the temperamental machine would be operable and could be seen making its rounds, spewing a trail of sheaves as it slashed through the waving expanse of golden wheat. Nothing was more novel than to watch what appeared to be a lone binder whip travelling on the horizon under its own power, until the accompanying horses and binder burst into view. However this was not the time for resting and wondering, but the time for stooking, an operation where every minute counted. Anyone able to lift a sheaf of wheat, old or young, male or female, was pressed into service. Visitors who showed up on the farm during this busy season were no exceptions and did their stint. Although the pace was hectic, it did slow down or stop entirely on occasion, as this story from the Elbow S.D. (Elbow, Sask.) shows.

During harvest one year, when both girls of a respected family were home from town for a couple of days, they donned overalls to help out with the stooking. Spying a man on horseback heading their way and not wishing to be seen in male attire, they crawled into a stook and left the boys to talk to the visitor. He stayed quite awhile and some of the sheaves that had been stacked hastily to cover the girls' hideout toppled over, causing the observant young man to remark about the poor job of stooking. When he finally left, the "proper" young ladies were glad to crawl out of their cramped quarters.

The climax of the agricultural season came with the threshing. This was the time everyone looked foward to — even the women, who had to cook for large gangs of men and to bring out meal-sized lunches to the threshing rigs. It was also the interlude during which neighbors, more than at any other time, got together and helped one another.

The demands of threshing were especially challenging for the young farm boys, as many looked forward to fulfillment of an ambition in the act of pulling up to the feeder of the separator with a full load of wheat sheaves, wrapping the lines around the standard with a flourish, and pitching the sheaves into the ravenous jaws of the growling separator, with the blades whirling and chopping into the bundles. It required a few days of toughening up and getting familiar with the rigid routine but by the end of the threshing run the lad felt he could pitch bundles for the rest of his life and not get tired. And then there was the joy of stopping off at the lunch basket and knowing full well, for the first time, that he had earned his lunch and had it coming. It also meant a good deal to the rookie to become an accepted member of the threshing crew. Now he went to bed in the hayloft or bunk car with the men, instead of being relegated to the farm house like a child.

The men who worked beside him were often interesting, if not always pleasant. There was always the one character in the gang who had a knack of telling stories and cracking jokes, someone else who possessed enough musical ability to be able to sing or to play a mouth organ or comb, and then there was the inevitable truth-stretcher who no one could believe. The fine spirit that characterized a good gang made the experience an enjoyable and broadening one for a shy farm lad.

Once the threshing and tidying up was completed, the routine changed to fall field work interspersed with sessions of digging potatoes and garnering the rest of the garden produce. In the main, the farmers directed their attention to fall plowing or discing to reduce the work that would have to be done in the spring. Such work continued until freeze-up.

Low temperatures signalled a solid roadbed for heavy wagons, so trips were made to the coal mines or to the grain elevator's coalsheds in the nearest town, to lay in a supply of coal for the winter. Besides, there was wood to be hauled and cut, green feed to be stacked, butchering to be done, and the ice-house to repair. In fact it was a relief to see the snow come, if the farmer was ready for it. Any change was welcome after driving an outfit in the field all summer, stooking and threshing all fall, and hauling coal and wood after that.

Winter, despite the snow and the cold, was a restful time on the farm. There were still a few demanding tasks, such as taking care of the livestock and hauling the grain to market, but the hours were never as long or as tedious as in summer. Most farmers remember lighting the lantern and walking out to the barn every evening to check on the stock. They dawdled along the feed alleys admiring the animals and throwing back into the mangers any hay or green feed that had been pushed out. The horses and cows seemed to be so contented, warm and snug in their stalls. This was quite a contrast to the livestock running out in the cold, or the farmer who had to haul grain to the elevator all winter.

It was no easy task to shovel grain by hand from the granaries into wagons or sleighs in the winter time, then sit on the load exposed to the elements for hours as the team walked all the way in with the heavy load. The drivers often walked most of the way as well for it was too cold to remain inactive on top of the grain tank. Once the wheat was unloaded at the elevator, the horses were driven to a convenient spot near the livery stable, unhitched, watered, fed, and rested before the return trip was begun. Once at home, the farmer immediately loaded up again and made any other necessary preparations for getting an early start the next morning. This routine continued all winter or until the necessary amount of wheat had been hauled into town. Some farmers lived so far away from any elevator that they required two days, or more, to make the round trip.

In addition to these seasonal duties there were others from which there was no periodic reprieve; some had to to be done every day. These included such essential chores as milking, separating, feeding and watering the livestock, cleaning and bedding the stalls and pens, fixing fences, checking on the well-being of every animal on the farm, and repairing at a moment's notice anything from the burnt-out grates on the kitchen range to the broken piston rod on the wind mill.

Few men who took up farming had much practical experience, so the vocation was spiced with challenges for them. It was through trial and error, hard work and love for the land that they eventually succeeded in the innumerable activities that went into the make-up of farming.

For the women, the routine of homemaking and child care was marked by loneliness as they attended to the needs of the farm while their husbands worked long hours in the field or helped neighbors many miles away. They felt utterly helpless and alone when, as darkness fell over the prairie, they went outside to listen hopefully for the sound of a wagon rumbling in the distance, the screech of bob-sleigh runners on the icy road, or the rattle of heel chains, that would mean their men were coming home. They never knew what was delaying the men, and at times like this, the human mind conjures the worst. Telephones were few and since most women had babies and one or two other young children at home, there wasn't anyone to send out searching. All any woman could do was to keep a good light in the window and wait, wait and wait.

Added to all these uncertainties were other threats: strange noises in the night that might be a wild animal prowling around the farmyard; a sick child tossing fretfully in a fever, the mother knowing full well that medical help was scarce and not within easy reach. To many, raised off the farm, there was the additional burden of unfamiliar work. They had to do everything for themselves whether it was sewing, knitting, tending fires, making bread, milking cows, churning cream, raising poultry, canning fruit, gardening, or helping each other during times of birth and death. Yet these women took to the hard life without a backward glance and with a faith so strong that the transition to the new life on the farm was achieved because they steadfastly refused to admit defeat. They laughed, they cried, they dreamed, they worked and in the end most of them made good.

Myra Stilborn, a former rural schoolteacher in Saskatchewan, recalled these bittersweet moments of anxiety:

> Mother, every so often, went outside and stood in the dark and the cold listening for the sound of jangling harness. It didn't bring Dad any sooner but it helped unwind her tightening nerves. When he came, Duke barked with joy, and all the sounds in the house became normal again. As Dad ate his belated supper, he told us what happened in town, and then we gathered around while he read us the weekly news of Andy Gump.

For the rural children there was work too — plenty of it. But it wasn't called work when the youngsters did it; instead, it was called "chores". They never complained of boredom or of having nothing to do, for a multitude of these chores awaited them at every turn. Old railway ties or logs had to be held down while sawed into stove lengths, blocks of wood had to be chopped and piled, cows brought in and milked, pigs, calves and chickens fed and watered, water pumped, gopher poison set out, coops and barn cleaned, kindling split, slop pails emptied, coal buckets filled, ashes taken out, eggs collected, gardens weeded, horses groomed, rocks picked, straw stacks burned, and butchered hogs scraped. There seemed to be no end to the number of hand-cranked appliances on the farm that had to be turned: the grindstone, fanning mill, cream separator, washing machine, meat chopper, coffee grinder, gramophone, egg beater, ice-cream freezer, forge, grist mill, blacksmith's drill, the kitchen-range grates, and best of all — the crank on the new automobile.

At first it was a matter of helping their father or mother do them, but once the routine of doing a particular task was learned it became theirs and theirs alone to do. These small areas of responsibility usually started with calves and colts, and to make sure the children had a vested interest in what they were doing, they were given animals of their own. Thus they learned that the welfare of the calf, the colt, or the chickens depended on them and their ability to do a good job of caring for their new possessions. Children also were awarded the privilege of naming any newly-born animal and this gave them an added interest in the newcomer.

Mothers began teaching their daughters at a tender age to do the chores that usually fell to the farm women. Before girls were out of their teens they could build a fire in the range or heater, cook, bake bread, churn, kill, pluck, eviscerate and disjoint chickens, sew, mend, wash, iron, can fruit and vegetables, make beds and clean the house from attic to cellar. The training the youngsters received on the farm made the boys well-qualified agronomists and the girls home economists. By the time the children were

-- Ethel VanBrunt

Len Lukey and Jim VanBrunt make ice cream for the Sunday dinner.

ready to leave school, they knew that money had to be earned through làbor.

A rural education helped train the children to survive once they started life on their own. The children attended school and at the same time learned farming, home economics and family living at home. It is only lately that homes have commenced to abdicate these duties to others.

One principle responsibility delegated to the children was getting the cows. Although this was just a daily routine for a farm lad or lass, there are men and women today who trace their love of nature to the time in their youth when it was their responsibility to bring home the cows. It was good to be alone at such times. The sweep of the wide prairie beneath and the billowing white clouds against a deep blue sky above, appeared like a vast backdrop ready for the performance of some great pageant. Plants and animals seemed to abound everywhere and it was up to the twelve-year-old to condition his eyes to see, his ears to hear, his nostrils to scent, and his mind to notice and appreciate the wonders of nature. Sloughs, edged with colored profusions of wildflowers and lush greenery, dotted the landscape indiscriminately, while the quacking ducks and trilling blackbirds provided a melodious interlude. The smothering fragrance of the prairie rose and the sweet smell of the newly-mown hay contrasted sharply with the warm, yeasty breath of the cows. Even the cattle, plodding homeward with their patient, phlegmatic tread and swaying udders heavy with milk, loomed like gaunt shadows in the fading reddish tints of the setting sun. It was glorious

-- Mrs. B. Campbell

No matter how young a child happened to be, he was responsible for certain chores. Here is David Campbell, aged four, shelling peas.

-- Edwin A. Anderson

Feeding the pigs was an onerous chore.

-- Mrs. Phyllis McDonald

Feeding the calves had its problems.

to be able to enjoy God's good earth at a time like this. Not many rural people ever forgot such an experience.

Getting the cows was not without its serious or lighter moments.

One lad experienced difficulty in getting his milk cows out of the thick bush and separated from the rest of the cattle in the common pasture. When he finally managed to get them home, his father, who was at the gate to help him corral them, noticed a strange cow in the herd and scolded him for not knowing his own cows. An attempt was made to chase the intruder out but she absolutely refused to go. The boy was sure she belonged to them, but seeing the mood his father was in, did not dare voice his opinion. Eventually, the mother, wondering what all the fuss was about, came out to see, and after being briefed, looked the cow over carefully. She assured them it was theirs. The animal had lost her long horn that day and the father failed to recognize her. It took him awhile to live that one down.

A small girl in the Union Jack S.D. (Vulcan, Alberta) was asked to go for the cows as all the other members of the family were busy with the harvest. It took her longer than anyone expected. When she returned they understood why. She had rounded up all the steers as well as the milk cows.

One of the first major chores assumed by farm children at an early age was milking cows. To start with, they were given the responsibility for milking one or two of the more genteel and easy milkers, but as they gained experience and confidence they eventually ended up milking anywhere up to fifteen or more cows. There was no respite from this twice-daily chore. It didn't make any difference what the weather was like, whether it was a holiday or the Sabbath day, whether there were other jobs to be done, whether a person was returning or going to a dance, a party or picnic; the cows still had to be milked at approximately the same time every morning and evening. It was a disagreeable chore on a cold morning or evening, but probably much more disagreeable for the cow than for the milker. So who can blame the "critters" for doing their best kicking on such days. There would always be one "wise old girl" who stood quietly while the task was being performed, but as the milker turned and attempted to rise from the stool, she would land a foot right in the middle of his back. Under such circumstances it was difficult to maintain balance and at the same time prevent the milk from spilling. There was, however, one advantage to such physical and emotional outbursts: the milker felt a good deal warmer after such experiences.

Milking time had its compensations, as it was probably the most restful period of the morning and evening. The milker could work while seated on a stool with only the pleasant high-pitched sound of the streams of milk playing on the interior of the pail, and gradually deepening into throaty or gutteral tones as the pail filled and the head of foam built up, with the milk's fragrant heat rising like incense on the morning or night air. Evening milking in a corral was a good time to star gaze, meditate on the wonders of the heavens and enjoy the peace, solitude, and singular beauty of nightfall

-- Mrs. Strandberg

Youngsters learned to milk cows at an early age.

on the prairie. Training a kitten to catch a stream of fresh milk squirted at it always proved to be a comedy of errors. There was no lack of subjects for such fun, for it seemed the barn was the favorite maternity ward for most mother cats. Besides, these blessed events came thick and fast. It never took a smart kitten long to master the trick. Yet older people failed to see the levity of such a practice, so when the sportive child had to keep a wary eye on the parent while feeding the cat through the air, the result was often a kick from the cow and spilled milk.

It must have been vanity, but more than one milker believed that cows enjoyed his singing, humming, yodelling or whistling. Certain tunes apparently helped the milk to flow freely, while others agitated the animals to such a degree that they held back the milk and often aimed a vigorous kick in the direction of the would-be singer. Songs like "Schooldays" and "Over the Waves" went well, but "Bye, Bye Blackbird" and "Whistle While You Work" spelled trouble. People often wondered why some agricultural research worker didn't come up with a chart of the ten best songs by which to milk. Rural students often practiced for the Christmas concert while milking by repeating their lines for the play, saying their recitations, and exercising their voices for the Christmas choral numbers. Such rehearsals had a real and sympathetic audience — the livestock in the barn.

A scene that will probably never be repeated is that of the farmer carrying his milk pails and lantern to and from the barn on a winter's evening. The giant shadows cast on the snow by the man's moving body and legs and the swinging pails were grotesque indeed. To a casual observer, the blot of veering yellow must have appeared like a UFO flitting from house to barn and back, but not to the farmer on the next quarter section. He would turn to his wife and say, "I see John Young is a little late milking his cows tonight. I wonder where he's been?"

Separating the milk into skim milk and cream was the next chore and the cream separator, the machine that did the job, was not easy to operate. It usually stood in the back porch during the summer and in the kitchen in winter. As soon as the milk was brought from the barn after milking it was poured from the pail into the elevated supply bowl of the separator through a cloth or metal strainer. It took quite a bit of the farm woman's muscle to get the separator in high gear before it would work. As it was not uncommon to forget to place receptacles under the cream and skim milk faucets, occasionally the operator would find herself standing in a pool of skim milk (preferably not cream!) Once the cream had been separated it was poured into containers and lowered into the well or stored in the ice shed or ice well. Here it was kept sweet and fresh until it was made into butter or shipped to the creamery. The skim milk was fed to the calves and pigs, with smaller amounts retained for use in the kitchen. Again, if the housewife was neglectful and forgot to place drip cans under the two spouts after the pails had been removed, the floors, unless kept scrupulously clean at all times, became the breeding place for flies and bacteria. The back porch always had a milky odor about it, and this was very noticeable when a person first came in from the outside.

It might have taken a little time and energy to accelerate the cream separator to its working pitch, but once all the cream had been separated and the cranking had ceased, the smooth running gears continued to spin away merrily, and it was almost enough to give a person the "willies" to hear the grunts and groans inside the machine long after the separating had been completed.

The most boring chore, that of washing, scrubbing and sterilizing the various parts of the machine after each separating, was left for the women of the family. The sixty to ninety-five discs or cups, float, separation chamber, faucets, rings, supply bowl, strainer and all other such parts had to be rinsed in cold water, washed in hot, and finally scalded and set out to air. As the separator was a precision machine and operated at high speed, constant check had to be made of the oil-feed and lubrication systems. Any undue vibrations or telltale noises meant the man of the house had to take the machine apart and make repairs or adjustments. The cream separator had to be ready to operate every day, or it meant a financial loss to the family.

To the uninitiated and to the young farm boy, the assembling or dismantling of so many parts of the separator seemed very complicated. It only appeared that way. True, there was the outside chance of making a blunder, but the real secret of success was in making sure the cap on top of the separator chamber was screwed securely. A special two-prong wrench was provided for the purpose. When one considers the early methods of separating the cream from the milk, the mechanical separator must have been the invention of the century. As everyone knows, the oldest way was to set the milk in crocks or tin pans in a cool place and wait for the cream to rise to the surface. Another and later way was to set the milk in tall, narrow cans submerged in cool running water or ice water. The third method was to dilute the whole milk with a large quantity of cold water, thus causing the cream to rise to the top.

The ruralist's creed, "For youth, the three words of counsel are work, work, work," stemmed not only from necessity, but also from the fact that work dignified the individual. The dignity of labor depends not on what a person does, but how he does it. Once boys and girls learned to work, to respect it, and entered into it with some degree of enthusiasm, they continued to do so for the remainder of their years. Such a personal asset formed the basis for a happy and successful life. Many parents were firmly convinced that the devil found diabolic ploys for idle hands, so children were given enough work to ensure that the odious old gent was kept at a safe distance.

The following vignettes provide insights into the pedagogy of those years on the farm.

Elizabeth, a six-year-old of the Star S.D. 4071 (Wetaskiwin, Alta.), was responsible for getting the cows at milking time. One evening she got off her horse to chase a stray out of the brush, but found she couldn't get back on as she had been riding bareback. She tried again and again, even leading the old horse to a small knoll thinking she could mount from the top. It couldn't be done. In desperation she looked pleadingly at her four-footed friend. Finally, the wise horse knelt down on his front legs and lowered his head as if to say, "Now try it!" Elizabeth did. Using his mane for support, she climbed on his neck, then over his shoulders and finally to his back. Success was hers, but with some reservation.

A huge turkey gobbler was in the habit of chasing a couple of seven-year-old boys in the Rye S.D. (Dewberry, Alta.) The bird was so bellicose that the boys were told to take a club to it. They never did. Instead they waited for an opportune time to teach the rogue a lesson in their own way. Once when the gobbler was on the war path they were able to lead it into the toilet. There, within the safety of the confines of the place, they plucked its breast as clean as a billiard ball. The turkey never bothered them again. It carried the queer trademark for the rest of its life, as it never grew real feathers again in that spot; it only managed to grow a sort of humiliating down.

Very few people could see any use for a dead cow, except to drag it out in the field as bait for coyotes. This was not true of the children. As soon as putrefaction set in and the animal became inflated like a balloon, they had a ready-made trampoline. With a run and leap they landed on top and were bounced sky-high by the taut skin. It was fun! Some parents let the children discover the folly of their actions for themselves, others sounded words of warning. One can imagine the horrified mother shouting, "Girls, stop! What are you thinking of? The skin will split. Dad, you've no more sense than they have." "Well, if it splits they'd learn", was the likely philosophical reply.

Mistakes are a bitter part of learning as two girls in the Union Jack S.D. (Vulcan, Alta.) found out. They had been asked to burn one of the old straw stacks in the field, and as it was the first time they had been entrusted with such an important chore they were quite overwhelmed. No less impressive was the breath-taking beauty of the scene as they eagerly set fire to the mountainous straw stack. The flames flashed over the dishevelled surface. Where, but a moment before, there had stood a dark foreboding mound of straw, there now was red chaos out of which great flames leaped aloft waving snaky tongues of crimson and gold. Huge billows of smoke poured upward and, when caught by the night breeze, wandered off in all directions over the rubious and eerie countryside. It seemed fantastic that two little girls could cause such a cataclysmic spectacle. Imagine their disappointment after such a thrilling experience, to learn when they reached home, they had burned the wrong straw stack.

A fifteen-year-old lad was asked to take a truckload of wheat to the field and he remonstrated with, "I don't know how to drive it!" The simple advice he received was; "If you think it is easier to carry it, go ahead." He drove the truck.

The home was firm, decisive and a consistent schoolroom for the training of children. It wasn't unusual to see youngsters sent from the table for not behaving like ladies and gentlemen, or receiving a cuff on the ear for not rising respectfully to their feet the instant an elderly person entered the room, or extorted to give an apology if they passed in front of a person without saying, "Excuse me, please!" They were forbidden to carry tales about anyone. Boys learned to remove their headgear the moment they stepped into a house, or to tip their cap or hat whenever they passed adults they knew. The parents were obeyed without question and the majority proved to be demanding critics when it came to training their children in proper manners.

The teenagers of today wouldn't think much of what was considered a real treat by rural students of that day. Its realization came about when a boy was greeted in the morning with, "You can stay home from school today and do the harrowing." Such a labor of love consisted of driving four horses pulling several sections of harrows. The early models of drag harrows were not equipped with riding carts, so the teamster walked behind on the spongy cultivated soil, in the stifling dust stirred up by the horses' feet and the hundreds of teeth of the harrows. A lad couldn't be indolent on this daily fifteen-mile marathon, for admonition meant being sent back to school the next day.

A schoolmarm in the Myrtle S.D. 3942 (Kitscoty, Alta.) borrowed a horse and buggy to visit a neighbor who had promised to help her stitch squares for the afghan the school was making for the Red Cross. At noon the husband unharnessed the horse and put it in the barn, expecting to be in from the field to hitch it for the teacher in the evening. During the afternoon the teacher discovered a number of the squares were missing. She suddenly remembered that Olga had not been at school on Friday, so perhaps the remaining pieces were at her home. Since the girl lived three miles away, the problem was how to get there. Neither of the ladies nor the eight-year-old daughter of the farmer knew how to put the harness on the horse. As they sat around bemoaning their problem, the grade-two student suddenly came up with a suggestion. She remembered Eaton's catalogue and the pictures of horses and harness in it and thought they could follow the model. It was worth a try, so they took the book and hastened out to the barn to try their luck. By looking at the illustrations, they managed to get the horse harnessed and hitched to the buggy. The jigsaw puzzle must have been snapped together correctly for they completed their errand and sewing project with success.

Mrs. J. H. Junson, who attended the Bede S.D. (Melita, Man.) in the thirties, discovered, as thousands of others have, that living on a farm awakened her to the beauty and majesty of nature. She became increasingly aware of its kaleidoscopic moods and appearances from season to season.

What sweet memories I have of watching the wonders of a prairie spring unfold, as we bounced along to school in our little home-made cart. The first to be noticed were the big black crows cawing raucously as they flapped their way to a lonely tree. Then, a series of tinkling notes would announce that the little brown-horned lark had arrived, to scurry about in the short grass of the prairie. Soon after, on a fence post, would be seen a fat little meadow lark, his yellow vest and V-shaped black collar; tilting his head back he would proudly announce, "My wife's gone to Peterborough!" Who can ever forget the honk of the Canada geese, as those V-shaped wedges winged their way across the clear-blue sky, or the sudden shrill whistle piercing the early morning stillness, as a saucy gopher flicked his tail at you and called a warning to his friends?

Oh what excitement there was when we spied the first patch of beautiful mauve crocuses, wrapped in their furry gray-green jackets! Quickly, we would stop our pony to pick a few flowers for our teacher, and later for Mom on the way home. There was also the thrill of seeing the first pussy-willows, the wonders of a prairie slough, and the endless delights that made spring my favorite time of the year.

Another moving memory was the sight of an early morning mirage. A neighboring town, not visible the day before, was suddenly stretched out before our eyes along the horizon. How we marvelled at the sight!

Each season holds it treasured memories. In summer it was the tangle of gorgeous prairie flowers, and the graceful swooping of the sociable swallows from home, which often kept us company for a mile or more on our way to school.

In the autumn it was the plumes of bright yellow goldenrod, the waving seas of ripening grain, and the delightful fragrance of the fall. How excited we would be, when we turned into the last field on our way home, and discovered that the Kruger steam-powered threshing outfit had pulled into our field, in our absence. Can you not smell the fragrance of that freshly-threshed straw, as the separator spewed forth a golden stream to form a straw pile below? I can still see the racks and teams of horses dotting the field as the men gathered up the precious stooks for the harvest. Our school pony, Tiny, would then revert to her favorite job, as a cattle pony, and I would bring in the cows for Dad, who was busy with the harvest.

Bringing in the cows was my favorite job, too. I would sit and dream the sweet dreams of youth, as that little pony wound her way back and forth rounding up the cows. Then we would wend our way home through the twilight — a cowbell tinkling on the quiet air.

-- Mrs. Strandberg

Alf and Inga Strandberg feed a flock of chickens.

There are bitter memories, too. I remember days when our brave pony took us safely home through the choking dust storms of the 1930s. There were times when we could not see our home trees from less than one-eighth of a mile away. I can still feel the grit of sand in my teeth and eyes.

Bitter memories still persist of cold fingers and toes, as we made the trip to school in the not-so-pleasant late fall and early winter days. When the snow got too deep, Tiny and our trusty cart had a rest until spring time came once more.

A chicken may seem to be a mundane creature to the present generation, but to the farmer of the past it meant food, survival and some ready cash. Practically every farmer used to raise a few chickens for these reasons. In addition, the birds required very little care as they scrounged most of their own food during the summer, reproduced prolifically, and best of all gave the farm child his first major responsibility and viable interest in the farm when he began to look after the chickens.

Chickens were raised in the "natural way," or as most farm women preferred to say, "by hand". This meant setting ten to fifteen hens every spring, keeping an eye on them during the hatching period, and surveillance of the baby chicks. The latter often meant bringing the chicks into the house during a cold spell or when the mother hen deserted her brood, and bedding them down behind the stove in a box lined with old newspapers. If their stay became protracted, the routine of feeding, watering and cleaning grew into a demanding responsibility. There was also a note of sadness and loneliness expressed in the continuous cheeping of the forlorn chicks.

It was a common practice to borrow setting hens if the required number did not get broody in the group at home, or if it was the first attempt to start a flock. They were often carried in a sack on horseback or in a buggy, and settled on eggs after the trip. Occasionally a pleasant surprise awaited the farmer's wife. After missing a hen for several weeks and crediting the coyotes for the abduction, lo and behold the absent one would return proudly leading a flock of baby chicks.

The setting hen, one that will set on a nest for weeks and weeks, determined to hatch something whether there is anything to hatch or not, proved a nuisance and an economic loss if her services as a mother were not needed. Instead of laying eggs she was wasting her time and talent by just setting.

Margaret Charters of Livingston S.D. (Drumheller, Alta.) remembers the time her mother attempted to break the habit of such a hen and get it back into egg production. Wise neighbors had informed her that a sure-fire method was to immerse the broody hen in a barrel of water and leave it there for a couple of hours. This was done. Unfortunately the water treatment extended beyond the recommended time as the hen was forgotten in the excitement created by a fast-approaching prairie fire, and to all appearances it was dead. The mother, feeling rather guilty, wrapped the body in a gunny sack, took it into the house and placed it in the oven, hoping the heat would revive the bird. Once again it was forgotten, this time because of the fervent conversation about their good fortune as the fire had been put out before reaching the pasture. Their animated talk was abruptly interrupted with a loud squawk and there was the old bird standing straight and tall in the middle of the kitchen floor. It was put out with the other hens, but the next morning it was back setting on a discarded door knob, as if nothing had happened. Drowning and roasting failed to break the habit of a determined brooder.

Incubators and brooders gradually superseded the setting hen, and later when commercial hatcheries came into being, it spelled her doom.

A careful vigil had to be maintained over a flock of chickens as coyotes, badgers, weasels and hawks constantly preyed upon them. A domesticated fowl didn't have the self-protective instinct of a wild one. When coyotes came slinking into the farm yard, many housewives frightened them away by beating dishpans with iron spoons. Others found that scarecrows placed in strategic parts of their yards made the attackers more wary.

In the fall of the year most flocks were thinned out by butchering the old hens. All hands on the farm pitched in to pluck, draw and quarter the birds and make them ready for canning. The jars of chicken were boiled in a washtub or boiler until every piece was thoroughly cooked. When this point was reached, each sealer lid was tightened until the container became airtight. Then it could be stored without any fear of spoilage. There was nothing more handy or more tasty to serve than canned chicken if company arrived unexpectedly. In addition, stewed chicken could be prepared quickly for a special Sunday dinner without the difficulties and inconvenience attending the butchering of a live one. This was particularly true on a cold blustery winter's day.

Eggs could be used for baking or as a complete food in themselves. Yet for the early farmers there were other considerations as well; they might trade them in at the grocery store for supplies or sell them for cash. "Egg money" could be designated as the secret weapon rural people used to survive bouts of economic adversity. Traditionally it belonged to the mother, and no one, not even the father, knew its exact amount from year to year. Yet, when a present was required for Christmas, when donations were being solicited for a wreath, when a child was in dire need of a pair of shoes, when a pedlar displayed a much-needed item, when a broken part of a farm machine couldn't be fixed, when it seemed appropriate to have a family morale booster in the form of a box of chocolates, or even if someone in the family dreamed of becoming a teacher or nurse, the required money appeared mysteriously. A book could be written about the various ways the "egg money" smoothed out some of life's rough spots. It's no wonder the value of the chicken to mankind and the philosophy of life of people during this era have both been immortalized by the simple phrase, "nest egg".

The slow-paced transportation and the lack of good roads restricted the range of normal travel of the farmer and his family to the immediate district. As a result, they did not look beyond their home community and town for their business dealings, educaton, recreation, religious interests, cultural pursuits, or entertainment. Rural people always had time to stop along the way and visit with each other, while their horses were resting. This explains why the early farmers seemed to know everyone over such a wide area of the country. The flow of young people from the farm to the towns and cities was light, so the population of a rural district was fairly well balanced, with representation from all ages and sexes. This led to a feeling of community solidarity.

Life on the farm was not all work but was lightened by various timely get-togethers held in a neighbor's house or the schoolhouse. Here the young were taught resourcefulness. They made their own fun and thought nothing of driving a team and a democrat, a single horse and buggy, or a cutter if there was sufficient snow on the ground, to a dance, box social, card party, talent night, house warming, or some other social activity, ten to twenty miles away. Baby sitters were a nonentity then and things were done together as family projects. There were sleigh rides, house parties and skating in winter; in the summer there were picnics, berry-picking excursions, visits to fairs and ball games. If the family went to a "do" in the schoolhouse and the small fry could no longer keep their eyes open, they were put on the desks and covered with coats or blankets. Then, when the local musicians had played the last note of the "Home-Sweet-Home" waltz, the small children were wrapped warmly in their coats and blankets, loaded into the sleigh, and along with the rest of the family, all went home. While the father and the boys put the horses in the barn, the mother and girls put the tots to bed and banked the fires for what little time remained of the night.

Sightseers, when they gawk inside a one-room rural school or an old-time farm house, find it hard to believe that so many people found room to dance. They did and no one was ever turned away. In fact, with so little space inside, there was no room for division of people into children, teenagers, adults, senior citizens, or for the creation of a generation gap. The mixed voices and laughter of young and old blended with a background of old-time music, reflecting a vibrant community tempered by happy, thriving family living.

Community clubs, with their concerts, plays, spelling matches, debates, and other edifying activities, functioned successfully in most rural districts. The talent displayed was not of the highest order but the important consideration was that everyone, gifted or not, was given an opportunity to participate in the community social and cultural activities.

Then, of course, rural families visited. Any message was an excuse for a visit and the whole family went. The latchstring was always out and all visitors welcomed as friends, not intruders. There seemed to be more time then, and with no phones available, messages were carried in person.

Neighbors were dependent upon one another for assistance in all aspects of country life and help was unselfishly given and received. The fact that money was scarce didn't stop people from carrying out transactions. They were willing to share time, ideas and whatever they possessed. It appeared that each had something another needed and conversely, each needed something the other had. Thus farm life was characterized by a strong spirit of cooperation.

Frequent bees were organized by the neighbors for doing work that would have been formidable, even impossible, for one family alone. They were especially useful in times of adversity, when a neighbor was sick during the harvest season and unable to cut his wheat, or someone else had lost his house or barn by fire and had no resources to replace the loss. In no time at all neighbors met to cut, build, plough, cultivate, seed, stack, thresh, raise a barn or do anything else that would help an unfortunate neighbor. The young shared and observed, learning all the time.

However, it was the simple acts of kindness shown from day to day that characterized true neighborliness among rural people. They firmly believed, taught and practiced the homespun adage, "A joy shared is doubled and a trouble shared is halved." The following prosaic incidents illustrate such a mode of living.

Since radios and telephones were few and far between, and the few newspapers were not only old, but passed eagerly from hand to hand, the early farmers depended on marking off a day on the calendar every evening to remember the day of the week. On one occasion a couple that was expected for dinner on Sunday arrived on Monday instead. Rural homes, of necessity, always had a supply of food on hand, so everyone fared well, but not in the manner planned originally by the hostess.

A bachelor in another community made a similar error but he was more fortunate than the couple mentioned above. After a hard week's work, he hurried through his chores, got dressed up and went over to attend church at a neighbor's house. He thought it odd that no one else showed up for the service, but he sat around making small talk with the farmer's wife, who courteously didn't ask why he had come dressed in his best suit. Eventually when she opened the oven door and began pulling out the crusty loaves of home-made bread, the confused church-goer concluded it wasn't Sunday. This hostess baking on the Lord's Day? Never! His visit wasn't a complete loss, for once his calendar was updated, he was briefed on last Sunday's sermon and treated to generous helpings of fresh home-made bread and copious draughts of ice-cold buttermilk. The neighbors were amused by his error and chided him for months about being such an expert farmer that he could afford to gad about on working days. Such innocent teasing often had a salutary effect. It did for this shy bachelor.

Spending so much time out-of-doors, in constant touch with nature, enabled farmers to see the beauty of the world about them. It could have been the dazzling prairie sunset, the gently unfolding petals of a flower, the flight of wild geese, or feathery flakes of softly falling snow, but whatever it was they felt the inspirational presence of a spiritual power, above and beyond man. So it wasn't surprising to find that Sunday on the farm was quiet, serene and restful, for both man and beast, a day dedicated to God. Everyone attended the church services held in the district whether they were of a particular denomination or not. The services, which either alternated from home to home, or were held in the district schoolhouse on a permanent basis, were under the direction of an ordained or student clergyman. Many of these young men were not schooled to understand rural life so they found it very discouraging. The work was strenuous, as there were at least three different appointments, about ten miles apart, under their charge. Even with such a heavy responsibility they often found time to form young people's groups so they could join in Bible study and outdoor sports. This was a vital part in the education of rural boys and girls.

The attempts of these city-raised sky-pilots to adjust to country ways were not without their embarrassing moments.

A student minister in the Riverton S.D. 2128 (Dewberry, Alta.) was driving down the road during a rainstorm in a most unorthodox manner. He was sitting on the edge of his buggy seat, with the reins in one hand and an umbrella, carefully poised over the rump of the horse, in the other. "Say, Reverend! What's the idea of protecting the horse and not yourself?" shouted a mouthy passerby. "I was told on good authority that under no circumstances must I permit the rein (rain) to get under the horse's tail," came the concerned reply.

A church service was to be held in a home in the Livingston S.D. (Drumheller, Alta.) and the hostess had invited the minister and a few neighbors to stay for dinner afterwards. She took a lot of trouble to prepare a sumptuous meal for all her guests. The children had just completed their Sunday school so the inexperienced minister thought it prudent to excuse them from the adult spiritual repast. Well, lo and behold, when the hostess repaired to the kitchen to set out the physical repast she discovered the youngsters had eaten everything, including the dessert! The sheepish minister became a firm advocate of combining children and adults in one service after such a dual feast.

A rooster persisted in crowing at the door of a farm house in the Tangleflags S.D. (Lloydminster, Sask.) where the service was being held. The concerned minister asked a member of the congregation to remove the bird. This was done, but the remedial measures proved to be more disturbing than the original calls. The noise accompanying the flapping of the wings and the clucks, cackles and squawks of the excited birds nearly proved the undoing of the service. Eventually order was restored and the clergyman went on with his eclipsed message, but not for long! A baby on his mother's knee had become quite interested in the rooster and his flock, and finding that the crowing had ceased, decided it was the appropriate time to substitute for the rebuffed bird. The hilarity that followed when the baby's cock-a-doodle-doos rang out across the room put an end to whatever spiritual thought the pastor was trying bravely to put across to his grinning congregation.

A farmer's life was not easy. Farmers endured many hardships and discouragements and the young suffered with them. In the early years the army worms invaded the farm lands of Western Canada. They appeared like a huge green carpet moving unrelentingly from west to east stripping every vestige of foliage along the way. Farmers found it difficult to stop or divert such a stream of destruction and by the time they found out what had to be done, their crops were devoured. One method was to plow deep furrows along the boundaries of the fields and pour old machinery oil in them. The instant the army worms tumbled into the oleaginous liquid they were snuffed out like candles.

Plagues of grasshoppers invaded certain areas periodically, so the men of the soil rushed to mixing stations set up by the government to secure their supply of poison bait. This was spread over the land by whatever method the farmer could devise.

At times the gopher population increased to such proportions that the pesky creatures became a real threat to the crops. This menace was controlled by the farmers scattering gopher poison (strychnine) near their burrows, while the municipalities looked at the long-term aspect of the problem and offered a bounty of one to three cents per gopher tail every year.

One year the gophers in the Morning Glory S.D. 2612 (Munson, Alta.) were becoming depleted. The children became concerned about this turn of events for it meant a corresponding decrease not only in gopher tails but in spending money. First they learned not to snare, trap or drown gophers until the young were born. This wasn't good enough. A couple of boys came up with the idea of trying regenerations. They decided on a heinous practice of removing a gopher's tail and then releasing it, in the hope that one or two replacements might sprout, just like those from a horseradish cutting. Obviously, they were not successful. This only proved rather frustrating for the rest of the hunters to catch an occasional bobtailed gopher.

Infestations by sawflies left the wheat stems so weak that the plants simply toppled over. There was little that could be done to combat this scourge until the agronomists produced sawfly resistant varieties.

Adverse weather conditions often resulted in hailed, frozen or dried-out crops. If this wasn't enough, plant diseases such as rust and smut turned entire fields of wheat into valueless grain infected with red or black-colored fungi.

Working conditions for both man and beast were far from ideal on the farm. Small clouds of stinging, burning, flying ants often plagued the busy men during the haying season. Nose flies stung the horses' lips, badgered the animals into constantly bobbing their heads, while the heel flies chased cattle knee-deep into sloughs for protection against the onslaught. On warm days and evenings, swarms of mosquitoes harassed both the farm people and their livestock. The hundreds of sloughs that served as breeding grounds for these prolific insects loaded the prairie grass and air with masses of tormentors that caused constant tail switching and head swinging of the farm animals, and forced rural people to protect their faces with netting, which was draped loosely over wide-brimmed hats and fastened snuggly around the shirt collars. During cross-country travels people had to defend themselves with leafy branches, or else put a pail of smudge on the wagon or the stoneboat to smoke away the mosquitoes. Smoke and cool nights gave the mosquito victims their only relief. Farmers adopted the practice of lighting smoldering fires for the protection of their livestock. Wild sage, useless for anything else, proved to be excellent for making a mosquito smudge. It exuded an acrid smoke that irritated the lining of the nose, brought tears to the eyes, but repelled even the most blood-thirsty mosquitoes. The farmers often used oil cans, wired to their machinery, to hold such wild-sage smudges. In this way, the farmers and their horses were protected in the field as they ploughed, disced or harrowed.

One farm woman was telling a friend that she couldn't understand the mosquitoes biting through the bed clothes at night. Then, to her horror, she discovered that the real culprits were bed bugs. There seemed to be no sure way of getting rid of these vermin except by a nightly rampage until all were exterminated. Bed bugs were carried from home to home in clothing, and since it was common practice to deposit the visitors' coats on beds, most likely the transfer took place at that time.

Lice were also easily passed on, and although they caused a rash that itched unmercifully twenty-four hours a day, there was a standard method of control: all-around cleanliness. Every sheet, blanket, quilt, pillowcase and piece of clothing had to be boiled and every member of the family bathed, scrubbed and their hair washed with coal oil and combed over and over again with a fine comb. This delousing process went on until all signs of nits disappeared.

Then, as if to add insult to the injuries already wrought by the vagaries of nature, the farmers had to contend with periods of economic recession, like the thirties, when they received very low prices for the produce they were able to raise only after untold difficulties.

Yet, in spite of problems associated with their vocation, the farmers remained a happy people, satisfied with their lot, occasionally depressed but not defeated, inspired by the fact they were feeding the hungry millions of this world and in a sense were their brothers' keepers.

Such lifestyles have convinced many educators that children raised on the farm receive a well-rounded education that cannot be equalled anywhere else. This was especially true in the period extending from homestead days to the advent of World War II and the end of "the little white schoolhouse" era. The following are a few of the positive factors that accrued for children brought up on a farm. These factors will be referred to throughout the book as they occur in various frames of reference.

In order to feel his life is worthwhile, an individual needs to acquire a sense of inner harmony and meaning for his life; he also needs to love, work and play on a balanced scale. The rural child learns at an early age that work is essential in maintaining life; he begins to notice right from the beginning the close relationship of work to such things as security, standard of living, and his own comforts. He observes how his parents work with nature, and he can actually see the results of their efforts. Such self-evident conclusions instill a feeling of order and purpose to daily living. He feels that his work, the daily chores he does, is a necessary part of the successful operation of the farm, and in turn he perceives his own individual worth and importance in the scheme of things.

Since farm work involves a considerable amount of cooperation, the child spends a significant amount of time with his parents in such endeavors. This is all to the good. The physical presence of the father and mother over extended periods of time make the child feel protected, secure and wanted. Besides, the youngster can only identify himself with the life values his parents want to pass on to him if he has ample opportunity to observe how they react to others and their responses to hundreds of situations that occur daily on the farm.

A good community is one that functions in a give-and-take manner among its individual members and a farm child is bound to notice very early that the mutual exchange of help is a part of successful living. Such a community feeling teaches and shows the youngster that a good neighbor is often essential for his own success, if not for his survival on the farm.

The rural youngster witnesses sex, birth and death as natural phenomena. Eventually the cycle of life and death makes sense because of its simplicity and normalcy and does not bother him. His need for love in life is fulfilled in many ways, for he learns to love the land, the animals, the crops, the everchanging scenery and even his parents' partnership with him.

The value of finishing chores impresses the young child when he or she discovers that recreation and play can be enjoyed much more fully afterwards. This tends to develop a sense of responsibility and feeling of inner satisfaction in him as he realizes he must work first and then enjoy his leisure time afterwards.

All the farm child's experiences in regard to love, work and play, become part of his character. He is not apt to become confused about the meaning of life in general or his own in particular, because he is needed by his family, not merely supported until he is grown.

2

Around the Family Hearth

The old proverb that philosophizes, "Man works from sun to sun, but a woman's work is never done," was true in the case of most farm women. This couldn't be better illustrated than by the story vouchsafed by a team of university students making a survey of rural life on the prairie. They asked one housewife how she spent her time, and as she paused for breath from a recital of a seemingly endless list of her chores, they clarified their question by explaining they had meant only leisure time. After a moment's hesitation she answered, "Oh, that's when I find time to go to the biffy!"

Preparing meals took considerably more time than it does today. Much of what we now eat, the modern housewife buys ready to cook or even ready to serve. Meals in the early days were set on the table only after hours of hard, tiring work in the kitchen over a hot stove.

Farmers were self-sustaining to a marked degree. Outside of quantity purchases of such staples as flour, sugar, salt and baking powder, the rest of the food was raised, either directly or indirectly, on the land. They grew their own vegetables and meat, made butter and bread, canned saskatoons, gooseberries, currants, chokecherries, strawberries or whatever wild fruits were available, and bought other fruit to preserve.

Fresh meat was hard to come by on a regular basis so a few farmers would get together and organize a beef ring. A steer would be butchered, divided into various cuts, and a member allotted his share according to the number of children and adults in his family. Each member provided one animal to kill during the summer. This arrangement enabled some rural families to have fresh meat every second week. If a meat ring could not be formed, the housewife canned most of the meat and cured some bacon and hams. This required several days of tedious labor whenever an animal was butchered.

Keeping food from spoiling was a real problem for rural people as refrigerators and deep freezes were still unknown. Ice-houses were used. Ice was cut from the river, lake or slough during the winter and packed in sawdust, straw or coal dust in some convenient granary.

-- Fred Rall

Picture shows ice harvesting in the early days.

Another means of preserving food was the ice-well. A pit was dug in the ground approximately three feet square and ten feet deep, and the inside lined with inch-lumber. When the temperature dropped below zero, clean snow was packed into the well to a depth of a couple of feet and then saturated with water. As soon as the layer froze the process was repeated until the space between the ice mass and the top formed a compartment of suitable size for the specific needs of that farmer. Milk, cream, butter, fresh meat and other perishable foods were stored in the ice-well. Clean straw was stuffed over and around the containers storing the food to insulate the top of the well. This kept the ice from melting too rapidly during the warm weather. True, the level of the ice dropped considerably during the summer due to melting, but with care it lasted until the cool weather arrived again.

Preserving meat in winter was no problem. A young steer and a couple of pigs were slaughtered, cut up into usable pieces and the below-zero temperature did the rest. In the spring, whatever was left was salted.

Hearty meals were necessary because everyone worked hard. To provide a nourishing, appetizing meal on a limited larder taxed the ingenuity of the housewives. It was impossible to run to the store for every notion as is done today. Days often went by before anyone in the neighborhood had a real need to go to town. Farmers didn't make very many unnecessary trips in those days when they lived some ten miles away, relied on horses or a Model-T car for transportation and the best roads were no more than rutted trails. The careful family, as always, was able to anticipate its culinary needs weeks ahead and experienced few problems. Ready or not, everyone was welcome to drop in uninvited for a meal and enjoy the best that was on hand. During the winter months there were no fresh fruits or vegetables aside from the occasional box of apples. Dried fruits were so common for desert that the prunes were affectionately named, "C.P.R. strawberries." Diets and allergies simply were not mentioned.

Today's families do not have the unique "talking pieces" about food that rural families used to have.

The Ward family in the Riverton S.D. bought two cows which the children promptly named Molly and Jenny. The animals became real personalities to the youngsters. A year or so later when it was decided to butcher Molly, their grief knew no bounds. Not one bite of poor Molly would anyone touch! However, when the first roast began to spread its aroma through the kitchen, the mourners could scarcely wait for dinner time. Such is the fickleness of human beings!

It took more than human confidence to plan for a birthday cake when no eggs were available and the farm could boast of only one laying hen, but fate intervened! The guests arrived and waited two hours for the hen to lay an egg. A successful birthday party followed and featured the most delicious cake the children ever tasted. Disappointment turned to victory through the valiant efforts of a mere hen.

The hunger which children acquired for common foods was fantastic. One family had run out of potatoes and when a neighbor dropped in to say he was going to town, he asked a five-year-old girl what kind of candy she preferred. The tot answered, "I don't want any candy, just potatoes." She watched eagerly for his return and when he arrived, she could hardly wait for her mother to cook the potatoes. There were other foods on the table as well, but the child ate only potatoes and made a complete meal of them.

The kitchen range was a necessity in the farm kitchen and nothing could take its place for comfort. Besides being the main source of heat, it served its legitimate purpose for cooking. This 400 pound black monster had a high back and stood about a foot or more off the floor on four curved legs that resembled the talons of an eagle. The cat could often be found sleeping somewhere under the range and it was an ideal spot for setting out wet mittens, stockings and overshoes to dry. The warming oven over the top of the range was designed to keep meals warm for late-comers and was considered indispensable on the farm, while the copper-lined reservoir at the side held the only ready source of warm water.

Anyone could see at a glance that life centered around the kitchen stove. Pans of rising bread and crocks of sour milk for cottage cheese sat on the top of the warming oven, while "hot" sadirons reposed in disarray at the back of the stove. Even the alarm clock from its position of importance on the top of the warming oven seemed to say, "Life is lived right here!" The singing kettle and the coffee pot seemed to agree for they always stood ready to refresh any neighbor who might happen by.

A most peaceful scene materialized in the evening when the entire family gathered near the kitchen range. No modern heating device can compare with the therapeutic warmth generated by a wood or coal fire. The children usually sat with their feet in the oven, toasting their toes, and either reading or doing their homework. Mothers preferred to relax in the rocking chair as they teetered back and forth and sewed or mended socks, while fathers liked to stretch out on a cushioned chair beside the table where they could stack their newspapers. Sometimes the family pursued its activities by the flickering light from the stove top with one of the lids askew. This may have appeared romantic but it was usually because they were out of coal oil for the lamps.

A must in the kitchen was the woodbox and coat scuttle. Nothing gave the household more satisfaction than seeing these two containers filled to overflowing. Anyone who has had to go out in the snow, or on a cold rainy morning for dry kindling, can appreciate why such a chore had top priority. The grown-ups were always happy when a child in the family became old enough to accept this responsibility. In addition to this task, there was the reservoir to be filled with water, the top of the stove to be kept black with stove polish, the nickel trimming to be scoured, and the ashpan to be emptied once or twice a day. This last task had to be undertaken cautiously, for the moment the door was opened the ashes flooded the kitchen floor, and hot sparks burned minute spots in the linoleum. Many such lessons were learned in the kitchen, but the knack of using the cross-cut saw, the axe, and the chopping block was perfected behind the woodpile. It was a comforting feeling to have stacks of poplar, spruce and willow firewood, piled high against the back porch or fence, all exuding a refreshing woodsy aroma.

In wintry weather, several rocks or sadirons were placed in the oven after supper. Then, just before the family retired for the night, these warm objects were wrapped in flannel pieces and placed in the cold beds.

The children shed their clothes behind the kitchen stove, and in the process absorbed as much heat as possible against the dread of the icy dash upstairs. Stoking or banking the fire was the last chore of the night. It was not unusual for the fire to die out during the night with dire results. By morning the bed covers or feather ticks, as well as the rafters in any unfinished rooms, were covered with frost. Girls took several minutes to release their tresses from the circles of ice on the blankets formed by the condensation of their breath. Downstairs, everything perishable which wasn't underground froze solid. The water in the pail, the bread and the milk suffered the same fate. The linoleum curled up around the edges and billowed in the middle from the cold. To prevent such a thing from occurring too often, the parents sometimes stayed up all night during any extended cold spell and kept the fires going.

Myra Stilborn reminisced about going to bed on a cold night:

> Mother said goodnight and took away the lamp. I slid down under a pile of covers until my feet found the hot irons wrapped in Dad's old

socks. Snow slapped spastic hands against the windowpane but I felt safe and warm. I heard Mother singing, "Trus-tan-dough-bay," as she washed the milk pails in the kitchen. I took a long breath of cold air; my fingers relaxed their hold of the bed clothes and today was gone.

The farm family was up early in the morning as each member had specific chores. If anyone was still sleeping by the time the father went out to feed the stock and the mother to start breakfast, the clang of empty pails, the bang of the coal scuttle, the clatter of the stove lids and the whine of the cream separator, acted as persistent alarm clocks. Soon the fire would be going and preparations for breakfast underway. The kitchen became "toastwarm," steamy with coffee and bubbling porridge, and smoky from the frying eggs and ham. In this breakfast haze the mother or one of the older girls filled the lunch pails.

When breakfast was over, the children did the dishes, placing their dishpan on the top of the stove or the kitchen table. Hot water was obtained from the reservoir on the stove. The washing and drying of the dishes was done by hand. All too soon preparations for school took over from all other activities. The youngsters bundled up in coats, put on their overshoes, found their lost scarves and mitts, and in noisy but happy confusion, set off for school.

A typical prairie farmhouse, once it had passed through its metamorphosis of tent, sod hut, tar-paper shack and a one-story residence, eventually evolved into a two-story frame structure. It included a large

-- A. A. Elliot

This frame homestead house near Coronation, Alta. belonged to Joe Weiz.

kitchen, a parlor and a bedroom on the ground floor and two or three bedrooms upstairs. The downstairs was nicely finished but the entire house lacked insulation, and had no storm windows or storm doors. No special provisions were made for heating the building, so the kitchen range, and in some instances a pot-bellied stove in the parlor, had to do the trick. This wasn't enough! The rooms upstairs were very cold; the only heat reaching them either radiated from the chimney or stove-pipes passing through them, or the little that rose from downstairs through the doorways, the open stairways and the misnamed "hot-air" register. In due course a porch was added to the back and a veranda to the front of the house to provide additional protection from the flies, the mosquitoes and the elements of the weather, and for such ancillary purposes as a place for washing the clothes, separating the milk, churning the cream, stowing the slop buckets, starting seedlings, and storing a barrel or two of drinking or soft water.

The cellar under the house was little more than a hole in the ground. It had a hard dirt floor and earth walls. Access to this crypt was through a trap door in the middle of the kitchen floor. This arrangement sometimes proved dangerous; practically every member of the family, at one time or another, plummeted "down the cellar." Suddenly and without warning, the person would become aware of the startling fact that there was no support underfoot, and he was plunging into the dark void. Luckily no one was hurt badly but some still bear scars incurred in making the "drop" without the aid of a parachute.

The trap door itself was a menace. It had the uncanny habit of dropping shut with a determined bang and leaving one prisoner in the cellar, attempting to pry the heavy door open from the nether surface. Unfortunate also was the person who, laden with an armful of potatoes, carrots and a couple of jars of preserves, felt the full impact of the dropping portcullis just at the time when he was ascending the cellar steps. One teacher was nearly killed while descending into the school coal cellar to tend his sole companion — a pet cat. The trap door swung shut on his head, catching it between the door and the kitchen floor. He had a bruised head and neck to remind him of the odeal. When he was asked about the incident he philosophized tersely, "Trap door, m-m-m-m, well named!"

A ladder, or an open flight of steep stairs, provided the means for entry into the cellar. A person crawled down backwards, carefully keeping a firm grip on the first rung or step as he grasped for the second, and so on, until he felt his feet touch the hard-packed dirt of the cellar. There was a niche in the wall near the bottom of the ladder where a rickety lamp or a candle stub and a few matches were kept in readiness. The problem was to grope around in the dark, find the lamp or candle stub and light it. The alternative to this stratagem was to descend with a candle or lamp already lit. But what was a person to do with an unsteady hot lamp chimney, spilled coal oil, an open flame and no free hands to deal with such emergencies. The only sensible alternative was to have some form of light downstairs that could be put on the moment the person reached the down-under region.

Once down, there were the fruits of the farm harvest, all around on shelves and in bins. Cobs of corn, bunches of onions and garlic, hung from the floor-joists. The jams and preserves stood in their glass jars, a rainbow of color against the dark walls of the cellar. Piles of brown potatoes, rust-colored carrots, with a number of purple beets rolled against the green cabbages, glowed like opal in the dim light. In the shadowy corners it was possible to discern enormous spider webs with an assortment of flies and bugs trapped on the sticky silken gossamers. On more than one occasion some impressionable youngster blundered into the sticky dragnet, only to clamber back up the ladder, shrieking for someone to protect him from the monstrous, ferocious, ogling spiders.

Earth cellars are also remembered for their variety of good smells. The instant the trap door was opened the fresh aroma of apples and stored potatoes, carrots, turnips and onions gushed out like a fountain. Deep down in the cellar other scents were discernible: the acrid reek from the sauerkraut or pickle barrel and the spicy whiffs of the apple butter. An excursion into the cellar always meant a feast for the nose.

Bread was baked once or twice a week. Even if money was available for store-brought bread and it was convenient to obtain, people still considered it a sign of laziness or an unnecessary luxury to buy it. Bread-making was considered an art and if a housewife established a reputation as being a good baker, the bachelors in the district usually persuaded her to bake bread for them. They supplied the flour and she did the rest.

Fast-rising yeast was not available in pioneer days, so slower, homemade yeast-mix was kept viable at all times. Potato water was often added to the mixture to improve the quality and rising ability of the batter. No wonder the farm women had the strength in their arms to handle a team of frisky horses after the hours and hours they exercised their arms in working the sponge into dough and kneading it. In no time every convenient spot near the hot stove would be cluttered with pans of rising bread. It was imperative to keep the dough warm or it would not rise, and as early farm homes were not known for their warmth, various ingenious schemes were used to accomplish this. Some wrapped the bread pans in coats and blankets and snuggled them on chairs near the stove. Others stayed up all night and kept the fires going full blast. Some secured the necessary results by taking it to bed with them. However this method was not always foolproof as the following incident demonstrates.

The weather had been cold and a young teacher had made bread the day before. As he had no success whatsoever with it rising because of the low temperature in the teacherage, he took it to bed with him to keep the dough warm. While he slept the usual teacher's carefree Friday-night slumber it had risen beyond the confines of the mixing-bowl. When he woke up he was literally rolling in dough. It had entangled him and his bed clothes so well that it was impossible to distinguish which was which. Luckily it was Saturday, so he had time to scrape the bread dough off the blankets and his long winter underwear. Apparently he had enough bread-making experience, for later in the afternoon he was seen heading in the direction of the home of bread-maker for the district.

The reward for all the hard work and patience expended in making bread came when the oven was opened and the crusty, cinnamon-brown loaves of homemade bread pulled out. There is no aroma quite equal to newly-baked bread and the taste of light, expertly prepared fresh homemade bread is out of this world.

Farmers who made their own butter were able to sell or barter it at the stores in town in exchange for groceries, so most farms went in for butter making to some extent. Churning cream into butter was an exacting science and was of interest to the children until they were called upon to assist in the excitement, and then it waned to just another monotonous chore.

First the churn, the dash or barrel, the butter mold, the paddle and the butter bowl had to be scalded and placed in cold water. Next the cream was tested as to its temperature, for if it was too cold it required hours to churn; if it was too warm, the butter turned out to be too soft. The tedious routine of churning is self-evident. It involved supplying the physical power for the up-and-down strokes of the plunger in the earlier churns, or manipulating the foot-pedal or the handlebar in later models. The operator had to exercise extreme care during the churning for it was difficult to keep the dash from splashing over everything, and any carelessness in adjusting the capricious lid on the churn usually ended dramatically with buttermilk and butter coating the floor, walls, windows and ceiling of the kitchen. A less spectacular effect could be produced intentionally by removing the air plug at the strategic moment the greatest pressure had built up within the churn. The resulting geyser of buttermilk not only was something to behold, but the rushing gases emitted such eerie sounds that the most mischief-minded youngster was usually satisfied with the performance of his own particular brand of "Old Faithful".

Margaret (Ennis) Vincent of the Haunted Lake District (Alix, Alta.) related another common churning accident.

Churning butter was a weekly chore we loathed. Everyone had to take their turn, and many times the clock was turned back on an unsuspecting youngster so that he turned an extra five or ten minutes. One churning incident I've heard repeated many times happened in 1916. On this particular day Alice Roland had come over to help Jean and Myrle Ennis with the churning. Everything was progressing nicely but the fact that it was periodically necessary to let the air out of the churn. The three girls had forgotten. BANG! The churn blew its cork and thick cream went in a stream on the floor, walls and ceiling before the churn could be stopped and recorked. The girls were frantic. Father sent them all down to the lake to skate and when they returned the messy kitchen was spotless. He had called in brother Gordon's long, lean, hungry coyote hounds. They were more than willing to lick the floor clean and the walls as far as they could reach. Father cleaned up the rest. Everyone was happy, especially the hounds, who were always hungry.

Such incidents occurred when the inexperienced operator, fed up with the purely physical nature of his task, decided he could perform other activities such as reading, doing his homework, playing with the cat, or experimenting with the churn, in addition to his main duty of churning.

After a half-hour of arduous labor, if the operator was lucky, an encouraging thumping sound inside the churn indicated the butter was breaking. Sure enough, soon the yellow crumbs appeared. The unskilled labor was finished and now it was time for the expert to take over. The buttermilk was drained, the butter washed in cold water, and salt and a little coloring matter added. Later that day it would be ladled some more, packed in crocks or cast into pound-molds, wrapped in waxed paper and readied for the next trip to town.

Lack of good water, or any kind of water, was a great drawback for the inhabitants of the prairie farms. Reliable water supplies were hard to find. No matter how many wells some farmers dug no water was located, or at best a small supply of brackish water. Fortunate indeed was the homesteader whose efforts and luck culminated in a shallow producing well somewhere convenient to his buildings. It didn't take him long to crib and cover the well with planks. The water was usually brought to the surface by a square wooden pump, which later was replaced by a more efficient iron model. Nevertheless, many a housewife had to hoist the water required for her household from the well by a bucket on a rope.

More than one venturesome gopher landed in the well after burrowing under the cover. There was no telling what inquisitive creature would next find its last resting place down the well. Grasshoppers, mice and birds were common casualties, but farmers rescued larger animals, such as horses, cows and pigs from a watery grave.

Not too many farmers could afford the expense of a drilled well, but there was no alternative if the water existed at any great depth. It was common for the drillers to have to drill for two hundred feet before reaching a satisfactory supply of water. Windmills were generally erected to pump water from such great depths. If a dug, or drilled well, failed to uncover usable water, it became necessary for the farmer to haul it in barrels or in a tank from whatever source was available for him, near or far. Those who had to transport water for any great distance usually built cisterns under their houses and filled them with suitable drinking water before the snow got too deep to haul the precious fluid by tank wagon or sleigh.

Another solution was to dig a hole about ten feet from a slough and when the highly organic liquid seeped into the excavation, most of the bugs and other impurities were filtered out, leaving soft water for washing clothes or dishes. Water for drinking and cooking purposes still had to be hauled because the water from the slough had harmful organisms in it. The hauled water was stored in pails, tubs, crocks, barrels or anything else in the house that could hold it. Thus it can be seen that water was considered a rare commodity and to this day, people who were raised on prairie farms cannot bear to see water wasted.

The inconvenience and frustration of being short of water became a way of life as the following incidents document.

When a stranger stopped at a farm and asked for a drink of water he was told to help himself. The water pail and washbasin were located on an apple box by the door, so the thirsty visitor took a dipper of water, drank most of it and threw the rest out the door. The housewife showed immediate concern and said, "Say, Mister, what water you don't drink, empty in the washbasin. We haul that water eight miles!"

Before one prairie farmer succeeded in locating a good well his wife used to wash the dishes twice in the same water, break it with lye and then scrub the floors with this liquid.

One day a neighbor drove into a farmyard, tied up his team and went into the house to deliver a message. The team got loose and knocked over the barrel that was brimful of rain water at the time. The farmer's wife wept so bitterly over the loss that her children realized for the first time just how valuable soft water was. They had a difficult time of choking back their own sympathetic tears. Children never could forget such lessons in water conservation.

One farm girl took the theme of water conservation rather seriously. She had driven a team and stoneboat up to a well for a barrel but she had forgotten the lid to keep the water from splashing out. It was five miles from home and too far to return for the cover. What should she do? After considering the problem for a while, she smiled and then hoisted herself on top of the barrel where she sat all the way home. Not a drop of water was lost.

The water problem increased during the winter. Snow, if available, was melted to make up for the lack of water, but this was hard work when cattle and horses had to be watered. Yet there was a pleasant compensation in listening to the sound of snow dripping from the outside of the buckets as it melted and created sizzling spurts where it struck the hot surface of the kitchen range. There was something comforting and reassuring in knowing soft water was so near at hand.

A large part of the morning's work on the farm after a heavy frost was cleaning out water holes in the frozen spring, river, slough, trough, or whatever was the usual watering place of the livestock. The icy water was not beneficial to the stock and the refuse left on the ice was far from sanitary, so considerate farmers installed small heating retorts inside the water trough.

Pumping water for the stock was a large order, and if done by hand was hard work. Most children who lived on farms prior to World War II remember the many hours they had to stand and pump water for the thirsty stock. There was no shirking. As the youngster pumped, the stock drank, and the job was not finished until every animal was satisfied and the trough left full. It was impossible to cheat for if the water in the tank was low some resentful brute would announce to one and all the lad's inefficiency with reproachful bawls. The doleful message always reached the farm house and shortly after an adult would appear to investigate the cry for succor. Rural folk, just like a mother rationalizing the various cries of her baby, could tell from the vociferation of the livestock how the animals were making out in the barnyard or pasture.

Bathing was not a daily activity. It was an event. The washtub was trundled sonorously into the house and filled with hot water from the kitchen-range reservoir, or alternatively it was placed directly on the stove and filled with water to be heated. The latter method, although more cumbersome and time consuming, was preferred. The galvanized tub became heated as well as the water, so as long as the bather was wary of the hot metal he enjoyed his warm bath longer. The kitchen doubled as the public bathroom and was usually the only room in the house sufficiently comfortable on a cold winter's day to make bathing a pleasure rather than a torture. There was something snug and exclusive about taking a Saturday-night bath in front of the roaring coal fire in the kitchen. Privacy was discreetly maintained and members of the family not bathing would spend their time in other parts of the house.

It should be explained that to bathe in a round washtub for anyone over three feet tall wasn't exactly easy. The traditional and the only way of getting into the tub dictated that the knees be double and thrust under the chin and the back firmly pressed against the side of the tub. From such an immobile huddle the bather bravely attempted to scrub himself with the oily-smelling bar of coarse yellow soap, Fels Naptha or Sunlight, using a still coarser washcloth. There were sections of the human anatomy that couldn't be reached and hence escaped the lavation.

Many rural teachers who boarded with farm families can still recollect the "order of the bath" on bath night. It went something like this: the mother came first, followed by the daughters, then the teacher, and finally the male members of the family.

It was indeed a day to celebrate when a family could afford a full-sized bathtub. Of course they still carried the clean water in and the dirty out, but it was sheer delight, after years of squeezing into a washtub, to be able to stretch out and relax.

In the long intervals between the household-disruptive ablutions, the sponge bath was the order of the day. This meant retiring to an intimate corner or room with a basin of warm water, a bar of soap, a wash cloth, a towel, and then going over the body and limbs with the lathered moist cloth.

This was a quick and convenient way of getting ready for a social engagement, but at best was an ersatz sanitary activity.

A couple of rural teachers didn't believe in sponge baths but neither did they believe in emptying the washtub right after a bath. The result of this philosophy provided the community with a laugh, but was unfortunate for the two school marms. It happened rather innocently. They were in a hurry to leave for a dance, so after a refreshing bath in the teacherage, they simply pushed the washtub under the table. The next morning one of them was very thirsty and finding the water pail empty, used the bath water to make the coffee. The brew had a pungent, pleasant taste and quenched their thirst quickly, but it left them debilitated a couple of hours later. The soap in the brewed coffee had imbued it with laxative properties.

One cold day in winter in the Gledhow S.D. (Delisle, Sask.), Irma Hawkins was taking a bath in front of the stove in the kitchen with all the doors tightly closed to keep in the heat. A knock came at the door and, as was the custom in those days, her visitor just walked in. She gave one jump out of the tub, propelling it across the floor, and dashed for the hall where it was twenty below zero. Fortunately, the teacher who heard all the commotion from upstairs threw down a towel to aid her escape. The visitor was an elderly bachelor. Irma's sister, with a mop in her hands and doubled over from laughter, escorted him into the living room. The visitor knew something was up so he joined in the laughter as a matter of courtesy. Irma, from the safety of her retreat upstairs, yelled down she couldn't see anything to laugh at, she was so angry.

Irma had only one such experience but the teacher at North Star S.D. (Alix, Alta.) had to contend with such a problem on a permanent basis. The McCutcheon family boarded her in their two-room home, so of necessity the teacher had to have her morning wash in the kitchen completed before Mr. McCutcheon came in from doing his chores. This inevitably led to some hasty retreats.

The Walter family of the Sargent S.D. (Clive, Alta.) overcame the problem of any indecent exposure in a unique way. They placed the washtub in front of the oven door of the kitchen range and then suspended sheets from a rope line to completely enclose it. A boiler of hot water was kept on the stove and a barrel of cold water stood beside the reservoir, so there was no need for the bather to expose himself beyond his sheet sanctuary. The order of bathing was according to age, beginning with the baby and concluding with the head of the home.

The weekly wash day was tough. The back-breaking activity started the night before when the boiler was filled with water. This was not a simple thing, for the water had to be carried in pails from the water barrel in the farm yard or a nearby slough, or pumped or pulled by hand from the well, and then lifted bodily and poured into the boiler on top of the stove. Fortunate was the woman who could rely on a supply of rain water in the summer and melted snow in the winter as these provided the ideal soft water washing.

Once the boiler was filled, the soap was shaved or chipped and the bluing and lye made ready. Water was very hard due to its mineral content and using it to wash was a problem. It was "broken" or emulsified with wood ashes or lye. Not knowing the amount of lye to use, the occasional new housewife added too much and the caustic action resulted in the holiest clothes on the line rather than the hoped-for cleanest wash. Nearly everything was ruined. This was especially true where any white wash was concerned, as the women took great pride in producing snow-white garments and soaked them over night to do so. No wonder the first wash day was nothing but tears for many frustrated beginners.

In the morning the clothes were boiled, scrubbed by hand in a tub with a cake of soap on a glass or galvanized washboard, rinsed in clean water, and then wrung by hand or passed through a manual wringer. It took a strong back and arms to do a good job.

By the twenties, various hand-operated washing machines were on the market. They could best be described as "women killers", as the heavy wooden tub was trundled by turning a wheel or operating a lever. This mechanical device, however, did get the clothes clean a lot quicker. Within a decade farm homes were introduced to the gas or kerosene washing machines. These new labor-saving appliances were welcome, but they made a tremendous racket while operating and had the uncanny characteristic of skipping all over the kitchen floor or porch. Farm women were forced to become mechanically minded if they wanted to use these inventions successfully.

The washing machines provided some mothers with a unique way of teaching their children to work. If anything rattled inside the tub it was probably a nickel, a dime or a few pennies, and whoever dumped the water was the fortunate one.

Once the washing was finished it was strung outside on a clothesline to dry. If the weather cooperated, everything was fine, but a sudden squall, dust storm, or shower, could play havoc with the clean garments. A constant vigil had to be maintained during the period the wash was out on the line, and at the slightest sign of trouble the clothes were quickly gathered and brought inside. The farm wife had to be a good weather prognosticator if she wanted to choose the right day on which to do her wash.

In winter the clothes froze solid and it was a common sight to see a shivering housewife nimbly collecting ghostly apparitions from the clothes-line, spirit them inside, and then arrange them expertly on various supports in the house and porch. Every available inch seemed to be hung with clotheslines. Very little space was left for the living, with so much room purloined by the frosty skeletons. However, the pleasant aroma of newly-washed clothes and the anticipation of the invigorating feeling of wearing clean garments, more than made up for the inconveniences.

There were many problems associated with washing clothes in the early days and the following comments by women who actually used to wash by hand are worthy of note.

Clothes were scrubbed in a galvanized washtub on a glass washboard. Water for washing was hauled from a slough in barrels on a stoneboat pulled by horses. It was heated on a cook stove in a copper boiler. The white clothes were boiled in soapy water in the wash boiler, then this soapy water was used again to wash the clothes, and clean water brought in for the second washing. They were rinsed and passed through a hand wringer and hung outside on the clothesline in the summer. In the winter the laundry was hung in a granary, or in an attic to dry. Of course they would have to be finished off by hanging them in the house, but the freezing seemed to take a certain amount of the moisture out and also gave the white things extra whiteness. Aprons, print dresses and men's dress shirts were starched.

I heated water for washing clothes on the kitchen stove in copper boilers. Many buckets of water had to be carried for washing and rinsing the clothes and it all had to be carried out again after the washing was done. The ground in our yard around the house was quite level, and the used wash water had to be carried some distance in order for it to drain away.

The biggest chore of the week, especially for a mother of a large family was washday. The hard work of getting clothes clean with tub and washboard was always present. The invention of the wash machine meant less work, so was something every woman tried to obtain. These machines, however, were not altogether a blessing, for they jumped around like a Mexican jumping bean when in use. Besides, they were made with cypress wood held together by iron bands, and when not in use they would dry out and when washday came they would leak like a sieve.

Farm clothes such as overalls and denim jackets were heavy and got particularly dirty and greasy. They were usually the last of the many tubfuls to be put through the machine. Since the wringer had to be turned by hand such heavy garments meant the housewife had to expend extra manual work to get the heavy garments through the rollers.

Once the clothes were dry they were sprinkled with water and then they were ironed. There were three or four flatirons to a set; they were heated on the stove and as each iron cooled off it was exchanged for another hotter iron. Ironing was done on the same day as bread was baked, so the one fire would do. Often a cake pan was used to cover the irons to retain as much heat as possible. There was no thermostat to control the temperature of the iron, so the women improvised a test of their own to know when the iron was ready; they touched the hot iron with a moist finger, and the resulting sizzling sound, correctly interpreted, indicated whether all was in readiness for the particular type of material to be ironed. This was no job for the amateur.

The first irons were made of iron, handle and all, so they were uncomfortable to use. Later the sadiron was introduced with a detachable wooden handle. Although it was an improvement, women found it necessary to place one hand under the sadiron to carry it safely from the stove to the ironing board or table. Not infrequently the handle released its hold and the hot iron clattered to the floor, or landed on the person's leg or foot. No one ever could solve the mystery of why the iron was called "sad"; in fact, most people thought that the women who used them were the "sad" ones.

In those early farming days the ladies relied almost exclusively on what nature had endowed them with for their beauty. Artificial aids or cosmetics were few and far between and the one or two that were available, debilitated rather than glamorized women's faces. Thus, it was a simple thing to primp preparatory to going out. They frizzed their hair with the curling tongs heated in a lamp, or used rag curlers if they had more time. There was no problem in deciding which dress to wear as most women had only one good dress anyway. White powder applied to the face and neck was the only makeup used. The majority overdid the powder, and since it was applied in front of a small mirror and in the presence of a poor yellow light, instead of looking like reigning beauties, some looked as they had fallen into a sack of flour. Every district could boast of at least one fair damsel who always managed to faint at the most dramatic moments and elicited the oft repeated comment, "Alas! I'd sure like to wash the kalsomine off her face!" Such caustic remarks were soon outdated with the introduction of colored face powder and rouge. Deodorants were unknown in those days, but many placed their trust in washing with a cake of Sunlight or Fels Naptha soap. Others powdered their undergarments before they went to a dance to keep from offending and to appear dainty.

Haircuts for boys and men were considered essential prior to their appearance at any public function, such as a dance. Unless they were going to town before such a "do" and could visit the barber shop, home cuts were the order of the day. Frequently some person in the community was handy with the scissors and could do the job, otherwise it meant "learning on the job" and some volunteers snipped and snipped as long as the hair lasted. An expedient method was to place an inverted bowl over the person's head and cut off all the hair that protruded below it. Such tensorial experiments ended with the males looking like plucked chickens, but at least their neck regions appeared neatly groomed. Men, like the women, only had one good set of clothes: their "Sunday suit". Invariably it was a blue serge outfit consisting of trousers, coat and vest. In fact, the blue serge suit was so common that it could easily have been designated by the government as the farmers' holiday uniform. The suits lasted for years and years, and only the degree of sheen on the seat and knees of the trousers, and on the elbows of the coat betrayed the age of the attire.

This "waste not, want not" theory not only applied to clothes but extended to every possession, large or small. Things were looked after so carefully that it was considered a major catastrophe if something fractured, cracked, ripped, wrinkled, tore open, was lost or showed signs of unnecessary wear. Once their usefulness was jeopardized in any such manner they were patched or repaired and directed into new channels of serviceability. Empty flour sacks proved to be the best standby for such jobs. They could be made into sheets, pillow cases, mattresses, curtains, tea towels, aprons, under wear garments of all kinds, and excelled as patching or remodelling material. What the flour sack was to the housewife, the haywire and binder twine were to the farmer. These items were indispensable in an age that had yet to bow to the social pressures induced by self-interest groups declaring that certain products or customs were obsolete or out-of-date.

Children were taught frugality by precept and example. For instance, they were constantly reminded to lift their feet well off the ground while walking to avoid any needless wear on the shoes, to change into their work clothes the minute they came home from school, to wrap their school books in protective covers, to write on both sides of a piece of paper, to hang up or put away their clothes, to wear aprons over their good dresses while helping in the kitchen, or to keep their elbows off the table to prevent any soiling or needless wear of the sleeves. When any of the father's clothes wore out they were made to fit one of the older boys while garments that were outgrown were handed down to the younger children. Frayed collars on shirts or dresses were reversed to show their better side, old clothing was used to make hooked rugs for the drafty floor or pieced together to make quilts, and garment parts considered expendable were remodelled into useful articles. For example the tails and fronts of men's shirts were made into petticoats, and back pockets of overalls became patches for worn knees.

An amusing incident of such "a stich in time saves nine" way of living occurred in the Hamona S.D. (Spy Hill, Sask.).

A father hurried out to stop the boys sliding down the hill on their seats and wearing out their overalls, when all at once his feet slipped out from under him and down the hill he went. His method of teaching left much to be desired and besides, he was teased about it for a long time.

The success of any new convenience introduced in a farm home seemed to vary according to the amount of work put into it. The coal-oil lamps that replaced candles, for example, required as much understanding and care as a baby. Every morning lamps had to be filled, burners cleaned, the wicks trimmed and the glass chimneys washed and polished. There was also a knack in trimming and setting the wick to ensure a steady flame. At best, these lamps were not too bright and failed to throw much light beyond the immediate confines of the kitchen table. Perhaps that is why heads nodded early as it was a relief to close one's eyes in sleep. The lamps, however, cast huge, grotesque shadows on the walls to create a never-never land of giants. No wonder it took nerve for a tot to be the first to leave the table. That is why wise mothers always comforted these adventurers by saying, "I'll go first and and make the bed ready!"

The Aladdin lamp was a welcome addition to any home, but it had the undesirable habit of "turning itself up" at untoward times. The children, who were forbidden to tamper with this lamp, often sounded the alarm, "Mom, the lamp is acting up again!" "Aladdin", as it was called, was no more than a glorified coal-oil lamp with an umbrella-shaped mantle overhanging the flame. The luminescent fiber shed a bright, quiet, white light. This type of lighting was an improvement when it came to close work, whether it was reading, crocheting, mending, or school homework. Since the mantle was very fragile and easily damaged by fluttering moths, sudden jars, or the vagaries of children, extra care had to be exercised in its use.

Most homes had one gasoline lamp which hung from a hook in the center of the ceiling in the kitchen. Here was one lamp that had the power to light up the entire room. It burned high-test gasoline, exuded a white light from its two mantles and generators and operated with a constant hissing sound due to the high pressure under which the air of the air-gasoline mixture had been pumped in. Although the gas lamp produced the best light, it was a risky illuminant. Every rural resident can recall incidents of gas lamp explosions. Accidents most commonly occurred when a person forgot about the flaming monster overhead and knocked it off its hook with his head or shoulders as he got up suddenly from his chair.

Lamps were the beacons of life on the prairie. Their presence signalled that isolation and loneliness were at an end. They sent their message of hope to a person lost in a blizzard. They flashed the news that someone was sick, that a baby was being born, that a "do" was taking place in the schoolhouse, that a family had company, or a wife was waiting up for her husband to return from a wheat-hauling trip to town. On the other hand, if the farm home was dark, it foretold an absence, a sign of trouble or even death.

The open flame that was the integral part of every type of lamp always warranted care and respect. Accidents happened so quickly that before a person could blink an eyelid the room was engulfed in flames. One evening some boys were playing a game of tag and running around the kitchen table with their hands on it. In their excitement the coal-oil lamp was knocked to the floor. It broke and a fire instantly swept across the room, fed by the flooding kerosene. Their grandmother, the only one to retain her presence of mind, grabbed a large floor mat and smothered the flame. There were some very subdued parents and boys after the incident.

But lamps could be very helpful. A concerned neighbor put up a post to hold a lantern in order to guide travellers at night. If he saw someone going to town in the morning, he would watch for their return. If the expected one did not pass by before dusk, the lantern was hoisted on its pedestal. This was frequently done in winter and during blizzards.

Mail-order houses played an important part in the lives of rural people, so the arrival of Eaton's or Simpson's catalogue was eagerly awaited. Since it was found in every home, more than one minister hinted that it was more thoroughly studied on the Sabbath than the Bible. In fact, many a wit called it the "Family Bible".

Early in the spring, when the dirt-crusted snow still lay in drifts against the fences and buildings, it was an eventful day if someone returned with the mail and it included a large roll-shaped parcel wrapped in brown paper. Everyone knew what it was and clamored to be allowed to open it. However, the honor was reserved for the mother. She leafed slowly through the ponderous volume as other members of the family gathered around her and eagerly watched the unfolding of the world of new merchandise. Each new page brought forth its quota of canny observations: "A woman would be daft to wear such a flimsy dress;" "These overalls look just right for the boys;" "We better not forget to order some of this ointment;" "This one looks just like the hat our teacher wears to church on Sunday;" "Oh Mummy, please get me this." The catalogue was like having a whole shopping center spread out on the kitchen table. Many hours of looking preceded decision-making, and when the father and mother took out the special order form and started to fill it in, everyone stood around waiting to learn of the results. Most revelations were disappointing! Instead of the glamorous looking shoes or dress, the order turned out to be the dull, rugged kind. Nevertheless, an Eaton's parcel was eagerly awaited by the whole family. Then, when it arrived and was opened, the accompanying excitement, the deluge of wrapping paper, the appearance and aroma of the brand new goods, and the resulting good fortunes or disappointments, imparted a holiday atmosphere to the event.

Catalogue shopping thwarted any feelings of jealousy if some woman discovered two or three others in the district wearing a coat just like hers. She knew where the others had purchased it and the price paid, and since every farm home depended on the mail-order catalogue, she didn't mind.

The service provided by the mail-order houses was considerate and good, as may be judged by the following extract taken from a letter written on June 27, 1915 by a teacher at Baraca S.D. (Youngstown, Alta.) to his mother back home in Ontario.

> I tried Eaton's mail-order service and ordered a fifty-cent bicycle pump. They sent me one worth seventy-five cents because they were out of the other, and actually refunded some money because I had sent a little too much postage for the fifty-cent pump. There's business for you! I shall certainly deal with them again.

Shopping for Christmas presents via the mail-order catalogue was relatively easy. The children made it plain enough and soon enough just what they wanted; the prices remained the same, irrespective of the Christmas season; and emotions were not swayed by bargains, the bustle, the excitement or the physical exhaustion accompanying today's Christmas shopping.

Usually the father and mother sat down quietly after the children had gone to bed and made out the Christmas order, wisely and within their ability to pay. When the parcels and boxes arrived they were left unopened and carefully put away, a sure sign that they contained presents. The children didn't see the contents until the gifts mysteriously appeared on Christmas morning.

Youngsters were not lavished with gifts, but the one or two they received were appreciated. Young girls used to set their hearts on receiving one of the Eaton's Beauty Dolls, and if they did, their joy knew no bounds. Alice Brewitt of the Sunbeam S.D. (Delia, Alta.) was one of these fortunate youngsters. Upon finding her dream doll on Christmas morning she dashed into her parent's bedroom shouting ecstatically, "Daddy, daddy, look what Santa Claus brought me!" In her hurry to show off the gift she swung it around too vigorously and struck her loving parent square on the head with the hard-headed doll. Before long her father had his own unexpected Christmas gift to display: a lump the size of an egg on his noggin, courtesy of his appreciative daughter.

Besides a means of buying goods, a way of comparing prices, and a method of learning about new merchandise, the catalogues had many sundry uses. They made ideal doorsteps, and with a little ingenuity the pages could be used to fashion attractive homemade Christmas decorations. Children played by the hour with the hundreds of cutouts they clipped from old catalogues, and all the make-believe games of life could be played with the pictures of people and things they were able to collect. Young ladies studied its pages assiduously in order to keep informed about the world of fashions. No one found the catalogue more enlightening than the many bachelors, for they were able to dreamily compound their future brides-to-be from the scantily-clad models displayed in the women's section of the "farmers' Bible". Teachers looked to the catalogues for their teaching illustrations and as pre-primers for their non-English speaking students. A catalogue or two placed on the seat of an ordinary chair elevated a tiny tot until he was high enough to reach the table. When all else in the pioneer home had been read there was always the catalogue to browse through again; and no one ever seemed to tire of just looking and dreaming when the weather sent them indoors. Even when the catalogue came to its final resting place in the wee house at the back and was used as toilet tissues, people often sat with the door slightly ajar and reread the individual pages for the last time, particularly the smooth photogravure ones that were, for obvious reasons, the last to disappear.

The pedlars who used to travel from farm to farm plying their trade are legendary. At first they made their rounds with horses or teams and covered

-- Fred Rall

Fred Rall, the friendly Rawleigh man of Coronation, Alta, visits a farm home in midwinter, hopefully to sell some of his products.

wagons or democrats, but as the years went by, trucks became their standard means of covering their territory. The odd one walked with the huge pack of merchandise fastened on his back.

The arrival of a pedlar meant an exciting time for the family as they clustered around the back of the wagon or the mysterious packing-cases to view the merchandise. Carefully, and almost lovingly, the pedlar went through his giant valises, item by item, citing, without any high-pressure sale pitch, the relative merits of each article. Everything seemed to be there, from overalls to house dresses, from common yard goods to the finest silks, from buttons, thread and safety pins to jewellery and Waltham watches, from baby clothes to straight razors and strops. Whether anything was purchased or not, there was always something for the children. If a deal was made, the pedlar "threw in" an additional article. Giving something extra was quite customary in those days, perhaps because the majority of the pedlars were Armenians and they were simply following the business traditions of their homeland.

The "Rawleigh Man" could also be described as a pedlar, but his wares were more of a specialty. His suitcases were filled with containers of spices, extracts, ointments, cosmetics and remedies for every ailment suffered by man or beast. Rawleigh's liniment ranked as the favorite cure-all. It was as common as the aspirin tablets are today. These travelling self-styled amateur apothecaries were as publicity and good-will minded as their dry-goods counterparts. Brides were honored with gifts of hand lotion and in the following years received cans of baby powder or bars of scented soap, for each new arrival. At the conclusion of each visit, each youngster present was handed a stick of gum or a piece of candy. No wonder the children considered his visits as something to anticipate and enjoy.

These itinerant tradesmen were more than salesmen. They were treated as guests and assured of a meal or two and a bed for the night. In return for such hospitality they brought news of the outside world, told many human-interest stories, and shared the pleasures and sorrows of their hosts. Because of their friendly communication and relationship with the hundreds of the new self-imposed Canadians, the pedlars were often called the "emissaries of a fledgling nation."

Those who have had modern conveniences all their lives accept them without the devout gratitude which is their due. Telephones and radios were two such inventions that relieved perhaps the most difficult condition with which early prairie farmers had to contend — the feeling of isolation. The old "party line", whether it was the top strand of a barbed-wire fence or the regulation wire strung on a telephone pole, filled a definite need and played an important part in the life of a farming community.

Early telephones were equipped with a one-step switch and taking the receiver off the hook enabled one to be heard as well as to hear. When the telephone rang, no matter whose ring it was, everyone could listen. "Listening in" became a popular pastime. Housewives could ring up and chat with one another. When someone bought a new record for his phonograph, everybody on the line could enjoy the latest recording. In the Spy Hill S.D. 170 (Spy Hill, Sask.) a musical family was in the habit of entertaining friends on the party line. A neighbor usually rang the family's number and asked for a sing-song. The receiver was left off the hook and while the mother played the organ and the rest of the family sang, the people for miles around listened in. After an hour or so of singing favorite songs, the entertainers said goodnight to the unseen audience and replaced the receiver on its hook. Such diversions were varied and depended on the talent available along the party line. Entertainment might consist of organ music, recitations, readings, or Roy Embree and his fiddle.

Party lines contributed to more than one embarrassing moment. If a baby cried, or a clock struck the hour, or an adult snored or coughed, it wasn't difficult to identify the snooping household. Hence, it wasn't uncommon for a speaker to call a guilty party by name and tell him or her to get off the line. Of course the accuser was often answered curtly with, "I'm not listening!"

If any usable information was acquired secretly over the party line it was not pressed to advantage immediately. No one ever wanted to admit that he eavesdropped on the party line. There seemed to be something morally underhanded about such conduct. If one of these phone-tappers acquired the news that his neighbor was going into town for a load of coal, he permitted a discreet interval of time to elapse before putting in a private call of his own. "You don't know of anyone going into town today?" he would query innocently. "We ran out of coal oil last night." "Oh, you are!

That's just wonderful!" It was in this manner that the privacy of the party line, although non-existent, was tacitly honored.

All subscribers could be officially summoned to their receivers by a prolonged ring initiated by central. Such a general alert advised the farmers of tragedy such as a lost child, a drowning, a prairie fire, or a runaway. Such pleas for help never went unanswered. Not all general calls were concerned with dramatic events, for some merely announced an auction sale, the time of a funeral, a farmers' meeting, or a dance.

Radios became a new fad in 1922; then, within a couple of years, radios became a necessity. Excitement reigned supreme when the mysterious object was set up in the home. The early models were designed to be used with headsets, but it wasn't until the loudspeaker prototypes came on the market that radios captured the fancy of rural people. Now the whole family could sit around and listen at the same time.

Initially, radios were a mystery. Take the time a skeptic put on the headset for the first time and the receiver was turned on. He sat very still for awhile and then meekly whispered, "Is is all right for me to speak quietly, or will they hear me?" When there was an insufficient number of earphones to go around, people either took turns listening or the earphones were arranged in a large glass bowl to reflect the sound to the entire group.

People living within a fifty-mile radius of a broadcasting station popularized radio crystal sets. Such receivers could only be heard faintly with earphones. No tubes or batteries were required, but by adjusting a catwhisker until it made contact with the most sensitive spot on the crystal, the maximum volume or efficiency was secured. The use of crystal sets was limited, but as they provided a novel type of entertainment and were inexpensive, they were popular at the dawn of the radio era. Most people graduated to ownership of battery-operated tube models very quickly, once the crystal set whetted their appetites for radio entertainment.

Tube radios were operated by one car battery and three-power pack dry cells. Hence listeners learned quickly not to use the radio indiscriminately or the storage battery ran down within two or three days. Radio was the topic of many conversations: "I got KDKA, Pittsburgh, last night." "KOA came in like a ton of bricks!" "Did you hear the Charlie McCarthy show?" "I received my verification card from that Mexican station." "May we come over to listen to your radio this evening? Our battery is in town being charged." "All I got was static!" "My battery went dead in the middle of 'The Happy Gang' program." People were forced to become selective in their radio entertainment. They listened to the news and a few favorite programs, but as soon as they finished, the radio was carefully turned off to conserve the batteries.

Radios were not the efficient receivers they are today. Tuning, accomplished by turning a couple of dials, was accompanied with howls, whistles, squeals and no end of static. Such strident sounds quickly irritated people and the operators were censored in no uncertain terms. For instance, a mother would complain bitterly, "For goodness sakes, Dad, what are you looking for?" His reply, "A fight," probably got him just that.

In spite of all its faults, listening to the radio was a popular pastime. Those who owned sets in the district were proud to have their neighbors over for an evening of listening. The broadcast could have been the Dempsey-Tunney fight, Foster Hewitt's play-by-play account of the Stanley Cup Hockey Final, William Aberhart's "Back to the Bible" sermon, Gillette's World Series Baseball, or the CFCN Oldtimers.

Radio became so popular that the federal government felt the only way to keep a tab of all these potentially subversive gadgets was to license them. So in 1926 a new law required every owner to pay one dollar for a license, and to designate the permanent location of the radio.

From time immemorial man has devised ingenious signals whereby people separated by distance can still communicate with each other. Prairie farmers were no exception. A single sheet hanging on a clothesline could mean, "Yes!", two sheets, "No!", anything red, "We need help!", a sheet flying from a makeshift flagpole, "Time for the midwife to come!" Such a system didn't always work. There was the time a farmer, who had not been feeling well, let it be known he would hang a dark blanket on the clothesline if he became worse. He took sick during a blizzard. When his neighbors spotted the message after the storm, they discovered he had been dead for several days. However, the standard distress signal given by draping an article of wearing apparel over the front gate of the farmyard has brought succor to many people in trouble.

3

Going to Town

"Town" to the farmer and his family meant a convenient economic center served by a railway, irrespective of its official designation of hamlet, village, or town. Visits to town were infrequent enough to make "going to town" an important occasion, while a trip to the city was a rare event. Rural children soon became accustomed to town life, but they were a little afraid and unsure of themselves when confronted by the strange and busy environment of a metropolis.

No matter how many trips a prairie dweller made to town during his lifetime, he always experienced a feeling of exhilaration and anticipation the moment he got close enough to make out its familiar skyline. There seemed to be something fanciful about each prairie town, perhaps because they mushroomed into existence so quickly. One moment the farmer beheld the lonely prairie stretching endlessly as far as the eye could see, and then as if by magic, when he looked again, he saw ribbons of steel, a belching, smoking locomotive, and a collection of huts loomed on the horizon. A prairie town had just been born, so no wonder it snuggled so affectionately to its mother, the railway.

There is no town like a prairie town. Its row of grain elevators, like strange cathedrals, stand silhouetted against the sky, while its patchwork of homes and business places huddle nearby as if seeking protection. It doesn't take long for a regular visitor to recognize the characteristically red railway station, the rambling hotel, the spired churches, the spacious lumber yard, the somber-looking schoolhouse, the false-fronted stores, the old prosaic town pump, the screen-doored restaurant, the dark-interiored livery stable, the clamorous blacksmith shop, the poster-plastered community hall, the Chinese laundry with clotheslines filled with fluttering garments of all shapes and colors, the hair-tonic scented barber shop, and the busy post office.

The eye could rove in all directions but it met only the windswept prairie grasses, the large slough, the amber-colored grain fields and the rutted-trails converging on the town. Wire-bound board sidewalks and dirt roads crossed and recrossed the town with mathematical regularity. They seemed to bind the town together but, as everyone knew, after a good prairie rain the streets turned into seas of mud and made venturing forth rather harassing. And when the streets dried up, the deep ruts played havoc with wheel travel of any kind, and then in what seemed to be no time at all, clouds of dust whipped up by the everlasting breezes hippity-hopped up and down the streets like gleeful children. Now and then it tore around in miniature whirlwinds, whipped up weeds, straw, pieces of paper, and small pebbles and danced them gaily all over the town. Hitching posts sprouted fore and aft of every business premise and it was a common sight to see horses hitched to buggies and wagons fastened to them behind the biggest store and the hotel. The streets were never silent, for the musical ring of the blacksmith's anvil, the squeak of the metal sign over the front of the store as it swayed back and forth in the wind, the put-put of the diesel engine at the grain elevator, the rumble of horses' hooves on the livery floor and the occasional laughter from the bar room could always be heard. Any person with an adequate sense of smell had no problem distinguishing characteristic town odors such as the ammoniac reek from the livery stable, the yeasty breath of the beer parlor, the profusion of greasy-laden whiffs stealing through the dilapidated screen door of the restaurant, the putrid odor of the outhouses, the rather pleasant leathery aroma from the harness shop, the piney smell of the newly stacked boards in the lumber yard, the sweet essence of freshly-baked bread from the bakery, the smell of the forge and the singeing hoofs of the horses from the blacksmith shop, and the indescribable fetor from each backyard's tangled mess of ashes and sour garbage. These were unforgettable sights, sounds and smells and eventually grew to mean "my home town."

The general store was one place that intrigued most farm boys and girls, and since Saturday was shopping and visiting day for most of the rural folk, it was a convenient and ideal time for the youngsters to go along and explore the magical place. The store itself was a grocery, hardware, meat market, dry goods, haberdashery, furniture, millinery, harness and farmers' exchange shop all rolled into one to serve the needs of the people of the area. In such a heterogeneous shopping center it was possible to buy anything from a buggy whip to red flannels, bustles to binder canvasses, horse collars to chamber pots. Besides, if circumstances warranted, it was possible to trade butter, cream, eggs, dressed fowl, garden vegetables and other farm produce for factory-made goods stocked by the store.

The social side of selling was not forgotten but rather encouraged, by placing a few sturdy chairs, boxes, nail kegs or a bench beside the pot-bellied stove or near the large heat register. It was here farmers met to visit while waiting for the mail or for their grocery list to be filled. They discussed every topic, but in particular they talked about the crop prospects, the price of various farm commodities, the weather, and how satisfactory the government was being run. Not infrequently they helped themselves to morsels of cheese that they cut from the huge cylindrical-shaped portion which sat so invitingly on the turntable of the cutting machine. This snack was supplemented with crackers from the cracker-barrel. It seemed that more pieces of cheese and crackers were eaten "on the house" than sold. In the winter time the members of the hot-stove league were joined by story tellers, idlers and the occasional travelling salesman. Children loved to stand around and listen to the talk until the topic under discussion or the joke became a bit off-color, and then they were abruptly reminded that their presence was urgently required at home.

The people who owned these old general stores were a special breed of pioneer. They were a busy, hard-working lot, but they always knew who a person was and took a real interest in their customers. Personalized service became the general store's standard policy. The owner knew just about all his customers on a first-name basis. Therefore, when a farmer came in, the storekeeper usually knew exactly what to pick off the shelves for him, including the preferred quantity and brands of items such as tobacco and syrup.

The shelves, counters and the other store fixtures were arranged to lend a homey and neighborly atmosphere. Often there was a cat dozing by the stove, in the window, or on the counter, which helped to convey this atmosphere. The counters, highly-polished and sculptured smooth with numerous striations from years of use, stretched in a double line the full length of the store. The customers stood on one side and ordered their requirements from the shelves on the other side. The goods were ranged on

--Carl Rehill

Stores similar to the one pictured above served the needs of rural dwellers. Personal service and the variety of goods offered in bulk characterized these general stores.

these shelves which were built right up to the ceiling. If the desired item was on an upper shelf, the owner brought it down skillfully with a long pole, which had a clutching mechanism on the end of it. On the other hand, if the article was breakable or if there was no reaching-pole available, he retrieved it by climbing a ladder that was always there for such purposes.

The front of the grocery counter was subdivided into numerous rectangular display compartments fitted with glass to exhibit such staple foods as navy beans, rice, tapioca, raisins, macaroni, dried peas, and dehydrated fruits like apples, prunes, apricots and pears. Most of these groceries were sold by the pound. Fancy biscuits were displayed in tin boxes, with garish pictures of the variety inside. When a half-pound, or a pound of these delicacies was ordered, they were weighed out on the scales. The more discreet shopkeeper took the biscuits out of the tin box with special metal tongs; the less discreet used their fingers. The scales were always in use as few things came in packages.

A red hand-operated coffee mill and a guillotine-like cheese cutter usually occupied a place of prominence on the main grocery counter. The moment a customer entered the store his nostrils were treated to the odors of aged cheese and freshly-ground coffee. If coffee was ordered it was fascinating for the children to listen to the crunching of the beans and to smell the aroma of newly-ground coffee. The cheese-cutting machine was just as interesting. In fact it was considered an art to cut off a sector of cheese and come up with the exact weight ordered by the customer. The manner in which the shopkeeper, with an expert eye, set the machine, then grasped the handle of the hinged hatchet-like blade and nonchalantly cut off a piece from the huge hogshead of cheese resting on the turntable of the machine, was a sight to impress even the most skeptical rural youngster.

When bananas first became available in country stores, the large stock was suspended from the ceiling by a rope, and the clerk cut off the amount of fruit as ordered by the customer. A razor-sharp hook-ended knife that resembled a scimitar was used for the purpose. When not in use this wicked-looking tool was left embedded in the banana stock.

Merchandise was not prepackaged as is the common practice today; it was either put in bags at the time of the purchase, or wrapped in heavy brown paper for the customer. There was no person more skillful than the old-time storekeeper when it came to wrapping. In a flash of an eye he could tear off the exact length of paper from the large roll on the top of the counter; he would then make a neat parcel of any shape; finally he would tie it up criss-crossed with string obtained by pulling on the free end of a length that extended from the counter up to a topmost shelf where it unwound as needed from a huge cone-like spool.

The candy was displayed in large glass jars on the counter and the children made their purchases by pointing and saying, "I'll have three of these, two of those, four of this kind, and yes, one of the red ones in the last jar." The clerk, in the meantime, would remove the cover on the designated jars, select the required number of sweets, and pop them into a miniature paper bag. Boys usually didn't bother with bags, but hastily stuffed their sticky booty into their pockets. It was quite common for children to come into the store, put down their penny on the counter, and make their choice of candy, whether it was one, two, or three pieces for a cent. To the credit of most storekeepers, they waited patiently for these little customers — and it must be added, with a smile and a twinkle in their eyes — to make up their minds as to the color and kind of candy they wanted.

Liquids like coal oil and vinegar were stored in barrels, the former in the back of the store and the latter in the basement. Customers brought their own coal-oil cans or vinegar jugs to the store and the storekeepers filled these for them simply by going to the right barrel and turning the spigot. Usually, when a child came to buy coal oil, the cap on his can was missing, so the understanding clerk plugged the spout with a gum drop or a raw potato.

The farmers bought certain of their groceries in bulk, like large cans of syrup and molasses, one-hundred-pound bags of sugar and flour, boxes of dried fruit like apples and prunes, and cases of canned goods.

Some stores had glass-enclosed display counters and the smaller, rarer and expensive items were stored here.

The general stores also handled the few school supplies that students in those early days required, such as the five-cent ink scribblers, the giant-size pencil scribblers (newsprint pages, ruled or unruled), wooden pen holders, pen nibs, bottles of ink, rulers, pencils, pencil boxes and erasers. Pen nibs received the most attention and were stocked in a small glass-topped display chest with those of each quality, brand and size of tip, contained in a felt-lined recess of its own. A child felt important indeed when the lid of the case was opened and he was permitted to choose his pen nibs from the array on display at the expensive price of three for ten cents.

With all the modern ways of packaging things, the natural odors and good smells are stifled, but in the early stores they spread everywhere and gave the place a distinctive characteristic. The odors of harness leather, binder twine, roasted peanuts, rope, kerosene, vinegar, aged cheese, newly-ground coffee and spices waxed and waned depending upon what part of the store the customer happened to be in while shopping, but the strong antiseptic smell of the oily floor, especially on a warm summer day, never seemed to dissipate entirely.

Saturday night became a special evening in town for rural folk soon after cars came into common use. It seemed everyone came to town on that day and the stores stayed open as long as the customers kept coming. Even when the doors were locked at the official closing time, which could be anywhere from ten o'clock to midnight, people still inside could get waited on. Many purchases were large, because during the horse-and-buggy days one neighbor often did the shopping for as many as half-a-dozen families. Some farmers had the habit of leaving their purchased groceries in the safe confines of the store while they went to the dance, the picture show, the restaurant, or the beer parlor. Usually it was way after midnight when they returned to pick up their supplies, and in the meantime the storekeeper and his helpers waited, waited, and waited some more.

As the store was the recognized meeting place for everyone, a sense of warmth, friendliness and belonging pervaded such gatherings and people stayed on and on. It was only when the owner started to sweep up and put things in order that the crowd began to leave. People would slide off counters, rise from the slat bread boxes, nail kegs, or barrels on which they had been comfortably sitting and with reluctance move slowly toward the door.

Fortunate was the child who was present when the store account was paid because it was the custom for the storekeeper to give generous treats of candy or some other luxury items. Some storekeepers gave away sets of dishes, cutlery, dresser sets, or other such items as premiums. In addition, the tot invariably received something special for himself for just being present on such an auspicious financial occasion for the storekeeper.

As the economy of the prairies improved and the farmers' demands for goods increased, the shelves in the general stores became stocked with a greater variety of and more expensive products. The barter system of trading eggs for the few necessary store-bought goods almost disappeared, and for a few years business expanded rapidly. This was short-lived. Before long, the improved road conditions and the advent of better and faster automobiles made travel easier and shopping in the larger stores in the bigger centers more inviting. The general store struggled hard to compete with these new trends, but for the most part local trade declined to the point where the owner was forced to close his shop. Only here and there some general stores survived and continued to make their customers happy with their personalized, or in the words of the pioneer, the cracker-barrel type of service.

Each trade or profession has its unique or classical incidents to talk about and the old-time storekeeper was no exception.

For example, there was the time a young farm wife was shopping in the Elves Hardware (Cayley, Alta.) for a new bed. While she was being shown the various beds in stock, she suddenly remembered and informed the storekeeper that she also wanted to buy a chamber pot. The display area for such enamelware was nearby so the obliging salesman stepped over and reached into the supply cupboard for the required item. As he did so he asked, "What size do you want?" The customer, who still had her mind and eye on the beds, replied, "Big enough for two!"

Or there is the story about bartering in the days when cream could not be shipped as there were few creameries around. Instead, the farm women made butter, packed it in crocks or butter tubs and traded it in at the local store for needed supplies. One enterprising lady packed a five-pound stone in the middle of a tub of butter and received twenty-five cents a pound for it. But the storekeeper who found the stone was equal to the occasion: he sold it back to the same woman, neatly wrapped and buried in a canister of tea, charging fifty-cents a pound for it.

No prairie town was complete without a Chinese cafe. It was a peculiar institution, part eating house, part rest room, part store and part recreation center. Its appearance was never impressive in the early years, even though it boasted a vaccilating sign that attempted to advertise the fact that it was the best eating place in town. It's needless to add it was the only one for miles around. The interiors of these establishments were usually dark, floors bare and blackened from years of oiling, tables covered with oilcloth and arranged down one side of the room, with a counter and one or two glass display cases taking up most of the space on the other side. With the passage of time, booths replaced some of the tables and destroyed the companionship so often noticeable when no partitions separated the patrons.

There was an air of glamour and mystery about these so-called restaurants, no doubt generated by the strange containers of preserved ginger and China tea on the shelves, the rows and rows of glass jars that seemed to harbor the secrets of the East, the bright-red packets of fire crackers with their seemingly untranslatable gaudily-colored labels, the abacus and open Chinese newspaper under the counter or on top of it, and above all, the stifling odor of fried food drifting in from the kitchen. In summer the screen door did its best to keep out the flies attracted by the odors of cooking food, but gusts of wind and the careless customers forced the concerned proprietor to install a spring to pull it shut after each such mishap. The banging screen door and buzzing flies waiting impatiently to get in on hot, lazy summer afternoons, were sounds that few patrons were able to dissociate from the small-town Chinese cafes.

The kitchen, just off the main part of the cafe and separated from it by a swinging door with its characteristic peephole, was accepted as out-of-bounds to the general public, except for a select few who seemed to have some mysterious goings-on with the proprietor. Everyone knew that certain games for stakes were played somewhere in the "back room," but that was the extent of their knowledge; the rest was based on rumor.

Most cafe owners appeared to be the silent types; they were very, very patient, perhaps a bit shuffly, always over-solicitously ready to please, and they seemed to punctuate every response with stereotyped smiles. The moment anyone entered the cafe, the grinning, inquisitive face always appeared at the lookout window in the kitchen door. People often wondered when these people ever slept to maintain such thoroughgoing vigilance. No matter how early in the morning, how late at night, whatever time of the day, these human machines of energy and patience were always ready to serve a meal or a snack, sell a cent's worth of candy to some tot, exchange a licorice plug for a pop bottle, listen to the woes of old men and drunks, and accept the taunts, the jeers and the devilry of more than one gang of mischievous boys.

The cafe served a diverse clientele. There were the farmers who were shopping or hauling grain, the visiting salesmen who were in town making their usual business rounds, the matrons out for an afternoon cup of tea or coffee, the teenagers in for their bottle of pop and some boy-girl socializing, the little children drifting in to buy candy and hanging around to see and hear what they could, the hectic and happy crowd on a dance or show night, the drunks after the beer parlor closed. Then there were the regular town customers like the railway pumpman, the lawyer, the relieving station agent, the grain buyer, the three or four elderly men of leisure and the school principal.

Just because the cafe was full didn't mean that business was good. People could be visiting; some had come in to get warm; country women could be sitting and waiting for their husbands to come from the bar; children impatiently waiting for their parents; lonely old men resting and nodding and lapping up the joys of companionship of the people around them; and teenagers lingering at their favorite table sipping softdrinks through sodden straws, appearing to have nothing better to do. The entire atmosphere in the cafe was one fraught with friendliness and leisure, and did not encourage its patrons to merely eat and run, but to stay, relax and visit. Besides, if one of the paying customers stretched out his eating time long enough, he would be bound before long to meet a friend or two dropping into the cafe. It was a convenient meeting place for everyone from the shy lovers to the farmer looking for the grain buyer.

The small-town cafe was just as economically important to the welfare of the district as the general store, the post office and the hotel beer parlor. Word soon got around if the establishment served good or bad meals and the rural people, the townfolk and the travelling public over a wide area reacted accordingly. Steady patrons of the cafe soon learned what to order or not order once they had sampled the good and bad dishes served up by the cook. A change of chefs was always frustrating at the start because the regular customers were forced to experiment with the menu again until they discovered the strong points of the new cook. The attempts to save money by buying meal-tickets for a week or month sometimes backfired in such instances.

Oriental tradition seemed to dictate that each proprietor should enjoy a private joke on his customers. Wong Kai of Hesketh, Alberta, when asked what was for dessert would say pie and then ramble off the names of several kinds of pie, and invariably end his recitation with apple pie, which was the only sort he ever made. That was his joke. Nevertheless, his friends had their own buffoonery and let themselves be taken in by his witticism by solemnly asking what was for dessert, knowing full well what it was. Sam Wong, who used to run a cafe in Chinook, Alberta, had the habit of rhyming off in sing-song fashion a long and mouth-watering list of pies, and then in an almost apologetic manner and voice, conclude with, "Only have apple pie today!"

When cafe owners began hiring white girl waitresses to handle the increased business as well as to give the place an occidental flavor, the little private jokes took on a different style. The waitresses were instructed not to bother walking back to the kitchen to give their orders, but instead to call out, "Wagon wheels!" if hot cakes were wanted, or "Travelling grunt, cross eyes and stack 'em dry" for an order of bacon, eggs and toast. Such jargon, although not Chinese, bewildered the uninitiated and always proved amusing to those in "the know".

Farm youth enjoyed patronizing the cafe, for in their eyes it was a risqué gathering place for young people and enabled them "to live it up." After all, they could spend their hard-earned nickels to buy several "cigareetes" and another five cents for a package of peppermints to take the smell and taste away. Besides, puffing on the end of a five-cent cigar and blowing smoke rings, or chewing snuff and punctuating world-shattering remarks with a stream of brown spit, made them heroes in the eyes of their younger followers. It was illegal to sell cigarettes, cigars and snuff to minors, but this very fact made it all the more attractive to the small fry if they could persuade the proprietor to do some under-the-counter business. Sometimes they were permitted to use the den at the back of the cafe to roll their own cigarettes, chew tobacco, or smoke. In fact, the old-time cafe was a forerunner of the present-day coffee house and pizza shop as a preferred gathering place for teenagers. It was an essential part of their informal education.

What with one thing or another the owners of small-town cafes had plenty of problems on their hands while serving an ever-demanding and ever-complaining public. Even selling such a simple item as ice cream had its difficulties. The delicate confection, packed in three-foot high wooden tubs and topped with night-cap shaped canvas covers, arrived by train. The ice cream itself was contained in metallic or cardboard cylindrical vessels surrounded completely by a freezing mixture of natural ice and rock salt. It took hard work and plenty of patience to drain the water, untie the cover, scrape away the ice, pull out the drum of ice cream from its icy bed and immediately repack it with a fresh batch of freezing mixture prior to placing it in the ice-cream dispensary. With no artificial refrigeration, the cafe owner depended upon natural ice which had been stored for the purpose, to keep the ice cream frozen and solid. A constant vigil had to be maintained, for if the confection became too soft or melted, the cafe's sale of cones of ice cream would be jeopardized for that day. Most people can remember the empty ice-cream tubs, the pieces of ice, the deposits of rock salts, the ash pile, the myriads of flies, the collection of cases of empty bottles, and above all, the stench, that used to characterize the backyard of each cafe.

The bottle collection resulted from the fact that the cafe set up a sort of bottle-exchange depot to make up for its own shortages. A child could exchange a pop bottle for one or two pieces of candy or else receive one-cent in cash. These minute business transactions brought additional headaches for the proprietor, but he had the satisfaction of knowing he was making a profit no matter how small it was. The profit was managed in spite of the boys who occasionally stole bottles from his pile at the back of the cafe and sold them back to the proprietor as their own.

Although these Oriental proprietors had to cope with such incidents, they proved to be fine and able Canadian citizens and did their share in supporting community activities. One enterprising prairie community decided to raise money by sponsoring an oyster supper. When the fresh oysters arrived, not only did no one know how to prepare them, but no one knew an easy method of prying the shells loose to get at the jelly-like repulsive creatures. After a few disheartening attempts, the once-enthusiastic supper committee was ready to give up on the oysters and serve ham instead. Just at this critical moment someone suggested the Chinese cafe proprietor as one who might know the secret of the oysters. He not only knew, he prepared such delicious oyster soup that people kept coming back for extra helpings. So many people turned out for the special meal that the community basked in financial success. No better advertising could have captured the imagination of the general public than that of an organization planning a shellfish feed and then not even knowing how to extract the oysters from their shells. The people who laughed the hardest at the ignorance of the committee members were the very ones, who, with faces tensed, hesitated at first to down the succulent oysters.

To the child who lived on the prairies during the first half of the twentieth century, there were no words that carried more exciting anticipation than, "Let's go and watch the train come in!" Train time in those early years created quite a stir in a small town, and whether it was the tri-weekly mixed train or the twice-daily passenger, it appeared as if the entire population was at the station to meet it. Children even gave up their play time to watch the unending drama of the arrival of the train. Besides the crowd of mere onlookers, there were always the regulars, like the mail carrier, the drayman and the station agent who had to meet the train no matter what the weather or how late it was. Sometimes during storms or in extremely cold weather the mail carrier waited all night for the train to get in, for the royal mail just had to get through. It's too bad William Shakspeare didn't live during this stirring period of the railway stations, for he could have recorded the great dramas of prairie life as it unfolded in their waiting rooms, their ticket offices and on their platforms.

Passenger trains were the most interesting to watch, but there were others, although not seen as often, that could really excite the imagination. For instance, there were the silk trains that travelled at terrific speeds and it was rumored that they carried armed guards on them, but before a child could get a good look to see if he could spot one, the train had swished by and disappeared down the track in a cloud of dust. Troop trains appeared during the war years and always seemed to be carrying only happy, throaty service men; this was in sharp contrast to the hospital trains marked "Red

Cross", that were so silent and solemn. Work trains often stopped at the station and they invariably seemed to carry such intriguing machines as pile drivers, steam shovels, gravel spreaders, rail hoists, ice breakers, the mystical Spurry Car, the rotary snow plow and the weed sprayer. Fruit trains went by in the fall of the year and left an aroma of apples, plums or peaches in their wake. Auxiliary trains pulling huge steam cranes and other mechanical devices occasionally went by on their way to the scene of a wreck. In winter the observant person could always spot the snowplow train clearing the right-of-way; it seemed literally to sail through the snow like a boat in water, often sheathed in a self-created blizzard. The holiday excursion trains from the United States or Eastern Canada rarely stopped at small places, but through the wide windows of their dining cars it was possible to catch a glimpse of the tables covered with glistening white linen and set with sparkling glassware and silver, with waiters in immaculate white walking up and down the aisles. However the train that made fairy tales and dreams seem true was the flag-decked royal train carrying the king and queen and the two princesses across Canada. Last but not least, as far as the children were concerned, were the ever-thrilling and colorful circus trains headed for some nearby city.

It was an experience indeed to be one of the crowd on the station platform and hear the train herald its approach by a whistle in the distance, see it round the bend, roar past the yard-switch, and finally grind to a screeching stop just at the right spot in front of the station, enveloping everyone in a cloud of dust, cinders and smoke. Immediately the station platform became an exciting hive of activity with passengers getting off and on. The station truck was wheeled up to the baggage and express cars in turn; any company mail was exchanged, and the milk cans, egg crates, bread boxes, trunks and suitcases were swung neatly into the dark exterior of the car. In return, the truck received a variety of bags, parcels, boxes, rolls of newspapers, machinery parts and sides of beef wrapped in gunny sacking. It took an expert to stack everything on the express truck and not have some odds and ends fall off. Sometimes the station agent required the assistance of the trainmen and the drayman to wheel the over-loaded cart up the ramp-like threshold and into the freight shed. In the meantime, the mail carrier wasted little time in performing his duties as he tossed his soiled gray canvas bags into the mail car, retrieved several bulky ones in return which he piled in his cart, and in no time was headed towards the post office with two or three eager patrons close on his heels.

All too soon, or so it appeared to the bystanders, the doors on the train began to clang shut one after the other. The conductor, after looking towards the head of the train to make sure that all the loading and unloading was completed, swung slowly and with dignity back up on the steps intonating in a loud voice, "All aboard!" At the same time he pulled the signal cord which responded with a few consenting hisses and in no time the train started to move off silently. The people on the platform subjected

-- H. H. Cooper

Here is a typical scene at the Byemoor Railway Station (Byemoor, Alta.) near train time.

the passengers to close scrutiny which was returned impassively as the coaches passed by, moving ever faster and faster.

The train was a visible link with the outside world and for a few minutes at least, relieved the stubborn tension of the daily round of a hard and lonely farm life. Little did most rural people dream that two future world wars would carry them and their children from this very station across Canada many times, or that many would travel to distant lands across the seas from which a few would never return.

As the train gathered speed and gradually clacked out of sight, the departing sound of its haunting steam whistle seemed to be the signal for everyone to come out of their trances and to swing back into their daily routines. Children dashed out onto the tracks with squeals of delight to pick up and examine the nails and pennies they had so carefully arranged on the rail prior to the train's arrival, now flattened smooth and useless. The adults, still in deep conversation, straggled back up town in twos and threes, while the drayman, with his dray loaded down with as many noisy children as newly-arrived supplies, urged on his horses to the nearest store. Now, with the train out of the way and the platform cleared of express and baggage, the station agent entered his bay-window office to reset the semaphore signal and to report to the dispatcher that train number nine left his station on time.

Between the waiting room and the large baggage-express room in the familiar red station there was a smaller room with a bay window that bulged out on the platform; it was from this mysterious place that the station agent performed his miracles. The children envied him his station as it was linked to the outside world by telegraph, telephone, and best of all by the steel rails over which the important trains thundered. Farm children soon learned just how important this man wearing the green eyeshade and black sleevelets, operating and understanding the phenomenal telegraph gadgets was to them and to their parents. It was he who shipped their cans of cream, their crates of eggs and their carloads of grain. He was the one their parents saw to pick up the parcels from Eaton's or Simpson's, the cartons of baby chicks from the hatchery in the city, the crate of baby pigs from some farmer in Manitoba in response to an advertisement in *The Western Producer,* or to ship cattle from the railway stockyard. Besides shipping and receiving goods, he sold tickets to people travelling to the next town, to Toronto, or overseas to the Old Country. He was known to have written up tickets a yard long for some lonely farmers or section hands who brought back their brides from such far-off countries as the Ukraine, Norway, Scotland or Italy.

Station agents possessed two skills that impressed most young boys. One was their ability to receive and send the Morse Code. In the pre-radio era, if they wanted to know the score in a Stanley Cup hockey game or in the World Series baseball playoffs, he always managed to get it "off the wire" for them. Little did the youngsters know that through the telegraph wires of their railway station flowed many messages of business, death, disaster, happiness and surprise which concerned the people in the town and surrounding area. There is still the person around who remembers the agent's sad wartime duty of delivering a telegram from the defense department which commenced so formally and without a trace of feeling, "We regret to inform you that your son, or husband is missing, presumed. . . ."

The other skill that impressed youngsters was the way the station agent used a bamboo loop to pass train orders to the engineer as the engine thundered by the station. After copying and checking the train orders received over the wire from the dispatcher, he folded and placed one of the flimsy copies in the wire holder on the loop. Then, when it was time for the train to arrive, he went out onto the platform, walked up a short way, and stood waiting as close to the track as experience had dictated was necessary. Then when the train approached, he held up the holder for the engineer, who skillfully slipped his arm through the loop when the engine passed, removed the message, dropped the bamboo loop to the ground, quickly read the orders, and either high-balled the train, stopped it, or put it on the siding, depending on the orders he had just snatched up. Most imaginative boys who watched the impressive transfer between the station agent and the engineer were convinced that such messages were very secret.

No place in town could equal the station and its environs for an interesting and daring place to play. The railway right-of-way was the first stretch of prairie to lose its mantle of ice and snow and provide an excellent place for walking along the track. Then with the smooth, gleaming rails stretching in either direction for miles there was the opportunity to see who could walk farthest on the rail without slipping off. The competitors always appeared like a flock of birds on a roost as their outstretched arms dipped, rose and counterbalanced as they attempted to maintain their equilibrium on the band of steel. The gang could go down to the station and watch the way-freight shunt cars in the railway yard and at the opportune time tempt the engineer to scare them with a sudden blast of steam. Then there were the strange characters, such as bums, gypsies, boys who rode the rods during the depression, and the out-and-out laborers, who arrived in town on freights and hung around the station and the railway yard for no obvious reason. It was a bit scary for the children to come within hailing distance of these adventurers of the road for there was no saying what they might do to the boys and girls. The waiting room in the station could harbor a runaway boy, an escaped criminal, a murder, a would-be thief, newly-arrived immigrants, or depression-driven men and boys. The agent's family could never be sure who was passing the night in the public waiting room beneath them, but the inquisitive youngsters around town always knew, and what they didn't know they fabricated.

Interesting things had a way of happening at the station. Once a banana stock had just been unloaded from the express car, when out popped a huge tarantula spider, and before the frightened railway crew could decide what to do, it escaped to the freight shed. The section men were ordered to destroy it but couldn't find it. They spent days cautiously looking for it while everyone else gave the place a wide berth. It took the inquisitive son of the section foreman to spot the supposedly poisonous creature neatly coiled up under the platform of the express scales.

Then there was the time Mr. Rannie was ready to board the train at the Munson station to travel to Calgary, when all at once he exclaimed with alarm, "My teeth! My teeth! I forgot my teeth!" An understanding and friendly conductor held up the train for fifteen minutes while an embarassed citizen hurried home to retrieve his precious molars.

There was no end of things for an adventurous boy or girl to do "down by the railway track." He could hitch a ride on the handcar, pushcar or speeder, beg a handout from the cookcar of the extra gang, run on top of a string of box cars, get a drink of cold water at the water tank by turning the right faucet, play hide-and-go-seek or search for money under the platform, ask for a chance to see how it felt to sit in the cupola of a caboose or in the cab of the steam engine, and best of all — to get a ride on the engine as it travelled the wye to turn around.

Every time the children entered the waiting room of a railway station they were attracted by huge posters advertising various railway excursions, exhibitions and fairs. However, it was the one or two large color pictures of the company's ocean-going liners that delighted them the most. Even the dates of arrival and departure of the ships at Canadian and foreign ports were given, which further fascinated the young romantic minds.

Railway officials would have been both surprised and distressed if they had ever discovered the many uses to which their waiting rooms were put, apart from their intended purpose. Depending upon the understanding and the cooperation of the station agent, waiting rooms were used for school Christmas concerts, dances, card parties, afternoon teas, school board meetings and as plant nurseries, indoor play areas and merchandise display rooms. Waiting rooms were ideally suited for such public functions as they were commodious, had pot-bellied heaters to keep them warm twenty-four hours a day, and provided ample seating in the form of benches made of narrow, slatted wood.

Rural children took in all the scientific wonders exhibited in the station and by the trains on the rare occasions they came to town, but back on the farm whenever they heard the train whistle they rejoiced in its company and the realization that they weren't so isolated from the world of men after all.

It was an enthralling experience for a child to visit the blacksmith shop because the sights, sounds and smells were unforgettable. There was the shower of sparks streaming from the red-hot plow share every time it was struck by the trip hammer, the sizzling of hot horseshoes as they were plunged into the wooden tub of water, the deep-throated wheezings of the giant bellows as the handles were pumped back and forth, the true ring of the hammer on the anvil, the sizzle of the fire in the forge, the singeing hoof and the yellow fumes as the shoe was fitted, and the strong dank odor of the forge and the welding compound. Sometimes the horse objected to being shod and the resulting battle of wits between it and the blacksmith was better than any Wild West adventure shown on today's television.

The blacksmith shop was usually no more than a large shed equipped with a forge, bellows, hammers of all types including the mechanical trip hammer, anvils, a good supply of iron, soft coal and coke, a platform for putting iron tires on wagon wheels, grindstones, holding-stocks for unruly horses, and tubs of water and oil for cooling and tempering the hot metals. It always had a grimy and unkempt appearance, probably because of the horses, the amount of scrap iron lying around, and the smoke and soot produced by the Pennsylvania coal burned in the forge. However it was a busy place and was bound to be open at six in the morning, or sooner if required, and it didn't close until long after supper. All was not work, for the blacksmith shop was also considered as something of a social spot. So while the trip hammer tapped out its rat-a-tat-tat, or the perspiring grime-covered blacksmith swayed gently in time to his sweeps of the bellows, experiences were exchanged, a few know-hows shared, the concerns of mutual friends and neighbors were discussed, and the latest stories told by travelling salesmen repeated with some local color added.

A blacksmith shop could best be compared to a three or four-ring circus, for each part of it was set up for a special job to be performed. The chief actor was the leather-apron clad blacksmith who would fascinate the youngsters with his skill and even inspire them to wish for an anvil of their own.

Tire setting was interesting to watch. The steel tire was first removed from the wheel, shrunk with a special machine, and then placed in a circular fire box in which a hot fire had been built. After a period of heating the expanded hot tire would be lifted from the fire, slipped over the wooden felloe of the wheel, pressed and hammered into place, and then rolled into a special water trough to cool the iron and prevent the felloe from burning. The work required exacting skill, for the tire had to be shrunk to the proper size within a sixteenth-of-an-inch. If a tire was shrunk too much it would buckle the wheel after cooling and become lopsided. If it wasn't shrunk enough, the work would be in vain because the tire would become loose again after cooling.

Horseshoeing was a major part of the blacksmith's trade. The two metal parts were welded by melting them and then fusing them with the heavy blows of a four-pound sledge hammer in the hands of the brawny blacksmith, or the lighter and more rapid taps of the mechanically-operated trip hammer. People who lived in any small town or village in those days eventually became accustomed to the clanging sound of metal pounding on metal. They were awakened in the morning by the rit-a-tat-tat of the trip hammer and went to sleep at night with the same sound ringing in their ears. Horseshoeing was dangerous as some horses did not take too kindly to having their foot held knee-high for several minutes by a complete stranger fitting a piece of hot metal onto their hoof in addition to the cutting, filing, burning and hammering that went on besides. Although the blacksmith was an expert at quieting a nervous horse, at times it became necessary to employ an easy nerve rope on the head, an immobilizing kidney squeeze loop, shoeing stocks, or in extreme instances, to throw the horse by tightening a loop around his four legs and then holding him down during the shoeing process. Not many people would recognize a horse shoe in its original form. It is only after the blacksmith thrusts the ordinary piece of metal in the forge, gets it red hot, holds it in long pincers and shapes it to fit a particular horse's hoof that the horse shoe becomes recognizable.

One activity of the blacksmith that captivated the imagination of the smaller children was sharpening the plow shares or discs. Youngsters were intrigued by the forge flaring orange and red flames of red-hot metal, the sonorous pounding, the flying sparks, and finally, the traumatic appearance of the hissing hot metal when plunged into water or oil and sand for tempering purposes. The shares or discs were whetted on a foot-propelled emery wheel and the resulting profusion of sparks, enhanced by the dim interior of the shop, rivalled a miniature fireworks display, especially if the blacksmith wanted to impress his young spectators.

Besides becoming better acquainted with town institutions such as the general store, the cafe, the blacksmith shop and the railway station, every time they came to town, rural boys and girls also learned a few things about the livery stable. Their parents had little need to visit the livery stable on such occasions so the youngsters were not as familiar with it as with the other business centers.

Livery stables provided feed and shelter for the horses of travellers and if the travellers themselves didn't want or couldn't afford hotel accommodation, hay bunks were available for them as well. It was here also that people such as the doctor, the school inspector, the real estate dealer, the implement dealer, or anyone else could hire a saddle horse or a team of horses and a buggy or a wagon, to travel to some destination that could not be reached on foot so expeditiously. Most doctors owned their own teams, buggies and cutters, and found it convenient to keep their horses in the livery stable where the horses would receive good care and be readily available for a trip at any time of the day or night. The drayman also found it to his advantage to quarter his horses in the livery stable and most had an agreement with the proprietor which worked out to the mutual benefit of both parties.

Forty miles was enough for a team and a wagon on prairie roads, so most farmers hauling grain or travelling to town to purchase supplies or on some other errand, put up their teams or saddle horses overnight in the livery barn. It was also quite common for the hotel and the livery barn to have a working agreement with each other; once the guest registered at the hotel his team was taken to the livery stable and his driving robe and whip put away in the harness room for safe keeping.

The front end of the livery stable contained the office, which was furnished with a large pot-bellied stove, several wooden chairs and benches, a battered roll-top desk, and a wall cupboard containing such essentials as bottles of horse liniment, painkillers and cans of harness oil. The remainder of the stable consisted of rows of stalls on either side with a large service aisle down the center. Two feed alleyways between each wall and the stalls, extended the full length of the building and were complemented with a trough and manger at the head of each horse bay. A harness storage area, three or four feed bins and several utility rooms of various sizes completed the downstairs part of the stable. The loft was used primarily for the storage of hay, oat bundles, bags of oats and other feed; however, when necessary, due to its spaciousness it could easily be readied into a hall or impromptu sleeping quarters for travelling farmers. In the latter case it earned the name "sheep's pasture", no doubt from the clutter of men sleeping on pallets or straw or hay on the hard floor of the loft.

The hostlers, usually two or three men or boys who liked horses and didn't mind an austere life, did the stable chores of feeding, watering, bedding and grooming the horses as well as the everlasting and monotonous task of cleaning the barn. The proprietor or owner, from his headquarters in the office, met the public, kept whatever scanty records there were and in a general way looked after the business end of the operation.

A livery-stable office served as an informal meeting place and lounge for travellers, farmers, local business and professional people, and the town "characters" and loafers. It was the spot to go to learn what was happening or about to happen in town, in the surrounding countryside, and in the outside world. People realized the importance of the livery stable as a communication center. The walls inside and outside were plastered with a desultory display of notices and signs calling attention to such things as auction sales, a desire to buy a gentle horse suitable for pulling a school buggy, the services of a registered bull, a reward for locating a valuable horse that strayed from the owner's farm, a city dealer wanting to buy hides and raw fur, a spelling match to be held in the Stone Angel School, a fowl supper to raise funds for a family that had lost its home in a prairie fire, and a large colored poster announcing a forthcoming magician's show which featured the unbelievable act of sawing a woman in half. It behooved the reader of these advertisements to note the dates very carefully; the livery-barn staff was never noted for its promptness in removing old notices, so a few of the announcements were out-of-date by weeks or months, and in the case of attractive posters and calendars, by years.

The livery stable possessed its own distinctive smell which was a blend of horse, hay dust, oat bundles, buffalo robes, tobacco smoke, snuff, liquor, liniment, harness oil and the usual ammoniac whiffs of horse manure. There was nothing more efficient, especially on a cold winter's day, when people gathered in the office to keep warm, than the big heater which provided a generous circulation of these odors in this inner sanctum.

Communities that lacked a suitable public gathering place but possessed a good-sized livery stable quickly exploited the possibilities of using the loft for various purposes. Perhaps the climb up the ladder or the temporary stairs made it inconvenient, but once the summit was attained there were few halls that could equal it. All types of social, religious, educational and business activities could be sponsored in this unusual penthouse including church services, school fairs, variety concerts, dances of all types and public meetings.

The livery stable's many uses made it one of the most important places in town. Strangers, district farmers and town inhabitants made a practice of calling in at the barn first, no matter what other commitments they had. However, nothing remains unchanged forever, so when the motor car came into common use the importance of the livery stable declined. Some owners turned their attention to sales and feed promotion. Others, prompted by the drayman, the butcher, the Rawleigh man, the doctor during the winter time, and a few sportsmen, who still used horses mainly for sentimental reasons, tried to carry on the livery stable business. But "the writing was on the wall," for the parking area behind the barn began to show fewer and fewer buggies and wagons, and more and more cars. Smart livery stable proprietors, seeing this trend, started to meet the change by converting their premises into garages, and began by installing gasoline pumps. It was a sad day for the hostlers to see the obvious incompatability between the huge sign "Livery Stable" on the building and the gasoline pump out in front. But for good or bad, the public had made its choice.

Early towns were considered fortunate if they could boast of an adequate supply of good water. In fact such a resource was good for business. Farmers made a point of taking an empty cream can along each time they went to town on business so they could return with good drinking water. Frequently the need was the other way about: water was the main attraction for going to town and business was secondary. Rural children didn't take long to become familiar with this routine for they earned the privilege of going to town by being responsible for working the town pump and filling the cream can.

The "old town pump," as it was affectionately called, did not have a picturesque environment as it was surrounded by a wooden fence on three sides to afford protection from passing horses which were apt to dash in when they spied the water emerging from the spout. Rural youngsters found it more interesting to wander over to the town pump than to their own on the farm because there always was plenty of company and the jaunt wasn't mandatory. As regular as a clock the clerks from the stores, the waitress from the cafe, the bartender from the hotel, the hired boy from the livery stable, or the housewives from their homes, could be seen carrying their pails to the old pump. There was no need to look out to see who was getting water, for the characteristic jangle of the pail or the singular clatter of the way in which the pump was operated readily identified the water carrier.

Things had a way of happening around the pump; sometimes a person would fall off the pump platform with a pail full of water; lovers spooned there by moonlight using the doubtful pretext of a low water supply at home; visiting farmers were known to drive a horse into it on a dark night; neighborhood spats had a way of gaining a second wind near the pump; fires always brought out the bucket brigade; water fights usually occurred when two temperamental boys reached the pump with their empty pails at the same time; and like most public and business places of that day, the old town pump earned the status of a social center near which people met to pass the time of day, to banter, and to show concern for each other.

It was not always easy to get water in winter as the pump sometimes froze up, caused indirectly by someone forgetting to drain the water from the pump after using it. This could have been avoided by simply leaving the pump handle up. When such a misfortune occurred a perseverance contest materialized among the users to see who could last the longest without taking the initiative of bringing a kettle of boiling water to thaw out the frozen pump. All winter long a coating of ice would form around the pump causing people to complain about the dangerous situation, but no one did anything about it, least of all the village council. It took an accident like a broken or sprained limb, someone slipping and hitting his head on the ice and being knocked out, or a child accidentally spilling water all over himself and arriving home like a sculptured figure in ice, to bring action. Then a group of concerned citizens would take matters into their own hands and gather together with picks, axes and shovels and soon have the approaches to the pump cleared and safe again. The attitude of the village fathers towards such problems was always interesting; they would let the vigilantes do the worrying and the work. They figured that since the water was free, as responsible purse holders of public funds they could not afford to spend money when, with a little consideration and care by the water carriers, the problem would not have occurred in the first place. Yet, in spite of all the difficult or embarrassing situations the old town pump created, it provided good drinking water and that was what was important.

Rural children were fascinated by the wooden sidewalks that extended along both sides of the streets and avenues of most prairie towns. They considered them to be a work of wonder and didn't seem to tire of walking or running up and down these wooden thoroughfares and gleefully enjoying the loud reverberations.

The board sidewalks were about six feet in width, constructed of two-inch by eight-inch planks laid crosswise and nailed to stringers set in the ground, or where the ground terrain dictated otherwise, supported on blocks. Towards the outskirts of the town, the sidewalks had a habit of degenerating into two planks laid lengthwise. This forced the public to literally "walk the plank" and accept all the attending pitfalls.

The elevation of the sidewalk above the ground varied from perhaps six inches to almost two feet, a condition that often made it necessary for the smaller children to climb hand-over-fist, and the women to clutch their long skirts every time they executed the giant step from the street level to the sidewalk. Four crosswalks of heavy wooden planks placed lengthwise and buried just below ground level straddled each intersection and provided convenient footing for pedestrians walking across any street.

Wooden sidewalks, although possessing many advantages over the footpaths they replaced, had flaws of their own. Planks often became loose and tripped the unwary pedestrian, or worse still, flipped right up and delivered a nasty blow to the side of the head or body. Women often found themselves immobilized when the heel on one of their high-heeled shoes lodged firmly in the space between two consecutive planks or, even worse, broke off completely. It was not unusual in the spring, or after a heavy rainfall, for sections of the wooden sidewalk to float away like rafts and come to rest in the most awkward places; they might end up in the middle of the main street or block the doorway to an outhouse. The town fathers countered such wandering tendencies of their sidewalks by stringing and nailing heavy wire along the edges of the planks, thus anchoring all the sections together. Any time the sidewalks became wet or coated with ice and snow, they became very slippery and the pedestrians had to perform gymnastics to retain their balance on the narrow promenade. The alternative was to suffer the indignity of glissading to the street on the one side or into the patch of dirty weeds and rubbish on the other.

If the sidewalks were neglected for a few years they had a characteristic way of settling down into the ground as if from some form of melancholia, but physically it was due to the gradual decay of the supporting stringers underneath. Soon the sidewalk began to resemble a corduroy road and after a few more years would disappear entirely in a maze of grass, weeds, dirt and rotten wood.

Wooden sidewalks also had one serious drawback for the smaller children. This was the era of the small silver five-cent piece and as such a coin slipped so readily out of tiny clenched fists, minor tragedies occurred when it rolled around crazily and then with a final clink dropped out of view through a crack in the walk. Instead of the anticipated ice-cream cone, the chocolate bar, or a bottle of pop — nothing! Hence it was a common sight to see a number of worried tots on their hands and knees on the sidewalk peering through the spaces between the planks in the hope of seeing their lost treasure. Once spotted, the problem of retrieving it came into play. Sticks, wire, branches or strips of cardboard served as probing and fishing tools. Often these were tipped with a piece of chewing gum or a dab of saliva to raise the coin from its crypt under the sidewalk. If older children suffered the loss, more drastic actions were taken, for a crowbar or a claw hammer would be borrowed from the cafe and used to pry up a plank or two in order to locate the lost coin. Such measures often brought pleasant surprises, for not only was the original five-cent piece recovered but coins lost by other people were found as well. Another method employed by the small fry was to burst out crying the moment the coin was lost and continue until some sympathetic adult retrieved the coin for them, or else replaced it with one of his own. If none of the above methods brought results, all indicatons of the "fishing" were erased and the all-important position on the sidewalk marked in some secret fashion in the hope that no greedy opportunists had watched the unsuccessful hunt and would return later to retrieve the treasure themselves.

It is doubtful whether any social consideration entered the planning and construction of the wooden sidewalks, but preconceived or not, when friends met, the walks provided a convenient place to stop for any hobnobbing. They simply sat on the edge of the board walk just as they would have on the settee or chair at home. Well, there was a difference! The many slivers that protruded from the surface of the planks threatened the person who didn't examine the surface carefully before sitting down on it. In the business section of the town it was common during the dull period of the day for the shopkeepers to sit on the sidewalk outside their shops and chat with whoever happened along. If a prospective customer entered their premises, the barber, the bartender, the cafe proprietor, the harness maker or the store clerk, rose slowly, smoothed his distinctive trade apron, rubbed his hands and entered into business.

No sounding board recorded the activities going on in town better than the wooden sidewalk did. Without looking out the window, the housewife knew who was approaching by the sound of his tread, whether it was her husband, any of her children, the butcher next door, or the school teacher who boarded down the street. Strangers always gave themselves away long before they had sauntered any distance along the telltale board walk. Whether it was the sound of a passing bicycle, a perambulator, a cow, a dog, a wheelbarrow, the mail carrier's pushcart, a doll buggy, or the comforting tread of the doctor or the night watchman, the wooden sidewalks unerringly played back the symphony of life enacted in each prairie community for all who had ears to hear.

4

The Home as a Health Center

One of the greatest drawbacks to pioneer life was the lack of professional treatment for the sick. If your family was healthy, you considered yourself exceedingly fortunate. If they were not, that was just your own tough luck. The terrible fear of losing loved ones, especially small children was ever-present in those days. Communication, always a problem, became critical during any severe illness. Doctors and drug stores were hundreds of miles away at first, and as there was no telegraph, telephone, radio or even a railroad, a call for help would have to be sent with a rider and a tough horse. It has been told how people lay in their homes seriously hurt or sick for days before a neighbor chanced by. A person had to be very ill and almost at death's door before any thought was given to getting a doctor. On the other hand, these general practitioners were dedicated, and like the mail, travelled in rain or shine, through mud or snow, on horseback, in sleigh or buggy, to reach the sick no matter where they were. These doctors never refused to make a house call if it were possible for them to get there, knowing full well that their fees, if paid at all, would likely be in the form of farm produce.

Since doctors were out of reach for the majority of the people living in the rural areas, all illnesses and emergencies were cared for at home by wise, but sometimes panic-stricken, mothers. Of course they received some valuable hints from the old-fashioned doctor's book that occupied a prominent place beside the family Bible in most farm homes, and from the "old-wives" cures that started to make the rounds the moment some malady appeared. The sick also depended on the advice and help of their neighbors. Many of the women who had demonstrated nursing ability in the past were called upon to minister to the sick, or to act as midwives and help with childbirth. How wonderful it was to have a woman in the district who would give herself unstintingly to relieve the fears of those concerned! In the Adanac S.D. (Adanac, Sask.) it was Mrs. Baldwin who was the angel of mercy. The weather was never too stormy nor the road too long for her to come to someone's assistance. Somehow when she arrived, radiating confidence and cheer, everything seemed to be all right. She saved countless lives, especially those of expectant mothers. In fact, dozens of men and women living in the Adanac S.D. and elsewhere have at one time or another proudly boasted, "I'm one of Mrs. Baldwin's babies!"

One day a man drove up to her door and in a tremulous voice, "Could you come at once, Mrs. Baldwin, my wife is dying!" The mother-turned-nurse hastened and was ready in no time to find she had to ride sitting on a stoneboat with an old tub turned upside down on it. This antiquated platform was drawn by an old white horse; the worried and excited man stood behind her so she wouldn't fall off. Days later when Mrs. Baldwin was coming home, the beholden man said, "You'll never know how grateful I am to you Mrs. Baldwin, and I'm sorry but I haven't a nickel to my name. However, I do have a little pig I could let you have." "That will be all right," replied the tired nurse, "a little pig will eventually be a big pig, I hope."

The predominant attitude towards medicine in those days seemed to be that the worse it tasted or hurt, the better it was for effecting a cure. Also, if a little was good, a lot more was better. The pantry shelves provided most of these unpalatable homemade remedies. There was goose grease and turpentine for colds and sore throats, sulphur and molasses for the run-down feeling, a cloth soaked in British Troop Oil for croup, a mixture of brown sugar and laundry soap to bring a boil to a head, homebrew or whiskey and honey for pneumonia or influenza, coal oil on a lump of sugar for coughs, rubbed on for rheumatism or chilblains, taken internally for constipation, and immersed in it for an infection, a wad of chewing tobacco inserted in a tooth cavity to deaden pain, electric oil for earache, garlic as a general preventative for all diseases and a cure for colds, and castor oil or epsom salts for any illness not diagnosed.

A poultice applied to any ailing or injured part of the body was the commonest method of home medication. Each family had its own favorite poultice: flour and lard, soap and sugar, hot soaked bread and brown sugar, bread and milk. Any of the following applied hot served as a poultice: flax seeds, oats, onions or tea leaves. A sure-fire poultice for festering sores or slivers was fresh cow manure.

Every rural home had a good supply of sulphur on hand as it proved to be a reliable farm cure-all. It was mixed with molasses to produce a spring tonic, combined with lard to form a livestock ointment, blown down the throat with a straw for sore throats, and impregnated with cold cream as a skin-disease prescription. When sulphur was burned inside the house the resulting sulphur-dioxide gas disinfected the place and acted as a deterrent to such diseases as influenza, diphtheria and small pox. Itinerant farm-help often caused the spread of bugs, headlice, ringworm, impetigo, and the seven-year itch. Various sulphur preparations were used to combat the menace. The bane of all housewives, the dreaded bedbug, was controlled by fumigating the house with burning sulphur. In addition, many households kept the legs of tables, dressers and beds carefully set in tins of coal oil, certain death traps for the pesky bedbugs that might have lodged in various parts of the furniture.

It was not surprising then, with so many uses for sulphur, that once in a while some person would misinterpret the instructions and come up with rather doleful results. Such was the case of an early settler in the Brownlee S.D. (Broadview, Sask.) who, upon developing a severe rash on his body, took the advice of some kind person who suggested sulphur and molasses. The patient mixed the ingredients, but instead of taking it internally rubbed it over the affected parts of his body. The treatment did not cure his rash but it certainly played havoc with his underwear. His union suit was stiff as a board and just as brown.

Although much of medical folklore is now considered groundless, the early rural people were faced with the grim necessity of getting relief from their illnesses as best they could, so they were willing to try anything, no matter how absurd it appeared to be. Hence it was not uncommon to find such singular treatments as doctoring whooping cough by passing the patient through a horse collar three times, stopping profuse bleeding from the nose or elsewhere by the use of cobwebs, preventing mumps from descending to a girl's breasts and ovaries or a boy's testicles, by placing strands of flax around the girl's neck or the boy's waist, preventing injury to the eyes by forbidding the wearing of rubbers indoors, treating headaches or sore eyes by bathing them in fresh human urine. Communicable diseases were warded off by wearing a bag of camphor around the neck; leg cramps were relieved by turning the sufferer's shoes upside down under the bed, or by placing magnets at the foot of the bed; patients with tapeworms were starved in the belief that the worm would also starve, or else become hungry enough to desert the improvident human body; colds were prevented from descending into the lungs and developing into pneumonia by wearing a dirty or used dark stocking around the neck; intellectual power was enhanced by eating a brain food like fish.

Homemade remedies were gradually replaced by the patent medicines sold by the Rawleigh and the Watkins travelling pedlars. No distinction was made in medicines given to humans or to livestock. Someone always was being sent from the house to the barn, or from the barn to the house, to get the salve, the carbolic acid, the liniment or the painkiller, depending whether it was last used on man or beast.

Of great concern were the infectious diseases like measles, chicken pox, whooping cough, mumps, scarlet fever, and the real killers like smallpox, diphtheria and typhoid fever. All these required quarantining and fumigation. The latter was a weird ritual requiring the family to move out while fuming pots of a fumigant like sulphur or formaldehyde produced smoke, vapor or gas that supposedly found and killed the remaining offending organisms. Families under quarantine were confined to their own houses and yards for periods up to six weeks. A large gaudy yellow sign nailed on the front door or gatepost warned all and sundry of the drastic legal and medical implications of breaking quarantine regulations. If a victim of a contagious disease had no home to which he could be quarantined, he was confined for the six weeks to one of the pest houses or shacks located on the outskirts of the town or village. This danger zone was marked off with black and yellow flags and the doctor or the R.C.M.P. brought the mail and other supplies to the unfortunate patient for the duration of his quarantine period. Usually friends and neighbors brought food and treats and left them outside the fence were the sufferer could get them. Children were continually warned of the disaster awaiting them if they ever went near the pest houses.

Occupants of these pest houses, mainly people who had been in contact with smallpox while travelling by train to reach the particular town or village, told how lonesome an existence it was, as no one but the doctor was allowed to see them for six weeks. One such victim, destined to farm in the Last Chance S.D. (Cayley, Alta.) as soon as he started to feel a little better from his bout with smallpox, used to bundle up at night and walk to the cemetery where he was sure he wouldn't bother anyone.

If one or two members of a family caught an infectious disease, the rest were released from quarantine if they showed no signs of the disease during the so-called incubation period, and if they moved to a threshing caboose or a hastily contructed shack at a goodly distance from the house. Clothing, bedding, dishes and anything else required in the temporary home were arranged on the floor and disinfected by sprinkling them with formalin. The building was then locked and kept closed for eight hours.

In spite of such strict preventative measures, an occasional incident like the following often undermined the good work.

> There was the time when my baby was cutting his first teeth. He was not at all happy to be alone and seemed contented only around other children. I made a point of visiting as many families with children as possible until he seemed over his restlessness. I got the surprise of my life! What was thought to be first teeth turned out to be German measles. Needless to add there were few families in the district that did not reap the benefits of our little visits.

At one time it was compulsory for all pupils attending school to be vaccinated for smallpox. The vaccine, needles and antiseptic were mailed out to all the school districts and it remained for the chairman of the school board, the teacher, or someone delegated by the school board to vaccinate the children. Specific instructions of how it was to be done were enclosed with each individual shipment. The vaccination turned out to be sort of a do-it-yourself medical project for the school. The directions were simple and direct, and read as follows: "Sterilize a spot on the back of the left arm between the elbow and the shoulder. Now, using the needle, make three scratches up and down and three across until bleeding results. Now apply the vaccine and cover the area with the swatch." Parents vaccinated their own pre-school children, while in some schools the older pupils, after receiving the necessary instructions from the teacher, assisted the teacher and vaccinated the younger classmates.

Medical services for the rural population improved immeasurably when travelling medical clinics were organized in the late twenties. These were held in community halls in towns, villages and hamlets, with a doctor, a dentist and two or three nurses in attendance. It was a busy time for the local people as the building to be used had to be scrubbed, thoroughly cleaned and fumigated. Later they were employed to man the throat pumps, clean up and care for the patients recovering from their operations.

Patients were examined the first day in rooms constructed by curtaining off parts of the hall, and if any surgery was necessary they were instructed to bring beds or cots, sheets, blankets, wash basins and anything else required the next day. A kitchen table, with large mirrors placed above it, served as an operating table. Minor operations such as removing tonsils and adenoids were performed as well as dental work on both adults and children. It was quite common to see scared or crying youngsters lined up before a curtained room marked "DENTIST", awaiting their turn to have teeth filled or extracted. Most operations were performed in the morning and the patients returned to their homes in the late afternoon or evening. If they became very ill, they remained in the clinic overnight. In such instances little boys appeared in nighties with crocheted lace yokes or embroidered eyelets, part of their mother's trousseau, some with "Weyburn Flour Mill" stamped on them. This was an occasion which called for a nightgown and not all children had one.

Supplementing these clinics were the "remove something or fix something" days held in rural schools when offending or unoffending parts of the human anatomy, like tonsils and teeth, were dispatched or treated by a visiting doctor or dentist while the student sat in the teacher's chair in the classroom.

The dreaded outbreaks of infectious diseases continued to make their rounds in the early days, paralleled closely by the usual routine of vaccination, fumigation, quarantines and many saddened homes. At that time there were no vaccines for some of the diseases, so people lived in constant fear of catching something. Large families spent considerable time under quarantine, for the children wouldn't contact a particular disease at the same time, but at irregular intervals. So when the quarantine period for mumps had just nicely elapsed, someone else in the family would get chicken pox and start another period of confinement. This could be followed by mumps again and so on. The only sure way to miss school, other than to help with the harvest, was to get one of the infectious diseases and the doctor did the rest with his quarantine poster.

The Bavelaw S.D. 747 (Spy Hill, Sask.) was one school that experienced the ignominy of having everyone in the district quarantined. At the time, the students were practicing for the annual field day to be held in the town of Spy Hill, and as usual they were anticipating the event with much delight. To the non-athlete it meant a respite from lessons, and to the more active children it meant a chance to win ribbons. Sad to relate, during practice for the event, all students in the school came down with chicken pox and the Spy Hill Field Day for that year was over for the Bavelaw School.

Records, like this example from the Glenora S.D. 2314 (Viking, Alta.), show that every rural school at one time or another during its history, was forced to close due to the spread of some type of infectious disease in the district.

> The Glenora S.D. 2314 was closed October 30, 1918, owing to the raging epidemic of influenza in the province. It was also closed during the late twenties and early thirties, temporarily, because of an epidemic of infantile paralysis.

People became so quarantine conscious that schools were closed on the slightest rumor or evidence of an epidemic.

A crisis arose in the Echo S.D. (Irma, Alta.) in 1917 when all the school children of the district, except those of one family, broke out with a rash. The parents of the "clean" students immediately reported an epidemic and the school was closed. No one was sure what disease was rampant. This would never do! So one of concerned taxpayers loaded up all the school children in the wagon, epidemic or not, and took them to town for a medical inspection. It was learned that all the children, except those of the one family, had been wading in a slough and, according to the doctor's diagnosis, had contracted a severe case of the itch. The school was reopened the next day.

The Rockafellow S.D. 1510 (Blackie, Alta.) was not so fortunate in 1938. Thelma, the newly appointed teacher, opened the school as usual early in September, although she felt ill. After a few days she still felt miserable and went into town to see the doctor. After a brief examination he startled her by saying, "You have polio, and you'd better get out of town as quickly as possible before you spread it." When she told him that she had been teaching school for the better part of a week, he immediately notified Dr. Sommerville of the district health unit. The students and teacher were inoculated, quarantined, and the school was closed. It was an anxious time for everyone in the Rockafellow S.D. as most homes in the district were affected. However, no crippling or fatal cases resulted, and the teacher was the most thankful of all; she felt personally responsible for bringing and spreading the disease in the district

The reports submitted annually by the school inspectors to their respective departments of education invariably included comments of just how illnesses of one type or another seriously interfered with education. J. A. Fife, inspector of schools for the Edmonton area stated:

> The year of 1918 has been a very broken one for the schools of the province on account of the serious epidemic of influenza which visited

it, and the schools of this inspectorate suffered with those of the other parts of the province. On account of this sickness all schools were closed on October 21 and remained so until the end of the year. This caused a very serious interruption in the school work of the year, the results of which will likely be apparent in the midsummer promotion examinations in 1919.

Too much praise cannot be given to the large number of teachers who unselfishly devoted themselves during the time the schools were closed due to the influenza epidemic to nursing and caring of the sick. Many contracted the disease and a few died as a result of their self-sacrificing effort and work.

Three teachers from the inspectorate died from the effects of the epidemic: Mr. C. A. Curtis of the South Side High School; Miss Della Swales, of the J. A. McDougall School; and Mr. Arol Faulkner, of the Huron rural school. All three were making valuable contributions to the educational work of the province.

Inspector Walter Scott, of the Hardisty Inspectorate, summarized his observations in the following manner:

Down through the years boards of trustees have had to contend with various unusual circumstances. Early in 1918 measles and chicken pox became epidemic in many localities. These outbreaks were followed towards the close of the year by the plague of influenza which made it necessary to close the schools during November and December. Sickness of one kind or another has been unusually prevalent and the attendance has been seriously interfered with thereby.

Inspector H. R. Parker of the Foremost Inspectorate in the southern part of Alberta, was not as fortunate as the majority of his colleagues, for he fell victim to the influenza scourge and was not able to do any field work.

The inspector of the district contracted Spanish influenza on the second of November and was prevented from doing field work for the five weeks following. Also owing to the influenza it was necessary to postpone indefinitely the holding of the teachers' convention.

F. L. Aylesworth's report from the Olds Inspectorate explained just how serious the health problem was:

Outbreaks of measles, whooping cough and scarlet fever in the spring and summer months adversely affected school attendance and school progress. There do not appear to be effective measures taken to quarantine families in which these diseases appear. As a result these diseases drag on in a district, from spring to summer, and from summer to autumn. The need for proper medical examination of rural school children is very apparent.

The outbreak of Spanish influenza has had most disastrous effects, demoralizing school work and effort. We must face in some communities almost the loss of a year of school work, with all that this implies.

I wish to give the highest praise to the teachers who did such noble work in caring for the sick during the epidemic of influenza. Their help was given cheerfully and without renumeration, and was instrumental, not only in mitigating suffering, but in saving many lives.

The late thirties and the early forties saw the heartbreaking poliomyelitis epidemics sweep the country. Since this was before the discovery and general use of the Salk vaccine, the disease was feared by everyone except the most likely victims, the children. It is doubtful whether any rural school district escaped the disease entirely. Very little was known about poliomyelitis and the results of its ravages were reflected by wheelchairs, iron lungs, braces and graveyards across the country. Late summer and early fall were the contagious periods, and any congregation of youth in groups was banned during these times. School re-openings were delayed and picture shows and dances were closed to children. There are people today in their late fifties who still bear evidence of how dreadful infantile paralysis used to be before the Salk vaccine was discovered.

The influenza epidemic that swept across the world on two occasions in the period 1918 to 1919 was a nightmare to people living on the prairie. How or from where the germs came was a mystery, but like the bedbugs, they reached the isolated and scattered farm homes. Sometimes, whole families fell ill at the same time. Everyone who was well enough to be out, helped as many others as they could, by milking cows, feeding and watering the livestock, providing coal and wood, keeping the fires going, getting groceries and medicial supplies, and feeding the patients until they finally recovered or died.

With some, the influenza acted much like pneumonia; others became delirious with fever, and some had very bad nosebleeds. There were so many sick and dying that schools, community halls and other suitable buildings were converted into emergency hospitals. The Red Cross Society or the local health authorities supplied the necessary equipment. One farmer even brought his cow to supply milk for the patients. Instances have been recorded where several hayracks were drawn up near the doctors' residences and tents erected over them to serve as makeshift hospitals. The majority of these fever hospitals were staffed by teachers and other volunteer help. A canvass was made of every home to see who were sick and, if there were any who needed care, they were taken to the hospital. Sometimes they met with severe opposition, especially from those who were used to living alone, and at times it required the services of an R.C.M.P. officer to persuade such patients to change their minds. One stubborn bachelor described such an incident in this manner: "It took a health officer and a mountie to get me here, and it's going to take two health officers and two mounties to get me away from here."

The time the influenza epidemic was at its worst was grim, and few families escaped loss of loved ones. Very little work was done in the fields and neighbors wandered from door to door to find if the inhabitants were all right. In spite of such concerns, cases were reported of people lying dead in their homes for days before their bodies were found, and livestock dying when whole families became incapacitated by the "flu".

The usual treatment for influenza was aspirin, hot drinks, epsom salts, and a prolonged stay in bed. As the epidemic continued, aspirin tablets became in short supply and bulk powder put up in folds was used. The druggists got so they could almost fold aspirin in their sleep. Hot-water bottles were soon sold out and disappeared from the stores altogether. It was hard to buy lemons for the hot lemonade, while the butchers found it difficult to supply enough soup bones. A standard joke about butchers during these trying times was that they were watching the dogs closely to see where the bones were being buried. Liquor was one of the usual components of a hot medicinal drink; there was such a drain on provincial supplies that the problem was brought up in Alberta Legislature in Edmonton. The *Edmonton Bulletin* of April 4, 1919, reported the incident as follows:

> In the evening James Turgeon, Ribstone, moved the adjournment of the house to discuss the influenza epidemic in his riding. In one district there was no liquor to be had. Liquor was regarded as a medicine, which formed a part of the treatment in this disease. He thought it should be supplied in some way.
>
> Honourable MacKay said there was considerable influenza throughout the country. He had sent a doctor to the district complained of and hoped conditions would be better. He had been asked to send liquor to postmasters to distribute. He could not do so.
>
> Dr. State said that many doctors had been greatly embarrassed by not getting liquor.
>
> Honourable MacKay said there were certain bounds beyond which the department could not go. The profession had not abused the privilege granted them during the influenza. The motion for adjournment was withdrawn.

Preventative measures adopted by health authorities were many. All schools were closed until further notice and public gatherings of any kind were forbidden. No one was permitted to go anywhere without a gauze mask. This was a piece of cheesecloth sixteen inches by eight, folded to an eight by four size and worn over the nose and mouth. The effectiveness of the mask could be improved by soaking it in eucalyptus oil and boiling it each time it was used, to kill the germs.

A gentleman in the Byemoor S.D. (Byemoor, Alta.) diligently followed the instructions of wearing a mask of white muslin, but, as he chewed tobacco he found he had an insurmountable problem. His mask became so fouled with tobacco juice that it left much to be desired in its general hygienic appearance. In fact the local people were quick to comment that no self-respecting germ would dare go near him.

Health officials also recommended that homes and public places be fumigated regularly by dousing the hot coals in the stove with sulphur, sprinkling formalin on all the floors, or using a specially prepared commercial product like Vapo Cresolene. Gargling with a concentrated solution of salt several times a day was also a powerful deterrent to the influenza germs. Many people made the grave error of getting up and going back to work too soon. Just because they felt a little better didn't mean they had recovered completely, so the relapse that followed proved to be the undoing of many. In their weakened condition they were not able to put up much of a fight against the influenza germs that had in the meantime built up a resistance for man-made remedies. The majority of such influenza cases proved fatal when the patient developed pneumonia. This was the day before miracle drugs, so people had to depend upon their own resources or the advice of their neighbors to combat the influenza-pneumonia course of the disease. People who were unfortunate enough to get pneumonia after a bout with influenza had to wear thick red vests called "pneumonia jackets." Whether such treatment helped is of much conjecture today.

Thus it was not surprising to find that "a life lived for others" was the rule rather than the exception in every community. The benevolence of a couple like Mr. and Mrs. George Webber of the Kirby S.D. (Drumheller, Alta.) was typical during the epidemic. They initiated something that could be described as the modern equivalent of "Medicine and Meals on Wheels." The wife spent her days preparing a variety of foods suitable for people down with the "flu", while the husband, with his own money, bought whiskey by the case and aspirin tablets by the carton. Each morning he loaded his car with food and a supply of his "medicine" and spent the day visiting and doing chores for those stricken with influenza, especially the bachelors. A number of the patients because of their personal convictions, were reluctant to partake of his liquor potion, but usually yielded to persuasion, and in time all recovered from the "flu". In spite of wearing a cheesecloth face mask with a liberal amount of oil of eucalyptus sprinkled on it as required by the health authorities for anyone appearing in public, George Webber fell victim to the very disease he had battled so successfully. However, he used his own remedies, and before long he pulled through.

During the height of the influenza epidemic, provincial authorities issued orders that governed people travelling on trains. It required all passengers and train crews to wear gauze masks over the nose and mouth all the time they were on the train, whether in the day coach, diner or sleeper. Arrangements were completed with drug stores and departmental stores to sell them at fifteen cents each. The order also required that all cuspidors in the trains be removed, and in their place old gasoline cans filled with a bichloride solution as the only receptacle for expectoration. Health officers also travelled on all trains and aided the regular crews in enforcing the new regulations.

The influenza epidemic took an unusual toll of human life and left those who survived with memories that are both depressing and heartbreaking.

Thinking if we were going to die it would be better to do so in Ontario surrounded by family and loved ones, all six of us made the long journey back to Ontario for a three-month visit.

At one time or another all the members of the family became delirious and their unintelligible mutterings terrified me more than anything. It seemed to me as a child, when a person's senses departed it would not be long before life did likewise. Mother had hyacinths blooming in the windows in the kitchen and their perfume filled the house. To this day the fragrance of hyacinths brings to mind the time of fear, exhaustion and confusion I experienced during the "flu" epidemic.

In one family in our midst the mother, grandmother and daughter all died from the "flu" within twenty-four hours of each other.

Our oldest child died of the "flu" in October, 1918, when he was two years old. I had never seen him, as I was still in France with the Canadian Expeditionary Forces.

When Evelyn returned home for Christmas from the normal school every passenger on the train came down with the "flu", and in the course of a few days, our whole family of six children came down with it too.

Going for the mail that spring was like going to a funeral, for we often received word of relatives or friends who had not survived the dreaded malady.

After the epidemic was over and things back to normal, there were many familiar faces missing.

When passing a lighted farm house at night, our doctor always went in and invariably found someone sick with the "flu". When the epidemic was at its worst he went for a whole week without going to bed.

We remember with gratitude, the devotion of our doctor during the "flu" epidemic, who even had a driver at times, so he could sleep en route from farm to farm so much was his services in demand.

Double funerals and joint graves were quite usual. Some of the dead had to lie for a month or more before a volunteer could be found to bury them.

So many people were dying from the "flu" that it was difficult to get anyone to conduct a funeral service. I remember one time a funeral party leaving the cemetery meeting another one just going in with no one to conduct the last rites. The matter was solved by persuading the lay brother from the first funeral to repeat his service for the second.

Another malady that took the lives of many inhabitants of the prairie but is rarely fatal today was appendicitis. Deaths occurred that could have been prevented by prompt medical or surgical attention. Unfortunately such help was not readily available since the nearest doctor was so far away. Sufficient numbers of rural students became appendicitis casualties to warrant teacher training institutions teaching would-be teachers how to diagnose it if a child complained of a pain in the lower right region of his abdomen. If the teachers suspected appendicitis the parents and the school board were informed so appropriate action could be taken immediately.

Some cases of appendicitis were so serious that it was inadvisable to move the afflicted one to a hospital, so the doctor operated right in the farm-home in an attempt to save the patient's life. In spite of the far-from-ideal conditions prevailing in the ordinary home and the makeshift equipment that was used, a surprising number of such operations were successful. Yet appendicitis continued to reap a heavy toll among the rural people.

> Zelpha Giles died while she was teaching the Plain Valley S.D. (Blackie, Alta.) from a ruptured appendix. The children were broken hearted and were the flower bearers at her funeral.
> I recall so vividly how my father died after a very short illness. There were four other men all within a few miles of each in the Blackie district (Blackie, Alta.) who passed away within a few months of each other. The five cases were not identical but they were all appendicitis.

Health conditions in the one-room rural schools were far from satisfactory and for the most part depended on the knowledge and interest of the local school board and to a greater extent on the incumbent teacher.

The chief disseminators of disease germs, like vulnerable drinking water, dust and flies, abounded in most schools. Usually the water bucket sat on a bench in the cloakroom covered with a piece of cheesecloth during the fly season. For the most part, no one seemed to be concerned how long the same piece of cheesecloth lasted or how many times it was picked up off the floor. Unless the teacher insisted on the use of individual cups, every one used the same dipper to drink the water. Also, no one knew how many times the dipper went to the bottom of the pail or whose dirty little hands retrieved it.

Before the opening of the fall term the school floors were given a substantial coat of oil. But by Christmas time most of the oil had penetrated the shoes of the students, so when the muddy season arrived it was a case of going outside or slowly choking to death whenever the floor was swept. Flies streamed into the schoolhouse, for without any screens on the doors or windows, the pesky creatures found an open invitation to come in from their ideal breeding places in the barn, the outhouses and the ash pile. The following note from the Brown S.D. (Sunnynook, Alta.) indicates how distressing the fly menace could be.

Our teacher took us outside for an entire day while a schoolboard member sprayed the inside of the building with fly tox and swept up the flies. Sometimes in early spring huge blue flies made their appearance and were especially numerous after a hard winter when there were many animal carcasses around. The school's large south windows used to literally crawl with these fuzzy giant pests.

July brought the moth plague. No matter how carefully the floor was swept after school, by morning it was littered along the walls by the wings of dozens of dusty miller moths. The mice ate the moths and left the unpalatable scaly wings.

Incidents like the following indicate the wide range of health standards that could prevail in two neighboring school districts.

One of the boys asked a grade five student why she didn't clean her teeth. She simply told him she couldn't get them out to clean, so that was that!

I recall a health-check contest the teacher had in my early days. I was determined to win and my brother was determined to help me. One cold morning, as we were a mile-and-a-half from home, I remembered I hadn't brushed my teeth. The minute I told my brother, he reined in the horse, turned him around, and old Pat hightailed it for home. I hurriedly brushed my teeth and off we went again on our way to school. I won the health contest that year and as a prize received a couple of bars of Palmolive soap.

The gravest problem confronting most rural parents when one of their family became seriously injured or desperately ill was how to get the doctor or the required medicine. The roads were so poor and the modes of transportation so slow that extemporary measures had to be taken. For instance, a small girl living way up in the foothills near Cayley, Alberta, needed a special medicine to save her life. The farmers and ranchers living along the trail to the town of High River posted horses about fifteen miles apart, chose an expert rider, and he rode at break-neck speed from farm to farm, changed to a fresh horse, and made it to town and back in record time. The race for the child's life was won.

In the Silver Leaf S.D. (Sunnynook, Alta.) Harriet Campbell required stitches to close a wound she had received on her forehead from the heels of her school pony. With no doctor within miles, the task was ably performed by her teacher, Mr. Lonegran, who had completed several years of medical school. With the aid of a few hairs removed from the horse's tail, carbolic acid, a good supply of boiling water, and the assistance of her father and a concerned aunt to control the flying arms and legs, the operation was a complete success. Harriet was told later that she must have been present on every occasion the male members put up the stove pipes, for some of the words she uttered were not in keeping with a lady's vocabulary.

One of the greatest causes of suffering, especially to children and women who found it all but impossible to travel long distances to the city to have dental work done, was toothache. Very few people bothered much about taking care of their teeth as preventative medicine was just in its infancy. Toothache was not taken too seriously, except by the person suffering from it. It did not kill so there was little concern over the agony one could suffer year after year. The majority of rural school children suffered from tooth defects of one type or another, particularly caries. In fact, it was rare to find a child with a healthy set of teeth. When a tooth started to ache, the standard treatment was to administer a drop of oil of cloves or to rub it with a pain-killer. In extreme cases people would dig out the offending tooth with a darning needle, a jackknife, or pull it out with a pair of pliers. If the tooth happened to be loose already, a common method was to fasten one end of piece of strong thread around the tooth and the other to a door knob, so when the door was flung open, out came the incisor or molar. This method was often the one used to remove a child's bothersome baby tooth. It seemed as if every pioneer community could boast of an individual, usually a blacksmith, who had the knack of pulling an aching tooth. No anaesthetizing was done, so the pain suffered by the patient was excruciating. The best bet in those days was to have the local doctor, if there was one available, extract the tooth. To this day, many older people experience twinges of fear every time they visit their dentists. They still remember the pain of either their own or their friends experiences with the blacksmith dentist. Sylvia Broechel, who taught in the Napoleon S.D. (Chagoness, Sask.) from 1929 to 1934, described her frustrations with the many toothaches her pupils suffered:

> Many of my pupils needed eye glasses and all needed dental work. I used to keep aspirin on hand and filled many a cavity of an aching tooth with crushed aspirin, and usually laid the sufferer on a desk covered with someone's coat. I pulled quite a few baby teeth.

When a child found it hard to read due to poor eyesight and the teacher passed on this information to the parent, the youngster usually was taken to the five-and-ten-cent store on their next visit to the city. The concerned adult pawed through the display of spectacles and bought the pair their son or daughter could see with best. Unfortunately, most cases of abnormal eyesight were never spotted as no one took the trouble to administer the diagnostic Snellen's Eye Test Chart.

5

Adversity Was a Harsh Teacher

Prairie farmers had many hardships to overcome. Isolation, lack of farming experience, scarcity of money, poor transportation, slow communication, shortage of fuel and an inadequate supply of good water, were problems from the very start, but there were others that appeared unexpectedly. They could be described best as emergencies or scourges and included fires, epidemics, accidents, illnesses, vagaries of the weather, and diseases of man, plant and beast. They usually struck with lightning suddenness and left the farmer and his family flabbergasted and seemingly defenseless. Today a person would put in an emergency call for the doctor, police, fire department, ambulance service, poison-control center, veterinarian or the district agriculturalist and secure immediate and knowledgeable help. No such services existed for the early farmer. He had to rely on his own skill, wisdom and resources to combat the menace, or as some sage said, "with his own bare hands." His life was a test of faith and a trial of fortitude. Like gold, he was refined in the furnace of affliction. His job was one that only men of mental stability and physical soundness could hope to fill. Rural children were conditioned to these sterling characteristics and gradually absorbed them as their own.

The most dreaded hazard the early farmers faced was the prairie fire. There was a paucity of large tracts of cultivated land and graded roadways, so once a fire was started by lightning, a steam locomotive or a careless individual, the spot of smoke or the cloud on the horizon mushroomed quickly into a rolling ocean of flames. Even before it was visible its stifling acrid grass smoke alerted everyone for miles around.

It was an awesome sight to behold, as the wavy line of brilliant flame, sparks and burning embers advanced unmercifully. The head or the heart of the prairie fire appeared to fly ahead on wings that stretched out in an advancing fiery-V. It was a roaring, tumbling mass of flames, shooting chaotically scores of feet in the air, spewing burning clumps of grass and cow dung for hundreds of yards ahead of it. These flying torches ignited fires far in advance of the main conflagration. At times the billowing smoke covered the sky, completely blotting out the sun, then wavered, broke and passed on, brushing the sun with a delirious blood-red tint.

At night the sky glowed red and was visible from twenty, forty or sixty miles away. Farmers could not sleep at such times for they did not know how far away the fire was and they had to be ready to evacuate at any moment. In the meantime, out of consideration of their neighbors, they wondered who was in trouble now.

There wasn't a horse living that could run away from a racing prairie fire. Fanned by the draft of its own burning, it could speed along at more than forty miles an hour, but with an assisting wind the fire could do better than a mile a minute. With such momentum it jumped fire guards, rivers, sloughs; like a tide, the fire kept sweeping on its rampage of destruction.

Rural people soon were aware of the high toll taken by prairie fires, not only in grazing and haying lands, crops, fences, buildings, but also in livestock and wild animals and the occasional human being outrun or trapped by high-wind fires. At the first sign of smoke, farmers near and far dropped what they were doing, tied a supply of gunny sacks to their saddles and rushed to aid in fighting the dreaded monster. The R.C.M.P. often took charge and enlisted all men from the surrounding towns, villages and hamlets to help extinguish the fire. Such holocausts were taken very seriously and the law was ready to levy a fine of fifteen dollars from anyone within visual range of a prairie fire who did not rush at once to fight it.

Prairie fires were fought with matches, gunny sacks and plows. The plows were employed to gouge long furrows across the path and ahead of the fire. From these trenches backfires were started to burn slowly and under control against the wind towards the onrushing flames. The creation of this burned-over area stopped the advance of the fire when the two met, hopefully to devour each other. The small patches of fire that were left were beaten out with moistened gunny sacks, saddle blankets, slickers, or any other coverlets available. A mother in Tangleflags S.D. (Lloydminster, Sask.) for instance, helped to beat out a prairie fire with a new tweed skirt she had put on that morning. One effective method was to drag a heavy pliable object like a mass of small chains or half a carcass of a freshly-killed cow or horse over the flaming grass and stifle the fire. This was accomplished by mounted men taking up positions on either side of the blaze and pulling on the ropes attached to the object being towed. The riders were forced to change off frequently as it was hot and suffocating work for both the men and their horses. Several fire fighters on foot usually followed closely behind with wet gunny sacks, beating out any small fires that remained.

Fireguards were double rows, six or eight furrows deep, plowed around haystacks and buildings separated by stretches of grassed areas. Very few farmers neglected to protect their holdings or their schools in this manner. In case of fire, the grass between the furrows was burned off, thus providing a buffer zone between the advancing fire and the threatened property. But with the long grass and the fire-fanned winds, a careful vigil had to be maintained for fear the fire might jump the plowed firebreak. A barrel of water and several wet gunny sacks were kept close by in case such an emergency occurred. Usually it was the responsibility of the women and the younger children to guard the fireguards on the home front while the men and the older boys were miles away fighting the main blaze. These fireguards were so common and so important that a school district near Champion, Alberta, adopted the name, "Fireguard S.D. 3879".

A prairie fire was a mere puppet in the hands of the wind. Just when the fire fighters would conclude they had put it out and were happily on their way home, the wind frequently would resume and there would go the fire again. Conversely, when it seemed certain that a building or a feed stack would fall prey to the conflagration, the wind would change direction and drive it in the opposite direction sparing everything. Winds played multifarious antics with prairie fires; they divided and spread fires to all points of the compass, propelled blazing tumble weeds into hay stacks, switched directions promiscuously, tossed smouldering debris over fireguards onto the roofs of houses and barns, whipped small fires set to burn weeds, stubble, or garbage out of control and mushroomed them into capricious devastators.

Family members, no matter how young or old, were briefed as to what to do in case a prairie fire should come. If caught directly in its path, they were shown how to set fire to the grass on the leeward side and move onto the burned-over area. A lady in the Tangleflags S.D. (Lloydminster, Sask.) learned this lesson well, for she was seen carrying a baby under one arm while using the other one for backfiring. Such knowledge and courage saved both of them.

The scene at the fire front was one of feverish hustle and daring. Men arrived from all directions and by all means of transportation imaginable: horseback, buggy, wagon, democrat, stoneboat and foot. Upon arriving, they dashed out to meet the fire head-on, working like mad to beat it out with wet sacks. Right beside them and anticipating their every move was a teamster pulling a stoneboat loaded with barrels of water, frantically urging his nervous horses, attempting to move a little closer to the flames. Teams of horses were dashing across the land ploughing fireguards as they were needed. Nearby a group of men would be engaged in the gruesome task of killing a horse and cutting it in two with jackknives, preparatory to dragging the carcass over the line of flames. Everywhere tired men could be seen with singed moustaches and eyebrows, their faces and hands blackened with sweat and soot and their clothing scorched. The suffocating smell of seared hair and burned grass was everywhere. The horses fared no better than the men. Their scorched manes and tails resembled dried hay; the hair on their feet was bristly and dead; their eyelashes shrivelled, and singed spots loomed up their hides.

How desolate the prairie looked after a prairie fire! Where a short time before, green grass had covered the landscape, there was now only black as far as the eye could see, a veritable Dante's inferno. As soon as the ashes were cooled enough for children's feet, explorations would yield lessons on the harsher aspects of life and death. Children would find farm animals burned to death or left crippled, smoldering carcasses of mice, rabbits, grouse and prairie chicken, and in the distance they might see antelope wandering about in search of food and water. Any house, barn or haystack that remained after the fire, stood starkly alone on the blackened plain, a grim reminder of the many hopes and dreams that too were gone.

Lives were lost.

On April 14, 1933, a very windy day, a prairie fire was burning fiercely in the Morrin S.D. 2513 (Morrin, Alta.). Mrs. Oscar Devaleriola and her two daughters, Margaret and Ellen, had set out to take lunch to the fire fighters. The three were burned to death when they were trapped by a sudden shift in the direction and speed of the fire.

The most disastrous prairie fire experienced in the Endiang S.D. 2253 (Endiang, Alta.) occurred on September 30, 1909. When Mrs. Burress saw the fire coming, she hurried to warn her neighbor, Mrs. Grover, and help her take the six children to safety. They were well on their way when Mrs. Grover remembered she had left her purse back in the house. It contained all the money the family had, so she felt it to be her duty to return for it. Mrs. Burress took the baby and the older children with her and rushed on. They reached safety, but Mrs. Grover and her two little girls were hopelessly trapped by the flames and smoke. The mother tried desperately to shelter the two tots from the flames with her body. It was to no avail. When she realized that they were dead she tried to save herself, but it was too late. She was so badly burned that she died the next day.

Prairie fires, although depressing in themselves, were marked occasionally by humor which took a little of the misery out of them.

For Hepsey Collins who had recently come out from England to keep house for her two brothers, it meant the beginning of a romance. A bad prairie fire had swept into the Harewood S.D. (Dewberry, Alta.) and like all the others in the area, she went out to help fight it. Dressed in a pair of her brother's overalls, with her petticoats and all the other feminine accouterments tucked inside and her face blackened from fighting fire, she was proving herself to be an able fire fighter. William Anderson, a young man of the district who had been beating out the flames side by side with her, thought she was another man, and a good one at that. When the fire crept into a pile of wood, the pair worked together moving the logs to safety, William lifting the big end and Hepsey the smaller one. He complimented her by saying, "You're a h——— of a good man!" That was their first meeting, but by no means the last. William started courting the pretty young helper when he learned of her true identity; they eventually married.

No prairie fire could be described as mirth provoking! George Aune of the Anthill S.D. (Morrin, Alta.) didn't think so either as he spotted one in the distance. It didn't take him long to make up his mind as to what he had to do when he saw it headed in the direction of the Clark farm. He knew the buildings were not protected by a fireguard, so he drove his horses as fast as they could go, toward the endangered home, with the plough trailing behind him. He immediately proceeded to plough a fireguard. In a few minutes other neighbors arrived to help and the fire was soon put out. But the men couldn't help smiling at Mrs. Clark's efforts to help. She was alone, running from house to fire with a dipper of water in her hand each trip, and throwing the few drops that remained onto the fire. All the while tears streamed profusely down her cheeks as she worked herself into a frenzy at the thought of losing all the family owned. The fire fighters tried to humor her by saying that her tears did more good in putting out the fire than the little water she carried in the dipper.

Sometimes the levity of a situation wasn't appreciated until later.

There were many straw stacks in the Lennox S.D. 2368 (Drumheller, Alta.) after the good crop in 1923, so those that were not needed for feed were burned. Children often were sent after dark do do the chore. George Appleyard saw one such fire and thought it was the Ziegler home. He grabbed his coat and cap, ran to the barn, jumped on his horse, without a saddle, just a halter on it, and took off at full speed. Unfortunately, while taking a short cut through the schoolyard, the clothesline that extended from the teacherage to the outhouse caught him on the neck directly under his chin and swept him backwards off his horse. He slowly got back up on the horse, a little dazed from the sudden stop, and continued his race to the rescue. When he was halfway there he noticed to his chagrin that it was a straw stack. The next day, visiting the Ziegler home, he said, "Because of you kids, I almost broke my neck last night." He related what had happened and pointed to a scar across his throat to prove the veracity of his story.

Neighbors, irrespective of any danger to themselves or their homes, were always ready to help or warn each other the instant a prairie fire was sighted. Ole Erickson in the East Bruce S.D. 3691 (Viking, Alta.) was awakened in the middle of the night by the barking of his dog; he looked out the window and noticed the sky aglow. He could also hear a continuous rumble coming from the northwest. Dashing outside, he spotted a prairie fire several miles away, so he quickly rode horseback to warn friends who lived four miles north. When he arrived he found the family asleep, completely unaware of the rapidly approaching conflagration. They had to work frantically setting backfires to save themselves and the house.

Prairie fires were not always started accidentally; a few were deliberately set. To mention one such incident, several lads who were bored with school in the Lake Thomas S.D. 1166 (Viking, Alta.), set a grass fire hoping the school would fall prey to the flames. They overlooked one thing. The gentle breeze changed direction and directed the blaze away from their objective and into a pasture. Here the fire spread rapidly in the dry grass and bushes. By the time help arrived, the fire covered several acres. One guilty youngster, fearing the consequences ran after the fire fighters yelling at the top of his voice, "I didn't do it! I didn't do it!" The daring plan had backfired. Boredom was one thing, but their blunder made school much harder for them to bear for the rest of the term.

Sometimes, life and property were beyond human aid and only the intervention of a kind providence could bring succour. Ernest Litchfield related one such experience.

> I was going to do some ploughing and finding there was no wind I thought it would be an ideal time to burn the stubble. I got it going nicely when the wind came up and blew the fire directly towards a large stack of oat bundles, my entire supply of winter feed. No help was in sight so I removed my jacket and used it to try and beat out the flames. It seemed hopeless and I knew any source of intercession could only come from the Lord. I continued to fight the fire with all the strength I could muster and at the same time prayed that my stack would be saved. The fire moved on mercilessly until it reached the loose straw around the base of the stack. Then all at once the wind changed and blew the fire away from my precious feed. It was saved by a miracle.

It is estimated that one-third of all rural schoolhouses built on the prairie were destroyed by fire in one way or another. Some school districts experienced this tragedy as many as three times. This is understandable as the frame buildings were vulnerable to fire from both the inside and outside. Very little thought went into fire protection while planning the building. The building was vacant most of the time, had children as caretakers and firemen, and few of the teachers, whose duty it was to supervise the work, had any experience in tending heaters, least of all the temperamental pot-bellied type. Fireguards that were plowed around the schoolyards became overgrown with weeds and grass and proved to be more of a hazard than a defense in case of a prairie fire.

The annals of prairie schoolhouses abound in stories of school fires. Here are several typical examples.

Students of the Balmoral S.D. 292 (Red Deer, Alta.) spotted a prairie fire approaching their schoolhouse from the west, and they realized immediately that the mass of small willow brush that grew around the schoolyard created a fire hazard. Fortunately, Michelle Northly, a student in the school, had helped her parents do some backfiring a few days previously, so she was able to explain to the teacher, Mr. Landsdown, how it was done. Leaving one of the older students in charge of the smaller ones, the rest backfired a strip around the school using wet saddle blankets to control the blaze. The burned-over area prevented the prairie fire from reaching the willows and the buildings. Everyone in the district praised the

-- Mrs. S. Mein

A fire destroyed the first school in the Dunreath S.D. 2121 (Innis, Sask.) in October, 1928. Stage one: the fire is discovered.

-- Mrs. S. Mein

Stage two: The fire has a good hold.

— Mrs. S. Mein

Stage three: No chance whatever of saving the school.

— Mrs. S. Mein

Stage four: The charred remains of Dunreath School.

pupils and the teacher, as it was their ingenuity and effort that saved the school and barn.

The Wideawake S.D. (Endiang, Alta.) burned to the ground in 1927, evidently because a can of high-test gasoline was mistaken for one containing coal oil. In the explosion that followed, Mr. Hilton, the teacher was so badly burned that he died shortly afterwards. It was decided to rebuild the school right in the hamlet of Endiang, so if future accidents did happen, the victims would have a better opportunity of receiving treatment quickly.

John Von Sprecken of Filmore, Saskatchewan, a former student at the Dunreath S.D. 2121 (Innis, Sask.), reealled the fire that destroyed the first Dunreath School in October 1928.

> Cash being extremely scarce in those days, I was glad to be considered a man of means when I was accepted for the position of fireman of the school at twenty-five cents a day. Wes Brown was janitor and of equal status.

> All went well for us for a few years, although we couldn't seem to accumulate any great wealth. The sad ending came one Saturday in October when Wes and I decided to give the school an extra good scrubbing. We built a good fire in the old stove to warm the floor and then went to work with our mops and hot water. About two hours later, the job was done and the fire in the stove slowly dying. We mounted our horses and headed for home. About half-a-mile down the road, Wes missed his mop, so we galloped back for it, only to discover to our great dismay when we entered the school that a fire had started around the leaky old pipe in the attic. We panicked! Wes hollered, "Phone somebody!" I grabbed the phone and yelled, though I didn't know any rings. Luckily I got Russell Whyte, the local trustee, and told him the school was on fire. It wasn't long until the whole countryside was there. Everything was removed from the school, including the important telephone.

> Needless to add, Wes and I lost our jobs, though without a reprimand, as many times in the past we had complained to the trustees about the leaky old pipes in the attic. School resumed a couple of weeks later in the old Gray place a quarter-of-a-mile away, and Bob Byers was the new fireman and janitor with money jingling in his pockets.

The Wilson River S.D. 688 (Dauphin, Man.) lost its schoolhouse in February, 1909, under slightly different circumstances.

A number of bigger boys were at the school making final preparations for a concert that evening. Maud Coulter, the teacher, filled the stove with wood in the hope of having a warm school for the public. She seemed to be succeeding. The room became so warm the boys joked with her for making it so hot for them. All at once they began hearing loud cracking sounds overhead. One of the boys went outside to investigate the noise and returned immediately with the news that the roof was on fire. Instantly each person grabbed something and made a hasty retreat. Only one person appeared to be able to think sanely in the emergency. He was seen coming out of the blazing building with a globe under one arm and the register under the other. The rest carried out useless things: a vase of paper flowers, a dust rag, an empty ink bottle and the coal scuttle. The school which turned out to be a complete loss, was rebuilt on the same spot the following spring.

Any time a special "do" was held in a rural school, there was always the problem of providing better lighting than that supplied by the ordinary kerosene lamps. Usually it was solved by the neighbors providing one or two gasoline lamps for the occasion. Since these lamps used pressurized high-test gasoline vapor as fuel, there was always the element of danger in their operation, especially in a public place. Probably every rural school or farm home that used gasoline lamps experienced incidents of fire or explosion. The Plainfield S.D. 1550 (Carmangay, Alta.) was no exception. After Santa Claus had given out the gifts and treats at one of the school's annual Christmas tree programs, a gasoline lamp flared dangerously. It looked as though a tragic panic would result, with the crowd jammed to the door. Paul Frederick broke a window and began dropping children out onto the snow. Two other men followed his example as everyone else appeared to be headed for the single exit. But it remained for Syd Thompson who, after shielding himself against the flames with an overcoat, threw the blazing lamp out into a snowdrift. A tragedy was averted, and after a makeshift repair to the windows, the festivities continued.

School inspectors had their moments with prairie fires.

Inspector Parker visited the Riverton S.D. a day after a prairie fire had swept through the district and luckily had been stopped just outside the schoolyard. He found the teacher still very nervous from the traumatic experience. She was from the city and this had been her first experience with a prairie fire. She approached him the instant he stepped into the school and excitedly asked, "Mr. Parker, did you ever see a prairie fire?"

"Yes!" he said.

"Wasn't it awful?" she remarked and then explained emotionally, "Mr. Thomas came and we sent all the children home. Mr. Craige also came along and put me on a horse, that very thin one you see in the yard, and he whacked him all the way until we reached his farm way over there."

"Now, Mr. Inspector," she explained embarrassingly, "Now you see why I can't sit down today?"

The inspector, who was a stickler for the connotation of words, replied, "No! I don't see. But I can imagine."

The following fire tragedy didn't take place in a school, but since it involved a former student, popular with her classmates and a consistent medal winner in reciting, the students of the Whitla S.D. 2061 (Whitla,

Alta.) were shocked for days and wouldn't talk about anything else. They still recall the incident although it happened in 1916.

Mable Lyon was married one day to Albert Force and died tragically the next. As she was expecting company to celebrate the happy occasion, she put on her wedding dress and started to bake the all-important cake. The wood in the stove wasn't burning very well so she tried to remedy matters by pouring coal oil from a can onto the sluggish fire. The flames instantly flared up and her frilly wedding dress caught fire. Mabel dashed outside and rolled on the ground but she was so badly burned she only lived a day.

When the threat of prairie fires disappeared with the coming of winter and snow, another menace materialized: prairie blizzards. These two adversaries of man, although so different from each other, had much in common. Both reached dangerous proportions at the whim of the wind and their directions and speeds were dictated by the same capricious force. They struck without warning and any living thing caught in its path had to fight for its life against searing heat on the one occasion and freezing temperatures on the other. Man often was able to improvise methods of controlling, or even snuffing out prairie fires, but tactics against blizzards were superfluous. They kept sweeping and whirling across the prairie in their accustomed stubborn and heartless manner, in spite of any efforts to subdue them. The best man could do was to try and save himself if caught in the white maelstrom.

Children who used to attend rural schools had many harrowing experiences with blizzards, so today they have a wealth of such incidents about which to reminisce.

Joyce Nelson of the Red Cross S.D. (Vulcan, Alta.) remembers a bad blizzard that came up during a school day in November, 1929. It became so severe towards dismissal time they felt certain they would have to remain in the school overnight. They knew, from past experiences, it was foolhardy to attempt to go home or expect anyone to come for them. The fathers were hauling grain that fall, so when the storm struck on this particular day they were forced to remain in town. Just when the students and teacher were ready to accept the worst, Ed McFarland and his hired man came across the road to school by following fences and an old culvert. The two champions had the twenty pupils and the teacher link arms and then took the living chain through the storm to McFarland's for the night. Late that evening, beds of all types were improvised and everyone retired warm and well fed. The next morning porridge was made in a wash boiler and this, together with quarts of fresh milk and stacks of pancakes, fed the twenty-one unexpected guests. Once breakfast was over they were escorted again through the blizzard back to the school and their studies. The blizzard petered out by noon and sleighs appeared like magic at the schoolhouse door to take the students home.

A story about a blizzard in the Lone Plain S.D. is not so pleasant. The storm was more severe, the schoolhouse a mile away from the nearest farm house, and it ended in tragedy.

One February afternoon in 1919 an ominous silence settled over the little school, hardly discernible in the vast stretches of trackless snow. A few moments later irregular patterns of snow began swirling across the prairie and the birth of a blizzard seemed imminent. As if to emphasize the truth of this conjecture, the wind screeched around the corners of the school and flung sheets of snow across the windows.

All the students knew the dangerous implications of a bad blizzard. But the teacher, who had come from the city of Toronto that fall couldn't understand the feeling of suppressed excitement that prevailed in the schoolroom or the sudden change in everyone's mien. The boys blossomed into men right before her eyes. Some chained arms and made their way to the barn to feed the horses; others crept along the sheltered side of the school to a nearby shed to return with a large supply of wood and coal. The younger students gathered around the teacher in the hope of restoring a little of their feeling of security.

In the midst of this forbidding scene, little Marie Lerange rushed over to the confused teacher and pleaded, "Please, we leave room!" The teacher, not knowing what to do in such a situation, merely nodded her head. Immediately Marie and her sister and elder brother bundled into their clothes and in no time were out the door and gone, to the cheery accompaniment of a chorus of, "Keep hold of each other and hurry back!"

A few minutes dragged by, when suddenly the blizzard struck with all its pent-up fury. Everyone hurried over to the windows to see what it was like outside. They could just make out the shadowy forms of the boys in the shifting whiteness fighting their way from the barn, firmly gripping the school's only first-aid blizzard equipment, a long stout piece of rope.

In a frenzy the teacher counted them as they stumbled through the snow-shrouded doorway. Three were missing: Marie, her brother and sister. She couldn't believe her eyes. As if in a trance, she calmly took her coat off the nail and started for the door. The big boys pushed her roughly aside. Then as if by a prearranged signal, two of the boys looped one end of the rope around their waists and fastened the other end securely about a cupboard in the cloakroom. Everyone but the teacher seemed to know what to do; they played the rope out slowly and the searchers disappeared into the world of howling whiteness. After what seemed like hours of waiting, the rope began to quiver and soon they heard the pounding feet on the steps. But how many were returning? Eagerly the students crowded around the door but only two snow-covered figures staggered in. "They're not in the toilets or the barn!" came the terse news.

The blizzard raged all night, with the children and the teacher making pathetic attempts to cheer each other and keep from thinking about their lost classmates. Sleep was impossible and tear-stained and haggard faces were occasionally pressed to the windowpanes hoping for some miracle to happen. A white turbulence was their hopeless answer.

By morning the storm subsided and almost instantly parents began arriving at the school. A search for the three Leranges was organized on the spot and soon men were travelling in all directions from the school checking every snowdrift carefully. Half-a-mile away a concerned parent was preparing to travel to the Lone Plain School, when he discovered Emil, the eldest Lerange, huddled under an old buffalo robe on the straw in the back of a bobsleigh. The boy sobbed out his story, telling how they became lost in the blizzard, how the powerful wind separated him from his sisters, and how he stumbled on some ruts in a road and dragged himself along in them until he reached the safety of the sleigh. He was so exhausted by the strenuous work by then that he lapsed into unconsciousness.

The searchers found the two small sisters clasped and frozen in each others arms a short distance beyond the fenceless schoolyard.

It wasn't only in a blizzard that one lost his bearings on the prairie. People became lost under the most ideal weather conditions because to them the landscape looked the same in every direction. Every farmer can recall at least one occasion when he became lost. The following experience of Dick Shields of the Pandora, S.D. (Sunnynook, Alta.) was typical. He thought he would visit the Dixon family who lived five miles north of his place. Dick walked for a couple of hours until he spied the back of a shack. He thought, "I wonder who lives there? That looks a lot like my own." He walked around to the front and peeked in the window. It was his own. He decided quickly, "I guess I'll stay home. I won't go up to the Dixon's after all!"

The legendary homing instinct of the prairie horses probably saved many lives, especially if a black or white blizzard blew up and obliterated landmarks. School children learned very early in their lives to give the horses their heads if they were lost and in most cases were taken home, safe and sound.

It was strange, but the moment people lost their bearings on the prairie they had a tendency to circle rather than continue their journey in a straight line. The following story illustrates the anomaly.

Two farmers of the Stuart S.D. (Didsbury, Alta.) were returning from the coal mines and were caught in a blizzard. Their dogs met them and since they figured they were fairly close to home, the one who lived farther east and had a lighter load decided to speed on. Some time later, to the surprise of the driver of the slower team, he met his friend coming from the opposite direction. They both argued that the other was travelling the wrong way. Eventually they decided to leave the decision to the horses and both arrived at their respective homes without any further circling.

Smaller children found it easy to get lost. Once they escaped their mother's watchful eye there were hundreds of interesting places to explore.

This wanderlust was dangerous as livestock were everywhere, unsafe conditions prevailed at every turn and the country abounded in sloughs. A mother from the Harvey S.D. 1597 (Vulcan, Alta.) told about two such dramas.

Once we lost our baby girl. We hunted madly for hours and even went down our eight-foot well and felt around in the bottom. Our neighbors were notified and they rushed over and began searching the entire countryside on horseback. I, myself, dashed madly about with my hair hanging in tangles, searching in the ploughing and the sloughs but with no success. When I turned homeward I was beside myself with grief for I couldn't see how the child could be found alive as we had spend hours searching everywhere. It was in my moment of deepest sorrow, when the child, after being asleep for hours, raised herself from out of the seed-drill box.

Another time I had been sewing by the open door while my baby boy was playing with the cat. All of a sudden I realized he had disappeared from sight. I had been so busy I hadn't noticed where he had gone. I called and called but there was no answer. I ran to the spot where I had last seen him. Still no baby. However, looking beyond the barn I noticed the cat jumping up and down playing with something that was moving. I ran over and saw the bobbing object to be two tiny shoes twitching back and forth. I caught hold and pulled my boy from a badger hole. He was almost black in the face, with his eyes, ears and nose stuffed full of dirt. I had a very sick baby on my hands for weeks and I was still doctoring his eyes a month after the incident.

Here is another story involving a lost toddler, but with a horse playing the part of hero. It all came about in the Verdant Valley S.D. (Drumheller, Alta.) because little Jack Steward preferred to be by himself anytime company came. On this particular occasion his father had spent the noon hour with a machine agent and had not missed him. Mr. Steward went back to work, hitched the four horses to the plow and started down the field. Barney was the furrow horse; that is, he walked in the last furrow plowed on the previous round. The outfit had not travelled far when the horses stopped and refused to go on. Mr. Steward spoke to them sharply. Three of the animals made an attempt to move forward, but Barney braced himself settling back in his breeching and held them. By this time the driver was getting impatient, so he hit the horse smartly with the lines and calling out, "Get up, Barney!" Barney winced, but did not budge. Realizing that something was wrong, Mr. Steward tied the lines to the lever on the plow, got off and walked around to the heads of the horses. He soon saw the reason. There, at Barney's feet, lay little Jack fast asleep in the cool furrow.

Small children in rural areas didn't have many store-bought toys but they didn't mind. With real live, cuddly animals both inside and outside the house, who needed such cold lifeless things as dolls or teddy bears? Thus, when Rhodina Pahl of Solon S.D. (Hanna, Alta.) was old enough to toddle around her house, she had a very efficient nursemaid, toy and playmate in the form of Ginger, the farm dog. Rhodina couldn't get away with anything. If she strayed too far beyond the farmyard, Ginger would nudge her back; if she didn't turn around within a reasonable time, he tugged at her clothes until she did. Ginger taught her how to play catch by grasping the ball in his teeth, flinging his head back and tossing the sphere up in the air for Rhodina to catch. In addition, he taught her how to run; when Rhodina would try to catch him, he would stay out in front of her, just far enough not to discourage her, but move fast enough to bring out her best as a sprinter. As a result, when Rhodina started school a few years later, she became not only an outstanding track star in the Hanna Inspectorate, but as good a ball player as any boy in the school.

The Pahls remember Ginger for an entirely different reason. One time Ginger accompanied Mr. Pahl to get some cows that had broken through a fence, and in the interval Rhodina found it convenient to wander from the farmyard. She was missed soon after; the dog seemed to have vanished as well the moment he returned from herding the cows into the pasture. An intensive search of the farm buildings and the immediate area proved fruitless and by this time everyone began to fear for the safety of the little girl. They thought of the creek and the large slough at some distance from the farm, so the search was concentrated in that region. Sure enough, there was Rhodina doing her best to head for the water and Ginger doing his best to prevent her. It was fortunate that the dog won the battle, for it was certain the little girl would have lost her life if she had waded into the treacherous waters.

Accidents are accidents no matter whether they occurred sixty years ago or just the other day, but accidents of yesteryears have to be considered more serious due to the lack of rapid communication, transportation and the remoteness of qualified medical help. It was a matter of taking care of your own emergency or perish. Runaway horses, axes, hot water, open fires, mistaken identity of fuels, vulnerable machinery and the lack of any building codes, triggered most of the accidents.

In modern times few people are called upon to use an axe, a dangerous tool if there ever was one, but in early times every member of a family had the experience of using one. This lead to casualties involving lacerations of one type or another.

Martin Haug of the Bergen S.D. (Sundre, Alta.) was trimming trees to make fence rails when his axe caught on a willow and plunged into his foot, cutting it across from sole to sole. He wrapped both socks around it to staunch the bleeding and keep the almost-severed foot together, and hobbled to the nearest neighbor for help. Martin never visited a doctor and it was three months before he was able to walk on it. The wound was treated with a salve made from spruce-tree pitch and lard. Apparently the

-- John Evans

It was a day for rejoicing and celebrating when the fine large barn of John Evans was completed in June, 1918, Kelston, Sask.

-- John Evans

Two years later, in 1920, smiles turned to tears as a tornado swept through and destroyed the barn.

concoction kept the deep cut clean and free from infection until it began healing from the inside.The boys in the Poplar S.D. (Viking, Alta.) diverted the attention of the teacher while they borrowed the axe. It was kept in the library cupboard as a dangerous weapon. The youngsters required it only to cut down a tree to collect some crow's eggs. Of course the axe slipped and inflicted a bigger gash on the human limb than it did on the wooden one.

An incident that used to happen once in a while at country school gatherings was abetted by the routine followed in brewing coffee for the lunch. A wash boiler full of hot water would be brought over from a nearby farm house, or heated on the school's heater or cook stove, and brewed after immersing a bag of ground coffee in the boiling water. The danger occurred if the wash boiler of hot water or brewed coffee was ever set on the floor unattended. Every now and again some tot would fall into the boiling cauldron. The child couldn't be faulted, for he probably thought his mother had prepared his bath; these were the types of bath tubs used to bathe children in the pre-bathroom era. Such accidents with boiling water, if they proved fatal or resulted in serious injury, always had the sad effect of ending once and for all any further social functions in the schoolhouse.

Teachers in the rural schools had to be very resourceful. The mice in the Gladys S.D. 232 (High River, Alta.) became so bad, that when a stray cat came along the children didn't have any difficulty in coaxing it to stay. One day while this school pet was playing with a needle and thread attached to a sewing card, the needle somehow became lodged in the cat's throat. The school had several bug bottles in which the students put insects and bugs for preservation, so the teacher surmised these jars must have contained some anaesthetic material like ether. The cat's head was held closely over a newly-opened bottle of this liquid until its body and limbs stopped struggling and the needle removed with ease. It didn't take the school pet very long to revive, and it became even more popular than before the mishap had occurred.

Not too many prairie schoolhouses were protected from lightning by lightning rods and there were those who maintained that they did no good, others who said they did. The debate was endless. Nevertheless the annals of rural education include many references to schools struck by lightning.

On one occasion, J. M. McDonald of the Melita S.D. 1458 (Benalto, Alta.) dismissed school early because of a threatening storm, and sent the children home. It was well he did! While the children were still within sight of the school, they saw the lightning strike the brick chimney, shatter it, and scatter the bricks all over the schoolyard. The stove inside the school was also badly damaged.

The Willowdale S.D. 303 (Red Deer, Alta.) was struck by lightning in the spring of 1929. The bolt came down the chimney at the east end of the school and stunned the teacher, Ruth Comer, so severely that she was knocked to the floor. Fortunately, she was not injured, and her grade nine pupils who were studying after school also escaped any harm outside of shock.

The Diamond Coulee S.D. (Gladmar, Sask.) was struck by lightning in the summer of 1946 and much damage was done. The chimney was knocked down and a corner of the roof shattered; luckily no one was hurt, only badly scared. It happened on a sultry June afternoon when examinations were in progress. Mary Hartuhn was leaning over to hand her completed paper to the teacher just as the bolt struck. A large patch of plaster from the ceiling crashed down upon her desk, but as she was leaning away from the desk she escaped with only a cut finger. Since the school required extensive repairs, the trustees decided to do some renovating as well. They put in a new floor, installed insulation and repainted the building both inside and outside. When the students of the Diamond Coulee School saw the improvements that had been made to their school they agreed that lightning could be of some value.

On the other hand the children in the Jennings S.D. (Sunnynook, Alta.) were terrified of lightning, because in 1920 one of their classmates had been killed by lightning while riding on a load of coal. For some reason it was believed the lightning had been drawn to the boy by the iron rims of the wagon, so whenever a storm approached, the youngsters got in the habit of emptying their pockets of nails, knives, or any other metal objects. On one such occasion, a little fellow was unfortunate enough to have a nail replacing the button which held up his overalls. His classmates shouted to him to throw away this nail in order not to attract the lightning. He obeyed in double-quick time and spent the rest of the day holding up his overalls by hand.

Life was not easy and farm accidents such as the following were common. Nels Anderson, a bachelor in the Pendant d'Oreille S.D. (Foremost, Alta.), was hauling in loads of rye bundles for feed at harvest time. Mr. Shoemaker, the local teacher, was helping him. They were nearly finished, and had stacked the rack high with the slippery straw to get it all on the last load.

Mr. Shoemaker headed the team for home, and Nels walked ahead of the horse. Suddenly, the heavy load began to slip off the rack. The schoolteacher was pitched forward with the straw and fell down between the horses. The startled horses broke loose and ran. Nels saw what was happening and leaped at the horses to stop them before the teacher was trampled underfoot, but the horses knocked him down and pulled the wagon right over him. Mr. Shoemaker was lucky that day. He landed in the middle of the trail, and as the rack passed over, the wheels missed him. He was unharmed. But Nels was less fortunate. The heavy load crushed him and he lived only a few hours. The land that had once held for him high hopes of a better future, became his final resting place.

In the early years the winters were severe and everyone suffered from the extreme cold. Hattie Hutchinson, who came out from the east to teach in the Gladys S.D. 232 (High River, Alta.) just after Christmas in 1908 was no exception. She was met by a school official with a democrat and when the train pulled into the station it was nearly forty below zero. Her hat sat on top of her head and she wore kid gloves on her hands. Fortunately she had a muff which she held up in front of her face to keep it from freezing, but during the trip her hands were severely frozen. When she got into the house her gloves could not be removed so her hands were immersed in coal oil. Eventually her gloves could be peeled off gradually and at intervals the ice was stripped from her hands. Poor Miss Hutchinson spent many painful months with her hands swathed in bandages, but they did heal and were saved.

The world changes a little every day and the advent of the automobile in the early days was one of the more important changes. The transition from driving horses to driving a car for the first time was fraught with difficulty and danger. Some farmers never did master the art of driving cars, particularly the proper way of bringing the automobile to a stop. They had become so inured to calling "Whoa!" and pulling on the reins to stop a team of horses, that they still insisted on yelling "Whoa!" and pulling on the steering wheel whenever they wanted to bring the new mechanical contraption to a standstill. It never worked. People took their lives in their hands every time they ventured out with such drivers, for cars ran off grades, careened crazily across ditches, went through gates and fences, crashed into animals and buildings, streaked into grainfields, and not infrequently ended the wild escapade upside down. Usually the only reaction by the errant driver after such an accident was to call the car a "Beechy Devil" as if he was blaming an unruly horse. One inept driver went so far as to name his Model-T Ford after his wife because, as he said, "After I got it, I found I couldn't control it!"

After one family went for its first car drive this is how the daughter described the experience:

> After a short but pleasant drive, we returned home. Then it happened! We never dared to ask Dad if the brakes failed, or if he simply forgot that he wasn't driving the team, but he hollered, "Whoa!" and a split second later, we crashed into the gate.

Handcranking, the only way of starting the old-time car, was tricky and resulted on occasion in a broken arm or thumb, if the motor backfired and spun the crank in reverse. Motorists soon found out there was a right and a wrong way of holding the crank. Often, if the emergency brake wasn't set properly, the car advanced on the cranker the instant the first explosion occurred and forced him to hold back the raring monster by leaning his weight against it. Some of these first drivers say they can never forget the feel of the cars nuzzling them as if they were looking for lumps of sugar in their pockets.

The knack of starting the car in the days of no self-starters consisted of knowing how to set the ignition switch, how to crank, and when and how far

-- Mrs. Strandberg

Youngsters in the Netherby S.D. (Hanna, Alta.) help to harvest the garden crop.

-- Mrs. R. J. Johnston

A young girl helps with "bucking hay."

-- Mrs. Strandberg

Youngsters water livestock the hard way.

— Mrs. Strandberg

Orphan piglets receive their nourishment of milk through the kindness of Lloyd, Ken and Muriel Strandberg.

— George Allen

Oat sheaves are hauled by means of a stoneboat and a Shetland pony in the Surprise S.D. (Craigmyle, Alta.)

— Hanna Herald

A proud youngster helps with the seeding.

-- Mrs. Strandberg

Alf Strandberg mows slough hay in the Netherby S.D. (Hanna, Alta.)

-- Fred Rall

Rural youngsters earned a good deal of prestige when they were given the responsibility of driving a team of horses and a lumber wagon.

-- Fred Rall

Billy Kroeker, a seven-year-old boy from the Coronation District (Coronation, Alta.) seems to be enjoying the responsibility of driving a stoneboat.

-- A. A. Elliott

"Be it ever so humble, there's no place like home," even if it is a sod house. This one belonged to the Pontius family, Castor, Alta.

-- Thorence Kasa

This two-story frame house, with tar paper covering, was built in 1913 near Cereal, Alta. The erection of a veranda at the front and a utility porch at the back usually followed in due course.

-- Ken F. Cooper, *The Western Producer*
April 14, 1949

One of the main reasons for rural people going to town was to pick up their mail. Here a mailman transfers the mail from the mixed train to the local post office by means of a wheelbarrow.

-- H. H. Cooper

A common practice for farmers coming to town in the early days was to visit the railway station and watch a train highballing through the railway yard.

— Ken F. Cooper, *The Western Producer*
April 14, 1949

The railway station was the communication and transportation center for every community. Here W. G. MacLaren, the station agent at Shellbrook, Sask., sits in his office surrounded by a bevy of communication instruments.

— Ken F. Cooper, *The Western Producer*
April 14, 1949

Express is unloaded from a mixed train. The express included such things as hardware, auto parts, furniture, chinaware, cream cans, egg crates, food supplies, repair parts and items for the home, business and farm. The railway and the train were the lifeline for every community.

-- Mrs. J. L. Achen

Carloads of "joy" arrive for the farmers in the drought area at Midale, Sask. In the top picture the farmers gather around a carload of relief goods. One man, second from the left, can be seen enjoying an apple as he chats with a companion. Youngsters of the area are seen in the bottom picture as they crowd around a car of apples donated by Ontario people under the voluntary relief scheme.

-- V. R. Johnston

In 1936, food for livestock was so scarce because of the drought that Russian thistle was cut and hauled to the farm to be used as fodder. Here a group of youngsters from the Helmsdale S.D. (Oyen, Alta.) brings in a load of Russian thistle on a stoneboat.

-- Mrs. Strandberg

Alf Strandberg stands beside the skimpy Christmas tree that served the family in 1933. Due to the austerity that prevailed during the depression period, Christmas was not celebrated in any ostentatious manner. The Christmas spirit was still there, but the outward show was not too evident.

-- Mrs. J. L. Achen

Water was so scarce during the drought period that it had to be hauled great distances. One good way to transport it was in the old gasoline drums hauled by Bennett buggy; this was done by Jake Achen (Halbrite, Sask.); he was assisted by his children.

to pull the choke, a little wire protruding through the lower right-hand corner of the radiator. The engine always responded first with a few scattered and encouraging explosions, but ended with a tremendous barrage sounding like gunfire, which was checked quickly by racing to the driver's seat and retarding the throttle.

It was always preferable to have two people perform the starting operation: one to crank and the other to manipulate the spark and gas levers. If the engine did not fire at first, the cranker would yell, "Give her a little more, George!" and alternately, "Advance the spark a notch, will you, George!"

In spite of its stubborn nature, the early Model-T was affectionately nicknamed the flivver, Tin Lizzie, or just plain "she" by her growing army of buyers.

The dashboard of the early models was bare except for an ignition key, so the driver travelled blind. He didn't know the temperature of his engine, the speed of his car, the amount of gasoline in the tank, the amount of oil or oil pressure. They learned all this pertinent information, not through instruments, but through sudden developments. A good example of this was illustrated by the farmer who refused to buy a speedometer because he said, "When my car is running five miles an hour the left fender rattles; ten miles an hour, my teeth rattle; at fifteen miles an hour the transmission drops out. Now can you tell me why I need a better speedometer than these indicators?"

The owners of early-model cars never regarded their purchases as complete, for the market provided a limitless assortment of hardware that could be attached to the car to improve its performance or remedy some deficiency. They included such gadgets as clamp-on dashlights, sun visors, fan-belt guides, windshield wipers, speedometers, rear-view mirrors, anti-rattlers and dip sticks. Most motorists thought the rear-view mirror was a useless thing, reasoning that there was no reason to worry about what was coming from behind, when it would be be seen out in front soon enough. Only persons of a suspicious turn of mind installed rear-view mirrors.

The spindly, seven-foot tall Model-T Ford was of such rudimentary construction that almost any handy farm boy could fix it given a wrench, a hammer, a screwdriver and some hay wire. Apparently Henry Ford designed the Model-T with the rural dweller specifically in mind. The flivver's high undercarriage and narrow, tall wheels made it ideal for travelling along the rutted prairie trails and rock-strewn byways and even enabled it to get through mud. In addition, its strong steel frame and the almost complete absence of body-covering made it durable enough to survive plunges into ditches. Once the problem of pulling them back on the road was overcome, the majority of cars were able to proceed on their way almost immediately, no worse for the plunge. So its understandable why a farmer on his deathbed made the following strange request: he wanted his

Ford car to be buried with him, because he had never been in a hole yet, where his flivver didn't get him out.

Yet in spite of its many redeeming features, the Model-T had one flaw that no one ever seemed to be able to correct — it rattled. In fact the rattle eventually became the unofficial trade-mark of the Model T. Such jibes as "a rattle for baby," "the rear axle should be magnetized to pick up the parts that dropped off," and "Danger, 10,000 jolts" were common.

There was the occasional farmer who knew he couldn't make the transition from driving horses to driving cars, but he still purchased a car and left it standing in the yard for months as a sign of his progress. It remained for his wife or one of the older boys to learn how to drive it and fix it and exploit the white-elephant purchase. In no time at all farm boys educated themselves and one another and ushered in the period of farm-mechanization.

The more or less instant transportation provided by the relatively convenient and cheap automobile transformed a horse-and-buggy land of isolated farms into a mobile rural society. The new-fangled self-propelled carriage captured the imagination of the entire population and such folk songs as "Get Out and Get Under," "In My Merry Oldsmobile," "Toot Your Horn, Kid, You're in a Fog," and "The Automobile Honeymoon," became the rage.

Operating a car in those days was attended by activities that the modern motorist wouldn't even believe. Repairing tires on the road was one of these jobs, as punctures occurred with monotonous regularity. The offending corner of the car was jacked up, but instead of removing the wheel as is done today, one flange of the tire was pried over the rim of the wheel all the way around, and the collapsed inner tube was removed. This was inflated to discover where the air was leaking and the actual spot or spots located by spitting on all suspected leaks and noticing where the saliva bubbled. The area surrounding each hole was then sandpapered and a cold or hot patch affixed, the latter by clamping on a vulcanizing attachment that operated as a little fire burned. Next the repaired tube was inserted back into the tire, the tire itself levered back on the rim, and then inflated with a hand pump. There were no filling stations and no garages at first, so if a driver wanted to put air in a tire, it could be only done manually with a pump. The first garages that installed air compressors advertised their progress with a large sign that read, "Free Air".

If the car was to be used at night, the acetylene gas generated in a tank on the running board was turned on, the glass front of the headlights swung open and the hissing jets inside lit with a match. The gas usually popped sharply as it ignited and the road in front for a distance of five to ten feet became bathed with a white light. Later models had electric lights that ran directly off the car magneto, but when the car slowed down the lights grew dim. Anytime a traveller drew up to a road sign he had to race the engine so the lights would be bright enough to read it.

If he went on a trip of more than a hundred miles, the wise motorist carried an extra supply of gasoline, oil and water and such things as spare tires and inner tubes, auxiliary motor parts, a jack, and plenty of tools. The liquids were transported in cans on the runningboard, with a red one containing the gasoline, the blue the oil, and the white the water.

Model-T cars were so versatile that in a pinch they were known to operate on such propellants as coal oil, homebrew, wood alcohol, cider, paraffin dissolved in kerosene and oil diluted with coal oil.

As the gasoline tank was located directly under the driver's seat, it was necessary to remove the front cushion and unscrew the cap to find out the amount of fuel in the tank, and to fill the tank. The former was done by peering into the tank or inserting a graduated dipstick. It was not unusual for the inexperienced motorists to light a match at night to get a better look in the tank; however, the inevitable explosion that ensued and the resulting serious burns and the occasional death made everyone wary of such a foolish practice. Despite the publicity such incidents kept happening. For instance one report has it that "On one trip, when Arthur and Gus made a trip to town, they ran out of gas on the way home. Having had too many spirits from a convenient jug, they lit a match to see if the gas tank was dry. The resulting explosion left Gus with almost no hair."

The Model-T had a top of sorts. It folded down over the back seat and flopped merrily up and down every time a bump was hit, which was often. At least these vibrations shook the dust out of it. It was called a one-man top by some humorist, because it actually took two men to put it up. There were also side curtains of isinglass and canvas that could be snapped on in cold or wet weather.

The cooling systems on the early cars were not too good, and motorists going up long grades had to stop two or three times to let their motors cool and to fill the boiling radiators with cold water. Then again, since the gasoline flowed from the tank to the carburetor by means of gravity, it was often necessary to back up the car over a steep hill; in the forward position no fuel flowed to the engine, as it was on a higher level than the tank.

At first there were no car salesmen, no service garages and no filling stations. Cars were sold by farm-implement dealers who knew nothing about them, except the price. Terms were spot cash; when you saw a man driving a car, you knew that it was paid for.

Gas was obtained at hardware stores. A clerk would come staggering out with a five-gallon can of the fuel in one hand and a funnel in the other and proceed to pour the gasoline into the tank. In the early models the tank was located under the front seat; it was necessary to remove the cushions, which in those days were filled with curled horsehair and springs, to reach the gas cap. Later models had the gas tank located under the hood alongside the dashboard with the gas cap positioned on top just in front of the windshield. All canny motorists kept a piece of chamois leather handy through which to filter the gas, so that bits of rubber hose, water and other foreign material would not clog the gas line or the carburetor. Even at that, the carburetor had to be removed and cleaned once a week, because in spite of the chamois some dust still managed to get in.

In dry weather the country roads and byways were fairly hard and motorists could get around quite easily in the Model-Ts. However, if it rained while they were enroute, the mud, especially the gumbo variety, imprisoned their cars. There was only one thing to do at times like this, and that was to abandon poor Liz and get home the best way possible, either by walking or hiring a horse to take you there. Then when the roads dried up, the unfortunate driver would have to return to the scene of his misfortune and persuade some farmer living nearby to haul his car out of the mudhole. It's probably only a joke, but it has been said that it was during this era that unscrupulous farmers made a handsome profit by hauling water to mudholes to make them sure traps for unsuspecting travellers.

The Model-T had its faults: it was noisy, unreliable, smelly and unsafe. But the horse that the car was attempting to replace was no paragon of virtue, safety or sanitation. Wherever the horse went it urinated and dropped "road apples". Hordes of flies bred in these droppings. Until fairly recently, automobiles were stored in garages built as far as possible from the house because that was where the stables had always been located and the stables were there because the smell of horses attracted flies. Early farm garages had a pair of swing-doors on hinges attached to each end. There was a reason for this. If the car was approaching the garage and became uncontrollable and couldn't be stopped inside the garage, it was free to pass right through without doing any damage. This arrangement saved a little money on repairing shattered doors.

Even with their many imperfections, the early Model-T cars gave their owners feelings of luxury and prestige, never equalled since. Such people could extend hands of fellowship and appreciation to their friends by merely inviting them to go for a drive. Today the modern car means only one thing, and that is transportation.

6

Depression, Drought, Dust

Blazing across the years of the 1930 decade, came the greatest tragedy that prairie farmers ever encountered — adversity in three forms — depression, drought and dust.

The economic debacle of this accursed trilogy was triggered in 1929 by the crash of the stock market. Prices for all produce, particularly farm produce, fell rapidly to almost nothing accompanied by unemployment in the towns and cities. There was a growing scarcity of money resulting in a decline of purchasing power, a strangulation of trade and finally, widespread poverty. People who had never been out of work before in their lives found themselves without jobs. At the height of the depression in 1933, more than 1,500,000 out of Canada's population of 10,500,000 were on welfare, receiving a mere pittance for necessities of life. Men rode freight trains from one part of Canada to another looking for jobs that didn't exist. This particular type of job-hunting practice was called "riding the rods" and soon every community in Canada became used to the sight of a freight train passing through their town pulling boxcars swarming with men; their "jungles" or camping places were located near the town and railway yard where they stayed between trains and lived on handouts.

Life was arduous for the farmers. As soon as they had come through the trials and tribulations of the homestead days, the majority paid off the debts they had accumulated prior to 1922 and began to increase the size of their operations. Easy credit enticed them to convert from farming with horses to working with tractors, trucks, combines and other mechanical devices. Yet when crops failed and prices collapsed they found it impossible to pay debts incurred when wheat was $1.50 a bushel, with income derived from selling reduced quantities at twenty-five cents. Prices for other farm produce took a corresponding drop. For instance, prior to 1930 eggs paid for a farmer's groceries, but the price dropped so low, five cents a dozen, that it took several dozen to buy a spool of thread. Dairy butter sold for twelve cents a pound, a can of cream brought little more than a dollar, price of wheat fell from $2.20 to seventeen cents a bushel. In selling cattle at one cent per pound on the hoof there were times when the freight exceeded the returns derived from the sale and the selling price of a calf couldn't buy a pair of shoes. In fact it was cheaper to use butter for for axle grease than to sell the butter and use the money to purchase the grease. Over one-half of Western Canada's production came from the farms, so the basis of its economy depended upon the state of agriculture. The hopeful farmer expected that "prosperity was just around the corner," but year after year, agriculture in spite of promising interim signs, remained in despair until after 1937. The federal government introduced a scheme whereby single men were sent to bush camps where they worked for food, lodging, clothing and twenty cents per day. Others went to farms where they received five dollars a month from the government, who also gave the farmer five dollars for keeping him. Still others joined the lineups at the soup-kitchens or bread lines to keep from starving.

All that the farmers had acquired up until then seemed to dwindle away. Machinery either wore out before it was paid for, or finance companies repossessed them. Interest and taxes accumulated until their amounts came to more than the original principal. It was impossible to meet any debt payments. The resulting hardships and near starvation forced many to abandon their land and to seek a decent existence elsewhere. It was not uncommon to see a man with his family and all their possessions loaded on a hay rack or a wagon with an extra team and possibly a milk cow following behind, moving northward to where it rained. Other farmers admitted defeat and went to the cities for help where they became the people "on relief". Those who stayed on were faced with foreclosures. There were cases at foreclosure sales where the other farmers would bid twenty-five cents for a cow and turn it back into the farmer's pasture. Lands listed for sale under the Recovery Act used to fill four to six pages in each weekly newspaper.

Some farmers, however, managed to consolidate their taxes and thus prevent their land from being put up for tax sale. Under such an arrangement they had five years to pay their arrears and current taxes, so they held on hoping for better times.

The depression would have been a staggering blow in itself, but when combined with severe drought and destructive dust storms, the triple punch was too much to endure, and today it is evident that some areas never did recover from the combined onslaught.

Beginning in 1929, the below average rainfall augmented by the hot, dry winds, resulted in successive crop failures. All records for drought were broken and the burning sun continued to scorch the prairies day after day. Sloughs and wells went dry. The soil became so desiccated the seed did not germinate and the grain did not grow, so there was no grain to harvest. Pastures dried up and became as bare as ploughed ground. Farmers rushed to sell their cattle before prices dropped, but they were too late. The market collapsed and not infrequently the freight charges came to more than the selling price the farmer received. In the meantime, hundreds of thousands of cattle died on their feet from hunger and thirst, while many more were mercifully shot to save them from painful deaths.

In spite of the fact that the thirsty dry soil couldn't produce anything resembling expedient crops and pastures, and in spite of the fact the price of agricultural products had declined to a new low, farmers still had faith in their farms. They went about their daily tasks as if no disaster had overtaken them. They cultivated and seeded as usual, prepared the soil by summerfallowing it, put up whatever food was available, and harvested their beggarly crops. Russian thistle seemed to be the only thing that grew well in the dry years, so the resourceful farmers cut these weeds at the very young stage before they developed thorns and stored them as winter feed for their horses and cattle. During the summer the livestock, whose skins clung close to pointed bones and made them look like sawhorses, roamed far and wide to rustle for whatever food they could find. There wasn't even straw enough to put in a chicken's nest. Many animals, after a fruitless search, huddled around the sites of old straw stacks eating food that had no nourishment. At times they became so desperate for food they swallowed anything that gave them a feeling of being full. So such appalling fodder as machinery parts, door knobs, discarded pieces of wood, odd pieces of leather, grease and oil, found its way into the animal's stomach. Needless to add, hundreds of such cattle died during this period from indigestion. Farmers hated to remain within sight of the animals, for every time they did cattle mooed and horses whinnied, following them around begging for more food and water.

It was also during the thirties the winds on the prairies never quit blowing. They would blow all day, subside after sunset, only to come back the next morning as a huge dust storm. It was an awesome sight to see a solid wall of dust swirling towards the farm. Sometimes big black clouds appeared on the horizon and to all appearances looked like rain was in the offing. But invariably, during the "dirty thirties", the clouds turned out to be strong winds laden with dust so thick it was possible to reach into it and snatch a handful. Day was turned into night, making it necessary to light the lamps even if it was only mid-afternoon. Road allowances drifted over, ditches disappeared, fences with their array of trapped weeds were completely hidden, hedges were banked, and vacant buildings were filled with the shifting waves of fine silt. The blowing hot dust acted like a sharp razor on crops, garden plants and the grass in the pastures, shearing them to ground level, leaving the countryside like a desert. Trees that had been planted for shade and kept watered to save them from the drought, presented a weird sight, for they were void of leaves. In cultivated fields the wind gouged holes big enough to hide a car. It has been estimated that many farms in the Palliser Triangle of the prairies lost from 100 to 1000 tons of nutritious top soil per acre during the soil-drifting years of the thirties.

Cars became stuck as their wheels spun uselessly in the drifts of loose soil on the roads just as they did in snow drifts in wintertime. Others stalled when their carburetors became clogged with the dust or the lights couldn't penetrate the swirling dust, or the car couldn't generate enough power to move against the force of the wind. Stories were told of the wind blowing so hard that a log chain fastened to a corner of a hay rack was stretched out horizontally. There was the story of the frustrated hen sitting on her nest with her tail pointing into the wind, laying the same egg six times before the wind relaxed enough to let nature takes its course. A common fable was that the wise farmers kept a gopher or two in the house, and when they wanted to know whether it was safe to go outside in the dust storm, one of the animals was released. If he started to dig upwards when the door was opened, the family stayed inside knowing full well the dust in the air was still too thick, but if the gopher showed an inclination to burrow downwards it was considered safe enough to venture outside.

It must have been a prairie housewife who coined the phrase, "dirty thirties", for it was the homes that suffered most during the black blizzards. The fine silt found its way into every nook and cranny of the house, and although it might have been cleaned in the morning, by afternoon the pattern on the kitchen linoleum would be indistinguishable under its layer of grit. Wet rags placed around the windows and doors of the home still did not keep out the dirt. The fine dust clung to curtains, clothing and the walls. In fact, before going to bed it was often necessary to shake out the dust from the pillowcases, sheets, blankets and bedspreads. Dishes usually needed rewashing before they could be used and tables were not set until everyone was ready to eat. Washing had to be put out early and brought in dry almost immediately to escape the dust and wind that was bound to come sooner or later.

Men and beasts were choked and blinded with the dust, their faces black and caked with mud as tears ran from bleared and irritated eyes. Farmers began to wear goggles, but still their eyes were filled. Many tied handkerchiefs about their faces to protect them from breathing dust. Animals had no such protection and many died as a result of their lungs becoming filled with or clogged with soil. The dust sifted onto the stubble fields and pastures and horses grazing on the short grass and stubble ingested so much dirt that their stomachs became inflamed. Many farmers lost valuable work horses from this complication, which soon became known as "dirt colic".

To add to the inconvenience and harm produced by the dust storms, the sound of the wind was soul-searing and frightening, not because it was a roaring or shrieking wind but because of its sameness; it always sounded like the agonizing moan of a wounded or dying animal. Hour after hour, day after day, week after week, it was the same monotonous dirge. No wonder it did strange things to people who let themselves be carried away! A young woman took her child of a few weeks and drowned him and herself in the muck of a nearby slough; a young city man teaching in his first school went insane; patients in mental hospitals wailed continually when the wind blew, imploring it to stop.

Gradually and imperceptibly dust storms became a way of life.

A father in the Craigmyle S.D. (Craigmyle, Alta.) planned to surprise his family while they were away visiting his wife's folks. Since the weather was perfect he decided to paint the kitchen a snowy white and make his wife's ten year dream come true. No sooner had he finished the redecorating and was anticipating the admiration that his handiwork would receive than to his horror he saw that the sky to the west was completely black from a dust storm. The moment it rolled in, it sifted through every crack and crevice in the kitchen.

Betty, a pupil in the Plainsfield S.D. (Carmangay, Alta.), proudly invited her teacher home for dinner. She confided in the teacher what a good cook her mother was and what a wonderful meal was awaiting them. Unfortunately one of the worst dust storms of the thirties was raging in the district and the soil was sifting into the house so badly it was impossible to eat anything that wasn't covered. The mother, much to the disappointment of her hosting daughter, served one of the few foods that would remain clean in spite of the dust — boiled eggs.

Lavinia, a teacher in the Blusson S.D. 1781 (Champion, Alta.), described how difficult it was to keep a school clean during the dirty thirties:

> Many and many a day the children and I would have to spend an hour in the morning sweeping up pail after pail of dust before we could go to work. It was useless to clean the building after school, as the winds often blew all night. We pasted oilcloth over all the cracks around the window, and tried many other ideas, but the dust seeped in anyway.

The 3-D combination of depression, drought and dust was damaging enough without any complications. Yet complications in the form of grasshoppers, rust, army worms, saw flies, wire worms and hail kept cropping up to further test the morale and economy of the already overburdened farmers. The grasshoppers hatched by the millions and ate everything they could chew. Not even the clothes hanging on the line were safe from their ravenous appetites. One lady had a hole chewed in the stocking she was wearing as she drove along. A farmer went to a field to plow, took a syrup can full of water to drink, placed a cloth over the top and snapped on the lid; but, by the time he had gone a couple of rounds, the grasshoppers had eaten most of the cloth. A bachelor farmer had washed his shirt and hunt it out to dry. When he went to take it in he found it was gone. He thought somebody had stolen it until he noticed the buttons lying in the grass. Army worms were just as destructive and many times more hideous. They crawled over everything, eating every bit of vegetation in their way. Some of them crawled into houses and it was common practice to paint the door sills with kerosene to try and keep them from entering.

-- Mrs. C. M. Stange

A dust cloud swept across the countryside in a broad front near Claresholm, Alta. in the mid-1930s.

-- Mrs. A. E. Oldridge

A cloud of dust is travelling across the bleak and dried-out prairie near Oyen, Alta. in 1937. The foreground shows the devastating effect of wind erosion on the unprotected soil.

-- Mr. and Mrs. W. Reid

The ominous approach of a prairie dust storm during the thirties at Pearce, Alta., is captured in this picture.

-- Mrs. R. G. Vockeroth

A home-made packer lies partly buried in drift soil.

To meet such trials and tribulations farmers were forced to resort to a survival philosophy of "make it over, wear it out, use it up, make it do." They knew only too well what it meant to be without good clothes, new machinery, and luxury foods. Magically, second-hand equipment like plows, binders and mowers were made to run again with wrenches, a pair of pliers, a few twists of haywire and much ingenuity. With no money to buy gasoline to run their tractors or trucks, farmers went back to using horses as the motive power in those areas where they could at least grow feed for them. Very few people could afford to buy licenses for their cars, let alone the gasoline and repairs, so cars were just left jacked up on blocks to save the tires, or converted into Bennett buggies. The latter innovation meant removing the motor, the transmission and windshield and attaching a wagon tongue, whippletrees, neck yokes and hitching a team of horses to them. The sewing machine was perhaps the most treasured possession in the house for it could be used for making-over used clothing, as there was seldom any cash for even a few yards of new material. Father's worn-outclothes were cut down for one of the boys. Younger children inherited the outgrown clothes of older ones. Handerchiefs were made of empty ten-cent salt bags. Shoe laces were strong strings or binder twine soaked in ink with the ends waxed. Empty flour or sugar sacks were made into sheets, pillow cases, dish towels and undergarments of all kinds. Two oft-told stories were based on truth: there was the girl who took a tumble and displayed Pillsbury's Best, or Robin Hood's Best on the seat of her panties; then there was the lady pianist at a dance wearing a dress on the back of which was "98 pounds when packed." There was also the tale of a lady from the Byemoor S.D. (Byemoor, Alta.) who attended a convention in Calgary. As it happened, she had to share a bedroom with a lady from Red Deer, and when bedtime came and they started undressing, the city lady showed off her fancy underwear. The farm woman, telling her friends about it afterwards said, "And there was me, with one leg in Five Roses and the other in Lake of the Woods." Overalls for school were made out of old binder canvas and dyed by boiling it in strong tea. Things were patched, repaired, or remodelled into new usefulness, but never discarded.

Cash deals were replaced by barter and bills were paid with eggs and cream. Instead of buying flour, farmers took some of their wheat, if they had any, to the nearest mill and exchanged it for flour, shorts, bran and porridge meal. The mills accepted extra wheat to pay for the milling, or kept the shorts. Many such mills opened up in the larger towns at this time just to take care of such demands. Wheat and rye, if available, were also roasted and ground to make "coffee". Rhubarb and wild fruits, like saskatoons, were the main fruits eaten during the depression period and housewives adopted the policy of "eat what you can and can what you can't." In spite of the many trials and tribulations, most farmers kept a few cattle, pigs and chickens to insure there was food on the table. Farm women went back to the traditional way of raising poultry; that is, a broody hen and a setting of

-- Mrs. Chris Losing

The header proved to be the best farm implement for harvesting any crops of the thirties that were too short to tie with a binder. The heads of wheat were elevated into a special rack, and then unloaded in stacks for ease of threshing.

eggs. Once again, as in pioneer days, it was necessary to scout around in the district for setting hens, which when located were carried in a sack on horseback and settled onto eggs after the trip. In spite of the many hardships it created, most farmers kept enough grain in storage to serve as seed for next year's crop. Yet after successive crop failures, all the seed became used up and the government had to come to the rescue of such farmers and supply seed grain to those who needed it.

Farmers, in an effort to save what they could of the short, thin crops, designed crude "headers" by attaching elevators to their binders which hauled up the heads of wheat and deposited them into accompanying racks, or especially built box-like wagons called barges. A gate opened in the rear of the latter contrivance and released the stack of heads, while in the case of the former, they had to be unloaded by hand with a shovel or pitchfork and put up in stacks. These stacks were threshed later. Many times the crops were so poor, the farmer wandered around his field and picked up the few strands of wheat by hand in order to have some feed for his chickens.

Business and professional people often helped "carry" families until "next year" and most of these debtors were considerate enough to keep the bills to a minimum. Unfortunately, "next year" turned into many years and so some acquired bills they found impossible to pay. It is known that many friendly merchants and doctors wrote thousands of dollars off their books during this period and in time were no better off than their bankrupt customers.

It didn't pay to get sick during the depression, for without money it was difficult or even impossible to obtain any medical treatment. Just ask the people who lived in the Buffalo Horn Valley S.D. 930 (Swift Current, Sask.) during this period. Any time they went to a doctor or hospital, the first question was, "Have you got the money to pay for this? If not, make arrangements with your municipality first." Sometimes they were advised to treat themselves at home. A woman in the district also remembers the time her brother-in-law's broken arm was set without an anesthetic because he didn't have the one-dollar to pay for the ether. This person must have been unlucky in more ways than one, for he also had stomach ulcers and not even the Red Cross Society could advance him enough money to buy the baking soda to ease the pain.

Farmers who owned prized horses or cattle sold a head or two whenever cash was urgently needed. The ordinary livestock would not bring any money and by the end of the depression such owners found themselves dispossessed of their purebred stock.

"Sayings" often repeated by people during a particular era give a good insight into the general conditions prevailing at the time as well as into the character of the inhabitants. The depression period was no exception, and one often heard the following: "The only things you can raise now are kids

-- W. A. Malm

A farmer from the Scapa S.D. (Scapa, Alta.) prepares to leave the drought-stricken area in the fall of 1934 and trek to the Peace River area where moisture conditions were reported to be much better.

-- Ida Ryland

Very few people could afford to operate an automobile during the depression years, so the motor was dismantled and the chassis and wheels converted into the so-called "Bennett buggy." The above Bennett buggy operated in the Bissell S.D. 2745 (Vesper, Sask.) in 1932.

and gophers. They don't dry out;" "Then came the dirty thirties — no rain, no grain, no gain, all work in vain, just wind, wind, wind;" "Well, the hail took the crop so we may as well use the hail. Let's make some ice cream;" "It isn't the fact you're licked that counts, but did you fight and why?"; "Where there is a will, there is a way;" "We never bought anything we could make and never discarded anything we could repair."

The songs people sang or listened to also divulged their feelings. For instance, such songs as, "Brother, Can You Spare A Dime," "Revive Us Again," and "I'm Forever Blowing Bubbles" were hits during the depression years.

To those who did not live through these years, or who remember very little about them, they seem unreal, remote, impossible. Records of those years from minutes of town and municipal council meetings, school board sessions, newspapers, and the memories of those who experienced them, can at best present only an imperfect picture.

The wherewithal to survive the economic depression, drought, blowing dust, early frosts, hail, sawflies, grasshoppers, rust and the other adversities came from the doggedness of the farmers themselves, their concern for each other, and the token of relief provided by the various levels of government, the Red Cross Society, churches and private individuals. In spite of the hard times and the humble living standard, the 3-D era helped to strengthen both man's ability and faith in himself. It made people more resourceful, dependable and respectful of their fellow man. A real and friendly spirit of comradeship pervaded each community. A consciousness of "we're all in the same boat" arose that helped to overcome many difficulties and encouraged mutual assistance and cooperation. What little they had they shared with one another. Their little shacks became brightly shining stars in the dark and forbidding firmaments of the depression and drought.

In the Greenlawn S.D. (Dewberry, Alta.) a casket association was organized to help members with financial problems in time of death. Each time there was a death in a member's family, a new assessment was made and this lent financial continuity to the cooperative association. To keep costs down some of the skilled members went so far as to make and cover the first coffins.

People initiated their own entertainment; the minds and bodies of the young and the old alike were kept healthy by a variety of local activities. There were continual rounds of Sunday visits and house gatherings, when perhaps four or five families would gather at a neighbor's place for singing, games of five-hundred, church service, or just talking about their hopes for a better future for the farmer. Dances, card parties, concerts, drama presentations, ball games, sleigh rides, skating parties, picnics and similar social and cultural activities were held regularly in the local schoolhouse. Practically everyone in the district participated. People had time to relax, meet and enjoy each other and did not use the present-day excuse of being too busy. The price of admission was nominal and it was always possible to bring food or whatever else was required. The group of a dozen or more adults that made up a particular rural community took turns in hosting the various activities, and with this type of cooperation and participation, interest was maintained at a high level most of the time.

Relief measures, either sponsored by government or private sources, helped ease the situation for those who were suffering. Families received ten dollars relief for food for each month and vouchers to purchase a minimum set amount of clothing, shoes, coal, wood and other necessities. For example, each person received an allotment of one, and only one, set of underwear for the fall and winter. What the authorities expected the relief recipient to do while the union suit was in the wash was not indicated.

To qualify for relief feed for their livestock many farmers had to practically give their cattle away to obtain hay or greenfeed for the team of horses and the couple of cows each family was allowed to keep. The response of the more fortunate Canadians to the Red Cross and various church organizations working on behalf of the impoverished residents of the prairies was magnificent. Hundreds of carloads of food and surplus clothing were collected and eventually shipped to each needy district, where they were distributed by municipal officials. Relief trains brought hundreds of freight cars containing apples, cheese, vegetables, fish and surplus clothing, to the suffering people of the Palliser Triangle of the prairie provinces.

-- Mrs. Donaldson

Paul Seegar and his son Marvin, a couple of happy farmers from the Chinook district of Alberta, are shown on their way home after receiving relief supplies.

There were long lineups and occasioned mad scrambles at the railway sidings when the long-awaited relief trains arrived.

One such carload of relief supplies arrived in Hanley, Saskatchewan on November 5, 1937, and a local organization was hurriedly assembled; it consisted of representatives of the town, the municipality and the churches. The organization's job was to distribute the car's contents to those most in need. Some 250 families qualified. The shipment contained mainly potatoes, apples, nearly two tons of beans, and large quantities of canned and preserved fruits, jams and jellies, jelly powder, vegetables, honey, syrup, dried fruit, soap, some clothing, and even thread, pencils, envelopes and paper. These particular relief supplies had been assembled in St. Thomas, Ontario by a "Joint Committee of Churches for Western Canada Relief." Many of the donors included notes with their contributions, so some of the recipients undoubtedly wrote letters of heartfelt thanks for the gifts.

The fruit growers and the fishermen were especially generous with apples and salted dried cod fish. Although these two foods were very much appreciated and never wasted, they did cause the recipients some embarrassments. Each family on relief was usually allowed 100 pounds of apples per member, but without adequate refrigeration the only way to preserve the fruit was to can it. So once the relief apples were brought home, the housewifes were engaged for days in peeling and canning, and using the apples by themselves in as many different ways as possible, as there wasn't anything else in the cupboard to go with them. The carloads of salted dried cod fish created much more consternation than the apples. Unfamiliarity with the method of desalting and cooking these so called "snowshoes" or "horse blankets" made it difficult to know how to prepare them for eating. As conversational pieces the slabs of fish had no equal; everyone wanted to know what to do with them. However, they were never wasted and an occasional farm home on the prairie today can still exhibit one of these "snowshoes" as good as the time forty years ago when it was received from the relief train.

In spite of the tons and tons of surplus clothing that were distributed, the majority of those on relief wore threadbare garments. Women who had always dressed well wore the same clothes for years. Patches, and patches on patches, became a way of life rather than a sign of poverty as is the case in today's affluent society. It was even common for children to arrive at school during wintertime with their feet wrapped in newspaper inside their footwear.

Several families came from Calgary to settle in the hills east of the Willowdale S.D. 303. Many people felt sorry for their children who walked five miles or more to the Willowdale School. However, they seemed to manage and opportunities for the parents to find work were better than in the city. They left as soon as times improved enough for them to make a better living elsewhere.

Farmers were permitted to dig their own coal at so-called poverty mines, paying the government ten cents a ton for the privilege, or else fifty cents per ton at commercial mines that were also subsidized by the government.

The wounds of the 3-D years were deep, but like wheat in a bumper year bending under the heavy winds that strengthed it, so the prairie farmers bent beneath the onslaught of the depression and survived to come through strengthened as well. The experience provided an education in many things.

First and foremost came new methods of research, new farming practices, new farm implements, new experiments and the organization of new agricultural concerns that eventually led to the control of the prairie drought, soil erosion, and plant and insect pests. Such achievements should rank as high as any Canadian success story, whether it was the building of the Canadian Pacific Railway, the achievement of confederation, the promotion of democracy, the settlement of the West, or the organization of the Royal Canadian Mounted Police. The entire world has reaped benefits from this agricultural experience: semi-arid regions of the world have been able to increase food production with Canadian techniques, while the Canadian prairies continue to grow grain and to feed millions everywhere and avoid famine or alleviate hunger whether it is in China. India, Africa or any other country. Humanity caught up in the population explosion can thank Canada both for the lessons learned during the 3-D years and because she continues to be one of the major breadbaskets of the world.

The agricultural revolution took place gradually. The moldboard plow, the single disc and the harrows gave way to one-way discs, Noble blades, duckfoot cultivators, chisel plows, rod weeders and improved drills. Farmers knew they had to summerfallow in the arid Palliser Triangle to raise any sort of a crop, but if they did they also helped to create the dust bowl. The plowless-fallow practice of cultivating and leaving stubble and trash cover on the surface helped solve the problem of soil drifting, as did strip farming, planting of shelter belts and contour cultivation.

Agricultural authorities were able to convince the farmers of the importance of soil conservation and soon hundreds of thousands of acres of abandoned and unproductive land were regrassed with crested wheat and became valuable pasture areas. Farm dugouts, although crudely excavated and grotesque in appearance, proved their value in water convervation and their construction continued. Methods for controlling and combatting the spread of desert conditions, rust, smut, grasshoppers, sawflies, wireworms and gophers were devised and the information disseminated among thousands upon thousands of farmers through a massive scheme of government-sponsored short courses, farmers' meetings and the establishment of many experimental farms. When the recommended methods were adopted by the farmers who attended these agricultural courses, the rest gradually followed suit, once they noticed the good results. It was almost pathetic to realize that the various scourges reached their most destructive stages during the 3-D period.

Not many people today are aware that the 3-D period affected and is still affecting everyday life in Canada. The traumatic experience of living in that period became so ingrained in the people that their personalities changed more than they realized. The parents passed on these attitudes towards life to their children, not only by incessant philosophizing, but even more forcibly by the example they set in the way they lived.

The times were so hard that most people adopted the habit of saving just to survive. They did not discard anything or waste it for fear it would be useful in the future. Farmers saved apparently useless things, such as used binder twine, store string, old wrapping paper, tin cans, rusted stovepipes, out-dated magazines and newspapers, wire, shoe eyelts, worn-out clothing and the boards and nails of all wooden packing boxes. A farmer in the Scapa S.D. (Hanna, Alta.) put up some bales of greenfeed in the early thirties and saved them from year to year for the time that a shortage of feed might arise. In 1974, forty years later, when one son took over his father's holdings, the bales of greenfeed were still there in the corner of the barn, still usable, and still ready and available in the event of a food emergency.

Likewise, farm women never wasted anything in the kitchen and saved crusts, bread crumbs, fat, grease, bones, meat scraps, vegetable water, peelings and coffee grounds. Today, this saving habit instilled during the 3-D era is reflected in the practice of storing more food in the home than a family could use within the foreseeable future. Scraps of food and leftovers are not thrown out, but carefully packed in small containers and stored in the refrigerator. It is only when these bits of food become moldy and begin to stink in the refrigerator that they are thrown away. People were so hungry during the 3-D period that today they take every precaution, from force of habit, to prevent such a food dilemma from occurring again.

This same fear is illustrated by the individuals who must have money in their pockets or purses no matter where they are. This gives them the satisfaction, the confidence and the assurance of knowing they have some purchasing power. They don't want to risk a repetition of the depression years when they had nothing, not even a single cent on their person or to their name. The lesson they learned was to save their money, make every cent count, bank it, put it away in government bonds, be frugal, not to buy anything until they could pay cash for it, and always to look for bargains, for "a penny saved is a penny earned."

Another throwback to the 3-D era was the attitude towards money itself. Since money was scarce and jobs were insecure and difficult to get, earning money for survival became dominant in every man's mind. So when a person was successful in getting a job, no matter how menial, he stayed with it. The wages might have been small, working conditions unfavorable, the task tough and demanding, and his talents unsuited to the work, yet the fear of another recession kept him at the job for years. The employers were kings and no employee questioned their policies or decisons, that is if he wanted to retain his job. No job was secure anymore. After all, the administration could always find workers who would gladly work for a lower wage. Lawyers, teachers and engineers with degrees were vying with each other for ordinary positions as railway section hands, door-to-door salesmen and sales clerks. Work was something to be treasured. Man had been created to work, and when he didn't work everything about him went wrong. Under such circumstances no person could afford the gamble of trying for another job. So, each worker stayed with his job believing he was fortunate to be working, and that "a bird in the hand is worth two in the bush."

The child of the depression learned his lesson about the importance and value of money so well, that today when he is confronted with a bill of $7.50 for a steak dinner, $14.00 for a motel room, $43.00 for a pair of shoes, or his son asks him for $5.00 to take his girlfriend to a football game or to buy a hockey stick, his insides churn from frustration. He remembers vividly that ten dollars in relief fed a family of five for a month during the depression, or that the teacher in his Bryant S.D. 2533 (Blindloss, Alta.) earned a salary of twelve dollars per month, sometimes not able to collect even this meager amount.

The difference in the appreciation of the value of money also can be illustrated by the grandmother who spends a few cents to take the city transit to town, while her daughter thinks nothing of paying a couple of dollars in taxi fare for the same trip. Today's extravagance, the widespread use and availability of credit buying, the lack of genuine effort on the part of the workers, the presence of permissiveness in every segment of society, and people living way beyond their means, cause the people who lived through the depression to philosophize rather frustratingly that, "The present generation needs a depression to educate them in the error of their ways." An education in adversity gave people a greater sense of values, once they became graduates of the 3-D period. To see a beautiful field of grain reduced by the hot winds and blowing dust into a brown desert of drifting soil, to look for rain day after day which never came and to see livestock suffering from lack of food and water, were harsh experiences indeed, but they increased one's appreciation for the bounty of nature.

In the long struggle back to prosperity, many farmers who survived the 3-D period acquired more and more land, so that instead of half-a-section supporting a family, the population was spread more thinly, with one family farming one, two, three or more sections. Farming on such a large scale came about because the depressing and tormenting years of drought and blowing dust discouraged many farmers who abandoned their farmsteads and took what they could with them; they left with hopes of making a better living. The 1936 census reports that 13,900 farms and some three million acres of land were abandoned. It was unfortunate that it took such harsh experiences to help develop a workable settlement policy for the Palliser Triangle of the prairies. Now the area functions better agriculturally with its farming population dispersed proportionately accordingly to the potential productivity of the land.

The widespread unemployment, the hardships and the poverty of the 3-D years were responsible for the attempts of present-day governments to prevent such suffering among their citizens again. Hence today most state systems have been promoting increased spending and have augmented their money supply to keep the economy of their country viable. This has lead to the present inflation spiral. During a depression the reverse is true, for the abnormal rate of unemployment and falling wages tend to decrease demand and business is forced to lower prices in order to sell goods and services.

The 3-D years had a restraining effect on education, but social activities remained strong and in most school districts improved considerably. Teacher recruitment was not a problem, for there were hundreds of applications for each position, but the financing of schools and the searing effect of those years on human lives were the chief culprits. The exodus of farmers from the drought-ridden prairies left some school districts so depleted in population that not a child was left, so such schools were closed. In many other schools the number of pupils dwindled to a mere half-dozen, but had to be kept open. With so many farms vacant, the remaining farmers

-- V. R. Johnston

Putting on a school pageant for the people of the district taxed the ingenuity of both teacher and pupils. So, many rural schools, like Helmsdale S.D. (Oyen, Alta.), sponsored such events to dispel some of the melancholia of the depression of the thirties.

were unable to keep the taxes paid and the districts were soon hopelessly in arrears. The 3-D years imprisoned the inhabitants physically and mentally, shrinking their hopes and horizons and reducing their capacity for optimism. The sad effects could be seen in the eyes of the children, for they were often dull, listless and bewildered.

Some teachers succumbed to this lethargy, but the majority did not and seeing what was required, provided a window to the outside world and gave the students a chance to expand their cramped minds. These wise teachers stimulated the interests of the youngsters, fed their minds, devised fresh methods of teaching, and brought the great world to the classroom through the appropriate use of newspapers, books, magazines, pictures, radio and other media. The contact of the boys and girls with living, warm, inspirational and dedicated teachers brought many rewards, and educationally, the dust-bowl days were not all in vain. School districts, realizing the value of an education, continued to operate their schools at great sacrifices to themselves. The 3-D era abounded in examples of the resourcefulness and courage of the human spirit in providing the rural youngsters with a good preparation for living, notwithstanding the most adverse conditions.

The provision of an elementary education was difficult enough in those days, but some school districts sacrificed even still more to establish local rural high schools, so the children of the district could receive more than a grade eight or nine education.

Horace Allen, a teacher in one such school, described his experiences in the Ewelme S.D. 2829, (Fort Macleod, Alta.) during the 1934-35 school term.

> After four years of university training I was the successful applicant for the newly-opened high school room, grades nine to twelve inclusive, all subjects in the Ewelme S.D. 2829. Ewelme is some twenty miles south of Fort Macleod.
>
> The room was a converted threshing caboose, twenty feet long, nine feet wide and six-and-a-half feet high. Thirteen mature people occupied this space from 9:00 a.m. until 3:30 p.m. for five days each week. Anticipating modern trends in education the furniture, being home made, was of the innovative, utilitarian type. Two rows of benches were used in lieu of desks, with smaller backless benches serving as seats. The teacher had a kitchen chair and table. Any degree of mobility existed in the imagination of the occupants.
>
> Heat was supplied by a small coal stove located near the front of the room. During the cold, blizzardy days so common on the prairie, it was necessary to keep any fresh air strictly on the outside of the building. We were the forerunners of today's forced circulation, air-conditioned buildings, except that our air was circulated from person to person.
>
> The equipment and/or library was nil.
>
> My theoretical salary was the statutary minimum of $840.00 per annum, but to prevent me from exerting any inflationary pressure on the locality, $420.00 was deducted forthwith as payment for my transportation to and from my boarding place and school. However, teaching all the subjects to the four senior grades called for considerable preparation, so I remained in school long after the pupils left and then walked to my current boarding place.
>
> Nothing was new; today's credit cards are just an extension of the credit principle often afforded the teacher. Room and board was charged at the rate of $20.00 per month. It was paid by having me board at the homes of the parents of my pupils on a pro rata basis, the number of pupils in the family attending school decided the length of my stay. Payments for this service to the school district was made by a deduction in the school taxes. This accounted for $200.00 of my salary. Final payments of the $220.00 cash money was completed two years after my year at Ewelme.
>
> However, we made our own fun. The actual work in the classroom was very enjoyable and satisfying. In fact one of the lads in this school became the superintendent of schools in Milwaukee, U.S.A.

The report of the inspector of high schools on the Ewelme setup was far from complimentary.

Very few teachers were able to collect their full wages during the 3-D period, so like the rest of the inhabitants they also received relief orders that they turned in at the store for groceries and clothing. The arrival of relief trains laden with food and second-hand clothing afforded more than one teacher a measure of welcome assistance at various times during the thirties. Teachers organizations in Ontario went so far as to provide relief assistance in the form of ten dollars cash to any teacher in the drought area receiving less than $300 annually in take-home pay.

Teachers' salaries decreased with experience rather than increased. Dave Maitland's salary was reduced in the six years he taught in the Decorah S.D. 459 (Decorah, Sask.) from $1200 to $476. He was an understanding teacher and at a meeting on December 6, 1932, informed the trustees he would teach through January and February for no salary to keep the school in operation. There is a note in the school's minute book which reads as follows: "We, the trustees of the Decorah S.D. 459 deeply appreciate Mr. Maitland's offer to assist the school in this manner. Signed — Robt. F. Strouts, Chairman; J. A. Cameron, Sec. Treas."

The conscientious and dedicated teachers, as always, found themselves more concerned and consequently more involved in the lives of their pupils. Some learned they couldn't get the best results from undernourished children so they introduced many discreet methods of feeding children who

-- Horace Allen

The "box" on the horizon was the high school operated by the Ewelme S.D. 2829 (Fort MacLeod, Alta.) in 1934-35 during the depression years.

came to school without any lunch, so as not to hurt the feelings of their parents. They provided hot soup, especially prepared porridge, shared lunches, including the teacher's, had noon-hour picnics, or treats by the teacher. Whatever the scheme was, usually it was the teacher who managed to scrounge or buy the necessary food. There was no end to what a teacher could do. Lavinia Carlson, who taught in the Blusson S.D. 1787 (Champion, Alta.) for four years during the depression, reminisced about those times.

> Money was scarce and I found myself with numerous little tasks ordinarily considered above and beyond the call of duty. I found I had to be prepared to sew on a button, repair a tear, share my lunch, and provide a scribbler or pencil. I also entered the field of barbering, cutting hair for the girls, keeping their bangs trimmed, and providing hair ribbons. Jimmy Miller came in one day and asked for a haircut. He needed it but being afraid I might make a mess of it, I told him he would first have to get his mother's permission. The next morning he announced, "Mom says it's my hair!" He received his non-guaranteed haircut, but I felt I failed to come up to his expectation, for although he was very polite about it, he never asked for another.

A school lunch did not contain an apple or orange, or some other fresh fruit as it does today. A child considered it a treat if he found store-bought dried apples or a prune or two in his lunch pail.

Pupils in the Wild Lily S.D. (Elbow, Sask.) often shared their prunes with the teacher, and when she returned from her vacation she remembered them with a special treat of oranges.

During the 3-D period it became a common practice to keep schools open all summer so pupils did not have to attend when the weather was at its worst, as most of them didn't have clothing fit to wear when it got bitterly cold. Students who wore clothes without patches were considered fortunate; it was likely that some good relative in a more prosperous part of Canada had sent some hand-me-downs to them, or they had been lucky in the draw for the castoff clothing shipped in as a relief measure. Thus the children formed a motley crew as they played together outdoors at recess on chilly days; some wore their parents' old coats, mackinaws, or sweaters cut down to prevent them from dragging on the ground; some appeared in the clothing of their older brothers or sisters, some showed up wearing apparel made from the better parts of several garments; and some appeared in singular and inappropriate toggery acquired from the relief bundles. All the garments were too large or too small and made the wearer appear shabbily dressed. No wonder many teachers used their own limited financial resources to buy a pair of mitts, shoes, rubbers, or some other article of clothing for a needy child to alleviate any excessive suffering from the cold. Such assistance had to be given rather judiciously for some parents were so proud that they refused to accept charity and preferred to keep their children home from school.

E. 1. 22 (Form B).

GOVERNMENT OF THE PROVINCE OF ALBERTA—DEPARTMENT OF EDUCATION

REPORT OF INSPECTOR OF HIGH SCHOOLS

Ewelme   S. D. No. 2829   Date.   June 5   1935

Enrolment: IX-2, X-1, XI-6, XII-3   Total 12   No. of Rooms 1

Accommodation: The building cannot be called a class room; it is a narrow building, about 9' x 20' with ceiling only 6' to 7' 3 small windows on each side, with home-made desks, and a blackboard cloth only about 2'6 x 6'

Equipment:
     There is no equipment.

     The difficulty of teaching under such a low ceiling has to be experienced to be appreciated. I feel that a teacher is not given an opportunity to do anything approaching his best work under such conditions as obtain in this temporary building.

     I recommend that if high school work is to be continued in this district, and government grants paid to assist
General Organization suitable building be provided at once, up to required standards in respect to floor space, lighting, ventilation, heating and equipment; and that if this cannot be done, those students who desire high school courses be assisted in taking Correspondence Courses with the Department of Education or attend other schools, the fees in either case being paid in part or wholly by the district; that in any case the present building be no longer recognized as a class room.

H̶c̶B̶

-- Horace Allen

H. E. Balfour, the inspector of high schools for the province of Alberta, was not favorably impressed with Ewelme High School. His inspector's report of the Ewelme school board was anything but complimentary.

Teaching during the 3-D period provided teachers with experiences that served them well in the future, for they became the best educators that Canada has ever had. In their new capacities as department of education officials, university professors, inspectors, superintendents, principals, and classroom teachers, they brought a concept of concern, dedication, accountability, discipline and high achievement standards to education. They were responsible for what might be called "the golden age of education in Western Canada." This success continued until the majority of these stalwarts passed on or retired from the profession. During this golden age, demand for graduates of Canadian educational institutions came from all over the world. Those transplanted Canadians proved their worth in their adopted lands and soon assumed responsible positions in industry, agriculture, research, education, business and space science. Much was written at the time about the "brain drain" to foreign countries, but few chroniclers gave credit to the high standard of education that had been achieved by the graduates of the 3-D era.

7

Railways and Rural Education

The original contract between the Canadian Pacific Railway and the Canadian government, signed in 1880, contained a monopoly clause; the railway was to receive a subsidy of twenty-five million acres of land taken in alternate parcels of 640 acres each, from a strip forty-eight miles wide running along the route between Winnipeg and the Rocky Mountains. The railway was to have the option of rejecting land "not fairly fit for settlement." This option resulted in the rest of the grant being made up of reserve land located elsewhere on the prairie. It was not surprising then to find Canadian Pacific Railway land hundreds of miles away from its trans-Canada right-of-way.

The railway depended for survival on quickly settling the country, and in this way creating the traffic which it would carry. Both the government and the railway set to work immediately to attract immigrants, using such schemes as cooperative farms, humanitarian enterprises and commercial colonization companies. In addition, the Canadian Pacific Railway advertised the agricultural potential of the prairies by flooding the market with publicity pamphlets and posters of all sorts, and inaugurating an educational program designed to supply information about the new land. The latter was accomplished in a unique way. A passenger coach was converted into a classroom, which informed the public of the advantages of taking up farm land on the prairie through exhibits, pictures, hand-out material, and lectures. This classroom on wheels visited towns and cities throughout Eastern Canada and provided agricultural information both in English and French. Realizing that the expense of travelling to the "land of milk and honey" would deter many prospective settlers, the railway introduced special economy fares. The homeseeker's ticket, for example, enabled people to inspect land anywhere in the Canadian West, simply by requesting a homeseeker's permit from the nearest representative of the Canadian Pacific Railway. Special excursion rates encouraged new settlers to travel to their old homes at Christmas and other holiday times; it was hoped these people would spread the gospel of "cheap lands and good

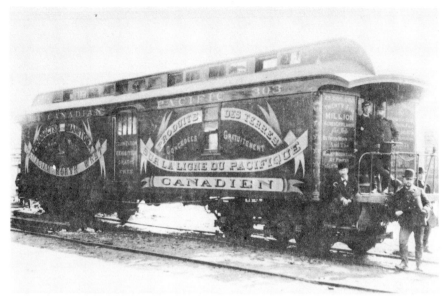

-- Canadian Pacific Railway

This is one of the railway coaches that was converted into a display classroom to advertise the farming possibilities of the Canadian prairies.

crops" and thus encourage further settlement. Visitors from Eastern Canada could also take advantage of these low fares.

The fantastic influx of the settlers and their families between 1901 and 1911 created a need for schools. Schoolhouses mushroomed everywhere and a cry went out for teachers to take charge of these schools. Normal schools for training teachers were few and far between in the West in those early years, so it was indeed fortunate that teachers from Eastern Canada, the United States and the British Isles answered the call. The railway made it easier for the teachers to come by permitting them to take advantage of excursion rates. A teacher travelling via a Canadian Pacific Railway harvesters' excursion paid a fare of twelve dollars from Saint John, New Brunswick, to Winnipeg, Manitoba, and an additional eight dollars from Winnipeg to anywhere west. The return fare was just as attractive. For example, there was a teacher who arrived in Alberta from New Brunswick in 1916 with his teacher's license. He was thirty-four years old and had been working in his home province for an annual salary of $250. He thought he had uncovered a fortune in the McKenzie S.D. (Tofield, Alta.) where he was offered $600. The cheap railway fare of about twenty dollars lured him to Alberta to see for himself what the country was like and discover whether there were any good opportunities for teachers. Both were to his liking, so he stayed.

Sometimes it was the desire for adventure that prompted a teacher to seek a teaching position on the prairie frontier. Euda, a former teacher in the Verdant Valley S.D. (Drumheller, Alta.), described how it happened that she decided to teach in Western Canada.

> One evening in 1904 I attended a sportsmen's fair being held in Boston, Massachusetts. Canadian Pacific Railway agents were there, passing out pamphlets describing the golden opportunities to be had in Western Canada. Upon returning to my married sister's home in Lynn, just outside of Boston, I told her that I intended to write to the Department of Education in Edmonton, Alberta, to find out if my diploma would permit me to teach in that province. She looked in utter disbelief at me and said, "Have you gone out of your mind? You don't know a living soul out there and how do you know what may befall you in that wild and wooly West?" A fellow in the same office where I worked as a secretary told me that an uncle of his worked one winter in Calgary, Alberta as a plumber and froze both his ears off when the temperature dropped to fifty degrees below zero. In spite of all the protestations against my going to Alberta, I came, I saw, and I stayed.

The special fares may have been an inducement to come west, but the railway coaches on harvesters excursion trains were not. Pioneer teachers travelled in crowded wooden passenger coaches fitted with uncomfortable wicker and slab seats arranged in pairs facing one another. At night it was possible to pull out these seats and improvise hard wooden beds, and just above each bunk was another wooden bed that swung down from the wall like a shelf. Bedding had to be provided by the passenger. One end of the coach contained a stove where water could be heated and food prepared, and the other end contained the toilet facilities, the wash basin and a supply of water in a tin reservoir. Since no cooking utensils were provided and as the fuel for the range and the water was always in short supply, the unwary passengers were forced to scrounge for food from fellow passengers, buy some at stores when the train stopped, or remain hungry for most of the trip.

Once the teacher reached the railway center nearest to her school, all her travelling problems were by no means ended, as there was the matter of getting from the town to her rural school. Unless the school board had made arrangements for someone to get her, it could evolve into a difficult situation, as the following incident indicates.

A teacher who had been hired by the Sundial S.D. and advised to travel to Lethbridge, Alberta, as it was the most convenient center from which to reach her new school. Unfortunately, the school board failed to tell her how to get from Lethbridge to Sundial. When she arrived in the thriving town, she stayed at the hotel for a few days but found no way to get to Sundial so she left. Two days later a party from the district called but found she had left town. They immediately requested the teacher agency at Regina, Sask. to get them another teacher, but this time the secretary-treasurer included the following note that was to be given to the next teacher hired for Sundial: "Dear Miss or Sir: This is to inform you that the only way to get from Lethbridge to Sundial is by stage, which leaves the Lethbridge Post Office on Tuesdays and Fridays at 7 a.m., arriving at Sundial about 4:00 p.m. the same day."

Annual reports sent to the Department of Education by the school inspectors in those pioneer days reveal that, in general, the competency and qualification of a teacher in any school seemed to vary with the distance of that particular school from the railroad; the closer it was, the better the qualifications; the farther away, the less satisfactory the qualifications. Teachers preferred to teach in schools as near as possible to centers of civilization. In fact, the only way the isolated schools could get teachers was for the Department of Education to grant permits to anyone who had at least a grade eight diploma and desired to teach. Education in rural schools was of an inferior quality. G. E. Ellis, an inspector of schools in Alberta, included the following comment in his 1908 report to the Department of Education:

> I have had more permit teachers during the past year, than for the two previous years. This is probably the chief reason that there has not been a more marked degree of progress. It is not intended that these teachers are to be considered indolent or even deficient in non-professional qualifications, but having little or no training, their work is necessarily defective.

The transcontinental railway lines of the Canadian Pacific Railway, the Canadian Northern Railway, and the Grand Trunk Pacific Railway became the lifelines for every new settlement that sprung up along them. However, it was the network of branch lines that stretched out like tentacles all over Canada that was important to the homesteaders; with branch lines, the isolation of many rural communities was brought to an end. The loneliness and emptiness of the prairies were soon to be legends of the past. The stories of the settlement of the Canadian West and the development of rural education were unavoidably linked with the building of railway lines. Branch lines were so important that a potential railway made a good political football. Myrtle G. Moorhouse of the Buffalo Horn Valley S.D. (Assiniboia, Sask.) described her experience.

> Every four years, there would be a couple of politicians come around in a hired livery and travel the entire proposed line from Assiniboia west, and tell us that if their party was elected, the railway would be assured. They got out of the buggy and examined every survey stake, adding news ones as the old ones rotted away, and visited with all nearby residents. We got excited about our future prospects. These politicians held meetings in all the schoolhouses and invariably were elected, but we never did get our railroad. The closest town is still twenty to twenty-five miles away.

— Mrs. Donaldson

The tri-weekly mixed train arrives at Fairlight, Sask. A close examination of the picture (taken in 1909) shows a teacher descending the steps of the passenger car, while the chairman of the school district is waiting on the station platform to greet her.

As soon as a branch line was completed and the trains started to run on it, all the nearby school districts experienced an improvement in the standard of education offered by the teachers. The success and progress in any school was, and is, just as good as the teacher in charge, so when competent and qualified teachers were willing to accept positions in these now no longer isolated districts, education benefited.

Mixed trains operated on these newly constructed branch lines until such time as the traffic warranted the introduction of regular freight and passenger trains. The term "mixed" was used to describe them as they carried not only freight, like coal, lumber, livestock, grain, settlers' effects and machinery, but also cream cans, egg crates, baby chicks, parcels from Eatons, packs of raw fur, the mail, as well as people. A day coach and a combined mail-baggage express car were tacked on the end of the freight train and made up the two-part passenger section of the "mixed."

The train crews were friends to all, and usually knew about all the people on the line. Passengers boarded the train at their nearest town's flag stations or at railway crossings if they could attract the attention of the engineer. Flag stations were unmanned, so the do-it-yourself technique was used to stop a train. This was accomplished by flying a red flag on the station platform during daylight hours, or showing a red lantern at night. When the engineer saw the danger signal he would stop the train and pick up the passenger. Regulations required that each such station be equipped with flags, a red lantern and a small heater, so if the would-be passenger had a match and could read instructions, he was able to wait for the train in comfort and be assured of having it stop. On the other hand, if the passengers were on board and wished to get off at one of the flag stations, they simply told the conductor and he did the rest.

At noon most early trains stopped at certain designated "lunch towns". Meals or snacks were served at one of the restaurants in town and the passengers were made aware of its location by a bell ringer who stood outside the cafe door, vigorously ringing an old school handbell.

Travel by a mixed train was casual and very slow. It stopped at every point along the line to spot cars on the siding or pick up others and add them to those they already had on the train. The shunting and switching took time so the passengers relaxed, visited with each other, played cards, read, or walked up and down the station platform. The day coach always turned out to be a social center, and before long everyone knew everyone else, as well as almost everything about each other. There was much kidding back and forth, and many remarks were directed at the conductor because of his slow train.

A woman passenger once told the conductor that the CPR "mixed" was mentioned in the Bible in the book of Genesis as "God created and loved everything that creeps and crawls." Passengers always agreed in verbal fashion that the cow-catcher was on the wrong end of the train as it was more likely for a cow to catch the train than for the train to catch the cow. A good illustration of the type of bantering that went on occurred on a mixed train in east-central Alberta. A pregnant woman was travelling on a CPR mixed train to the hospital at Consort seventy-six miles away. The train was so slow this day that soon everyone was snapping at the conductor to speed up the snail-like pace of the train or the stork would beat them. In desperation the worried offical blurted out, "Lady, if you knew how slow this train was, why did you take it, realizing your present condition?" The woman was not to be outwitted and exclaimed loudly enough for everyone in the passenger car to hear, "That's just the very trouble with your train," she said, "for when I got on I wasn't pregnant!"

The leisurely pace at which the trains travelled was a boon to the teachers going out to their schools for the first time. They had ample time to get to know each other, were able to get practical advice from experienced teachers and usually talked to passengers on board who could tell them something about the people and the district to which they were headed.

Perhaps no teacher experienced a more lonely feeling than when she arrived at some flag station and there was no one to meet her. The train would stop, the trainman open the door, help the teacher down the steps, and desposit all her luggage on the station platform with parting words of, "This is Excel! Good Luck!" The conductor, without getting off, would yell, "All aboard!" and pull the signal cord. Almost immediately the engine bell would clang, the train jerk into motion, pick up speed, and in a few seconds its twin tail lights would grow dimmer and dimmer, and the echoing hum of the wheels on the rails get fainter and fainter, until finally, like a flick of a switch all sights and sounds would end. Just how lonely these teachers felt standing alone beside the railway track on a dark night in a strange part of the country, had to be experienced to be understood.

It was as traumatic an experience to board a passenger train in the middle of the night as it was to leave one. A rural schoolteacher, who used to travel on the CNR Goose Lake line between Calgary and Saskatoon reminisced about her first trip.

> As it was about 2:00 a.m. when I got aboard, people were sprawled on the seats in every direction trying to get sufficiently comfortable to sleep. I got out the pillow my wise mother had given me and put it under my head. Since I had no blanket I covered myself with my coat, but I felt it was too indecent to relax like those all about me were doing. Sleep under such conditions didn't come easily, so it was almost daylight when I dozed off. I was startled into consciousness by a gentle rap on my chin and my mouth snapped shut. A man in the opposite seat was grinning at me and when I stirred he said, "Sister, your mouth was open!" I was so embarrassed and annoyed that all I could do was to turn my back and ignore him.
>
> Soon, as if by a prearranged signal, everyone awoke, smoothed out their clothes a bit, took turns going to a most inadequate washroom, and then ate some of the lunch they had brought. Apparently everyone must have had an orange for soon the air in the car was saturated with a pungent citric odor. A few waited until the train stopped twenty minutes or so at some station, and then they dashed up town to grab a cup of coffee and some toast. On this first trip I did not know of these long stops nor of the convenient all-night cafes usually located just across the street from the station, so I breakfasted on a couple of chocolate bars that my father had slipped into one of the pockets on my coat.

The majority of the pioneer teachers were a very special breed and could cope with such inconveniences. However, there were some who took the line of least resistance and returned to their homes as soon as possible.

Two teachers arrived in Delburne, Alberta, from Calgary; one was to teach in Cumberland S.D. 1616 and the other in the adjacent district of Bellgrove 2390. When they got off the train and discovered that they were about one hundred miles from Calgary, they took the next train back and said that they had enough of isolation and didn't want to be that far from civilization.

The arrival of a new teacher wasn't always on such a discouraging note, for in most cases the occasion could turn out to be full of pleasant surprises, as the following incidents indicate.

Margaret McLean had been hired via correspondence to teach the Arrowwood S.D. 1733 and was to come on the train as far as Blackie, Alberta. The last train to go through Blackie from Calgary before school started in the fall would be bringing teachers for all the surrounding rural school districts, perhaps as many as twenty-five new schoolmarms. Hence it was imperative for Jack Green, a member of the school board, to meet her at the train before some irreparable mix-up occurred. The neighbors had to go and see the fun of him picking out the Arrowwood teacher. One of the first passengers to get off was an old, stern, spinster-looking teacher, and he could hear someone in the background taunting him with, "Tackle her, Jack, tackle her!" He just let her go on her way and waited for some others to get off. Well, he had to make the break sometime, so when a pleasant-looking lady was making her way down the steps of the train, he walked up to her and asked if she was Miss McLean. She said, "No, but I've met a Miss McLean on the train and I'll get her for you." Mr. Green in turn helped his benefactor find who she was to meet at the train and then proudly took Miss Mclean over to meet the grinning neighbors. He felt pleased that the boys hadn't got a good laugh at him, at least on that occasion.

The most unusual teacher that Pollockville S.D. had was A. H. Keanne, who came in mid-term. The school board met the train as a welcoming committee, but no teacher arrived. Disappointed, the trustees went over to Gardner's store to have an emergency meeting, as school was to start the very next day. To everyone's surprise, when school opened the next morning the teacher was there. She had arrived by train all right, but no one thought the little seventy-one-year-old lady wending her way slowly along the station platform was the school teacher. The school board had accepted the application of an A. H. Keanne, but thought it would be a man. They felt rather sheepish about making such an error. Life could be hard for trustees no matter how well-meaning they wanted to be!

The coming of the railway into any community influenced the lives of the children in may ways. Ida (Balmer) Rylands, a former student in the Bissell S.D. 2745 (Vesper, Sask.), described some of her early experiences with trains.

> The railroad played an important part in our school days. The track that ran from Vesper to Simmie was about half-a-mile west of our school. We often watched the train at recesses or noon, whenever the weekly event occurred. The Thursday train rarely kept to any timetable so we never knew when to expect it. One time my mother made the trip to Swift Current and was to phone her relatives the moment she arrived at 2:30 p.m. They were eating supper and given up all hope of seeing her when she phoned at 6:30 p.m. explaining, "I just arrived. Can you come and get me?"
> On another occasion I made the trip from Swift Current to Vesper and expecting to arrive a little late, purchased some fresh fruit before I

boarded the train. I was fortunate I did. We should have arrived at Vesper at 11:00 a.m. but as it was a beautiful summer day the CPR took advantage of the fine weather to unload nine carloads of cinders along the track. We finally reached Vesper at 2:30 p.m.

Sometimes special excursion trains were run in the winter for the convenience of the settlers. The train would make the trip to Simmie early in the morning, pick up passengers there and all the way back. After a day in the city the shoppers were brought back again at night. The CPR was kind in that they also stopped at railroad crossings, picking up any passengers who were waiting there.

I took my first train ride on the occasion of my seventh birthday. It was during the depression and as this particular year was a good one for rabbits, everyone trapped them. The waiting room at Vesper was full of bags of rabbit skins. I remember that some lady with a baby tripped over one of them, but neither she nor her baby suffered any injury. Since rabbit skins seemed to bring in the only ready cash we had in those years, we affectionately called our train, "The Rabbit Special."

Hundreds of rural schoolteachers have said, rather dotingly, "Thank goodness for the train whistle!" The sound of it was so much company as well as reminding them that they weren't too isolated. Many teachers confessed that they were able to retain their aplomb while living and teaching in some isolated rural school district because there was always the train whistle to reassure them. They knew the train was on its way to some city; the whistle meant home, friends, romance, adventure and everything else associated with the society of man. It was an emotional nourishment that enabled them to live contentedly as well as inspiring them to become better teachers, as everything that mattered was not that far away after all.

Some railways, particularly on their northward runs, passed through sections of country that were deficient in both developed natural resources and in people. This resulted in stretches of trackage anywhere from fifty to one hundred miles in length with a succession of diminutive communities ten or fifteen miles apart, with not a single good-sized town among them. The population of these centers was made up of the railway section men, the foreman and his family, two or three government employees from the forestry and Indian departments, the proprietor of a small general store, and maybe a trapper or two. There were probably no more than a total of twenty-five men, women, and children. If there were any children of school age in these hamlets, the parents found it extremely difficult to provide them with an education as the establishment of a local school was out of the question. Some railway officials, realizing this problem, arranged for a school car for the territory, with the help and the cooperaton of the department of education. A large section of a passenger coach was converted into a classroom and the rest into living quarters for the teacher. Doctor Robert M. Stamp of the University of Calgary wrote a splendid description of these "schools on wheels" in an article entitled, "The Railway Car Schools of Northern Ontario," in Volume 1, Number 3, Spring 1974, of *Canada — A Historical Magazine.*

The cars themselves were a model of compactness and efficiency, each containing kitchen, living quarters and classroom. The kitchen was equipped with the latest in conveniences — metal sink, refrigerator, food larder of two to three weeks' capacity, spacious cupboards, "the whole layout to equal that of the best appointed home." The living room combined living, dining and sleeping quarters, "with beds concealed from view and convertible by night into comfortable sleeping accommodation." A fully equipped nine by nine feet bathroom adjoined. The largest of the three rooms was the classroom, thirty feet in length with desks for fifteen young pupils. Not as roomy as many southern Ontario homes, but certainly more comfortable than the accommodation many teachers were able to find in remote northern Ontario settlements of the day. And the seemingly cramped quarters did not inhibit Fred Sloman and his wife from raising five chilren during their lengthy career on the cars.

This school on wheels was better equipped than most of is earth-bound one-room counterparts, especially in such matters as library books, reference materials and extra-curricular facilities. It was hauled from place to place by the regular trains operating on the line, and visited each designated community on a regular basis. Generally, the school remained at such places for a week or so, with the children attending for longer periods of time each day than that required by the ordinary schools. Just prior to the scheduled time of departure, the teacher assigned enough material to keep the students busy until the car returned again, three or four weeks later. In the meantime the school continued its scheduled appearances at the two or three other centers on the line.

Because of the "school on wheels," equality of educational opportunity was provided for a large number of children living in sparsely settled areas along the right-of-way, in the timber and pulpwood camps, and in various isolated spots chosen by the hunter, the trapper, the itinerant farmer, and the fisherman. But it must be realized that the "schools on wheels" did more than simply impart basic skills to the children; these institutions provided citizenship training and combatted Communist influences. In the early years of the twentieth century thousands of non-English speaking immigrants from continental Europe settled in these remote sections of the country and schools were regarded by many as the only force that would bring about cohesion, unity of spirit and purpose among such a heterogeneous population, and produce loyal and law-abiding Canadians. In fact, the schools were regarded by many as the first line of defense against communistic influences.

A study of the G. Howard Ferguson papers and the annual reports of the Minister of Education 1926 to 1928 reveals that Ontario political and educational leaders of that day firmly believed that "schools on wheels" were successfully combatting Communist influences in the isolated communities in northern Ontario. For instance, G. Howard Ferguson, premier and minister of education, boasted publicly:

> The foreign-born, both parents and children, trained in an atmosphere inimical to Canadian ideas of citizenship will quickly develop into loyal and law-abiding Canadians.

> The communities are being wrought over into the fabric of loyal Canadian citizenship.

> Bolshevik propaganda finds no place or acceptance wherever the school car operates. The next generation will fall naturally into their places as loyal citizens.

The night classes that were taught along with the day classes provided some with an opportunity to learn the basic skills of communicating in English; for others it meant viewing films and talking about events happening in the outside world; finally, it gave some people a second chance in life. Many found that with the learning of basic communication skills they were in line for promotion in their jobs. But for everyone living along the remote railway lines, the arrival of the school car provided a most welcome break in the monotony of isolated living.

Through these school cars, the government discharged its responsibility of providing schooling for every child no matter where he lived. The railways in turn were satisfied with the arrangements, for they solved their ever-present problem of placing their right-of-way employees in centers that were able to provide schools. Thus the railway found it feasible to provide the car and move it from point to point free of charge, while the department of education, as its share, paid for the furnishings, and the school equipment and hired and paid the teachers without any cost to the communities served.

Northern Ontario led the rest of Canada in providing such travelling classrooms. Beginning in Nandair, Ontario on September 20, 1926, the school-car system expanded until by the end of the first year, there were two such travelling units on the Canadian National transcontinental railway line. Two more cars were added in 1928, and two more in 1935. The service reached its peak in the late 1940s when 226 children were attending school in seven such cars: four on the Canadian National lines, two on the Canadian Pacific, and one on the Timiskaming and Northern Ontario Railway.

The school car continued to be a way of life for many northern communities for another twenty years, until advanced communication and the appearance of larger settlements rendered them obsolete.

-- Canadian National Railway

A geography lesson is in progress in a typical school car.

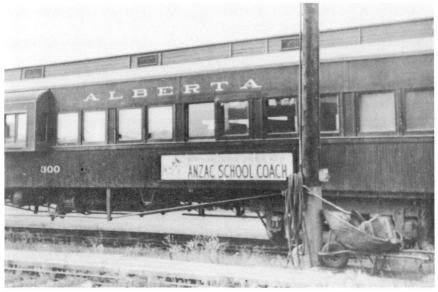

-- K. R. Perry

The Anzac School Car of the Northern Alberta Railway company brought native children from along the line into Anzac where they attended classes during the week and then returned in the same car to their homes on Friday afternoon.

The Northern Alberta Railways Company, with headquarters at Edmonton, Alberta, also launched a school car on its Waterways subdivision between Lac La Biche and Fort McMurray. However, its purpose was to transport students rather than to instruct them. Known as the "Anzac School Car," it brought children from along the line into Anzac where they attended a central school during the week and then returned in the same car to their homes on Friday afternoon. The youngsters lived in old bunkhouses of an oil company while attending school in Anzac. K. R. Perry, general manager of the Northern Alberta Railways Company, described this unique method of assisting the children along the line to get an education and concluded by saying:

> This service was only provided during 1960 and has long since been discontinued as the native people did not wish their children to be away from home to the extent that was required. The car has since been scrapped.

A unique type of early educational service that proved of value to the early homesteaders was one initiated by the Department of Agriculture with the cooperation of the railway companies. It was an agricultural demonstration train that visited hundreds of prairie villages and towns providing information and instruction about farm implements, methods of prairie farming, farm buildings, water wells, various breeds of livestock and strains of seed and other kindred topics. The objective of sending out such a train was to provide answers to the problems that were besetting the farmers as well as to indicate any future trends to them. The demonstration train carried the cattle, horses, sheep, pigs, chickens, and the latest in farm machinery and everything else that would be of value to concerned farmers. The exhibits were displayed at each stopping point and qualified instructors pointed out the merits and weaknesses of each animal, plant or machine. The visit of the demonstration train to a particular community in the homestead days was equivalent to a modern "field day", and was the forerunner of today's experimental farms.

The following two newspaper accounts from *The Saskatoon Phoenix* dated May 31 and June 1, 1920, explain the value of demonstration trains in more detail.

BETTER-FARMING TRAIN LEAVES FOR TOUR OF PROVINCE
Made Up of Twelve Coaches With Six Sections; Demonstrations to be Given Every Day

The Better-Farming train which was at the C.P.R. station yesterday, left last night for a tour of the province. The train is made up of twelve cars and is being conducted under the joint authority of the Department of Agriculture and the Department of Education. The CPR is cooperating by supplying the coaches, engine and the crew of the train.

Six sections, all of interest to the agriculturist, are in the twelve coaches. There is a section for livestock, one for grains, farm machinery and engines, poultry, and a section for the boys and girls, and another for household science.

The train will go from here to Macklin, right near the Alberta border. It will then make a tour of the province, finally returning to Saskatoon. Two demonstrations will be given daily.

Professor Shaw and Professor Greig are in charge of the train and will do the demonstrating. They are experts, and the farmers will get the best advice.

The moving-picture car, which was a popular feature of the train last year, will again be the leading feature of attraction for the boys and girls, and splendid new films have been secured, the best of these being the moving pictures of pelicans, blue herons, terns and other curious birds, which were taken at Lake Johnston last year under the direction of F. Bradshaw, chief game guardian of the province. There will be two coaches fitted up for men's lectures cars, a coach for women's lecture car, a nusery car fitted up with sand piles, slides and cribs, and with capable nurses in charge, so that tired mothers can leave their children in care while they are attending lectures or visiting the various exhibits on the train. There will be three large coaches used in displaying field husbandry exhibits, and another car to display dairy, mechanical, building and poultry exhibits.

The Saskatoon Phoenix
May 31, 1920

BETTER-FARMING TRAIN HAS FIRST STOP AT MACKLIN: RAIN LOWERS ATTENDANCE

The Better-Farming train, consisting of 13 cars, started on its tour of five weeks duration at Macklin, Sask., yesterday morning. The train will finish the tour at this city.

There was a heavy rain lasting all forenoon, and although it was a blessing to the crops in the Macklin district, it made for a small attendance. Another demonstration was given yesterday afternoon.

The exhibit and lecture cars are filled with demonstration material attractively arranged for instructional purposes. There is no question but that the train is better equipped and arranged for its purpose than any time during the five years in which these trains have been run.

F. H. Auld, deputy minister of agriculture, followed by Captain Acheson, of the agricultural department of the Canadian Pacific Railway, opened proceedings with brief addresses, explaining the purposes of the Better-Farming train. After the addresses the crowd of interested agriculturists dispersed to attend the various lectures and exhibits.

The government never had a more brilliant idea than the Better-Farming trains to give the farmers new ideas on all branches of the work. The CPR cooperates by giving the train and the crew.

The Saskatoon Phoenix
June 1, 1920.

There is no getting away from the fact that prairie farm surroundings in the early days were bare, drab and unattractive. It didn't take the homesteaders who planned to stay on the land and the agricultural authorities long to realize that the answer lay in landscaping the farms and farmyards with trees. So gigantic tree-planting programs were launched in Western Canada.

It is doubtful whether it is possible to find a person who has lived on the prairie for any length of time during the past forty years, and is not familiar with the "Tree-Planting Car" sponsored by the Canadian Forestry Association. Ross A. Evans, who was in charge of such a car during 1951, 1952 and 1953 as it toured Manitoba, Saskatchewan and Alberta, wrote the following interesting account.

The coach was donated to the Canadian Forestry Association by the Canadian Pacific Railway and both the Canadian National Railway and the Canadian Pacific Railway hauled the car free of charge. In addition the Canadian Pacific Railway took on the responsibility of its maintenance and upkeep. The Canadian Forestry Association is supported by individuals and companies interested in conservation.

It was one of the early Canadian Pacific Railway coaches, built almost entirely of wood. No one I ever talked to seemed too sure as to when it was actually built. It was coach No. 54 when I knew it, but that was not its original number. It was renumbered when given to the Canadian Forestry Association in keeping with the Canadian Pacific Railway policy of numbering all their "official" coaches below 100. In 1960 it was replaced with a steel coach.

Depending on where you encountered the car you knew it as the "Tree Planting Car" or the "Forestry Car." When working in the prairie region the words on the side read "Tree Planting Campaign" but when the car was moved into forested areas the wording was changed to "Forest Conservation Campaign" by sliding panels into place on the sides of the car which covered the words "Tree Planting."

I started on the coach at Langenburg, Saskatchewan, on June 1, 1951 and ended that year's run in southern Alberta in early November. The next year I began in Regina in late March, and after travelling much of south-eastern Saskatchewan and southern Manitoba, moved to

Alberta for the fall. Travel in 1953 followed much the same pattern. It was the practice to arrange to be in southern Alberta in the fall of the year because the weather there was usually milder.

Most of the time the operator was alone on the coach. About sixteen feet of one end was fitted up for living accommodation, with a stove for heat, a two-burner gas hot-plate for cooking, overhead water tanks, a chesterfield-bed, tables and cupboards. There was also an icebox. If you were on the good side of some trainman he would bring you ice from the nearest divisional point, otherwise you did without. A furnace at the rear of the coach provided heat for the theatre when this was necessary. I was fortunate in that I was usually moved by passenger trains. In later years when the passenger trains were taken off, freights moved the coach and I understand the service was not too reliable. Occasionally I had the experience of being moved by a freight and discovered you got the smoothest ride you could ask for when the coach was next to the locomotive with a long freight behind. I never liked to think about what would have happened if he had stopped quickly. The roughest ride occurred when the Forestry Car was placed on the end of a long freight. I've often wondered how the trainmen stand it riding in the caboose.

The usual procedure when the coach arrived in town was to contact the station agent, if there was one, or an elevator agent. From these sources it was possible to find out the name of the teacher and any other information that might be helpful. The schools had all been contacted ahead of the time of arrival so they knew we were coming. Sometimes the teacher and her class would be waiting to meet the train, but more often I went to the school and arranged for the children to visit the coach. In a large school we sometimes arranged to show our films in the auditorium, but if this wasn't possible, we scheduled several showings in the coach, until all had been accommodated. If the coach arrived in town early enough in the day we tried to get the children to the coach that day so they would go home and tell their parents about the evening program.

The program, whether for adults or children, was mainly films and exhibits supplemented with a talk. If it was to children the information given was mainly about conservation, if for adults the talk was more about tree planting and landscaping. In the forestry programs, conservation of all natural resources and forests in particular was stressed.

The railway companies, noticing the success that attended their educational services of providing colonization exhibits, agricultural demonstration trains, school cars and conservation programs, were now ready to cooperate in promoting many other such pedagogic schemes.

If it had not been for the four or five-car circus retinue that was moved by the railways from town to town, and even to the most isolated parts of the country very few rural youngsters would have had the opportunity of attending a circus and learning at first hand something about such strange animals as elephants, lions, bears, seals, camels and giraffes. No prairie youngster will ever forget the excitement created by the arrival of the circus train in his town, not to mention the novel manner in which the various cages and equipment wagons were unloaded from the railway cars; sometimes an elephant was used for the purpose.

Chautauqua, a touring educational variety show that played three or four night stands in most towns, found ready acceptance, as opportunities for entertainment of any cultural value were few in the early days. New performances were held every afternoon and evening in the familiar big brown Chautauqua tent. At the conclusion of its engagement period the show moved on, by car, boat, train, or any means of conveyance available at a given time and place. The railway, in particular, was relied upon for transportation between the various distant unit headquarters that had been set up all over the country. An enthusiastic railway official when commenting on the Chautauqua said, "I feel that the Dominion Chautauqua is one factor in making life liveable on the prairies, and we of the railway are proud to have had a small part in its success."

No child who was fortunate to see the royal train that carried the king and queen and the two princesses across Canada in 1939, will ever forget the thrill of seeing the train, newly refurbished in royal colors, and flying the royal ensign, steam proudly into a flag-draped railway station. Patriotic fervor was in evidence everywhere, and no more so when the youngsters caught glimpses of the royal family. It was almost like seeing a fairy tale come true. Best of all, however, it inspired devotion to Canada. It was well that it did, for a short time later our country was involved in the life-and-death struggle of World War II.

Most people may recall the six-car Confederation train that toured Canada from the Atlantic to the Pacific to celebrate the country's centennial year in 1967. A centennial anniversary is a proper time not only for lively celebrations, but it is also a time for serious thought about the entire course over which the country has travelled and the direction in which it is headed. The Confederation train did this through colorful and comprehensive exhibits. These told a story of primeval beginnings, explorers and pioneers, successes and failures, peace and war, happiness and sorrow — a story of great development and a bright future. Thanks to the government and the railways for conceiving such a unique way of telling Canada's story, many youngsters learned something about Canadian history for the first time.

Several types of the smaller rolling stock were designed by the railways for the use of their maintenance-and-way employees, to assist them in covering their allotted trackage. These on-the-job transportation units included the handcar, velocipede (speeder), and the push car. The railways had strict regulations covering the use of these track vehicles. One in particular stated they could only be used by their employees during the course of their normal work day; in other words, no extra-curricular activities after hours.

Understanding railway officials must have closed their eyes, or else some of their employees must have been experts in covering-up some of these activities, for these small track carriers were often used in ways and at times contrary to the regulations contained in the rule book. Hundreds of incidents similar to the following indicate that early railways were concerned with personal service, leaving their imprint on people, homes and communities throughout the country. Canada was better for such humanism.

In the Bjorkdale Valley S.D. (Tisdale, Sask.) during the winter of 1930, Alex Lalonde and his two section men picked up a sick farmer and brought him to the hospital at Tisdale; they used a handcar. A blizzard was raging and there was no other way of getting the patient to the doctor. They saved his life, for he was choking with a bad case of asthma. Upon returning from their mission of mercy, the section crew faced the storm all the way and had to push the handcar from Crooked River, walking in about a foot of snow.

At Talmadge, Sask., James Doyle took a teacher into the hospital at Weyburn, Sask. on a speeder in a blizzard. She had broken her arm and that was the only way to get her there quickly.

Railway employees of the early days have chronicled many such experiences in which the railway, through its local transportation facilities, was able to cope with emergencies that otherwise might have ended in tragedy. Doctors often rode on the speeder or handcar to deliver a baby, set a fracture, treat a serious injury, remove an appendix, prescribe for infectious diseases, or deal with any of a hundred maladies or impairments that might have occurred to endanger someone's life. If it was impossible to get a doctor, the patient was taken by speeder or handcar to the nearest hospital. The handcar was often called "the little angel of mercy" by people who lived near the railway right-of-way in the early days. It was well named! No matter what the emergency or how severe the storm, it was always possible by means of this little track carrier to get the doctor to the patient; if conditions warranted, it was used to get the patient to a hospital.

Since the section foreman at The Gap, Alta., and another one at Anthracite, Alta., each had sons ready to start school, they decided to send them to the Canmore S.D. 168 (Canmore, Alta.). Each Sunday afternoon-during the school term, Mike from The Gap, six miles east of Canmore, and Roman from Anthracite, eleven miles west of Canmore, were brought to town by their respective fathers via speeder or handcar, and taken back

-- A. E. Oldridge

Two views of a handcar are pictured above; the carrier was used by railway maintenance-of-way employees in their work. Handcars may appear to be a simple means of transporting workmen, but they proved invaluable in taking people to the nearest doctors or hospitals when other methods were not feasible. Teachers often referred to them as "the cars of mercy."

--Canadian Pacific Railway

A velocipede, more commonly called a "speeder," also proved invaluable in providing emergency transportation in the early days. This particular picture of a speeder was taken in front of the railway station at Banff, Alta. in 1900.

home on Friday evenings. During the week the two tots boarded in town with relatives and attended the grade one class in the Canmore school. The education of the two boys, when it counted most, was made possible through the use of a railway velocipede.

Most people today know that the caboose, with its characteristic glass-enclosed cupola, is a special railway car attached to the rear of a freight train for the use of the crew, but few have had the experience of riding in one. In sharp contrast, the pioneers used it quite frequently as there were very few regular passenger trains, and the freight trains sometimes was the only means of getting from place to place. Conductors permitted passengers to ride in the caboose, and furthermore, the regulations permitted them to collect fares from such travellers. Rural teachers in particular found the caboose of a freight train a ready way of travelling to reach their new school, to get home for Christmas, to attend a teachers' convention, or in the case of serious illness or injury, to be taken to the nearest hospital. Nellie McClung, who taught in the Hazel S.D. 365 (Somerset, Manitoba) in 1890, described her experience in riding in the caboose of a freight train between Somerset and Wawanesa during a blizzard to get home in time for Christmas and said, "It was a delightfully different but harrowing way of travelling."

Bob McCrea, the editor of the Hanna *Herald,* remembers an incident back in 1932 when he and members of a minor hockey team travelled from Hanna to Craigmyle in the caboose of a freight train to play a hockey game. Blocked roads made rail travel the only possible way of getting to Craigmyle, and a generous Canadian National Railway superintendent gave the team permission to ride in the caboose of the freight. The hockey players returned to Hanna around midnight on the No. 10 daily passenger train that ran between Calgary and Saskatoon in those days.

The caboose of a freight and the express car of a passenger train were the best carriers available in transporting stretcher cases to the city, so it was a common sight in those days to see an ambulance parked on the station platform awaiting the arrival of the passenger train or the freight, ready to take the incoming patient to the hospital.

If a rural school happened to be located near a railway, a number of students always found it convenient, especially during the winter, to walk to school along the track. The right-of-way was always kept clear of snowdrifts, whereas most country roads, once they were drifted over with snow, remained that way for the rest of the winter. In addition, if the students timed themselves properly, it was possible to meet the section crew on its daily patrol, and depending on the mood of the section foreman, get a ride on the handcar. Sometimes these accidental meetings became routine and on cold, stormy mornings the men often waited to pick up the school passengers. Benevolent section foremen have been known to plan their work activities on the track in such a way as to be in time to transport the students home after school.

-- Canadian Pacific Railway

The railways kept their lines of transportation open under the most adverse climatic conditions. Snowplow units, similar to the one shown above, made it possible for freight and passenger trains to operate successfully, even during the worst winters.

-- Canadian Pacific Railway

It wasn't always easy for the snowplows to keep the lines open, especially after a blizzard filled in the "railway cuts."

-- Canadian Pacific Railway

The railways persisted in the work of removing the snow after a blizzard until even the most remote branch lines were made passable.

Not all such modes of railway travel were prompted by emergency or educational needs. For instance, a number of orchestra players travelled from Cayley, Alta. to Nanton on a combined railway conveyance made up of a handcar shoving a pushcar. One musician in describing this unique mode of travel said,

> If anyone has ever tried to sit on a handcar with a violin case, he will know that it is not the most comfortable way of travelling. Our contribution to the concert was much appreciated, so we didn't mind the rather precarious trip. If it hadn't been for the cooperation of the section foreman and his crew we never would have been able to get to Nanton, for not many people in our district owned cars, and the few that did, never operated them during the winter.

The young people in Sunnynook, Alta. used to go to dances in Pollockville, Alta. fifteen miles away during the winters 1920 to 1925 whenever the escorts had the money and could persuade the section foreman to take them there on the handcar. It was a cool trip but the dancers always maintained it was worth it.

The diversification of railway operations is well known today, but some of these operations, which used to be of considerable value to the pioneers, are no longer possible. At one time the railway station was the only source of the correct standard time. Rural teachers relied on it. There was no more frustrating experience for them than to have students arrive at school at all times because of the different settings of clocks and watches in their districts. There were no telephones or radios by which the correct time could be checked, so most districts operated on what was called the "school time" or the "teacher's time". That referred to the time the teacher's clock or watch showed irrespective of whether it was right or wrong. Hence teachers were always hearing that their time was too fast or too slow, depending on the time shown on the clock in a particular farmstead. The annual ratepayers school meeting could always be depended upon to have the problem of the "correct time" on its agenda. The discrepancies in the time in a school district not only led to many embarrassing situations, but also to numerous controversies. Just imagine the confusion if some members arrived for church, an important school meeting, a social engagement or to meet the train, an hour or so too late or too early. Needless to add, most teachers made genuine efforts to avoid all this and operated their schools by the correct time. Therefore, any time a person from the district went to town, one of his first duties was to call at the railway station and get the "correct time". Everyone knew that the station agent received the correct time daily and that he set the large wall clock accordingly. If there was any doubt about the accuracy of the station's clock, the lettering "Correct Standard Time" appearing on the glass front was enough to dispel any disbelief.

Annie Siddall, a teacher in the Mound Lake S.D. 754 in 1903, recalled how she solved the "correct time" problem.

> The school board wanted to use the $18.00 that had been raised at a box social to paint the schoolhouse, either inside or outside. I insisted that we needed a bell for our very fine belfry. Most had but one timepiece, so when it stopped they went outside, looked at the position of the sun in the sky and then set the clock. When I admonished a child for being late and he said, "Well, I started on time by our clock," there was nothing more to say. We got the bell, a very good one, and its musical notes rang over the hills and valleys in the district and we had no more trouble about tardiness. The settlers learned to set their clocks by the bell.

Many forward-looking school boards, comprehending the difficulty of the entire district having the same time, took steps to remedy the situation even before the schools were built. They insisted that their new schools have belfries and bells. James E. Loucks, an inspector of schools in Alberta, included the following information on school belfries in his 1909 annual report to the Department of Education.

> In two of these, bells have been placed, the sound of which may be heard from end to end of the district and serves a very useful purpose in summoning the pupils to school at the right time and in reminding the parents of their duties towards their own and their neighbors' children.

The flexibility of "school time" however, did have one advantage, espcially during the winter; the teacher could manipulate the time to suit local conditions. Horace Allen, who taught in the Greenvale S.D. (Onion Lake, Sask.) in 1929 described how such a scheme worked.

> Following the usual custom, the oldest boy in the Greenvale School acted as the janitor, but since it took him hours to attain any degree of warmth in the building, I innovated and kept setting the clock back to a mythical nine o'clock. When spring arrived I found that the "school time" and the "standard time" at the railway station in Frenchman Butte, Sask., differed by slightly more than an hour.

The waiting room in a railway station had its official uses, but its off-the-record functions, such as those associated with education or social gatherings, were of more importance to the local community. The Canadian Pacific Railway station at Lake Louise, Alberta, prior to 1930, was a good example. During the summer its waiting room resounded to the footsteps of thousands of tourists from all over the world as they detrained from the various transcontinental passenger trains, passed through the station compound, and caught the two railcars that took them via the narrow gauge tramway up to the Chateau Lake Louise. In the winter, however, only the shuffling steps of Ed Braun, the caretaker, echoed in the empty corridors. It wasn't until a few days before Christmas that the waiting room came to life again, but just for one evening. That was the time the one-room Laggan School presented its annual Christmas concert. The plush waiting room of the Lake Louise Station had many advantages over the small schoolhouse as a place in which to hold the affair: there was plenty of room for everyone; the oak benches provided splendid seating accommodation; the inside washrooms made ideal dressing rooms; and best of all, a very large Christmas tree could be put up to celebrate the occasion. Hence the Laggan School, like many other rural schools conveniently located near railway stations, often made good use of station facilities to provide new educational experiences for the children.

School inspectors used railway travel regularly to get from town to town to carry out their inspection work. Upon arriving in a town they set up their headquarters in a room in the hotel, hired a team and buggy at the local livery, and in the course of a week or so visited every rural school within driving range of the town. Then they moved on to the next village or hamlet on the railway to inspect the schools in that particular area. The process was repeated throughout the year until the inspector had visited every school in his inspectorate. The high school inspectors were a bit more fortunate as most secondary schools were located in towns or villages along the railway, so they did not have to rely on the horse-and-buggy type of transportation to any great extent. However, their areas of jurisdiction were larger than those of the local inspectors, so they were forced to spend most of their time on the road, using passenger trains, freight trains, or even handcars and speeders to get them from high school to high school. In those days school inspectors were as well-known to the travelling public as the salesmen or the train crews, because of the wayfaring nature of their job.

An item in inspector A. J. McCullough's report concerning the Wadena Inspectorate in Saskatchewan in 1911, provides some indication of the distance most inspectors travelled in the course of their duties during a school year. He said, "I drove my own horse and we covered about 1300 miles. I also travelled some 300 miles by rail."

In spite of the fact that early railways possessed a virtual monopoly of all passenger traffic, they kept encouraging more people to travel. One way they did this was to offer lower rates during certain specified times. There were reduced fares for Christmas, Easter, weekends, or any other time when special events, like exhibitions or fairs, were taking place in some nearby cities. Rural teachers in particular took advantage of these low return fares to go home for holidays, visit the city, attend conventions, or travel to the coast. The mere fact that they were able to get away from the scene of their work, even if for just brief periods, boosted their morales, inspired them with new ideas and made them better teachers. No one will ever be able to know exactly just how much the railways contributed to education in this way alone, but it must have been enormous.

C.P.A. Form 18W (revised)

CANADIAN PASSENGER ASSOCIATION TEACHERS' AND PUPILS' VACATION CERTIFICATE

☞ TO BE ISSUED ONLY TO TEACHERS AND PUPILS OF SCHOOLS OR COLLEGES IN CANADA.

To be filled in by ticket office

I HEREBY CERTIFY that_____ whose

(Fill in Name, also age when under 12)

signature is written in my presence is a_____, of this

(Fill in "Teacher" or "Pupil")

institution and is entitled to any reduction in fares that may be made for teachers or pupils, as provided in tariffs.

From_____ to_____ and return.

(Fill in starting point)   (Fill in destination)

This certificate is issued for the ☐ **CHRISTMAS**   ☐ **EASTER** vacation, which commences

_____ 19___, and ends _____ 19___

(Fill in commencing date of holidays)   (Opening date of school or college)

(Signature of Principal, in ink)   (Fill in name of school or college)

(Name of Place school or college located at)   (Signature, in ink, of Teacher or Pupil named above)

Received ONE Special Ticket {FIRST CLASS / COACH CLASS

Form_____ Number_____

Between the points and in the direction named opposite.

Purchaser's signature (in ink)

FARE AT WHICH SPECIAL TICKET WAS SOLD

STAMP OF AGENT SELLING SPECIAL TICKET

$

READ CAREFULLY—Tickets will only be sold upon dates authorized in railway lines' tariffs. Information as to going dates should be obtained from ticket agents.
IMPORTANT NOTICE—Principals, teachers and pupils should read carefully the instructions on back hereof.

-- Canadian Pacific Railway

This Canadian Passenger Association Teachers' and Pupils' Vacation Certificate enabled teachers and pupils to purchase return tickets at reduced rates.

More than one rural youngster took advantage of the low weekend fares to travel to the city regularly to take music lessons.

A student attending a university, a college, a normal school, a technical institute, or even a high school, away from his home, found the railways rather philanthropic. By having an official from his particular educational institution sign a special form, he was able to purchase a return ticket between the college city and his home town at a special student rate. Such reduced fares definitely helped financially and made it easier for parents to provide higher education for their children.

In those days any freight, express, baggage or mail was usually transported by the railways. Hence the physical essentials that made education possible in the rural areas of the country all arrived at the nearest siding by rail, including the building material to construct the schoolhouse, the furnishings for its interior, and the books, supplies and equipment used by the teacher and her students. Mail, the rural teacher's lifeline with the outside, came the same way. There were letters from home and from friends, official communications from the Department of Education and the inspector of schools, registered packages containing the grade eight or nine final examinations from the examinations branch, the all-important school grant from the provincial treasury, the bundle of readers from the book branch, the current mail-order catalogue and the parcels from Eatons, the teacher's classroom helps from the publishers of educational material, and last but not least, the weekly newspaper and a magazine or two.

It was the prerogative of people anywhere in Canada to petition the federal government to establish post offices in their districts, so as more and more settlers came to the prairie, the number of rural post offices grew. One of the duties of the rural postmaster or an appointed mail carrier, was to travel to the nearest railway center, whether it was ten or sixty miles away, and pick up the mail.

-- Ken F. Cooper, *The Western Producer*
April 14, 1949

The common method of bringing in supplies to a community in the early days was by means of the railway. This picture shows how freight was unloaded from the mixed train at Canwood, Sask. Conductor Cliff Wilbee and trainman W. G. Rosser struggle with a bulky piece of freight, assisted by the man who had placed the order.

Some such rural districts were more fortunate as they were located along the railway and although the trains did not stop, they were able to get their mail via the unique "catch post". The post, erected by the side of the track, had a cross-arm on it, from which the mailbag could be hung, and as the train whizzed by, an armed hook from the open door of the mailcar caught the bag. The incoming mailbag was simply tossed out on the ground, where the local mailman picked it up, took it home, and sorted it into several compartments of a box nailed to the wall in a convenient place in his house.

Before the advent of the telephone, the sole means of rapid communication was by telegraph, so it was common to see a person go down to the railway station to send a telegram. The greatest thrill the early teacher experienced was when she received a telegram from some school board or other notifying her that she was the successful applicant for the position of teacher for the school, and to notify the board of her decision as soon as possible. Usually telegrams were used by the general public only when emergencies occurred or when business urgency required it. For the teachers, however, the mere fact that telegraphic communication was available, even if it was several miles away, made life more tolerable.

A high-school lad, by working on the railway during the summer holidays, was able to earn enough to purchase his school books for the next term, or even finance a part of his higher education. Most such unskilled and sporadic jobs were with the maintenance-of-way section crews or extra gangs. The manual work involved was hard, but the students who were able to stand it realized very quickly just how preferable a higher education and a skilled job would be for them. At no other period in Canada's history did manual work on the track have so many applicants as during the depression. Clerks, teachers, university students, all those that could be termed white-collar workers, were willing to accept any kind of labor. Such employment was considered a godsend. Many railway officials, realizing how important it was to university students, hired them if jobs were available. In fact, some railway extra gangs during those hard economic times were composed of university students planning to become doctors, engineers, dentists, lawyers and teachers. Although the manual labor for such people was hard, it was paving the way for better things for them in the future. Even today, hundreds of university students flock to the various holiday resorts during the summer to accept jobs as waiters, bus boys, bartenders, bus drivers, clerks, and office personnel with hotels operated by the railways. The railways did, and still do, help the conscientious student to pursue a higher education by providing him with opportunities for seasonal jobs.

The above examples showing how the railways, directly and indirectly, contributed to the growth of rural education in Canada in the last seventy-five years, could be multiplied scores of times, for every pioneer living today is able to relate many more such incidents from his own experiences. Hence it can safely be concluded that our contemporary life never would have reached its high standards without the patronage of the railways in education in the early days.

8

Bachelorites

In the early days, when school districts were first being formed, there were many bachelors holding land within these areas. They "proved up" their homesteads, saw the region filling up with settlers and decided to stay and continue farming. It wasn't easy, living in small lonely shacks, baking their own bread, doing their own washing, putting up with lack of variety in their food, irregular mail, little entertainment, and not even a comfortable chair or bed in which to relax. The bachelors found the summers tolerable for they spent long hours working on the land and about their premises, but the winter season, with very little to occupy them, left them lonely and distraught. Many took jobs in logging camps and coal mines or, if they had the money, hibernated in some city during this off-season. Those who stayed on the farm put in time as best as they could. They played cards with neighbors, visited, hobnobbed with other bachelors, did a considerable amount of sleeping, read and reread all available newspapers, magazines and books, and attended dances at the district schoolhouses. Many did not even dance, but went to meet friends, listen to the music, and enjoy a lunch which they did not have to prepare themselves. Often they would travel long distances on foot for companionship. A bachelor in the Ridgeway S.D. (Carmangay, Alta.) whiled away some of his time shooting at flies on the wall with a small caliber revolver while lying in bed; a little more ventilation of the shack made little difference. Yet these same bachelors, eccentric as many were, influenced education in diverse ways.

The organization of a new school district was the prerogative of the residents living within its proposed boundaries, so if there was a large bachelor fraternity, they had the voting power to determine whether or not such a proposal came to pass. No prophet was required to foretell that the existing two dollars per quarter land tax would rise if they voted in favor of establishing a school. To the credit of these pioneer bachelors, very few areas turned down attempts to organize school districts and build schoolhouses. Now and then, if they persisted in turning down school-formation attempts, they were outwitted by the other residents. Such a plot materialized in the Buffalo Horn Valley S.D. 930 (Swift Current, Sask.). There were many unmarried men within the boundaries of this proposed school district and only three families with nine children of school age among them. The situation appeared hopeless. Meetings were held about establishing a school, but the bachelors being in majority, voted it down. Mr. Isaacs, one of the family men, had some lawyer's training and devised a plan. He advised his two cohorts, "We'll wait until after harvest when all the bachelors turn out their horses for the winter and go east to their homes. We will call a meeting then and it will be passed." Everything turned out the way Mr. Isaacs predicted. The schoolhouse plans were approved and the bachelors returned to find an important decision had been made in their absence.

A story from Innisfail, Alberta describes what happened when the vote in such a matter became close. J. H. McArthur was dismayed when he was refused inclusion in the Calder S.D. as the small school building was already filled to overflowing. With characteristic determination he set about to create a new school district. Naturally there was opposition to his idea from the bachelors. When the proposed area was canvassed, the deciding vote lay with one of these bachelors, and to Dick Hollings' everlasting credit he said, "Aye!"

At its original meeting on June 11, 1906, the Ryckman S.D. 1502 (Carmangay, Alta.) honored one of the bachelors in their settlement by naming their school district after him. Mr. Ryckman was a bachelor who farmed about one mile north of the site of the school and was a man who was indeed highly interested in education. He realized the value of having a school in the community and did more than his share in supporting it through the years.

In the Kitchener S.D. the bachelors received a setback to their plans after they voted in favor of the school. Although they were loathe to inflict taxes upon themselves, they were thinking of the possible social benefits that could accrue from having a school. They thought of the dances, card parties, fowl suppers, and concerts that would likely be held in the school; but most of all, they thought of the young ladies they would meet at such social functions. The bachelors also felt that the responsibility for school affairs should rest with those who had children and voted them into the offices of trustees and secretary-treasurer. Imagine their disappointment when the first ruling of the new board was, "No dances or other social functions are to be held in the school, for these would mess up the new building!" It was said that the Kitchener school was one of the best kept schoolhouses in the country.

The young bachelors of the Elstow S.D. (Unity, Sask.) were of the same mind as those of Kitchener S.D., but they approached the problem in a slightly different manner. They were willing to give their support to the building of the school in the district on the condition that they could hold dances in it when it was completed. The necessary motion was passed and

-- Edwin A. Anderson

Bachelors are ready to go to the dance at Mizpah S.D. (Sunnynook, Alta.) in the fall of 1924.

the district got its school and the bachelors their dances. In fact the bachelors became so enthusiastic that they volunteered their services in the construction of the building to speed up their plans. Kitchener may have been the best kept schoolhouse, but Elstow became known as the best dance center in the country.

Once school was underway in any district the trustees were confronted almost immediately with the most vexing of their responsibilities, that of collecting the school taxes. The land, as yet, was making but little returns to the homesteaders and their sacrifices were great. What money there was, was earned by the farmers' outside labor at lumber camps, railway construction sites, or coal mines. Collecting taxes under such circumstances was a hard job and hard men had to do it. Kind and amiable fellows who are fathers as well can be surprisingly severe when the needs of their children are at stake. Many bachelors felt that schools were of no personal benefit and went so far as to swear that no power on the prairie frontier could make them pay. In such districts, if the trustees were equally as determined to collect the taxes, they undertook to knock the idea out of these delinquents' heads, and the taxes were collected or the district became embroiled in trouble of one form or another. On the other hand, if the job of tax collector was assigned to an irresolute individual, the financial returns could be far from satisfactory. Hugh Johnson of the Braemar S.D. (Cowley,Alta.) was given such a task; the first year he brought in a greater amount in arrears than in current taxes, but in the following years, as he gained experience in dealing with people, he reversed the balance in favor of the current taxes.

A somewhat eccentric taxpayer in the Rosebud S.D. (Drumheller, Alta.) argued that since he was childless he should not be required to pay school taxes. It was only when his beloved cattle were seized, that he reluctantly paid his overdue municipal taxes. But he was not truly repentant, for his school-tax arrears continued to accumulate in the following years and eventually he lost his farm for failure to pay them. Arrangements were made for him to reclaim the land but he never did.

Inspectors' annual reports to the Department of Education revealed just how difficult it was to collect taxes and finance schools. A 1910 report in Alberta read:

> A bachelor, for example, files on a quarter section and spends very little time on his homestead. He has no stock or implements and is merely trying to hold his claim without improving it too much. He does not want a school and will not pay his taxes. He has no goods or chattels which can be distrained and the secretary reports the case to the Public Works Department. The tax becomes a lien against the land and for two years at least, the district does not receive any revenue from it. It often happens too, that the homesteader has a quiet understanding with a friend that he will abandon his claim on a certain date and give him an opportunity to file on it. When it is finally abandoned, the land becomes the property of the government and the taxes due the district are no longer a lien against the land and the school loses the amount due it.

A 1917 inspector's report indicated that after seven years the problem of collecting taxes had not been resolved:

> The majority of the holders are bachelors who are averse to paying school taxes, while the men with families are not as a rule in affluent circumstances, and often allow arrears to stand over from year to year unless compelled to make payment.

In 1924 the inspectors of the Department of Education were still reporting the same difficulty:

> 1924 was in some respects a rather unfavorable year for the farmer, even although prices were relatively high. The success of the rural schools depends largely on the tax collection.

Sometimes a protest would be made against the taxes levied on the landowners within the district; some bachelor or childless couple would complain that they were not fairly treated because they had to pay to educate the neighbors' children. Since the status of these people could change very quickly, nothing was ever done about it.

As might be expected, the bachelor population in most school districts dwindled with the passage of time. In the Ridgeway S.D. (Carmangay,

Alta.) for instance, the original population of thirty dropped to a mere one. What happened to the rest? A number sought their fortunes elsewhere, but the majority relinquished their state of single blessedness, married, and remained in the district to find an honored place among the rest of the populace.

There was no more undesirable life than that of a bachelor farmer. It was a lonesome existence under the best of conditions; there was no one to assist with the housework, cook the meals, help with the chores or to talk to. In such an environment a few bachelors developed what was called "homestead insanity" and wandered off leaving everything as it stood, while others had to be taken by the North West Mounted Police and sent to mental hospitals for treatment. Perhaps they were no more peculiar than other men, but they did not have wives to cover up for them. Most of them, however, remained undaunted, preserved their senses of humor and planned to overcome their solitary existences at the first opportunity. This usually occurred when the new teacher arrived to assume her duties in some nearby district school. Young, single women were scarce in rural areas so the teacher usually got a lot of attention. Strange as it may seem, most bachelors were recognized authorities on school affairs, and they were particularly informed about the teachers. The almost yearly tenure of female teachers provided them with something akin to a local matrimonial bureau. Several school districts boasted, "No teacher leaves here single. We marry them off."

Teachers in rural districts were always appraised as to their value as prospective brides upon their arrival. They were classified as either attractive or useful, although the occasional one possessed both characteristics. The former were pretty good dancers, but sort of naive; the latter were practical and reliable. When it came to matrimony, the bachelors often took the girl who could milk, drive a team, bake and sew in preference to one who appeared to have all the attributes of a Hollywood movie star or model. However, sometimes the bachelors were not noticeably astute in choosing their schoolteacher wives.

In the early days the trustees had to engage new teachers almost on an annual basis. This yearly change may have been an education in personalities, but it did not contribute much to the learning of reading, writing and arithmetic. It was such an accepted practice that one mother who didn't approve of her daughter changing schools every year, after being informed by her daughter of her decision to marry, offered the following cryptic advice, "Well, there's one thing I hope you've considered. Once you're married you do not resign at the end of June!"

The rivalry for the attention of the schoolmarm was keen. Indeed, a comely teacher reigned as a veritable queen with an assortment of bachelors coming from near and far to pay their homage. She could choose from the elite among them. Few teachers remained unmarried for any length of time;

although not all teachers were greatly sought after, any teacher could marry if she wished.

There was little doubt that many influences played a part in the selection of teachers; some were of too personal a nature to be of an educational value. All too often, where there were young bachelors on the school board, applications of young unmarried women took precedence over others. The various departments of education contributed a great deal to agricultural development by training and supplying school teachers who very often became the wives and mothers of the country's pioneers. Many rural school districts, after being sent a male, a married woman, or an elderly spinster as teacher, petitioned their respective departments of education for young, unmarried replacements. How, they demanded, could their districts be expected to go ahead and prosper if they were not supplied with marriageable schoolmarms? The departments, in their turn, wanted to know why they should be expected to educate and train a never-ending supply of girls in their normal schools just to stock up the remote and unsettled parts of the country. The departments must have been replying officially with "tongue in cheek" for eventually single, attractive school-marms would be wending their ways to the hinterland school districts. This was a way of life in early Canada, so historical research material abounds in stories such as the following:

The first teacher at White S.D. (Lethbridge, Alta.) was Florence Robinson, who married Bert Tiffin. In 1909 Alberta Wight taught there and later married Jack Tiffin. One of the reasons given for the teachers marrying Tiffins was that one of the original trustees of the White S.D. was a Rubin Tiffin, and he made sure that the teachers hired were attractive enough to appeal to his sons.

When the Medicine Hat S.D. (Medicine Hat, Alta.) was first organized Mr. M. Grimmet was hired as teacher. The bachelors were not happy and later petitioned for a lady teacher. They got their wish! Applications were called for, but unfortunately as each letter of referral was received, a practical joker affixed a picture of some actress or model. The selection committee, composed primarily of bachelors, had an extremely difficult time making a choice from the bevy of beauties pictorially displayed. When the chosen teacher did arrive, there were many disappointed young blades because she was not as attractive as the picture enclosed with her letter of application.

Competition for the hand of each new teacher coming into the district forced the bachelors to vie with each other to be first to meet and perhaps to impress the newcomer. They hoped to gain a strategic advantage over any other rival for the girl's favors. This would give them time to convince her to marry them.

Some school districts facilitated matters for any bachelor who might want to be the first to meet the new teacher. In fact, the trustees were willing to pay his travelling expenses to the nearest railway station to pick up the

-- V. R. Johnston

The saying, "Schoolteacher marries a bachelor", was re-enacted hundreds of times. On January 11, 1928, Russell Johnston married Louise Vogel, a schoolteacher who had come to Helmsdale S.D. (Oyen, Alta.) to teach.

teacher. One of the unusual expenditures listed in most rural schools' financial statements was the periodic payment of approximately five dollars to one of the local men to meet the train and then to take the teacher to her school district. In a few school districts the privilege of getting the teacher became so important that the trustees, to be fair, were forced to draw up a roster of names and give each bachelor a turn. Quite frequently these young girls married and remained in the district and often the groom turned out to be the fellow who met the train. In the Helmsdale S.D. (Oyen, Alta.) for example, Russell Johnson was fifth on the list of local bachelors delegated to meet the new teacher.

Although Russell had to wait several years before his turn came up, he had a feeling all along that whoever the new schoolmarm happened to be, she was destined to be his wife. It turned out exactly as he had anticipated. He first met her at the railway station at Oyen, Alberta, and remembers thinking how fortunate he was, for if first impressions were correct, she was both pretty and intelligent. Johnson, the bachelor, soon became Mr. Johnson, the married man. In future years his wife contributed much to the rural education by assuming such important and responsible positions as: president of the United Farm Women of Alberta, member of the senate of the University of Calgary, and the rural representative on a number of provincial commissions on education.

Anna M. Bailey described her meeting, romance and marriage with a bachelor in this rather matter-of-fact way.

> The Newell School, located about eighteen miles south of Coronation, was built in 1914. Debentures were issued by the district in order to finance the lumber and the other materials needed for the erection of the building. All these supplies were freighted out from Coronation with horses. Every able-bodied man turned out to help, with more bachelors than married men participating. A carpenter was hired to superintend the job.

> When the building was finished they advertised for a teacher. At the time I was teaching in the Sprott Shaw Business School that had just started operating in Calgary. My wages were so low I had barely enough to pay for my board and room, so I wrote to the Department of Education at Edmonton to see it they would give me a permit to teach in the public schools for a year or two. They sent it right away with no questions asked. Immediately I began scanning the papers for Teachers-Wanted advertisements and came across the one from the Newell School. I sent in my application and out of thirty-eight others they selected mine, so away I went to Coronation.

> I was met there by a young fellow, Wilbur Rogers, who was the secretary for the new school. He took me out to the farm of Mr. and Mrs. Small, where I was to board. He told me there was to be a meeting at the school the following evening and I was expected to

attend. I guess they wanted to see what their first teacher was like. I don't remember what the meeting was for, but I recall they were clubbing together to send to Eaton's for produce like apples, onions, prunes and other dried fruits. I don't think anyone had a garden, which probably would not have grown anyway.

Fourteen children attended the Newell School and most of them had a long way to go. I taught here until Christmas time when the school was closed for the winter months. However I was fortunate to be hired for the Burns School a few miles farther south and taught there until the summer holidays in 1915.

The people in both the Newell and Burns school districts all seemed happy, in spite of the hard times and the lack of money. We (Wilbur and I) used to go miles to the dances which seemed to be the only form of amusement. One evening when we started for a dance, the snow was so deep that the horses couldn't see to follow the trail, if there was one, so we did a lot of circling before getting back on the trail to take us home. We didn't get to that dance! On Monday morning when I arrived at school there was a drawing on the blackboard of all those tracks in the snow with the caption, "A Chinese Puzzle." I never found out who drew it but it was all in fun anyway.

Most of the children were so far behind in their studies I used to assign them homework to do, as I felt sorry for them. One morning, a little fellow, who was an adopted child, did not have his homework done. He explained, "My mother said you were paid to teach me and she doesn't have to!" That ended his homework but the rest made good progress in catching up.

I resigned my position at the Burns School at the end of the term and returned to my home in Nova Scotia. Wilbur Rogers came to take me to catch the train in Coronation. He had acquired a buggy by that time so I took a picture of him sitting proudly in it. The mosquitoes were so bad that he, buggy and the horses were covered with them. They even showed up in the picture for quite a long time but gradually faded over the years.

By this time we were engaged but I stayed in Nova Scotia for a year-and-a-half before returning to Calgary. We were married on January 17, 1917. In the meantime Wilbur's father had visited him and decided it was no place to take a young bride so he gave him a half section of raw land in Acme district, twenty miles south-east of Carstairs. Wilbur moved over there in 1916 and built a house where we lived until 1943 prior to moving to Calgary. We celebrated our 57th wedding anniversary in January 1974 and I have no regrets whatsoever of marrying my prairie bachelor.

Another way of answering the burning question so prevalent in every district at the time school opened, "Have you seen the new teacher yet?"

was for the bachelor to call at the school. If he happened to be a member of the school board all was well and official, but if not, he made up an excuse for the visit. It could be anything from looking for stray cattle to an urgent message for one of the students. In the Westward Ho S.D. a determined swain used the "being a stranger" excuse. Sadie Coulson had just come out from Ontario to teach in the district and on the second afternoon as she was teaching she heard a pounding on the front door. When she opened it she saw a handsome smiling cowboy with all the trimmings, sitting on a spirited horse. He had ridden up the steps onto the entry platform, a western custom she thought. He apologized for his intrusion but confided he had lost his way and wondered if she would be so kind as to direct him to a certain ranch. Miss Coulson replied that she too was a stranger, but maybe one of her pupils could show him the way. When he rode off, the youngsters laughed and said that Jack was no stranger and that he knew his way around the district better than most people. He just wanted to see what the new teacher looked like!

Most first meetings between the new schoolmarn and the bachelor were contrived by the lonely male but others were of the unpremeditated variety.

The schoolyard at Pleasant Grove S.D. was not fenced in 1909 and the teacher was experiencing difficulty in keeping the cattle away from the school. One day when she and some of the students were shooing off a small herd, Henry Streeter, a bachelor, rode up just as they had the cattle nicely stampeded. He was very disturbed as they were his cattle and he didn't like to see them frightened. In the midst of all the noise and excitement he suggested to the young teacher that she obtain some posts and wire, and fence the schoolyard. She in turn informed him that she had been hired to teach, not to fence. That was their introduction and at the end of the school term they were married.

Arlie Woodward, a bachelor, had the habit of dropping in on the Fredell family to pick up his mail. During the school term 1909-1910 Caroline Archibald, a young teacher from Nova Scotia, came to teach in the local school and boarded with the Fredells. Apparently Mr. Woodward's purpose in visiting changed from mail to female. Miss Archibald returned to Nova Scotia at the end of the school term in June 1910 and did not come back until 1916, when she became Mrs. Arlie A. Woodward. Arlie must have used the mails to advantage to convince her to make such a decision.

Occasionally a teacher was attracted to a particular bachelor because of the compassion she felt towards such a hapless and hopeless individual. She somehow came to the conclusion that it was her mission in life to make things more pleasant for the unfortunate individual. Florence, of the Elbow S.D. (Elbow, Sask.) was such a teacher. She, and some of her friends had visited Pete's shack to sample some of his hardtack when she first arrived in the district. In no time at all she realized the adverse and lonesome conditions under which he lived and began to feel sorry for him. So before the people in the district realized what was happening, Pete and Florence were married in Moose Jaw, Sask. She continued to teach in the district and it was certain Pete relished the charming company and the fluffy bread and buns that were placed on the table before him from then on.

Every rural school held box socials to raise the much-needed funds for the Christmas concert, the purchase of an organ for the school, or some other worthy project. The women in the district worked hard to decorate and fill their boxes with delicious sandwiches, cakes, pie and other goodies, hoping to bring the highest bid. The honor usually went to the school teacher, as the bachelors, competing for her hand, paid terrific prices to get her contribution, even though it seldom contained anything very special in the way of cooking. The box social presented a wonderful opportunity for the shy single male, who did not have the nerve to speak to the teacher, to bid on her box, after he was fortified with some woodshed courage. When the intentions of any man became evident, it was common practice to make him pay dearly for his prize. It was alleged that in addition to buying a lunch the bachelor bought the shoolmarm as well. Many romances began in this way and some ended successfully with the teacher eventually becoming a permanent resident of the district.

Another occasion on which it was possible for a shy bachelor to make his affections known to the teacher was the school's annual Christmas concert. Here he could try to impress the schoolmarm by placing a gift, perhaps a box of chocolates, on the tree for her. The entire community would know about it before the evening ended and in all probability it heralded the beginning of a new romance.

At most Christmas concerts it was difficult to coax anyone into playing the part of Santa Claus, so if a bachelor accepted the role he was indeed in love with the teacher. If he refused, he wasn't serious in his intentions. In the Mooreville S.D. 3357 two Santas later married the respective teachers who had persuaded them to play the part at their particular concerts. Evidently new talent was discovered in the way they assumed their roles as Father Christmas.

Friendly rivalries developed among the bachelors in any community for the chance to court the new schoolmarm. This arose partly from the fact that marriageable girls were few in number and that the teacher seemed to outshine the local possibilities.

In one school district there was not only a scarcity of girls, but a scarcity of buggies for courting as well. There were but three suitable vehicles in the entire district, so when one enterprising bachelor invited the new teacher to a dance, one of his colleagues, learning about the date, borrowed all three buggies for that particular day. The fat was in the fire for most of the afternoon, but after having his fun, the jokester relented. On another occasion, when the joker of the previous incident was taking the same teacher for a Sunday afternoon drive, all his so-called friends escorted the couple on horseback.

Most former teachers of rural schools will be able to recall attempts to interfere with romances similar to the incident described below. This type of buffonery was perpetrated easily, possessed the element of suprise and gave the community a good laugh, but it is doubtful it achieved its purpose of breaking-up romances very many times.

The bachelors in the Gavrelle S.D. 3910 in Saskatchewan were a progressive lot. Some had been farmers near Indian Head, Saskatchewan and brought to their homesteads a few of the ideas and methods they had seen used at the experimental station and forestry farm there. John Burrell, one of these bachelors, sent back to Indian Head for some shrubs and seeds, and then planted trees, started a vegetable garden and sowed a few sweet peas. That summer his sweet peas bloomed beautifully. It was also just about this time that May, a pretty young lady from Abernethy, came to visit the Lyster family. With the average number of females to males approximately one to twenty-six in the Gravelle district, the competition among the bachelors for May's hand was understandably keen. John attained a favored position in this contest when he brought the lady a bouquet of sweet peas. There was no way the other rivals could match such a move, so the best they could do was to bide their time. One time, when his brothers were watching, John picked more sweet peas, carefully wrapped them in an old newspaper and set them under the buggy seat before making a visit to the Lysters. The envious swains saw their opportunity of dulling Cupid's arrow. They broke off some potato tops, wrapped them in a newspaper, and while John was in the barn harnessing his horse, they substituted the potato vines for the sweet peas. As it happened, the Lysters had relatives visiting from Eastern Canada; they were eagerly awaiting their first sight of prairie-grown sweet peas, after May had told them how scented and beautiful they were. There was some discomfiture and dismay when the newspaper was unwrapped.

The following incident is interesting as it was motivated and characterized by the age-old customs of other lands.

Two sisters decided to teach in adjacent school districts, live together in one of the teacherages, thus avoiding loneliness. As it happened, the districts were settled mostly by people from the Ukraine and very few of the parents spoke English. Early one Sunday morning a middle-aged stranger arrived at their teacherage. He entered without an invitation, took off his coat and cap, extracted a gaily-wrapped parcel and sat down. The purpose of his visit was soon apparent to the two girls. He had heard that a couple of unmarried school teachers were living in the district and decided that one of them, it did not matter which one, could marry him, move into his bachelor shack, keep house for him and continue teaching. The parcel contained the engagement gift, which in this particular case turned out to be a piece of bear meat that he, himself, had cured. Each girl in turn was asked for her hand in marriage, but both refused him as politely as possible. Before leaving he promised the girls he would come back again to repeat his proposals. Fortunately, the neighbors got wind of the marriage bid before he returned and explained to him in no uncertain terms that courting customs in Canada were different and certainly were not business propositions but based on mutual love and respect and that his offers were not appreciated. The two girls did not see or hear from him again.

Although many romances blossomed into marriage, a few faded into oblivion because of indiscreet bachelors. They were just not conversant with females.

A bachelor in the D'Arcy S.D. (D'Arcy, Sask.) purchased a new buggy and had invited the teacher to go to a dance with him. He drove to the house where she was boarding and told her to get ready. He thought she would be out in a few minutes, but he didn't understand how long it took a girl to get ready. Thinking she had changed her mind about him, he left.

Charlie Sheppard of the Prairiedale S.D. (Dewar Lake, Sask.) was more understanding than the bachelor from D'Arcy. Charlie had a glittering new top-buggy, and his horse, Morgan, was groomed to perfection and as proud as his master to call on the teacher, Grace Bradford, to take her for a drive. They waited patiently for an hour or more, but were rewarded with the appearance of Miss Bradford; she had dressed for the occasion and off they went, looking lovely in the finest clothes. A few hours later Miss Bradford's landlady saw a desolate parade approaching from the west: Charlie had white alkali mud to his knees; Morgan was white almost to the backbone and his tail looked like only a horse's tail that is full of alkali mud can look; and Grace was mincing along in tiny shoes. The buggy was not in sight. Charlie, in order to impress Grace with his cleverness, had decided to take a shortcut through Archison's slough and the horse and buggy became mired. He had to cut poor Mogan loose from the shafts, carry Miss Bradford to shore, and abandon the lovely new buggy bogged to its axles in the mud.

Courting the teacher could have annoying and embarrassing repercussions for the bachelor who also happened to be a member of the local school board. His moral responsibility to the school district and his own personal interests often clashed and left him bewildered, not knowing whether to follow the dictates of his brain or heart. In 1917 Edna Steve was the teacher in the Kincora S.D. (Glidden, Sask.) and Arnold Jackson, Jake Adams and Don Blair were the trustees. In discussing the work of the teacher at one of their meetings, Arnold and Jake agreed that she was satisfactory, but Don, who was courting her, refused to make any comments. Arnold, the chairman, jibed him with, "It is your turn, Don. Tell us what you think of her!" Don evaded the loaded question and kept quiet. Sometime later, George Mackay, who was acting as Santa Claus, got a parcel for Don and shouted out, "This is for the silent trustee!" It didn't take long for the story of the incident at the school board meeting to make the rounds of the district and beyond.

With so many teachers and bachelors courting, every school district had its favorite story of "unrequited love".

A bachelor in the Conquest S.D. (Outlook, Sask.) invited everyone around to come to his wedding. The minister arrived to perform the ceremony and the bride was to be brought out by livery from Outlook. The schoolhouse was crowded but word was received indirectly that the bride, instead of coming out to the Conquest School, had decided she didn't want to get married after all. She had taken a train the same day and had gone back East. Everyone was disappoined at the turn of events, especially the poor groom, who found it most embarrassing to be jilted in such a heartless fashion. He had to go home to his shack alone. Shortly after this, he sold his homestead and left the district.

A common type of broken romance often occurred at the time the school opened in the fall. Usually a very attractive schoolmarm, who had been a drawing card for the young and ardent bachelors for miles around the previous term, failed to return. This always turned out to be a nasty shock to the more optimistic suitors, for during the holiday interlude some had made special preparations which they hoped would give them a chance for the girl's affections. These endeavors included learning to play a guitar or some other musical instrument, purchasing a new buggy or a Model-T Ford, building a new home, acquiring some prize horses, investing in a diamond ring, accumulating an impressive bank account, outfitting himself in an eye-catching set of clothes or refurbishing the shack. If the suitor happened to be an older man, he often attempted to make himself appear younger by getting a set of teeth, a toupee or a pair of horned-rimmed glasses. One bachelor explained his manoeuvering when someone asked him why he was building such a nice house and barn. He replied, "You got to have a cage to catch the bird!"

Imagine the chagrin experienced by any one of the serious suitors when he discovered that the object of his affections had not returned and that all his plans and preparations had come to naught. It is certain that the guitar never twanged again and the toupee was never used. A man doesn't get over a disappointment like that in a hurry, and it didn't improve matters much to hear a sympathetic observer say, "I guess it's been this way since Adam's time."

Each school district had its usual middle-aged bachelor who had tried, without success, to court each new teacher, year after year. It was true he needed a wife. He was lonely, had all kinds of work to do on the farm, and the assistance and sympathy of a woman would have helped him immeasureably. True, he was getting older, but he always hoped to marry one of the young teachers fresh from normal school, any one of whom was young enough to be his daughter, or even granddaughter. Such men became positive pests, for whatever social affair the teacher attended, they also attended. They appeared even if the young teacher had turned them down a number of times. These characters usually were poor dancers and were not satisfied with a few dances an evening, but asked for every third one. They were determined to marry a teacher, no matter which one they got, so they kept hounding the current teacher in the district until she consented, married someone else or left the community. There was no other alternative for the frustrated young women.

Many teachers taught school as a stopgap until some young farmer proposed marriage and if too much time elapsed she accepted an older bachelor, or failing that, a widower. Sometimes well-educated girls with good family backgrounds married coarse, slovenly, foul-mouthed, selfish and tight-fisted bachelors. They were ashamed to go out with such husbands, yet stayed with them. A normal school education did not necessarily mean that these wives had a good all-round education. They may have had sufficient academic knowledge to get by, but that was all. In most cases these girls used more creditable English than their spouses but had fewer and less varied interests as well as a poorer grasp of affairs than they did. The discrepancies in education, age, social graces and background did not necessarily separate the couple for they had the work on the farm to keep them together. Each became indispensable to the other as far as operating a successful farm was concerned. There was no need to feel sorry for most of the young schoolmarms who married bachelors, for their prospects of happiness and success were at least average. The demands of the farm left them with no doubts as to their usefulness. Besides, they usually became the leaders in their districts and the ability to influence is sweet to nearly any person.

Farming, no matter how efficient, will not succeed for any length of time without a community structure around it. In turn, since a community structure is dependent on the family for its basic unit of operation, the schoolteacher and bachelor-farmer wedlock contributed much to the success and welfare of early rural districts.

A bachelor who was matrimonially minded but unsuccessful in convincing a local girl or woman to settle down with him on the farm, continued his quest by using the mails.

A homesteader in the Bergen S.D., tiring of the solitary life, answered a lonely hearts advertisement in the newspaper and was soon on his way to Calgary to get married. The schoolteacher bride turned out to be a childhood sweetheart from Scotland.

Nick Nicholson, a former apprentice carpenter in Sweden and a well-known bachelor in the district, after living on his lonely homestead for a number of years decided it was time to get married. No sooner said than done! After meeting his new wife, his friends wondered where he found her and how she had found him. Nick, unabashed, informed them that he had advertised in the paper for a wife. He received more than a dozen letters in response to his press notice and one captured his heart, or rather his stomach. She informed him of how many things she could make out of carrots, including carrot pie, carrot cake, carrot soup, carrot relish, carrot pudding, not to mention boiled carrots, stuffed carrots and carrots with peas. Well, carrots was one crop Nick had been successful in raising on his homestead, so he wrote for her to come and share his bed and carrots.

A courtship conducted across the miles by letter was difficult to detect, so it wasn't until the bachelor returned from a mysterious business trip, already married, that the district first learned about it. However, there were revealing clues of an impending marriage if a sharp-eyed resident kept a careful watch on the conquering hero's manoeuvres. Here is an example from the Riverton S.D.

One of the sharp-eyed bachelors in the district appeared at Tom Lee's farm and excitedly announced that Keast was getting married. Tom couldn't believe it, for he and Keast were good friends and not at any time had he seen his friend write or receive a single letter from any girl. But when Tom was told that Keast was building a toilet behind the house, it looked a bit suspicious. The erection of a biffy for a lady in those days was equivalent to presenting her with an engagement ring. The next morning when a few neighbors investigated, sure enough they caught Keast in the act. The small building was up and he was busy finishing the inside servicing with a draw knife. The blushing bachelor had to admit, with the evidence staring him in the face, that he was getting married the following week.

Another obvious sign that a bachelor was soon to be married was disclosed the moment he appeared in the barnyard to do his chores draped in something resembling a skirt and the top of his head swathed in a colored kerchief. He wasn't acting strange, but was conditioning his farm animals to the future presence of a woman. The bachelor reasoned that when his prospective wife went to milk the cows, water the horses, or feed the pigs, the wary animals would accept her without becoming uncooperative because of the strange attire.

There was always the bachelor whose education had not been too extensive, and since he found letter writing difficult or even impossible, he sought assistance. He dictated and the volunteer secretary transcribed the information. It was difficult for these men of the soil to find words to say precisely what they wanted to say, especially if it was to a strange woman. However, the letter writers often took things in their own hands and inserted romantic portions which had not been dictated. This was necessary, as accounts of the number of cows being milked, the breaking of a new horse, the amount of feed put up, or the visit of the threshers told very little to the woman who wanted to hear whether he loved her. Often an understanding and skillful correspondent brought about the desired results, with the bachelor going back home to marry his boyhood sweetheart, or the arrival of a strange woman in the district ready to marry the man who expressed his sentiments for her so tenderly. On the other hand, some scribes through ignorance or by carrying out their assignments in jocular fashion, precipitated ludicrous or distressing human situations.

Courting by mail could have tragic results. Mr. Koltzheimer of the Elbow S.D. (Elbow, Sask.) had walked to Davidson to get a letter from his sweetheart; he was overcome with the cold and froze to death on the road. He was buried along the road as there were no cemeteries then.

Families with youngsters of school age always took more than a passing interest in the matrimonial prospects of the local bachelor. If the bride turned out to be a widow with children, there was always the chance that the number of children of school age in the district would reach the required minimal number, enabling the community to go ahead with plans for building a schoolhouse and hiring a teacher. It was an exciting prospect!

The following drama, which could be entitled, "The Bachelor Marries a Widow With Children and Saves the School," was repeated in so many communities across the country at the time of the founding of school districts, that it could be considered part of prairie folklore.

The rumor making the rounds in the rural district was that Bert, a bachelor, was returning from North Dakota on February 10, 1922, bringing a wife with him. It was also understood that he had married a widow with children. There was no doubt the people in the district were beside themselves with excitement at the prospects of having enough children to start a school. The most interested person was Ralph, the chairman of the newly-formed education committee. He stood in his parlor with a number of school supporters about him peering out the window. Soon he focused a pair of fieldglasses on a lumber wagon a couple of miles away travelling in the direction of Bert's homestead. Chivalrously, the tense chairman handed the glasses to his wife. Soon she was giving a running commentary to the group about what was happening at Bert's place. "There they go. Up to the front door, no less. John was alone when he left for town for a load of coal early this morning. Whoa, they've stopped. John gets down. Now, Bert is also climbing down. My, there's a lot of heads bobbing up and down in the wagon box. Now there's a regular scramble to get out. That must be the widow still in the wagon. Say! I can see, one, two, three, and there's another one, four children all of school age dashing around in front of the house. My, oh my, I'm so happy I could cry. We can now have our school. Just imagine, we were saved by a widow!"

In the Dunreath S.D. (Froude, Sask.) the trustees were so interested that all of them went out to meet Mr. and Mrs. John Spracken at the railway station to find out the number of children of school age the newcomers had. They were pleased to learn that there were seven, more than enough to get the school started. The Spracken family never received a heartier welcome from any community than that summer in 1912 when they first arrived at Froude, Sask. from Iowa.

A type of romantic bachelor that drifted into many rural communities during the early days was the remittance man. English families of substantial wealth and high social standing made a practice of sending any sons causing them undue grief or problems to countries like Canada, and providing them with handsome allowances as long as they stayed away. These bachelors had gracious old-country manners and were better educated and possessed more worldly ways than their local counterparts. Thus they offered keen competition for the favors of the local girls. The ordinary bachelor just couldn't compete with these dashing young men from the Old Country. If so disposed, they had the ability and the training to make valuable contributions to the educational and social life of the district. Eventually, some returned to their homes overseas, others moved to cities where the hectic life was more to their liking, while some remained in the districts to live singular and lonely existences.

The bachelors with their idiosyncrasies, their love of company, their jealousy of the married man, and their unique senses of humor, harvested a crop they didn't know they planted, friends. Their exploits frequently provided their communities with something to talk about, scoff or laugh at, profit by and perhaps remember for a long time. During the difficult homestead and depression periods their dramas or comedies helped people to maintain proper perspectives about life. It is said, "Misery likes company" and, "No matter how badly off a person is, there is always someone worse off than he is." Bachelors proved to be good examples of both these maxims as the following stories will illustrate.

Wallace Braithwaite of the Grenfell S.D. (Grenfell, Sask.) was a bachelor of high character, although he was somewhat eccentric. With no family to care for, he lavished all his affection on his horses, treating them with unusual thoughtfulness at all times. The horses were stabled in a long building for many years and when it became necessary to erect a new barn, he constructed it right over the old one. He felt that his temperamental horses would feel strange in a new barn, so in this way it was possible for him to remove the old one, a log at a time, and his horses would not notice the transition.

Another bachelor was just as considerate as Mr. Braithwaite but it led indirectly to his demise. One very cold morning when he took his horses out to water, he thought it rather cruel to slip the icy bits into the mouths of the horses; instead, he put the harness on without this gear when hitching them to his wagon. No sooner did he say, "Get up!" than he discovered he had no control over his team. The horses ran away and unfortunately he was thrown out of the wagon and killed.

A farmer in the Red Cross S.D. (Vulcan, Alta.) needed some help, so he drove over to his neighbor, a bachelor, to ask him for assistance. He found the bachelor still in bed and any attempts to get him up proved fruitless. The indisposed bachelor kept saying, "You go home and I'll follow." The concerned farmer was afraid that if he left, the volunteer worker would go back to sleep, so he refused to leave. Eventually the bachelor, in desperation and with much embarrassment, threw back the bedclothes and revealed the cause for his unwillingness to get out of bed.

The weather had been cold and the bachelor had made bread the day before. As he had no success with it rising because of the low temperature, he took it to bed with him to keep it warm; the results were highly successful, but distressing. The dough had risen so well and so rapidly that it had entangled him and the bed clothes.

Most bachelors had strong feelings about certain things. One such middle-aged farmer placed his order for groceries with Mrs. Dove in the Sunnynook Store (Sunnynook, Alta.) and then asked for Mr. Dove. He was away. The bachelor waited all day in town, returning occasionally to ask if Mr. Dove had returned. Towards evening, hesitatingly and with much embarrassment, he drew Mrs. Dove aside and whispered, "I'd like to buy some underwear. You know, men's underwear." She respected his modesty.

Another bachelor, Charlie Curry of the Huxley S.D. (Huxley, Alta.), carried on a perpetual feud with the storekeeper's wife over the unwanted butter and vintage eggs with which he insisted on paying for his groceries. He was an unforgettable character! Once he was asked by an inquisitive visitor why he kept his plate and cup upside down on the table. He replied that since he was the only one using them, and as long as he kept the flies off them, there was no need to wash them. All of his bedding was sewn together to reduce bed-making to a simple procedure, although no one knew how or when he washed it. No wonder most girls in the district were teased about Charlie as a prospective husband.

Time and again a little scrawny bachelor in the Verdant Valley S.D. (Drumheller, Alta.) would appear at some home in the district just as a meal was being served. Of course he was always asked to eat with the family. "No thanks," he always said, "just got up from the table, couldn't eat a thing!" He was served a full meal anyway, and always ate it. One noon when the family saw him coming they planned a little conspiracy: "We'll ask him just once. If he says, 'No!', let's not set a place for him. We will see what he does." They followed their scheme explicitly, and after the usual refusal, the family sat down at the table. The father said grace and commenced to serve everyone but the stunned visitor. He gave startled looks to each member of the family and started to edge his chair towards the table. Finally, when he got to the table, he said, "Well, I might be able to eat a bite!" The mother felt sorry for the lonely little man and got up immediately to set his place, although she turned away to hide her laughter.

A bachelor in the Vulcan district of Alberta used the excuse of getting drinking water as the reason for visiting. His homestead did not have a water supply, not even a slough, so he carried his domestic water supply from his neighbors. He used a four-pound jam pail to carry it in, and he usually turned up at, or just before, meal time. The lonely man and his battered tin container travelled far and wide, but he did not visit the same place too often. He was a good storyteller, a superb amateur entertainer, and could take his guests into another world for an hour or an evening.

Most homesteaders were just as lonely as he and as they were starved for some form of amusement, they loved his visits. In time he felt free to make his rounds without the telltale pail. He had a good thing going for him, but it was just possible that he gave more than he received.

Horses were still scarce and very valuable until about 1912 when the machine age loomed. Sometime prior to this, two farmers in the Silver Stream S.D. (Armley, Sask.) had their two mares bred in an attempt to increase the number of work horses. The spring of 1910 found them anxiously awaiting the outcome. Some weeks prior to the date circled on the almanac, Frank, the bachelor, took up sleeping quarters in his barn to ensure that all went well. George, the family man, chose to make occasional visits during the night to look after Old Nell's welfare. The difference in vigilance resulted in the first colt flourishing, while the second one was found dead. George's wife was disappointed and upbraided her husband for his carelessness by reminding him that, "Frank slept out in the barn with his mare!" The reply she received was a gem and it ended the argument, "Yes, but Frank hasn't a pretty wife to sleep with!"

Through the years most bachelors maintained memories of their childhood days, their companions, their boyhood sweethearts, the old folks, and the familiar buildings and streets of their home town. Such cherished memories and hopes for the future sustained them during periods of disappointment, loneliness and hard labor of the homestead years. Hence their ambition was to harvest good crops and return in style for a visit to these familiar haunts. Yet sometimes this proved to be their very undoing. They left for their former homes with hope in their hearts and stars in their eyes, but failed to realize the changes that time had wrought during their years of absence. For most bachelors it was like visiting a strange town: no relatives; no friends; no familiar scenes; in fact, people just stared when they mentioned their names. It was usually dejected, depressed bachelors who returned to their farmsteads after having their dreams shattered in this manner. They thought their lives weren't worth living after such disap- pointments and the resulting delusions often led to departures from the normal way of thinking and acting.

A few bachelors gave the impression that they would never marry and hence earned the label, "confirmed bachelor". They were usually over forty-five years of age, well-off, self-sufficient and wary. They outwitted any attempts to corner them at box socials, dances, dinners or house parties. Their philosophy seemed to be, "there is safety in numbers" and they skillfully avoided attempts to pair them off with unmarried females. They always managed to be on their way home from any social function before the older people or the guardians of propriety retired for the night to leave the younger generation to its own resources. One bachelor explained his single-blessedness by saying, "The women I wanted I couldn't get, and the ones who want me, the devil wouldn't have!"

Contrary to what might be expected, most bachelors liked children, had a way with them and were not bothered by their everlasting fussing. Therefore, it was not surprising to hear of a bachelor marrying a widow and acquiring a ready-made family. Sometimes one would see a former confirmed bachelor carrying a baby and taking care of its most personal needs, while his wife was busily engaged with the rest of his newly-won family. A high percentage of such marriages often proved more successful than those with single girls as the man's love for children provided an additional basis for the marriage.

It didn't require a marriage for a bachelor to show his love for children. Take the case of one bachelor in the Ryckman S.D. 1502 (Carmangay, Alta.) who was a generous person, although he could ill afford to part with the little he possessed. On one occasion, knowing that a particular family could not provide Christmas presents for their children, he gladdened their young hearts by playing Santa Claus. He continued to do this for many years and the youngsters revered him for his generosity and thoughtfulness.

The money required to purchase Christmas presents for the children attending the Sunny Alberta S.D. (Hutton, Alta.) was obtained, as in the majority of rural school districts, by soliciting donations from each family in the community. The bachelors were not left out, and since most of them had more than passing interests in the spinster schoolteachers and a liking for children, they donated most generously to the Christmas fund.

Bachelors visited each other quite often, but in the long run preferred to call at the homes of the family men. They were eager for a taste of the good cooking of the wives of their fortunate hosts. It didn't take long to tire of the typical bachelor meal of bannock, made by pouring water and other ingredients on top of the flour in a sack, stirring until it was of the right consistency, removing this batter, and finally baking it. The next meal was made by repeating the process after rolling down the flour sack a little more. Usually an old unwashed black skillet was used to fry one meal after another. In addition, most bachelors ate from the pan while standing in front of the stove on cold days, so it was indeed a pleasant change to sit down at the table with a family.

Sometimes, for something to do, the bachelors in the district joined forces and put on special parties for their friends in the community. In the Central Butte S.D. (Craik, Sask.) William Ratcliffe baked a fruit cake for such a social gathering and placed it on a chair to cool. In his excitement, he forgot about its location and sat on it. Although the cake was never seen by the guests, it was the source of much merriment and added a real "bachelor" flavor to the party. One of the bachelor's favorite tricks was to steal chickens from neighboring bachelors and serve fried chicken at these parties, with each bachelor wondering if he was eating his own chicken. After the meal was over and the dishes were washed, the guests participated in various activities. They played card games such as crib, five-hundred, whist or bridge; listened to music or played any available musical instruments; danced; joined in sing-songs; told or read stories; and played such games as charades.

In some districts the bachelors were so numerous and active that they founded social clubs comprised exclusively of bachelors. To be a member, each applicant had to be at least thirty years of age and the owner of property. Each individual also promised to avoid the pitfalls of matrimony, although some forgot their vows when the right women came along. The bachelor's clubs soon became so well established that the members began receiving invitations to the various homes in the district for suppers and social evenings. In return for such hospitality, it was the practice for most clubs to sponsor annual banquets and parties in the schoolhouses, barn lofts, or large farm homes, to which all their friends were invited. These used to be considered the social highlights of the year in many districts.

One of the most successful bachelors' clubs on the prairies was organized in the Dalum S.D. (Drumheller, Alta.) in 1929 and continued to function successfully until 1947. Yet the Dalum Club, from an original membership of over thirty, was reduced to a mere three in the twenty years that it operated. There was no telling when even the most avid bachelor would eventually fall prey to the wiles of some woman. This happened in the Verdant Valley S.D. (Drumheller, Alta.) when Gale Schiefla, one of the confirmed bachelors of the district and Miss Boone, the elderly school-teacher, started going together. The entire district was thrilled when romance blossomed between the elderly pair and ended in marriage. So is it any wonder that there is no record of any of these old-time bachelor clubs existing today! The vast majority of members broke their vows and married. Hence it would be impossible for an incident like the following to occur today.

A man knocked on the door of a farmhouse and when the housewife went to see who it was, the stranger asked her if she could be so kind as to do something for him. The frightened woman said it depended on what it was. Apparently the bachelor was on his way to a dance had crawled through a barbed-wire fence to take a shortcut and ripped the seat out of his only pair of trousers. She instructed him to go into the bedroom and toss out the torn pants. She repaired the pants and then threw them back. The thankful dance-goer was soon on his way again, decently attired. His benefactor's only comment to her family that evening was, "That's what I call an embarrassing moment!"

Today the era of the homestead-bachelor is no more. Yet the unique and valuable contributions these singular men made to rural education are remembered by present-day middle aged and senior citizens who used to attend the country schools.

9

Influence of Teachers

Society has been slow to learn at least one obvious lesson. It has taken man centuries to understand that to train and educate the child is infinitely easier than to labor with the deficiencies of the adult, with his crystallized habits and morals. There are many educative experiences outside of school and, of course, all involvement, no matter how apparently insignificant, still teaches, but what goes on in schools is the real education. Here education is organized, structured and variously assisted so as to be more effective and efficient than any random activity in the world at large. The school is the very foundation of society, and the teacher is its nucleus and guardian.

The success and progress of education in any school depend largely on the personality, scholarship and teaching ability of the person who is placed in charge of the pupils, and hence the problem before all educational authorities is that of securing the services and cooperation of capable teachers. Society must attract a sufficient number of men and women who have the required scholarship, high ideals, and the power to inspire children with ambition to develop their own self-respect, by living up to their ideals of conduct in work and play. The society that lets incapable people teach it while its capable men and women feed, cloth and amuse it, is committing intellectual suicide.

J. A. MacGregor, an old-time inspector, in his 1913 annual report to the Department of Education, emphasized the fact that the rural teacher, in his experience, was the grass roots on which education thrived.

> The character of the work done in the schools is, I find, just as good as the teacher in charge. Some teachers are absolutely incapable; others are capable but indifferent and there are those, fortunately in the majority, who are capable and conscientious, and are putting forth their best efforts towards making a success of their work.

No matter what any department of education, its officials or its supervisors legislated or did, it was what actually happened or didn't happen in any particular teacher's classroom that produced the educative results, good or bad. The teacher-training institutions, the so-called normal schools, realized this; they attempted in the short span of the three to nine months that they had the student-teachers to prepare them for such responsibilities. Even the admission requirements were geared to attract the best candidates possible. Here are a few such regulations:

1. Teachers-in-training shall submit to such rules and regulations respecting attendance, classification, conduct, and examinations as may be prescribed by the principal of the Normal School and approved by the Minister of Education.
2. Teachers-in-training shall lodge and board at such houses as are approved by the principal. Men and women are not permitted to board at the same "certified boarding house".
3. Any person holding a card of admission who fails to be present on the opening day of the session shall forfeit his right to attend.
4. No card of admission shall be granted until the applicant has submitted to the Department of Education a certificate of moral character signed by a clergyman, or some other responsible person.
5. Applicants for admission shall submit certificates to show that in the case of females they are over sixteen years of age and in the case of males, over eighteen.

In addition to the instructional programs and the practice teaching that characterized the normal schools, the student-teachers were imbued with the necessity of teaching manners and morals to their pupils. The future pedagogues soon became aware that it was the teacher's duty to see that the students practised conduct which demonstrated a sense of the proprieties of life, as well as politeness, which indicated a genuine respect for the wants and wishes of others. It was the teacher's responsibility to turn the attention of pupils to the moral quality of their acts and to lead them into a clear understanding and constant practice of every virtue. This was achieved through their own influence and example, the narration of suitable stories to awaken the right feelings, the memorization of lines embodying noble sentiments, memorization of maxims and proverbs containing rules of duty, and direct instruction.

Although the liaisons between the normal-school instructors and the school inspectors out in the field were reasonably good, there were many forces working against the success of the rural school that could not be remedied. Teachers changed schools very frequently so that much time was lost by both teachers and pupils in the process of adaptation to new conditions. It was difficult to secure and retain the services of qualified and competent teachers. In fact, teachers were so scarce it was impossible to weed out misfits who put neither energy nor enthusiasm into their work, and derived neither pleasure nor profit from it. Many teachers failed to meet successfully the needs of the rural school as they did not exercise a proper professional spirit. The extreme youth of others, together with their lack of knowledge of rural conditions and needs, worked against them in their dealings with teenage pupils; and, as a rule, they couldn't play any considerable part in making the school a social center. There were some schools in the charge of teachers who were homesteaders and although some of these did faithful and efficient work, the majority became negligent; the pupils in their care did not receive the full benefit of the training these teachers were capable of had their interests been centered only on their school work. Some teachers, like J. M. McDonald of Melita S.D. 1458 (Benalto, Alta.), practiced moonlighting. The salary for a teacher between 1905 and 1918 was about $325.00 a year, so to augment his earning this teacher engaged in several side-line occupations, along with his teaching. He sold insurance and did considerable butchering for the inexperienced homesteaders in the area. To the delight of his pupils he often dismissed school at 2:00 p.m. and on one occasion it was 11:00 a.m., so he could attend to his other duties. Mr. McDonald was a familiar sight as he drove to school and about the country in a buckboard pulled by Old Sam, a strawberry-roan, or, later by Old Frankie, a fast trotter.

Permit teachers who were hired when qualified teachers were not available had little or no professional training; hence, their work in most cases was defective.

Permits were both the answer and the bane to the teacher shortage. They did, however, allow teachers with complete training from other parts of the world to teach in Canadian schools without having to attend normal schools. But permits also were issued to high-school students who were sent into schoolrooms without formal training; in many cases such youthful mentors had malevolent influences on education in their particular schools. Some of the more conscientious students, before taking up their duties, spent a few hours with the local inspectors to discuss such subjects as teaching methods, tactics, expedients in discipline, timetables and the course of studies. Needless to add, such consultations proved of considerable value to any would-be teacher who lacked normal-school training. Mr. M. O. Nelson, an inspector of schools in 1910 for the Department of Education in Alberta reported:

> With reference to the character of the work done by the permit teachers, I might say that those who possessed grade eleven or grade twelve diplomas, and who, before entering their schools, call on the inspector for advice and practical suggestions, do very well indeed; otherwise, their work is inferior, lacks purpose, and suffers from poor organization.

The rural teacher had to be a very special breed to be able to cope with anywhere from five to eight grades in one room. It called for a type of personality that rarely exists today. Most were sincere young people who

-- Sylvia Wick

Sylvia Wick, an understanding teacher of the Devonshire S.D. (Youngston, Alta.), plays fox and geese with her pupils.

-- Jeanne Cody

Students in the Meadowlands S.D.(Hanna, Alta.) had individual drinking cups and towels as part of their teacher's effort to teach health consciousness.

worked under incredibly difficult conditions; yet, through thick and thin, heat and cold, good times and bad, they carried on. They came from all parts of the country, from all sections of society, and most were rural girls. Their pay was meager, their boarding places not always adequate, and the teaching equipment in their schools next to nothing, but somehow they managed.

If anyone earned the right to be called the efficiency expert, the teacher in the one-room country schoolhouse did. She had to be able to ride a horse and know how to take care of it; referee any type of game; organize school picnics; play the piano or organ; teach singing; operate the Waterman and Waterbury heater; put on a good Christmas concert; babysit pre-schoolers during the farm busy seasons; act as nurse or doctor; settle disputes; teach all grades from one to ten. She did all this for the $840.00 minimum, if she was lucky enough to get it. It was never what she could add to the course of studies to enrich it, but what she could delete and still feel she had covered the essentials. She was her own curricula maker and improvisor.

Great credit is due these pioneering schoolteachers. They were the hub of the wheel that was set turning by the influx of settlers and homesteaders. Each and every teacher in her own way played a part, large or small, in the building of each rural district. Many times today when recognition is given to a great man or woman for his or her outstanding achievements, mention is made of the fact that he or she began his or her education in a little one-room school. The bottom rung on the ladder leading to his or her success was earned by learning the three R's as taught by one teacher for eight grades in a rural public school.

Once a would-be teacher successfully completed the required normal school course and received the coveted teaching certificate from the Department of Education, the matter of securing a position had to be considered. Most relied on the services of a teacher agency, the normal school facilities, the inspector, or the "Teachers Wanted" advertisements in the daily newspapers and the local weeklies, to learn of current vacancies. The teachers' agency in Regina made a practice in the early days of sending letters to members of normal-school graduating classes in Eastern Canada, inviting them to apply for teaching positions in the west, where there was a shortage of teachers; the east had an overflow. Experienced teachers in Canada and those from abroad found the teachers' agency in Regina a convenient way of obtaining a school if they wanted to teach in Western Canada; they could also apply directly to any of the school boards advertising for teachers in the various newspapers across the country.

During the latter part of the twenties and the early thirties there was an oversupply of teachers and it was difficult, if not impossible, to secure a position. Muriel (Greene) Clipsham, who was graduated from the North Bay Normal School in 1925 with a second-class teaching certificate, described the torment she went through in her attempt to get a school.

All summer long (1926) I had answered advertisements and made personal applications. In two or three districts they seemed favorably impressed, but then a teacher with experience came along and I was left out. By late summer there was only the occasional advertisement, but somewhere was the school in which I was going to prove I was one of the best in the profession. I prayed for a school. I broke wishbones for a school, and every evening I wished on the evening star. I was on the lookout for the mailman every afternoon but never, never did he bring the letter I wanted. September arrived and just as a gesture of contempt, thumbing my nose at fate, I got my hair cut in the boyish bob fashion. It didn't matter now if I had the circumspect appearance of a schoolmarm or not. Nevertheless I continued writing application after application in my most painstakingly correct hand.

"This is surely it," I thought one day. "This is the school I'll get as sure as can be." I went out to the kitchen. "Look, Auntie, observe this application! It's unique, different, it's going to bring me a job, just wait and see."

She put it on the table beside her gooseberries and looked earnestly at it. "Well, for the life of me I can't see a thing different from all the others you've written."

"Oh! but it is," I said. "This is my one hundredth application."

"Goodness! I don't know how you can keep on. I'd think you'd be discouraged by this time."

"I am," I said, "but I've got to get a start somehow. I can't spend the rest of my life bumming amongst relatives. One summer's bad enough for you all. Dad has had another crop failure, pretty soon all vacancies will be filled and I honestly don't know what I'll do."

"Don't be discouraged," she said, "maybe the one hundredth application will be lucky."

"Maybe," I said, "but I'm taking no chances. Here goes one-hundred-and-one, one-hundred-and-two; that's all the ads in yesterday's paper."

Gordon E. Taylor, another would-be teacher, must have agreed with Shakespeare's famous lines: "There's a Divinity that shapes our end, rough hew them how we will." After submitting some 400 fruitless applications for a teaching position, it was a chance encounter with a farmer on the street in Drumheller, Alberta that brought the desired result.

"Well, as the fellow said, you can have the school if you teach for $700 a year!" The speaker, a big burly farmer named Homer Lamb, was talking to the newly-graduated teacher, Gordon E. Taylor, in front of a grocery store in Drumheller one fall afternoon in 1930. "I accept," said the teacher, almost too enthusiastically. His eagerness was not due to the salary offered, but as he already had written more than 400 applications to schools throughout Alberta, and as it was the third week in August and the coal mines were not working, he was relieved to hear of a job. "Well, as the fellow said," Mr. Lamb went on, "in that case the school is yours." The teacher was overjoyed and hastened home to tell his folks of his good fortune. Ten days later he arrived at Lake McKee School to start his teaching career. As the door was unlocked he quickly went in to see what the school looked like. It was just an ordinary classroom with a big pot-bellied stove at the back, but to Gordon Taylor it was the most wonderful school in the world.

The first, as well as the most colorful of a series of thirty-four teachers who taught at one time or another in the Big Rock S.D. 592 (Okotoks, Alta.), was Kate Creighton. Her abounding energy and love of adventure made her a local legend. She used to ride the three miles to her school sidesaddle attired in a riding habit. In wet weather it was said she had three such outfits: one at home, one at school, and one in which to go out in the rain. She was an excellent teacher, was held in deep respect, and was a leader in the social and cultural life of the Big Rock School District. Her pretty clothes and hairdo were subjects for discussion and even emulation. Yet the way in which such a fine teacher secured a position was another twist of fate. She was dancing with Robert McClaren in Okotoks, Alberta one evening, and in the course of her conversation mentioned that she was looking for a job. Imagine her surprise to be told immediately that she was hired to teach the Big Rock School.

The majority of rural school boards frowned on hiring local girls as teachers for their schools, reasoning that such action would result in trouble. "Familiarity breeds contempt," was the usual reason given. The trustees of the Washington S.D. 1431 (Carmangay, Alta.) broke with this tradition and decided on a home girl whose certificate was not as good as the others that had applied; but she had ties, presumably a boy friend, that would keep her in the district. Their experience in the past made them decide that one who would stay would be better than one who was apt to leave at the end of the school term.

Was a teacher's life dull? Never! Things started to happen the moment she got off the train at her destination.

One problem was the confusion in directions resulting from the railway journey. Unless the teacher made a mental note of all the twists and turns made by the train during the course of the trip, when she arrived in the unfamiliar surroundings the train seemed to be travelling in the wrong direction. It appeared headed back in the same direction from which it had come when it left the city terminal a few hours before. The world seemed to have done a complete flip during the course of the journey. It was bewildering to say the least and took much concentration to resolve. Some travellers never did become oriented! So during the time the teacher remained in the district, the sun, unaware of the confusion created, rose in the west and set in the east.

Annie Louise Siddall, who had been hired to teach in the Mound Lake S.D. 754 (Red Deer, Alta.) in the fall of 1903, got off the train at Red Deer, Alberta and was greeted by a heavy downpour of rain, driven by a brisk wind. There were no sidewalks, so she gathered up her long skirts and made her way by leaps and bounds to the Alberta Hotel, which was across from the station. She was about to enter, when a gentleman passing by said, "Oh lady, I think you are making a mistake. This is the door you are looking for!" To her great dismay she noticed that she was about to step into the barroom, and for a strictly temperance girl, it would have been a reprehensible way to commence a teaching career. The secretary-treasurer of the Mound Lake School District was at the station when the train pulled in, and as there was only one lady getting off, he followed Miss Siddall to the hotel and watched her register. He then introduced himself and made arrangements to take her with him next morning to the Mound Lake School, thirty-six miles from Red Deer.

When she was about to turn in for the night, Miss Siddall found she had no key for the door to her room, so she went downstairs to inform the clerk of the omission. She was kindly informed that the hotel never did have a key for that door, but she would be all right. This teacher didn't take anything for granted, so she barricaded the door with everything moveable in her room. But as the clerk had said, she was all right!

According to the arrangements made with the secretary-treasurer, she was in front of the hotel just before eight o'clock the next morning to meet him for the long drive to her new school. Since the barroom was about to open, there was the usual group of men waiting for the morning's refreshments. When she looked up to the spring seat on top of the double-box wagon, she wondered just how to climb up there without providing a peep show for the watching throng. But Louise was a resourceful young lady and soon was seated safely beside the driver and on her way to Mound Lake.

Most teachers suffered from intense loneliness when they first arrived at their prairie schools. However, the absorbing task of working with and for the children soon put an end to such emotional bouts. Take the case of Agnes Douglas who came from Ontario in the spring of 1897 to teach at the Battle Lake S.D. (Wetaskiwin, Alta.). She arrived in Wetaskiwin during the bleak, chilly month of April. As she waited in the Draiard Hotel sitting room and gazed across the barren, flat country, her pioneer enthusiasm foresook her. Travel weary, alone, and with an entire continent between her and home, she succumbed to homesickness. She sat weeping bitterly. The kindly bartender tried to comfort her by telling her she would soon feel differently. "My wife felt the same way as you do," he said, "but now she likes the country and doesn't want to go back East." Miss Douglas didn't ever expect to feel differently, but the man's deep concern embarrassed her enough to enable her to get herself under control. Presently she was taken out to Hans Finsen's farm where she was to board.

The teacher was far from a cheerful supper guest and everything seemed to be conspiring against her, even the furniture. When she attempted to push her chair back from the table it tipped backward and flipped her onto her back with her feet in the air. In the voluminous skirts which the ladies wore in those days, she was quite helpless and acutely embarrassed. It was some time before she could be restored to balance and dignity. The accidental diversion was just what she needed to break her spell of loneliness, for soon after she made up her mind to stay and unpacked her baggage. She also presented each of the Finsen children with an orange. Bessie Finsen was seven and it was the first orange she had seen.

The bartender had prophesied about Miss Douglas's loneliness correctly. Jim McLaughlin soon persuaded her that she was too good a cook to waste her life teaching school. They were married in March of 1900 and made their home in the Battle Lake S.D.

No matter in which part of rural Canada or the United States a young teacher found herself in the early days, she could always expect adverse living and working conditions. Mrs. Hubert Lester of Renfrew, Ontario, described some of her experiences as a young teacher in a remote community in Ontario during the school year 1932-33.

> As a new teacher in this isolated community I was the center of interest and was very much like an exhibit on display. Everyone tried to be the first to catch a glimpse of me, or to be the first fellow to date me. Soon gossip had it that a young man was courting "the teacher", which incidentally was what I was called rather than by my name. The mysterious Romeo was able to back up his claim that he had been visiting me frequently as he had become a "peeping tom". He was in the habit of coming to my boarding house in the evening and peering in through the window, watching and noting my every moves. I wasn't aware of this, until one night as I was sitting at the kitchen table I noticed a small red glow through the curtain. It was the end of his lighted cigarette. Without saying anything and appearing as natural as possible I wrote on a piece of paper that I thought someone was outside spying on the household, and passed it across to the man of the house who was reading at the time. He jumped up and rushed outside as quickly as possible only to see my prince charming disappear in the inky darkness.
>
> Some of the homes in my district didn't even have an outdoor privy. Fortunately I was lucky to be boarding quite close to the school and used the one there. The porcupines had gnawed at the seat to such a degree that any visit to this outhouse was never prolonged nor

comfortable. Nevertheless I considered myself better off than the women in the community who used the squat method in any spot concealed from public view.

Besides teaching I was expected to fill the role of anything from a midwife to a janitor. A new baby was on the way at the home where I boarded in December, and when the birth was imminent, which was at 4 a.m., I was asked to get up and stay with the mother, until the father returned with the mother-in-law who lived some miles away. Then I was expected to be "bright-eyed and bushy-tailed" for school at 9 a.m. after my all-night-vigil.

The winter was the worst for me. For three months it was impossible to get home or even leave my boarding house for a day. The telephone service might as well have not existed, for if I wanted to make a call my message was relayed through three people via the Forestry Branch Telephone Line. There was no such thing as rural mail service and it was necessary to bring the mail to the village some six miles away, twice a week from the nearest railway station. I remember once we didn't get any mail for sixteen days.

My landlord didn't go to the store in the winter and depended upon the neighbors to get such essential things as coal oil for the lamps. As a result, I was without light for two weeks, but luckily my mother had sent me some candles, so I as able to work by candlelight for part of that time.

One worry I had during the long winter was what would happen if I took suddenly ill, or even worse, died. There was no way of getting out of the district when the snow was deep. Not even the horses were able to travel between the stopping places in order to get to the railway station. A local carpenter made coffins and skis, and happily I bought and used only the latter.

Even prior to the arrival of the schoolmarm in a rural community she became the subject of wagers placed by the young and the not-so-young men in the district. Would she be pretty? Blond or brunette? Old or young? Tall or short? Plump or thin? Who would be the first to take her out, or dance with her? Sometimes the bet was ludicrous, as this incident from the Galarneauville S.D. (Hanna, Alta.) described by a young lady schoolteacher illustrates.

For two nights in a row I couldn't sleep very well as if something had been disturbing my slumbers. The third evening I was determined to catch up on my lost sleep so I retired rather early. I was sound asleep when I was awakened by music. It was "Let Me Call You Sweetheart," and seemed to come from the outside. By the time I was fully conscious all was silent. There wasn't a radio in the entire district and I decided I had been dreaming and went back to sleep. But next morning, sure enough, there were tracks in the snow leading from the road allowance to my window. I had been serenaded, the only time in my life, in a little prairie teacherage thirty miles from town, in the middle of a cold winter's night with the temperature about forty degrees below zero. My mysterious visitor won his dare — a two dollar bet!

Maisie Emery Cook, a pioneer rural teacher in Alberta, described her teaching experience in a comprehensive and interesting little booklet entitled, *Memories of a Pioneer Schoolteacher.* Her description of one of her boarding places is especially revealing.

In the middle of August, 1907, I started teaching in a district adjacent to the one in which my sister had been teaching for some time, near the present city of Wetaskiwin, Alberta. My boarding place was a mile from school and quite comfortable except during the winter. The husband and wife who were my hosts were fairly young, educated and moderately well-to-do. My board and rent was twenty dollars a month, so I was amazed at the end of the first month to receive an itemized account of all visitors during the month and a bill for horse feed and stable use, as well as a charge for keeping the minister, who had called during a storm. Added to my board the total bill came to nearly thirty dollars, which was half of my salary. On inquiring, I found they were not in the habit of entertaining company and felt that was the reason for the visitors coming.

The husband, who was also the secretary-treasurer of the local improvement district of that area, always seemed to need help with the books, so I put in many hours some evenings helping him to keep the financial statements balanced correctly. My assistance was never recognized remuneratively, and during the third month my bill included twenty-five cents for a ride to school on a stormy day, on an invitation from him, as he had to make a trip past the school. He wanted to keep our relationsip on a business basis he explained.

When the newly-trained teachers reached their rural districts to begin their teaching careers, their enthusiasm suffered a severe shock. They discovered that the ideas of the normal school staffs and the ideas of the school boards who hired them and to whom they were directly responsible, were entirely different. So after periods of bewilderment they lapsed into the vicious circle of "teaching as they were taught." They wrestled with timetables and the almost impossible task of making teaching theory fit into the concrete problems of reality in eight-grade one-room rural schools.

In most schools, fairly good timetables were in evidence and when these were faithfully followed, satisfactory work was usually done. Unfortunately, some teachers were not acquainted with the provisions of the School Act regarding timetables and consequently they neglected to prepare them, and their work was conducted in a more or less careless, slipshod and haphazard manner. Whenever inspectors discovered a teacher operating a school without a timetable, they gave her a few suggestions as to how to make one, and then required the teacher to prepare one and forward a copy to the school official concerned. However, it was one thing to have a timetable posted in a conspicuous place in the classroom, and another to follow it explicitly day by day. Teachers learned through experience about the art of juggling classes. To be a successful country schoolteacher, one had to have eight lessons in action, eight others ready to spring full-grown from one's repertoire the moment needed, and eight others held in reserve. Such an achievement could only be attained by intensive preparation before and by complete concentration during school hours.

One of the worst handicaps for rural teachers was the lack of reference books. It was rare to find a rural school that had an encyclopedia of any kind and it was even rarer to find a home in the district that boasted of this educational amenity. Perhaps the *Books of Knowledge* were the most valuable sources of educational material for both teachers and pupils in the days of the rural school. These splendid publications were available thanks to the persistent efforts of book salesmen who visited the rural areas time and again to peddle their informative wares at reasonable prices and attractive time payments. It was well for the teachers to have a set of encyclopedias, the *Books of Knowledge,* or some other reference material, for invariably she would be asked hundreds of questions prefixed with the diabolic statement, "You should know, you're the teacher!"

In pioneer days in a school district some sixty miles east of Edmonton, the Ukrainian farmers in the area used to stop at the schoolhouse as they drove their stock to the market in town and ask the teacher to estimate the weight of the animals and the price they should bring. This was a new venture for the teacher, but with the help of some of the older knowledgeable boys, they came up with fairly good estimates; the results were so good, the teacher gained the title of "Dobre Proffesorca" or "Good Lady Teacher". It was not unusual on the homeward trip for one of the grateful men to stop at the school, doff his cap, bow low and kiss the teacher's hand as a sign of the respect in which she was held for having so much knowledge and education.

Country teachers found that they had deep concern for and close relationships with everyone in the district, and if tragedy befell any of them, they felt the impact in a personal way. Eva Hewlett Mein recalled one such incident which happened while she was teaching in the Dunreath S.D. (Griffin, Sask.).

> The tragic death of Jimmy Brown is foremost in my mind in recalling our second confinement at the school during a blizzard in 1916. Mr. Brown had come early in the afternoon for Jimmy, but in the interval the storm became worse. When he reached the railway track his cutter was struck by a snowplow, unseen and unheard in the raging dense

whiteness. Jimmy, my seven-year-old student, was thrown out and killed. When school resumed a few days later, I wept silent tears at the sight of the empty little desk!

Sometimes it was the teacher herself who met with misfortune, and she in turn became beneficiary of community help and sympathy. Jeanne Huntley, one of the earliest teachers in the Plainfield S.D. (Carmangay, Alta.), suffered a back injury in a fall from a horse and was unable to walk any distance. She boarded with a family just across from the school and missed very few days during the time of her disability. The children were delighted with the daily scene of her considerate landlord taking her to school everyday in a wheelbarrow.

When schools were closed for a few weeks during the influenza epidemic of 1918-19, teachers were expected to make up lost time by teaching on Saturdays and during the Easter vacation if they wished to receive their pay for the time lost.

It wasn't financial remuneration that bothered the teacher at Galarneauville S.D. (Sunnynook, Alta.); it was the wallpaper in her bedroom. Just before Christmas the weather turned ominously warm and the snow began to thaw. As a result the paper in her upstairs room became damp, loosened and began to sag from the ceiling. By the time she went to bed there was an occasional drip, but she managed to contort herself into a position to miss it. Around midnight the deluge increased to such a proportion that she could no longer escape it by the way she lay on the bed. The wet blankets didn't bother her much as it was quite warm. Finally, in desperation, she got up, opened her trunk, found her umbrella and raised it over her pillow; from then until the time she got up all was well.

May Comer of Happy Valley S.D. 1018 (Didsbury, Alta.) almost gave up her teaching career because of a ram that her landlord owned. Every time she made her way back to her boarding place from the school, the rambunctious animal obstructed her path by challenging her with his playful butting. Miss Comer found it anything but amusing. One afternoon she was rescued from her place of refuge behind a telephone pole; she had just smashed her lunch bucket over the ram's head. Her nose and one foot were bleeding but her injuries were superficial. This particular ram seemed to have had an aversion to schoolteachers, for the next teacher in the Happy Valley S.D. also had confrontations with the jocular beast.

No teacher escaped jokes or tricks played on them at opportune times by their students. In the Britannia S.D. (Pollockville, Alta.) the bigger boys trapped a skunk and let it freeze so that it appeared poised and alive. They placed it on the school steps and when the teacher arrived at school she was afraid to go in. It was nearly eleven o'clock before the teacher discovered the ruse and started classes. The youngsters concerned paid dearly for their initiative as they had to stay in after school every day for a week.

In the Humboldt S.D. (Drumheller, Alta.) the pupils preferred to sweeten their pranks with flowers. One noon hour in early spring some of the boys, while playing around the hills, found some crocuses. They thought it would be a good idea to pick a few and prepare a bouquet to give to their teacher, Ivy Price. When they returned to school, they found it was an ideal time to present their crocuses as the teacher and most of the girls were sitting together enjoying the spring sunshine on the roof of the low coalshed. She was very pleased to receive the flowers, but as the boys dumped the blossoms in her lap, a dead mouse hidden in the bouquet fell out. The reaction of the females could only be compared to a crew bailing out of a burning aircraft.

Inexperienced teachers soon learned to give instructions open only to one interpretation. It was usually after a few incidents like the one experienced by Muriel Greene in the Craigton S.D. (Munson, Alta.) that such a decision would be quickly reached. She had told her grade one pupil to color a certain picture in the work book with crayons "if she liked." Returning a half-hour later, Miss Greene found the picture still uncolored and asked, "Why?" The reply she received was more pertinent than any advice she ever received at the Calgary Normal School, "You said I could do it if I liked and I didn't like to!"

Winter was the time for playing in the snow and this brought forth problems which arose from wet clothes. After each recess and the noon hour it was a common sight to see a whole row of stockings and mitts draped over the partition behind the pot-bellied stove. As this partition between the heated classroom and the cloakroom was not built right up to the ceiling, there was ample space for the students to sit and dry out their pant legs while they read or studied. On cold mornings there would be several pupils sitting there like chickens on a roost, as it as the warmest place in the building.

A teacher had to keep a wary eye on activities in the school barn at all times. The older pupils considered it a convenient place for boy-girl fraternization, and younger ones found it an ideal locality for watching any improprieties, or to practice some of their own. Occasionally the teacher would catch some of her pupils in the barn involved in situations somewhat short of propriety. The embarrassed culprits were brought to justice immediately and punishment was administered. Punishment usually took the form of either getting the strap or staying in after school for several days, but depending upon the nature of the impropiety, sometimes the parents of the children involved were notified. At least once a year some of the boys took it into their heads to experiment with smoking or chewing tobacco. It was alway done secretly in the barn, and frequently the aftereffects were severe enough punishment without being caught as well.

In the early days, school grounds were not fenced and this often created problems. During severe storms range cattle had the habit of drifting with the wind toward anything that provided shelter, like school buildings. Soon a large herd would surround the school and mill around the door and out-buildings. If this invasion occurred near dismissal time, it created a problem for the students and teacher: How could they evade the wild range cattle and make a dash to the nearest grazing-lease fence? Such a situation occurred in the Hannaford School located in the ranching country south of Hanna, Alberta. When the teacher and pupils were ready to go home, they quickly opened the door, started to beat loudly on their lunch pails and at the same time yelled and screamed. The cattle took fright at this sudden onslaught and ran away from the school, giving the teacher and her pupils an opportunity to make a run for the safety of the fence a quarter-of-a-mile away. The group didn't have much time to linger, for when curiosity got the better of the cattle, they turned around and in a rather surly mood started towards the offending humans.

Visitors to an isolated rural school were few and far between, so if one did appear, it was due to some extenuating circumstance and often proved to be a matter of anxiety for the teacher.

In the Poplar Hill S.D. (Viking, Alta.) the students noticed a tall man hurrying to their school just after dismissal time. He made signs to them not to herald his approach, and then still by pantomime, invited them to tiptoe into the school with him. It looked like a lot of fun, so the children complied with his suggestion. Jean Stuart, the teacher, was enjoying a few moments of relaxation at the organ, so the music drowned out the sounds of the approaching retinue. The stranger crept up behind the preoccupied teacher and suddenly clapped his hands over her eyes. Steely-nerved Miss Stuart emitted a scream and the frightened children did the same. The escapade ended well, for the stranger was the teacher's brother who had come to pay her a surprise visit.

Georgia Trotter, a first-year teacher at Rockafellow S.D. (Blackie, Alta.) in 1912, also had an unexpected visitor, but this visitor did not arrive in a stealthy manner. The stranger, a man with a heavy Scotch brogue and a badly turned-in eye, stopped at the schoolhouse to purchase, of all things, two dozen eggs. Georgia informed him that the building was a school and not a farmhouse. Undismayed, he asked her if the students would sing "Nearer My God To Thee" in memory of his brother who had gone down on the Titanic. Such a request was hard to turn down, so Miss Trotter played the organ and the children sang. The visitor went over and stood by the organ and sang with them. Soon after the incident, a concerned neighbor appeared on the scene. He explained that two men, who had obviously been drinking, had stopped at his house, and when he saw them turn in at the school gate he left quickly to investigate. The teacher had been too naive to recognize a drunk when she saw one.

Teachers put up with many offensive odors; some they could control, others were chronic. In the Hesketh S.D. (Drumheller, Alta.) for instance, the pupils like most rural youngsters, used to eat wild onions. Some didn't like the taste, but as it was a matter of self-defense, they indulged in the practice. After eating an onion or two they did not notice the fetid breath of the others. The poor teacher was the one who suffered most and eventually was forced to ban onion-eating during school hours if the novelty persisted.

Every rural school at one time or another in the course of its history had the frustrating experience of being visited by skunks. The animals themselves were not offensive, but the odors they exuded when distraught certainly were. Besides, the smell remained for weeks after their sojourn. Most attempts to break their underground leases in the neighborhood of school buildings proved fruitless and usually resulted in a more concentrated scent of skunk musk. Ida Stuart, a former teacher in the Millerfield S.D. 3383 (Dorothy, Alta.), could vouchsafe for all the nasty things said about skunks. After all, she spent an entire year with a family of them under her teacherage. Their nocturnal digging and wandering habits gave her many sleepless nights. Frequently they became agitated by her tenancy so near to theirs and made their displeasure known in their usual unsavory fashion. After several spraying sessions the teacher's possessions became putrid with the smell. Eventually the school board decided to do something about the skunks. One weekend when Ida went home, they attempted to smoke out the pests. The men lit a smudge fire at the entrance to the skunks' burrow, but the skunks also had decided to leave for that weekend, so the strategy failed. In fact, it backfired, for the teacherage ended up full of black, pungent smoke, in addition to the skunk musk.

If a student was sprayed by a skunk, the rest of the school had to suffer as well as the unfortunate human target. It didn't matter whether his mother scrubbed him with various scented soaps, doctored him with the most powerful deodorant, and doused him liberally with perfume; whenever the classroom became the least bit warm, the unmistakeable odor of skunk came to the fore. When Robert Offord picked up a baby skunk at school by mistake, thinking it was a cute little kitten, Miss Brown, the Golden Grain S.D. (Munson, Alta.) teacher, suggested he go home and change his clothes. She wrote a note to his mother, explaining what had happened and what to do with his clothes — bury them..

Rural schoolteachers took these various hardships in stride. "It was hectic, adventurous, soul-stirring and at times very monotonous," they said, but in the same breath vouchsafed, "Remember Arbor Day? Remember this . . . ? Remember that . . . ? Not only did they have much to remember, but they also left much for future generations to reminisce about as well.

In replying to how they liked teaching, most teachers said, "Teaching is fine, the first time around, but by the time you say the same thing fifty different ways it gets tiresome." An old-time doctor, after hearing the above answer, laughed and commented most appropriately with, "My dear girl, when you're my age, you'll know ninety percent of a job can be sheer drudgery. It's the other ten percent that is the leaven."

The annals of rural schools are filled to overflowing with this "leavening", like the following stories that could be prefaced with, "Do you remember when . . . ?

On the morning of the opening of Cotham S.D. (Armley, Sask.) although the pupils arrived rather early, Miss Oliver, the teacher, a medium-sized woman with snow-white hair, was there first. She stood in the doorway and after introductions were made, the youngsters were permitted to enter the school only after saying, "Good morning, Miss Oliver!" Each morning no one was allowed to pass by her without giving this greeting. She stood as straight as a sergeant major and demanded respect at all times. One result was that the pupils learned exceptionally good manners. Some fifty years later a teacher who taught the Cotham School said, "The children, mainly offsprings of the original pupils, were the best-mannered of any I have ever taught!"

Miss Dear, who taught in the Fallen Timber S.D. (Didsbury, Alta.), gave the community something to talk about when she first reached town on the train. On the day of her arrival a young fellow, Purcell Blain, took a wagon and went to the railway station to meet her. He found her dressed in the fashionable hobble skirt of that day. The teacher immediately saw that getting into the wagon would prove quite a problem, so she politely asked Purcell to turn his back while she rolled in.

Hilda Sloan, a teacher in the Clearview S.D. 638 (Red Deer, Alta.), also did some rolling, but for a different purpose. In the 1924-25 winter the snow was so deep that the fence posts simply disappeared under the snow and roads were where the first travellers made them. Hilda tells of meeting a team while walking on the road to school from her boarding house. Clad in her fur coat, she decided that rather than plunge into the deep snow she would use a more strategic manoeuvre. She lay down on the snow and rolled to the roadside and returned the same way after the team had passed.

When the Sunset Valley S.D. (Mossleigh, Alta.) was opened in the fall of 1915, the contractor forgot to leave the key for the new school with anyone in the district. He lived in Edmonton and could not be reached before school opened. Undaunted, the new teacher and pupils entered and left the building through the windows for three weeks until the key was returned. The windows were large and all on the west side. In fact, it was so convenient that the boys took advantage of the novel situation and set gopher traps in the yard; it was possible to keep an eye on a large portion of the area adjacent to the school and they could pop out immediately to attend the traps when needed.

The name of a school district could cause a teacher some embarrassment. Wild Lily S.D. near Elbow, Sask. was no exception. When the new teacher called at the Elbow station to pick up a package of school supplies, a stranger was relieving the regular agent, and this man's knowledge of local names was nil. So when the schoolmarm asked, "Is there a parcel here for

Wild Lily?'', the man could only laugh and ask, "Wild Lily? Who is she?"

In those early days teachers were allowed to assist parents in bringing up their children "in the way that they should go," and there was no sparing the strap or any other methods of correction. The School Act permitted corporal punishment; it stated that:

(1) All pupils shall be responsible to the teacher for their conduct on the school premises, and also for their behavior on the way to and from school unless accompanied by one of their parents or guardians, or some person appointed by them; and

(2) to conform to the rules of the school and submit to such discipline as would be exercised by a kind, firm and judicious parent.

The latter part of this regulation could be variously interpreted and the result was that the methods, severity and standards of discipline vacillated from school to school, with teacher to teacher. This lack of uniformity is illustrated by the examples that follow.

One of the first teachers in the Grand Centre S.D. was known for the severe disciplinary measures he used. He often lifted the guilty students out of the seats by the hair and dropped them, or flayed away at them with his yardstick or whatever textbook he had in his hand at the time.

On one occasion the boys in the Dryboro Lake S.D. (Crane Valley, Sask.) selected Charlie Brown to steal the teacher's strap and throw it down the well. The teacher, however, cunningly outsmarted the conspirators. She asked them the bring ten cents each for a proposed school party, and bought another strap with the money. The activity of the promised party turned out to be a severe strapping of each of the fifteen guilty boys with the new piece of belting.

It was a fine spring day so the students of the Brookside S.D. (Fairmede, Sask.) went down to a small ravine during the noon-hour recess to play on some logs. Two of the youngsters, Lothe and Ethel, got soaking wet. They both lived about half-a-mile from school and had ample time to go home and change their clothes, but they had a better plan. They asked Wilfred, who was always an obliging classmate, to build a fire in the pot-bellied heater in the school so they could dry their clothes. He did an excellent job, and when Mr. Nelson, the teacher, returned from dinner, he was met with a hot blast of air when he opened the school door, for the inside was like an oven. Being concerned, he rang the bell and then asked, "Who lit the fire on a nice day like this?" Wilfred's hand went up. "All right, Wilfred," the teacher declared, "you take this chair over close to the stove and sit down!" the girls sat and giggled all afternoon, while poor Wilfred sweltered, mopped his brow frequently, and suffered in silence.

Many pioneer teachers encountered the problem of the children using the language spoken at home rather than English. Such a practice could be disconcerting to any teacher not familiar with that particular language, for the students could make disparaging remarks about her, or plan nefarious activities, right in her presence. Henry Irwin, a teacher in the Lennox S.D., heard little German spoken around the school after one incident he still finds amusing.

> I had just finished sweeping the school and had accumulated a pile of summerfallow dirt in the cloakroom preparatory to scooping it into the coal bucket, when one of the grade-one boys barged in, followed by a strong draught of wind that had been shaking the old schoolhouse all day. The neat pile of refuse was blown into the schoolroom again. I roared the only German I knew, "Close the door!" After this, no one knew to what extent I understood German, so it was seldom spoken in my hearing.

It didn't take long for rural teachers to learn that an inanimate and harmless looking thing like a gatepost could be a bit of a health hazard to her pupils. Aside from the school itself, the gateposts proved to be the most enduring things around. The majority of children who drove a horse and rig, and even some who rode horseback, managed to connect with one post or another at least once during their school careers, with varying consequences. If an enthusiastic driver got a good start from the barn, Old Dobbin was able to work up quite a speed by the time the outfit reached the gate. When the vehicle did sideswipe or collide with one of the gateposts, it was the teacher who kept her presence of mind and administered first aid to anyone who was injured; she then would have the damaged rig temporarily repaired, or made arrangements for getting the children home some other way. She was forced to assume the dual role of policeman and ambulance attendant when such mishaps occurred.

Since teachers changed schools frequently, many had the dubious pleasure of following good teachers. It took real efforts on the part of the newcomers to enhance their own teacher-images while time mercifully dimmed people's memories of the paragons. Vina (MacKenzie) Crone, who taught in the Greenlawn S.D. (Viking, Alta.), didn't realize how difficult it was for the teacher who followed her until she happened to meet her and was told about it in no uncertain terms.

> I recall being introduced to the teacher who succeeded me at the Greenlawn School at a convention and her first words were, "You know, I hate the very sound of your name." I asked, "Whatever for, I've just met you?" She replied haughtily, "I followed you at Greenlawn, and no matter what I did, it wasn't right. "Miss MacKenzie didn't do it that way." Even at my boarding place, I got the meals you preferred whether I liked them or not!

No one ever knows by what thread popularity dangles and rural teachers proved this time and again.

John Parker who was in charge of the Poplar Hill S.D. for a time, became accepted because he proved he was a down-to-earth individual and was just like one of the farm folk. One day he appeared in school with a dishcloth happily dangling from his back pocket. In the Hesketh S.D. (Hesketh, Alta.) it was J. Fitzpatrick who captured the imagination of the pupils. He used to play ball with his pupils, but as there were not enough players for two teams, he acted as catcher for both, and being right on top of all plays he acted as umpire as well. Trading bites of lunch goodies was an accepted practice in rural schools. If the teacher found the custom distasteful but still wanted to be respected, she usually hid her feelings and traded bite for bite. She was always a favored trading partner because the pupils were sure the teacher had the best lunch.

John Morrison, the Buffalo S.D. 1700 teacher, went all out one year and, with the help of several residents, staged a stampede in conjunction with the annual school picnic. A number of men of the district collected a sum of money and dared the teacher to ride a bronc. He accepted their challenge and although he didn't stay the ten seconds required for a qualified ride, he showed he had spunk enough to help make his show a success. In addition, he earned his spurs as a popular teacher.

Farm children were always delighted when the teacher could saddle her own horse, or harness one to a buggy. Such a simple accomplishment gained her respect and admiration from her pupils. Usually city girls were afraid of horses and rural youngsters were critical of them as a group with the somewhat cynical remark, "All the teachers want to ride, but none even want to learn how to tighten a cinch!"

The Sulitjelma S.D., located some forty miles south-east of Edmonton, was settled almost entirely by Scandinavians, divided equally between Swedes and Norwegians. John Warcup Morrison, the new teacher, was intrigued by the opportunity this offered him to learn languages new to him. He eventually learned both tongues to the point where he could speak, read and write them quite fluently. This linguistic accomplishment endeared him to every parent and child in the district. He had become one of them!

The panorama of the prairie with its sweep of vastness and emptiness may have been an artist's or a poet's delight, but to a teacher new to such an environment it often proved to be a nightmare. It looked flat and the same to them wherever they walked or rode; hence, it was easy to confuse directions and get lost. The teacher who was able to travel alone in the area without losing her way was considered a gem, while the one who always seemed to end up at the wrong place no matter how carefully the directions had been spelled out to her was referred to as, ". . . that fool teacher! She's lost again." Some teachers learned that a horse could find its way home, so if they were not sure which way to go, they knew enough to give the horse a free rein and usually "old faithful" got them home.

Teachers had to be very discreet in any of their love affairs, for it seemed that every person in the community had a personal interest in the progress or regression of such romances. In fact, the teacher's success in the classroom depended in part on the diplomatic manner in which she handled

-- Mrs. N. Charyk

Teachers on the station platform at Bankhead, Alta. in 1915 display fashionable teacher attire of those early days.

her affairs of the heart. A rebuffed suitor could often turn the entire district against her, no matter how well she performed in the classroom. So, it is understandable why the annals of rural schools contain many interesting stories of teacher romances.

In the Tangleflags S.D. (Fort Pitt, Sask.) a couple of young brothers went courting one Sunday afternoon with the same girl, a young schoolteacher. They had a team and buggy and she sat between her two admirers. A rug had been brought along to cover their knees as it was rather a cool day. After awhile, one of the lovers wanted to hold hands, and then the other had the same idea. The girl, being quite a sport, manoeuvred their hands toward each other, and it was quite a time until they found out to their astonishment that they were holding hands with each other.

An amusing incident occurred in the Melita S.D. 1458 (Sylvan Lake,) Alta. when Miss McGregor was teaching there in 1906. Mr. Wylie, a trustee, had occasion to write to her, inviting her to accompany the family on a picnic to Sylvan Lake. Miss McGregor answered the letter promptly, however, she accidently sent him a love letter written to her by her fiance regarding their forthcoming marriage. Imagine the teacher's chagrin and embarrassment when Mr. Wylie returned her letter in person.

All in all, no group of people worked under more adverse conditions than the rural teachers; yet they managed to do creditable jobs. They made no promises of a life of ease and security as a student's reward for attending school regularly and working hard, yet the little white schoolhouses turned out men and women second to none. The pioneer teachers gave their all in the name of education and received very little in return. Although some of them were disappointing, most were sincere, and their personalities and devotion to their work left lasting imprints on the students. Children thrive in an atmosphere of harmony and rural teachers, due to their close relationships with everyone in their communities, were able to provide this through a loving understanding of all the youngsters and their problems. The homes, in turn, maintained constructive interest in the schools and supported the teachers, which helped immeasurably in the proper development of their children. At an early age, rural students, due to the multi-grade situation in the classrooms and under the guidance of the teachers, learned to help themselves, a most valuable lesson in living. As an Oriental sage once said:

> Give a man a fish,
> You feed him for a day,
> Tomorrow he'll be hungry
> In the same old way.

> Teach a man to fish,
> You feed him for his life,
> Tomorrow he'll be feeding
> His children and his wife.

Teachers instilled spiritual, moral and academic values, thus firmly embedding basic decencies in the minds of their scholars. Among other things, the students were taught discipline, consideration for others, respect for their elders, a sense of sportsmanship, love of good literature and correctness of speech. An experienced and concerned classroom teacher is the only one who knows how far the child has progressed educationally, and what he still can achieve; year after year she has worked with new groups of children and this experience enables her to have some expertise in estimating any child's potential. Rural teachers were in a class by themselves in this field as they could watch the student's development over several grades rather than a mere one.

Very few records have been kept of these pioneer rural teachers and though unhonored and unsung, they contributed much to the development of Canada and the country will forever be indebted to them.

10

School Officials

The early settlers did not come to close grips with all the problems and responsibilities of full citizenship. Everything was most benignly taken care of by key men in Ottawa or in the provincial capitals who had been selected by politicians from the various electoral districts. Thus the work of administration throughout the land was carried on by efficient departments, leaving little opportunity for the ordinary rural citizen to exercise his political flair. There was, however, one small exception. The state had magnanimously decided, that should the ordinary citizen decide to do so, he could deal at close quarters with the great social enigma, responsibility for education. To the credit of these pioneers, they seemed to adopt the motto, "Life is pretty much what you care to make it." As there were enough promoters of education around, school committees were formed, school districts organized and trustees duly elected. Soon little schoolhouses dotted Canada's countryside; these eventually provided citizens with the opportunity to help the country reach world-wide recognition.

The various Departments of Education throughout Canada spelled out the duties and responsibilities of the trustees and their appointed officials in a governmental document entitled the "School Law". Hence the effectiveness of the educational program conducted in any district depended upon the manner in which the local trustees interpreted the regulations and followed them, the conscientious way in which they carried out their duties, their initiative, their philosophy of education, and last but not least — their own educational backgrounds. The mass of official correspondence with the Department of Education sorely tried the patience of ordinary men and women wanting plain answers to their plain questions, and wanting them quickly. Usually the local trustees received replies referring them to this or that clause of some act, to section so and so, and to this amendment and that supplement, until the original problem or question became lost in the maze of official jargon. Ironically, each letter ended with a magnificent flourish of assurance and sincerity with the words, "and having the honor to be, your obedient servant." In time, all the official rigmarole was interpreted in one way or another and the devoted trustees set to work to solve their problems in ways they thought the regulations stipulated.

The recommendations contained in the official directives were not always in the best interest of the residents as local conditions often made the advice impracticable. For instance, the Department of Education, in its wisdom, had decreed that each rural school was to be built in the exact geographical center of the district, but the exact center of the Twin Coulee S.D. (Vulcan, Alta.) occurred on a place surrounded by such a concentration of coulees and other bogholes that it made the spot almost unapproachable for much of the year, except if the person went on foot or rode horseback. After much discussion on an alternative site, and a few more recommendations from the Department of Education, the stalemate was finally resolved by building the school on the central site, coulees notwithstanding. The location of the school proved to be a bugbear for years to come for the children attending, as during foul weather the approaches became hazardous and difficult to navigate.

When a school was first contemplated by the settlers near Cayley, Alta., people homesteading to the west wanted it built on their side of Squaw Coulee, while those living on the east side were equally adamant that it should be erected on the east side of the Coulee. The school authorities who came to organize the district were unable to do so because of the location deadlock. Finally an ultimatum was issued to the district indicating that this was their last chance to resolve the problem. The two factions got together and decided to build the school on the bench-land near the base of the hill, approximately in the geographical center of the district, as originally recommended by the Department of Education. The residents also agreed on a most appropriate name for their district: Last Chance School District. Thus, the name became a constant reminder of its unique historical beginning as well as the bureaucratic nature of the Department of Education.

It doesn't take more than a cursory examination of the School Law and the School Ordinance of the early days to convince an interested person that the duties and responsibilities of the trustees were many and varied. Even excluding the main one, that of school financing, a comprehensive list still remains. Here are a few examples:

1. To procure a corporate seal for the district.
2. To purchase or rent school sites or premises and to build, repair, furnish and keep in order the schoolhouse or houses, furniture, fences and all other school property; to keep the well, closets and premises generally in a proper sanitary condition; and to make due provisions for properly lighting, heating, ventilating and cleaning the schoolroom or rooms under its control, and if deemed advisable to purchase or rent sites or premises for a house for the teacher and to build, repair and keep in order such house.

3. To select and provide from the list authorized by the Minister all such reference books for the use of the pupils and teachers and all such globes, maps, charts and other apparatus as may be required for the proper instruction of pupils.

4. To provide separate buildings for privies for boys and girls. The buildings shall be erected in the rear of the schoolhouse and at least ten feet apart, their entrances facing in opposite directions or otherwise effectually screened from each other.

5. To erect and keep in order if deemed advisable, suitable stabling accommodation.

6. To require that no textbooks or apparatus be used in the school under its control other than those authorized by the department.

7. To provide for the payment of teachers' salaries at least once in every three months.

8. To suspend or expel from school any pupil who upon investigation by the board is found guilty of truancy, open opposition to authority, habitual neglect of duty, the use of profane or improper language or other conduct injurious to the moral tone or well-being of the school.

9. To see that the law with reference to compulsory education and truancy is observed.

10. To provide wholesome drinking water for the use of the children during school hours.

11. To provide when deemed expedient a suitable library for the school and to make regulations for its management.

12. To settle all disputes arising in relation to the school between the parents or children and the teacher.

13. A teacher shall not be engaged except under the authority of a resolution of the board passed at a regular or special meeting of the board.

14. It shall be the duty of the trustees and their successors to cause to be erected and maintained on the school grounds a flag-pole with all requisite attachments for raising and lowering a flag, and to furnish a flag which shall be the British Union Jack to be no less than four feet long and not less than two feet wide, and to cause said flag to be displayed from such flag-pole upon all such days as may be prescribed by regulations, and when not so displayed to be hung upon the wall inside the schoolroom.

15. School shall be held between nine o'clock and twelve o'clock in the forenoon and half-past one o'clock and four o'clock in the afternoon of every day, standard time, not including Satur-

day, Sundays or holidays, but the board may alter or shorten the
school hours upon receiving the permission of the Minister.

16. A recess of fifteen minutes in the forenoon and the afternoon shall
be allowed the children attending school.

17. The board of any district may direct that school be opened at 9:30
a.m. during the whole or portion of the months of November,
December, January and February; and the board of any rural
district may direct that only one hour's intermission be taken at
noon, in which case school shall be closed at 3:30 p.m.

18. All school library and reference books purchased by the boards
for the use of pupils and teachers, except those received from the
Department in lieu of grants or those contained in school library
lists authorized by the Department, shall be subject to the
approval of the Minister.

The school was usually the first communal effort in the district and left
everyone with a feeling of belonging. The elected trustees, imbued with the
same spirit, performed their duties at the start of their terms of office with
enthusiasm and dispatch. But once the school and the other buildings were
erected, the furnishings, equipment and supplies procured, the teacher
hired, the business procedure of tax collection and payments resolved, and
the day-to-day school activities functioning well, an atmosphere of apathy
and well-being seemed to settle over the district. Only the school boards that
had dedicated, public spirited trustees who firmly believed in the value of
education continued to perform their duties effectively. The annual reports
submitted by school inspectors to their respective departments of education
often berated school boards for their incompetence, ignorance and lack of
application and foresight.

Inspector M. O. Nelson's 1914 report to the Alberta Department of
Education stated:

As a rule the grounds are well-fenced, but here the effort to improve
them ends. In only a few instances has any attention been devoted to
beautifying the grounds by means of tree-planting or school-garden-
ing. It is to be regretted that trustees and even parents and teachers so
often fail to realize that bright, cheerful and attractive surroundings
are important factors in awakening and strengthening the aesthetic
side of child nature. The school as the district center should be an
object lesson in cleanliness, orderliness and attractiveness, but one is
forced to admit that in many instances the school is allowed to fall
below the general standard set by he community.

Inspector P. H. Thibaudeau's 1910 annual report alluded to the
unsanitary conditions that prevailed in most rural schools:

There is no getting away from the fact that most of the rural schools
are unsanitary, to say the least. It is evident in the majority of cases

that when rural school trustees pay $60.00 or $70.00 a month for a teacher they feel as if they had gone their limit and could not possibly carry the additional burden for a part-time caretaker.

The prescriptive nature of the School Law should have facilitated the work of the trustees, but in actual practice this did not turn out to be the case. Local problems often had a uniqueness that did not relate to any of the general regulations, thus forcing the trustees to grapple on their own with an endless variety of issues associated with the operation of their schools.

In the Buffalo Horn Valley S.D. 930 (Swift Current, Sask.), it was the irregular attendance of the teacher that confronted the school board. She had the habit of going home on weekends and not always getting back on Mondays. Once she missed two consecutive days. The trustees, in their wisdom, sent the secretary with a strong warning that she must attend more regularly. She became haughty and said, "I don't much care whether I teach or not. I want to go to Japan and become a missionary!" The secretary replied, "Well, Japan isn't where the trustees told me to tell you to go, but I guess if you go to Japan they will be satisfied!"

An episode in the Ardath S.D. (Conquest, Sask.) created a good deal of controversy in the district when the school board set an age limit for children starting school. In spite of the regulation, one family insisted on sending a little girl who was much too young to commence her schooling. The teacher was instructed, "Just ignore her!" One day when the youngster sat dejectedly in front of her home, a curious visitor asked her how she liked school. The child replied, "Well, they ain't larned me nothing' yet!"

When the Panorama SD. 251 (Cabri, Sask.) was first erected in the spring of 1912, some of the young people in the district decided it was about time to have a dance. The members of the school board passed a motion to the effect that no dances were to be held in the new school, and advised the young people accordingly. In addition, on the night scheduled for the dance, the trustees went to the school, barricaded the door on the inside and departed through a window. When the dancers arrived they did not hesitate to enter the school in the same way that the board members had made their exit a little earlier — through the window. In no time the barricade was removed and the dance started. They had a wonderful system of lighting that night as everyone attending brought along a stable lantern. The music was supplied by Mr. Droper on his fiddle, so there was no lack for an orchestra. Just when the activities were well on their way, the school-board members arrived to put out the intruders and enforce their edict regarding no dancing in the school. The officials failed miserably, for not only were they outnumbered many times, but since the dancers were having such a fine time they were in no mood to be deprived of their fun. It is sufficient to add that the dance continued all night until broad daylight. The activity was such a success that it was decided to hold another one. Soon posters appeared advertising the second dance. They read, "There will be a dance in the Panorama School on Friday, June 4. Gentlemen are requested to bring their boxing gloves and the ladies their running shoes!" There wasn't much the school board could do but stay away from the dances as a sign of their displeasure.

Most school boards were confronted at one time or another with the problem of finding board and room for their teachers. It didn't take long for the trustees to discover that the school districts that had a teacher's residence, or a good boarding place near the school, had the least difficulty in securing teachers. The school board members of the Crowfoot S.D. 2393 realized this and provided their teachers with a portable residence. This home could be moved anywhere in the district to suit the convenience of the teacher after she had secured boarding accommodation with some family.

At times, conscientious rural teachers became frustrated when they realized that no matter how hard they worked with the pupils, the results were far from satisfactory, because of the mental capacities of the youngsters. Then it was up to the school boards to take cognizance of the situations and lend moral support to the discouraged teachers. One perplexed schoolmarm described her untenable situation in this way:

> School was no comfort to me. I strove to supply the knowledge, incentive and ambition, but half the pupils made no progress whatsoever. Each morning I would say, "No matter how little I accomplish today, I will not let it upset me!" In half-an-hour the utter futility of it all would have me bordering on frenzy. Fortunately, the school board understood the circumstances. When one of the parents complained, the chairman replied, "No carpenter can accomplish much if he must work with poor lumber."

Unless the teacher concerned herself with the activities that went on during the daily recesses and the noon hour, they turned out to be periods for creating trouble instead of opportunities for relaxation and recreation. Unsupervised recesses created more problems than they ever solved. The minute books of thousands of rural schools and almost every inspector's annual report to the Department of Education contain numerous references to "recess high jink".

The sixth annual report of the Alberta Department of Education issued in 1914 contained the following pertinent instruction to all educators concerning the supervision of all recesses.

> We talk a great deal at conventions and read in school journals of developing character and training for good citizenship, but what character are we developing by merely making a boy sit quietly when in the schoolroom at his studies, and then let him run riot in language and deeds on the playground?

Mr. M. O. Nelson, an inspector of schools in Alberta, included the following observation about recesses in his 1913 report:

The playground is the child's kingdom, and here he is taught some of the highest duties of citizenship. How often does the inspector find the teacher sitting unconcerned inside the school during the recess and noon periods, while the children are running about the school premises without proper restraint or else standing listlessly about.

Incidents similar to the following one from the Hillsgreen S.D. 2610 (Morrin, Alta.) were bound to occur in an unsupervised schoolyard. Pete Notlands lived across the road from the school and was often called upon to carry out his duties as trustee. One day while he was working in his garden, he heard sounds of crying coming from the direction of the school. When he investigated, he discovered a small boy standing nude in the outhouse doorway. The board member exercised his authority then and there by retrieving the boy's clothes from the fence some hundred feet away where the pranksters had hung them. He also discovered that the teacher was unaware of the boy's predicament; she wasn't even aware that he was missing when school was called after the morning recess.

Irregular attendance of boys and girls and the indifference of parents concerning the education of their children were two weaknesses that characterized most rural schools. In spite of the fact that the School Law stated it was compulsory for children between the ages of seven and fifteen years living in the district to attend school, local authorities found the regulation difficult to enforce. During the fall and spring both younger and older children were kept at home to herd cattle and assist in the garden or in the field. Every farmer was doing it, including the trustees, so such instances of irregular attendance seemed entirely unavoidable and were overlooked. School inspectors and truant officers were responsible for dealing with this problem. Mr. M. M. O'Brein, the chief truant officer for the province of Alberta in 1914, visited the Quarrel S.D. 1504 to deal with the problem of poor attendance. He reported as follows:

> In the Quarrel School District during the second term of 1913, there was an enrollment of 12 and an average daily attendance of 5. I personally visited this district during the first term of 1914 and found that there were over 20 children of school age in the district, and these children had been in the district during 1913. I called on a number of parents and served warning notices in certain cases. As a result of the visit practically all the pupils of school age were enrolled and attending regularly. In two cases, however, the attendance was perfunctory and the parents of these children were called up before a Justice of Peace and a fine imposed. During the second term of 1914 there was an enrollment of 24 students in the school and an average attendance of 15.

Financial grants based on the number of days the school was kept open during the school term, the enrollment, and the regularity of attendance of the students, provided much of the incentive for the school board to try to

-- A. A. Elliott

Rural schools were given very little financial assistance from their school boards to purchase playground equipment. The Grand Ridge S.D. (Coronation, Alta.) was fortunate to have a ball and bat.

-- V. R. Johnston

Vernon Johnston, a pupil in the Helmsdale S.D. (Oyen, Alta.) imagines he's spying from a crow's nest on a ship's mast.

-- Horace Allen

The students and teacher (Horace Allen) of Ewelme High School stand proudly in front of their threshing-car caboose school.

— Phyllis McDonald

The Model-T Ford, in spite of its many idiosyncrasies, possessed some advantages over the horse-drawn lumber wagon or democrat, in taking the family for a drive.

— Mrs D. Parks

Pupils in the Rush Center S.D. 2769 (Esther, Alta.) travelled by covered sleighs constructed by fathers and sons, as no money was available during the depression period to purchase factory-made cutters.

— Ken Christiansen

This homemade two wheel conveyance was known as an "Anderson cart." It was made from parts of Model-T Fords by the Christiansen Family.

-- Peter Fehr

This Bennett buggy was made from a regular buggy frame with the spindles from a Model-T Ford welded to the buggy chassis. This unique transportation unit was used in the Balfour S.D. 4151 (Blumenhof, Sask.) by the Fehr children in 1931.

-- Mrs. J. H. Junson

Noreen, Beverley and Ian Robinson are pictured with their pony, "Tiny," pulling a cart made by their father, J. B. Robinson. They are ready to start out for the Bede S.D. (Melita, Man.) during the 1930s. Mr. Robinson made this light, bouncy cart from the metal-rimmed wooden wheels, axle, and springs of an old Model-T Ford, the iron piping from an old gate, some boards, and pieces of scrap iron. It was unpainted, but who could afford paint in those days!

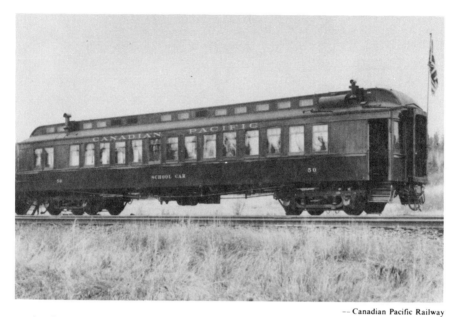

-- Canadian Pacific Railway

A school car was merely a classroom on wheels.

-- Ross Evans

Children entering a tree planting car anticipate learning something about trees and conservation.

Swift Current-Simmie Branch Line is under construction near the village of Vesper in southern Saskatchewan. The coming of the railway invariably brought an improvement in the type of education the rural schools were able to offer. The better-qualified teachers sought schools that were near centers of good communication and transportation.

-- Ken F. Cooper, *The Western Producer*
April 14, 1949

Cliff H. Wilbee, the conductor on a mixed train out of Prince Albert, is busy taking tickets.

-- Irene Wahl

Teco Lindstrom takes Irene Wahl, teacher in the Rocky Hill S.D. (Hanna, Alta.) to town in his homemade open-air car in 1932. All went well until they were within a few miles of Hanna, when a terrific dust storm arose. Irene, commenting about that particular trip, said, "What a mess we were by the time we reached town!"

— Mrs. J. W. Rogers

Wilbur Rogers, a bachelor, comes to court the young teacher of the Burns S.D. (Hanna, Alta.), as well as to take her to Coronation, Alta., so she can catch the train to her home in Nova Scotia. The mosquitoes were so bad, that he, buggy and horse were covered with them while the picture was being taken.

— Mrs. N. Charyk

Dorcus McGrath and Mary Bradley, two women who used to teach in the Laggan S.D. (Lake Louise, Alta.), found that because of the heavy snowfall in 1930, the only way of getting to school was to use skis or snowshoes.

— John C. Charyk

Most rural districts were served by competent and faithful school officials. Here is Lorne Proudfoot, the dedicated secretary-treasurer of the Chinook Consolidated S.D. 16 (Chinook, Alta.) who served the district well for thirty years. He is reading minutes at one of the annual ratepayers' meetings.

— Sylvia Wick

The pupils and teacher in a rural school were usually like a large happy family. Here the students and their teacher, Sylvia Wick, of Devonshire S.D. (Youngston, Alta.) celebrate the birthday of Fred Webber.

-- George Allen

The two-room brick school that was erected in the Surprise S.D. 2142 (Craigmyle, Alta.) in 1922 made it possible for two teachers to teach all grades up to and including grade eleven.

-- John C. Charyk

The attractive school built in the Chinook Consolidated S.D. 16 (Chinook, Alta.) in 1916 served the following rural school districts: Buffalo Plains S.D. 2316, Crocus S.D. 3355, Popular S.D. 2631, Carpathia S.D. 2963, and Bison S.D. 2824, for more than forty-five years. The brick building contained four large classrooms, an auditorium, a lunch room, a science area, an ancillary room, and a principal's office.

-- Mrs. R. Morrison

Clarence Collins raises the flag preparatory to the patriotic exercise of saluting it in the Albermarle S.D. (Rosetown, Sask.)

— Mrs. R. Morrison

Students salute the flag at the Albermarle S.D. (Rosetown, Sask.) in 1940.

— Mina (Klein) Tobin

The pupils of the Vindictive S.D. (Meyronne, Sask.) proudly display the coronation banner that won them first prize at an area field day in 1937.

keep school attendance at its highest possible percentage. When the Old Fort Macleod S.D. (Fort Macleod, Alta.) was first organized in 1885, Mr. A. F. Grady used to find it necessary to "round up" the seven pupils every morning in order for the district to qualify for the government grant. The work of Mr. Grady could be considered as the first parent-teachers' association organized in the territory that was eventually to become Alberta, for the express purpose of promoting education. The fact that the Fort Macleod School continued to run and draw its government grant speaks well for the effectiveness of Grady's parent-teachers' association.

Incidental things that could have facilitated the effectiveness of the overworked teacher were either overlooked by the school board or considered insignificant. The *Hanley Herald* rebuked the trustees of the Hanley S.D. (Hanley, Sask.) for one such oversight.

> It would be a good idea if the school trustees would have piled near the schoolhouse some firewood of such length that could be put in the stove in order that the teacher will not have to see that the wood is cut each day. The schoolteacher has enough to do without seeing about the wood.

One of the first purchases made by most rural school boards was *Webster's Unabridged Dictionary.* The size of the volume may have been impressive to the uninitiated, but such an unwieldy reference book was of little use to the children. So year in and year out the huge volume gathered dust and suffered wear and tear, not from any legitimate use, but from deleterious handling and student pranks. A smaller dictionary could have served the purpose much better, but not one in a hundred trustees had the foresight to discern this.

A disagreement arose in the Glenora S.D. 2314 (Viking, Alta.) as the teacher, Miss Norris, was giving religious instruction after school hours. She did it for the benefit of the Catholic children and did not solicit any converts from the other faiths. As the Protestants objected strongly to this, the school board decided to put it to a vote by all ratepayers and it was defeated by a narrow margin. The event caused bitterness between the Catholics and Protestants for many years to come, whereas before the referendum, there had not been any friction. The distressing situation could have been prevented in the first place if the school board had used a little diplomacy instead of forcing the district to take sides.

The idea of women's suffrage was not readily accepted in the early days. James Hosegood, who had a good boarding-school education, after serving on the school board of the Rugby S.D. (Didsbury, Alta.) for over eighteen years, finally resigned. He didn't mind one woman on the board, but he objected to serving with two of them. The minute book of the Morrin S.D. 2513 (Morrin, Alta.) contains a number of resolutions on this issue: "Moved by Mr. High, and seconded, that the chairman procure a muzzle for Mrs. High. No vote was taken." Also, "Resolved that the board will not in the future engage married women except as substitutes or under unusual circumstances."

When ratepayers' meetings were held to consider school business, they had the uncanny habit of turning into melodramatic affairs and certainly far removed from what one might expect from a gathering concerned with a purpose as serious and vital as education of the children of the district. For example, there was the time Herbert Coulson was chairing a special meeting in the Dauphin Plains S.D. 873 (Dauphin, Man.) for the purpose of electing a trustee. It appeared as if a close contest was shaping up and feelings were running high. According to some of the astute observers, it was apparent that the chairman would have to cast the deciding vote and thus incur the enmity of one or the other group of supporters. Such incidents in the past had been known to divide districts into two factions and it appeared as if Dauphin Plains would be next. A freak accident saved the situation. Minutes before the poll closed at noon, a farmer was seen approaching the school driving a horse and buggy at great speed. Just as he passed the school a wheel came off his vehicle. The driver, forced to stop until repairs could be made, came into the schoolhouse for help, and having nothing better to do in the interval, cast the winning vote.

Fate also played a part in procuring a school for the Arbogast S.D. (Langdon, Alta.). In 1915 the parents in the district who had children of school age were making a concerted effort to get a school established. Milton Doan, one of the concerned persons, travelled throughout the area and gathered up all the children of school age and called a school meeting at his place. He succeeded in getting eleven children, sufficient evidence, he thought, to convince everyone of the necessity of starting a school. As things turned out, it was a very heated meeting and the Arbogast School would never have come into being if one of the residents, who could not read, had not put his "X" in the wrong place.

Some school meetings in pioneer days proved to be almost complete farces. The secretary who recorded the minutes of the annual meeting of the Washington S.D. 1431 (Carmangay, Alta.) held in January, 1918, captured some of the ludicrousness that often characterized such gatherings.

> Very poor attendance owing to the fact that nearly everyone is in California at the present time. However, there was one person present who was willing to serve as a trustee in place of Mr. Griffen, whose term had expired, that being himself. Therefore he was elected by acclamation amids hearty applause from the ratepayers. As the books had not been audited the auditor's report was not available, and as the inspector had not turned up during the past year, we were also deprived to hearing his report. The weather was mild and balmy like a summer's day and the air fresh and pure as if it had been wafted from a bed of roses.

The financial burden of school support, then as now, was an ever-present problem for most school boards and took up most of their time. After all, the success of any rural school depended largely on the tax collections in the district, and to a lesser extent upon the grants received from the government. Under such a setup the equality of educational opportunities was impossible, for any advantages enjoyed by a particular child were determined by the wealth of the community in which he happened to reside. His capacity and his ambition were not always the factors which determined his success or failure.

Rural school boards seemed to drift from one financial crisis to another in their attempts to provide the best educational opportunities for the children of the districts. Many rural communities had new settlers who did not speak or understand English readily. They were quite at a loss when the word "taxes" was used. Their children went to school, but the parents didn't understand what was implied or involved when called upon to pay school taxes. The secretary-treasurer of any pioneer school district was the scapegoat for all such misunderstandings and remonstrations, but unlike the goat of the scriptures, he could not escape into the wilderness. He had to stay and take it. Undoubtedly it was expedient for the school board that he should be the target for any criticism, dissension or retaliation.

Rural schools were considered such a personal responsibility that at times a resident of the district was willing to put his own resources on the line to permit the school to continue operating. Stories of personal sacrifices for the cause of local education were common in the first part of the twentieth century. A couple of examples follow.

One year the Bellgrove S.D. 2390 (Delburne, Alta.) found itself in financial straits and was considering closing the school for the fall term. The problem was overcome when two residents of the district, Ernie Wallin, the secretary-treasurer for the school, and Mrs. Herve Johnson, a member of the school board, went to the bank in Delburne and signed personal loans to provide funds for the school to continue operating.

When a school district was suffering from a lack of funds to continue operating, it was usual for the worried secretary-treasurer to append a personal footnote to the tax notice, explaining the crisis and pleading for help. The "tax notice" below, issued in the Claremont S.D. (Gainsborough, Sask.) in 1903, is a good example of this type of stratagem.

School District of Claremont No. 164, North West Territories

To: Wm. McClung,
    Gainsborough, Sask.

You are hereby notified that you are assessed in the Assessment Roll of the above-named School District for the year 1903 for 320 acres of land, the tax on which at the rate of 1¾ cents per acre amounts to

$5.60, and you are further notified that the arrears of taxes due by you to the said District amount to $ ____ and you are required to pay the same forthwith.

Dated at Gainsborough, N.W.T. this
14th day of December, 1903.

T. A. Natrass
Secretary-Treasurer.

Teacher is going away next week and we need all the taxes to pay her off. Please help us out and oblige.

Yours truly,
T. A. Natrass.

The thirties were trying times indeed for most rural schools. It was a wonder that so many were able to carry on in spite of the economic recession. The debts incurred during this period, particularly teachers' salaries, took years to repay. There were instances where teachers did not receive final payments of their back wages until the good crop year came along, or until the wartime prosperity of the 1940s. Minute books and financial statements of school districts, perhaps better than any other documents, tell of the struggle that most boards had in trying to keep their schools open. Unfortunately, each such financial setback meant a corresponding decline in the type of education that the children received. It was the youngsters who suffered the most, and through them the nation's potential.

The fire insurance of the Diamond Coulee S.D. had lapsed in 1934, and in the interval, when the school was uninsured, the following motion appeared in the minutes of a board meeting:

> That from this date on, until a new insurance on the buildings is secured, any person using the school for any purpose other than school purposes, shall be required to put up a bond to the value of the schoolhouse. Carried.

In the same year, 1934, the following self-explanatory motion was also recorded: "That application be made through the Relief Commission for fifteen tons of coal. Carried."

Money was scarce and difficult to collect, so bartering became a way of life. If the farmers who took turns in boarding the teacher wanted to pay their school taxes but had no money, the school board charged these amounts against the teacher's salary account. This bookkeeping strategy enabled the trustees to pay the teacher a part of her salary, the farmers to pay their taxes, and the teacher to meet her board-and-room commitments. No cash was involved in any of the three transactions, yet each party received a receipt for fulfilling their financial obligations. Labor, professional services and many commodities like meat, potatoes and eggs, were bargained in this manner.

A sampling of rural school minute books always reveals the same story; namely, the vexatious financial situation.

> Moved by Mr. Hemstock, seconded by Mr. Greenwood, that the Board engage Mrs. Grimes as teacher at a salary of $500.00 a year, providing she is willing to accept instalments on her salary according to the ability of the district to pay. (Dundee S.D. 4326 [Hanna, Alta.] September 4, 1934)

> Moved by R. Chidley that the school be closed for the holidays and not be opened until a survey is conducted of how the school is going to be financed, and further we appoint J. Wallace to look into the question and report back to us. (Corinne S.D. 2497 [Hanna, Alta.] June 30, 1934)

> Moved that W. L. Cole interview Miss Tedford regarding tendering her resignation as her present salary is too high to suit present conditions. (Craig Murray, S.D. 3202 [Cereal, Alta.] December 20, 1930)

> The secretary reported that no monies had been received so it was moved by H. Hansen that the secretary pay all bills when monies, if ever, are available. (Merrickville S.D. 4114 [Oyen, Alta.] December 15, 1936)

> Due to financial difficulties a petition be sent to the Minister for permission to close school for the months of January and February, 1934. This permission was granted under the date of December 26, 1933. (Esther S.D. 4038 [New Brigden, Alta.] December 11, 1933)

Perhaps the most pathetic of all schoolboard minutes was formulated at the final meeting of Liman S.D. (Sunnynook, Alta.). The board decided they had had enough of organized education and turned in their official audit and all the rest of the records to Larry Helmer, a municipal official. In looking over the minutes of the final meeting of the board, Mr. Helmer's attention was drawn to the last resolution, passed unanimously. It read as follows:

> Moved . . . and seconded . . . that we close the school, the buildings be painted red, a white elephant drawn over the door and the school steps colored brown so as to blend with any deposit that might be made upon them in the future.

School boards considered hiring the teacher as one of their more important functions. Hence it didn't take them very long, after one or two sad experiences, to discover that the quality of education in the districts depended almost entirely on the teachers they selected. In the earlier years most school boards relied on the services of teacher agencies to get them applicants. These teacher's bureaus, organized in connection with provincial departments of education, gave free services to boards of trustees and teachers. Their role was to act as intermediaries between teachers looking for positions and school boards with vacancies to be filled. This service proved beneficial to both trustees and teachers. Later, school boards depended on the normal school facilities, the inspectors, friends or relatives of teachers, and extensive advertising in daily papers and local weeklies, to secure contacts with prospective teachers.

Once in a while a school board thought it could do a better job of selecting a good teacher if they held personal interviews with two or three of their more promising applicants. This method was slow, time-consuming, exasperating and expensive, so very few rural school boards used it. One school board that relied on this method of selecting its teacher had a unique method of doing it. On the day set for the interviews, the trustees scattered two or three books on the floor at the front of the schoolroom and then took their places at the back to conduct the interviews. Teachers who stepped on or over the books were told bluntly they did not qualify. The first one who picked up the books and fastidiously placed them on a desk or table was hired. Apparently this board figured that the person who demonstrated neatness, order and a respect for books, would prove to be the best teacher.

Another school board that put its faith in the interview method used to ask the applicant something about the students and parents in his former school. If he was critical or uncomplimentary, he was not hired; but if he spoke highly of his previous pupils and school, he was accepted on the spot. This board felt that a teacher always reflected the kind of school and community he was himself.

According to the 1913 annual report submitted by Inspector J. A. MacGregor to the Alberta Department of Education, many rural school boards were not sufficiently on the alert in the matter of engaging teachers.

> In these districts the secretary is instructed to advertise for a teacher, which he accordingly does, and receives one or two, possibly more, applications. He may not get his mail regularly, and by this time two or more weeks have elapsed. He then calls a meeting of the board, and they finally decide upon one of the applications, only to learn after another week or so that their choice has been engaged in some other district for some time previously. I have in mind a district that has accepted three different teachers since the new year, and their school is still vacant, simply because the trustees have not acted with dispatch. This condition of affairs could, to a large extent, be avoided if school boards authorized one of their number to engage a teacher,and in doing so to choose, if possible, a member who can be reached by telephone.

The accent of a teacher in the Livingstone S.D. 1685(Brownlee, Sask.) led to so much misinterpretation by the students that the board decided to get another teacher. On August 3, 1908, the following motion was passed to prevent the recurrence of such a problem.

> That we accept the application of Mr. Nelson Hanna as teacher for the remainder of the school year provided that he has no objectionable brogue, and if he has any objectionable brogue, then we accept the application of W. H. Hegland, and that if we employ either one, and he gives satisfaction, we promise that he shall be re-employed for 1909.

During periods of economic adversity teachers were plentiful and school boards would receive anywhere from thirty to several hundred applications in reply to their advertisements for a teacher. Then it became a matter akin to drawing the winning ticket in a lottery in selecting a teacher. Irrelevent and insignificant criteria would be used to determine the successful applicant: handwriting, quality and color of the paper on which the application was written, the name of the teacher's home town, the occupation of her father, a catchy phrase used in the letter, or even her picture if she was good-looking.

No matter what the challenge was, most trustees accepted it and tried to do their best. One foggy evening, Will Priest, one of the three board members of the Gledhow S.D. (Delisle, Sask.), set out to attend an important meeting in the schoolhouse, a mile south of his place. His dog followed him in spite of his efforts to send it home. On the way to school Will became hopelessly lost in the fog. He turned to his faithful canine and this time in a more friendly tone said, "Let's go home!" She guided him home safely. Still thinking he could find his way to school, he started off again. Once more he became lost and had to rely on his dog to guide him home. After this, Mr. Priest decided he had tried enough and gave up the idea of attending the meeting.

The school board of the Bristow S.D. 3488 (Islay, Alta.) transacted its school business in January, 1920, in spite of the fact that one of the hardest winters in Alberta's history made it impossible for them to get together for a meeting. They accomplished this by holding a meeting by telephone. The board members, W. Urquhart, S. L. Potter, N. Stone and the secretary-treasurer, A. Chambers, were all present on the line and conducted their business as usual; it took less time than ever before. Ratepayers who were lucky enough to have telephones were able to listen in on the proceedings. This was probably the most democratic school board meeting the trustees ever held.

A chairman of a rural school was not happy with the lackadaisical manner with which the board members paid attention during the course of their meetings. He eventually came up with a solution. Instead of having the regular secretary-treasurer take the minutes, he made the following startling announcement at the beginning of one of their regular meetings: "From now on, to insure your individual attention, I'll indicate at the end of each meeting who will write up the minutes." The chairman succeeded in his subterfuge, although his action never received official approval from the Department of Education.

No history of rural education would be complete without some reference to the work of school inspectors. Records indicate that most of the labor of organizing, establishing, furnishing, administrating and operating school in the first half of the twentieth century was accomplished largely under their guidance and supervision. However, their main function was to inspect, and that entailed criticism. Unfortunately, the majority employed a negative approach in their evaluations. Their work could have been more constructive if they had commented on any of the short-cuts or improvements they saw the more experienced and better teachers using. It was the advent of the "inspector's report" that forced the school inspectors to be strict scrutinizers of what was happening or not happening in each rural school. It was necessary for them to direct their attention to the work of the teacher and to a lesser degree, the efforts of the school board. Each inspector must have filled out volumes of these "inspector's reports" during his years of service.

Did these reports serve a useful purpose? Department of Education officials of those early years felt they did. In particular, they pointed to the fact that the documents had a way of prompting better teaching in the classrooms. They firmly believed that the reports served as a spur to the weak teacher to strive for higher efficiency and as an encouragement to the strong teacher to continue the good work. The school boards soon considered the inspector's report as one of the best yardsticks for determining the ability of a teacher and began the practice of asking applicants to enclose with their applications, copies of their last reports from the inspector. If good, these reports constituted the best testimonials applicants could submit. Teachers also felt more confident knowing the complete report by the inspector, whereas formerly there was always some doubt as to whether the report to the school board was the same as that given orally to the teacher. A written statement of the excellence and defects of a teacher's work, with suggestions as to the means of improving weaknesses in management or methods of instruction, was of value and of use to the conscientious teacher.

Erstwhile inspectorates were very large and contained up to 175 school districts. It was all the inspector could do to visit each school once a year; in addition, he had to attend to his office work or to any emergencies that required his attention. In 1909 for instance, the Edmonton Inspectorate, later known as the Strathcona Inspectorate, contained 160 schools and all but three were visited once and ten of them twice during the year by John Ross, the inspector.

J. F. Boyce, an Alberta inspector of schools, made the following shrewd observation in 1914:

It would be a great boon to rural education if an inspector had only about 75 schools in order that he might visit more frequently, remain longer, become better acquainted with the pupils and people of the district and be more helpful generally to the teacher, trustees and all concerned. It is strange, yet true that, notwithstanding an inspector may have visited some districts ten or twelve times, but because of so many changes taking place, each visit is practically the same as his first visit to a newly-organized school.

The inspector's buggy in summer and his cutter in winter were a familiar sight to thousands of rural school children and their teachers during the early days of the history of Canada. Travel by horses was slow and consumed a large portion of the inspector's valuable time as he made the rounds of the schools in his area. No one was more pleased than the school inspectors when the automobile came into common use. Perhaps the best statistical comparison between the inspector using car transportation as opposed to using horse transportation was given by Inspector J. A. MacGregor in 1918 when he resumed his duties in the Three Hills' Inspectorate of Alberta after an absence of some three years.

Since resuming the work of inspection in September last, after being out of it for practically the duration of the war, I'm impressed with the use of the motor car in carrying on inspection work. Prior to the war, a horse, or a team of horses and a buggy, was the standard mode of conveyance used to reach schools located away from the railroads. To visit a school twenty miles away and to return to the starting point would mean that six hours of the day would be spent on the road, and having inspected the school, with night coming on and a tired team of horses, a special effort was necessary to pay a visit to the secretary-treasurer, and by so doing several extra miles would be added to the journey. With the motor car all this is changed. The time spent on the road is one-third of what it was, while with no effort it is possible to visit not only the secretary but also other members of the board of trustees.

Rural teachers were apprehensive of school inspectors and over the years often posed the question, "Why are they such bogies?" The following stories might provide at least part of the answer.

Emma Rabourn of Medicine Hat, Alberta looked back on her ten years of teaching in rural schools in Saskatchewan, and decided to put on paper some of her observations and experiences for other teachers to read, in the hope that the information would provide a pleasing potpourri of inspiration, recreation and practical education. This month by month diary-like account which she entitled, "Ten Years A Teacher," was recorded in two old-time scribblers and contains many interesting ideas and suggestions. One day in March she had her first visit from a school inspector.

Queer what little crazy details one's mind retains and what important ones it forgets. For instance, I remember distinctly that I was working a problem on page thirty-eight in the algebra textbook when I had my first call from a school inspector some twenty years ago. I probably remember the page so well because during the interval from the time I answered the door and welcomed our guest to when I resumed my lesson, I lost my place in the book and was so nervous that it took me, what seemed eternity, to find the page again.

Mr. Leoppky was one of the kindest men I have known and made very little disturbance in the classroom routine during his visits; besides, he had taught me how to pick out noun clauses when I was in grade six and inspected schools when I was a pupil during most of my childhood, so I had no reason to be afraid of him. You young teachers will know how it is by this time! Anyway, Mr. Leoppky straightened out my glasses for me and informed me of a great truth. "You know," he said, "individuals who were good pupils do not always make good teachers!"

I'm afraid that as time went on he considered me a good example of this bit of wisdom. A year or two later, when I was teaching at the Memora School, a very embarrassing incident occurred. Some children had brought a dead long-legged, long-billed bird to school on this particular morning expecting that the teacher, who knew everything, would be able to identify it for them. As it wasn't one of the common birds in the district I was "stumped". We nicknamed it "The Pelican" for the time being and I promised to look up his real name in a bird book I had at home. By the time Mr. Leoppky arrived after dinner I had forgotten there ever was such a bird.

Things sailed along on a fairly even keel throughout the afternoon, although I expect it was a day when I had my lessons rather sketchily prepared because that always seemed to be the day inspectors had the habit of dropping in. After school was dismissed, we had a nice cosy chat about things in general, and by the time I was ready to bid him good-bye at the door, I was glowing with self-confidence and the thrill of success. My pleasure was short-lived. On opening the door we both noticed flapping at the upper end of the flagpole, not the good old tattered Union Jack, but Mr. Pelican. Was my face red?

Louise M. Laas recalls Mr. O'Brien, an inspector who was stationed in Regina and inspected schools in the area north of Humboldt, Sask., during the twenties and thirties. She remembers him first while attending a rural school as a pupil, and later as a teacher in his inspectorate. Her impressions were brief but trenchant.

Inspector O'Brien drove a horse and buggy in summer and a cutter in winter. He invariably scared "hell" out of the kids and the young teachers, then gave a good report.

Milton Miles, who started school in the Centerview S.D. (Bentley, Alta.) in 1905 had a similar opinion of his inspector.

> I must tell you of our inspector. He was a very large man, past middle age, and quite stout. He always had a scowl on his face and was just as crabby as he was big. I think I can truthfully say I never had such a fear of man or beast as of this inspector. The other pupils were as scared of him as I was. I believe most of the teachers were afraid of being clouted by him as well.

Most visits of the inspector ended with the young teacher shedding tears. Nina Harris, a former pupil in the Mica S.D. 2728 (Lomond, Alta.), who started attending the school in 1922 remembers her school inspector with some trepidation.

> The yearly visit of the inspector was looked on with apprehension by each teacher and left most of them in tears. We felt sorry for the teacher on such occasions and tried our best to please the stern invader so he would not be so hard on her.

Much of the dread of inspector was provoked by emulation. The older students passed on their fears to the younger ones, and they in turn to their primary-grade successors. E. Taylor, a grade one student in the New Berghtal S.D. 779 (Carstairs, Alta.), realized this but still acquired a fear complex from her schoolmates.

> The school inspector, poor soul, was held in great awe and fear, but never in admiration that I can recall. Personally, I never could see what was so fear-striking in the gentlemen that came to our school about once or twice a year, but the older children acted as if he was one of Frankenstein's monsters, and the rest of us accepted this travesty without question.

Perhaps women inspectors could have changed this attitude, but no ladies ever made it to the inspector's post. The travelling involved and the rough-and-ready type of living while on the road wasn't always what a woman would find easy or care to do.

Not all teachers or students had derogatory opinions of school inspectors. Maude Silverthorn, a teacher in the Longview S.D. (Rouleau, Sask.) in 1912, for instance, found the visit of the inspector agreeable and of assistance.

> The inspector was welcomed and helped me with my teaching problems. You could always see the strange horse and buggy coming more than a mile away and had time to tidy your hair and prepare the children for the crucial morning or afternoon. He usually had a bag of candy for the children and frequently knew someone from my home town which made us look forward to his annual visit.

The following story concerning Hugh Robert Parker who was appointed school inspector for the Vermilion area in Alberta in 1910 and continued to hold this position, with the exception of a couple of years, until his retirement in 1936, came from so many sources that it must be true. At the time of the incident Mr. Parker was regarded as the "dean of Alberta school inspectors."

Any time Mr. Parker visited a school he had the habit of asking the pupils to prepare a composition on some topic he thought pertinent to the time of year that he was inspecting the school. On this occasion the subject was, "A Prairie Blizzard", and as was his custom he wrote the title of the topic on the blackboard. Soon the students were hard at work on the assignment. The youngsters were given their usual recess and when school reassembled after the break, everyone instantly noticed that the "B" had been erased from the title on the blackboard, making it read, "A Prairie lizzard". Such a breach of discipline, especially during the inspector's visit, required immediate action. The frustrated teacher called the most-likely troublemakers into the cloakroom and questioned them about the matter. Since no one confessed to erasing the "B", all were strapped and asked to stay in during all the recesses for a week. In the meantime the compositions were turned in, checked by Mr. Parker, and in due course the incident was forgotten. But the mystery of who erased the "B" remained unsolved and continued to haunt the thoughts of the children.

Years later, one of the pupils who had been strapped for his supposed involvement in the "B" matter was recognized by Mr. Parker.

"Did your teacher or any of the students ever find out who rubbed the 'B' off 'Blizzard' the day I visited your school?" asked the inspector.

"No! We never did find out who the mean, nasty rascal was," replied the young man haughtily.

"Well, I did!" boasted Mr. Parker.

During the years when the country was being settled, the school inspectors, whatever their shortcomings may have been, were still the guardians of the very foundation of society, the schools. To them fell the responsibility of ensuring that the new nation developed steadily through the educational nurture supplied by the thousands of one-room rural schools that dotted the country. The rural schoolhouse type of education, in spite of its weaknesses, was a proud moment in the building of Canada.

Mr. J. J. Stapleton, a school inspector in the Regina area in 1918, made the following thoughtful observation of the growth of education on the Canadian prairies:

> The smiling blue skies, the vast, lonely prairies, the all-enveloping glorious evening solitudes together with the ever-present struggle for existence against the fickle and adverse climatic conditions, working through contrast and antithesis, are rapidly developing a type of mankind peculiarly at home in this broad west. Sublimely optimistic, patriotic, freedom-loving and impatient of restraint under whatever guise it may appear, these people are passionately interested in the

education of their children and restive under the handicap of present conditions.

The settled parts of rural Canada continued the practice of organizing themselves into school districts each from sixteen to twenty square miles in extent, each with its own school board and each an autonomous unit of administration. Such a system of administration represented decentralization of authority to the greatest possible extent and suffered all of the weaknesses of uncorrelated effort. By 1935 it had become apparent to those who had made any comprehensive study of conditions, that educational progress, especially in rural areas, had reached its practical limit unless there were developed some sort of administrative unit which could deal with problems over a larger area and with the ability to bring greater resources to bear upon them.

It was also clearly evident that there were vast differences in the educational opportunities afforded rural children, not only over the whole country, but even in adjoining districts. Most schools were too small to make even the least attempt to provide advanced and diversified courses of instruction. There was great variation in the incidence of taxation. There was no schedule of salaries for teachers and no channel of promotion for them other than that of shifting from one employing board to another. Administration and the relationship of the communities to the schools in far too many districts were at a very petty level.

Successful experiments already had been made in the centralization of rural schools in Great Britain and in the United States. The province of Alberta tried it out in the Berry Creek Area, a drought-ridden southeastern part of the province, and in Turner Valley, an industrialized oil-producing region south of Calgary. These trial runs in two such vastly different economic areas proved to be so successful that the minister of education of Alberta was determined that legislation should be provided which would enable him to extend the principle of centralization throughout the province. In 1936 the legislature amended the School Act to provide for the establishment of large units of administration. This was the first move of its kind in Canada.

Each unit, which eventually became known as a school division, consisted of sixty to eighty districts, with some smaller ones necessitated by geographical considerations and sparseness of settlement. The boundaries were determined only after a careful consideration of topography, transportation facilities, population, marketing centers and community congruencies. There was considerable opposition to the idea, but within ten years some of the vocal objection subsided and changed to passive acceptance.

The affairs of a school division were administered by a board of trustees, three or five in number, each representing a subdivision and elected for a period of three years. The divisional school board not only did for each school what the local board was expected to do, but in addition was able to provide for its component units services which, as individuals, they could not have obtained without this correlated effort, such as: high-school education for every child, which in the past had been almost entirely a matter of parent responsibility; vastly-improved library facilities, especially in the number of up-to-date textbooks, reference books and free-reading materials; increased health services; greater diversity of programs that could be offered in the schools; and more and better equipment. Systematic repair programs covering both buildings and equipment were introduced, and where necessary many one-room schools were replaced by more modern buildings. It was found that the business operation of 60 or 85 districts from one central office proved to be much more economical than the administration of these as separate entities. Even the wholesale purchase of supplies of all kinds, whether it was paint, coal or dictionaries, proved to be a great saving over the retail method that had been employed by the individual local boards.

When low attendance warranted the closing of a school and it was within daily driving distance of another, that school would be closed, transportation arranged and the disused building moved to another site or otherwise disposed of. Now, one building, one teacher and one set of equipment was able to do the work of two or more schools. This type of area centralization continued everywhere, until the one-room country schools disappeared almost entirely and in their stead were a few graded schools located in strategic localities throughout the division. The distance problem was solved by the use of buses to transport the children from their farm homes to the closest central schools. Sometimes, when it was not feasible to provide bus transportation, dormitories were operated for the benefit of the rural students. Thus centralization spelled the end of the era of the one-room rural school.

The introduction of the larger unit of administration changed the duties of the school inspector so dramatically, that in keeping with his new role, he was designated as the school superintendent. Probably the most revolutionary innovation was in the official's attitude respecting teachers. Since he was no longer expected to inspect, it was no longer necessary for him to grade a teacher in his inspection report. As a result, the reports themselves became less formal and eventually lost their former importance and sting. It was now possible for the superintendent to take time to give help and encouragement to the teachers. He could visit them as many times as he thought necessary to work with them to overcome any weaknesses, and stimulate them in their duties. However, it took many years for the teachers to become convinced that the superintendent was no longer there to inspect them, but to help them become more effective teachers. The dread of his visit was still there and probably always will be, but since he kept in touch with the teachers to an extent unknown before, he came to be accepted as a vital part of the process of maintaining, improving and inspiring education in the schools for the benefit of all boys and girls.

11

Beyond the Classroom

One of the educational highlights in the lives of prairie children until the mid-thirties was the Chautauqua. This was a travelling professional cultural show that provided a once-a-year treat for people during the summer and fall months in every hamlet, town and city from one end of the country to the other. Many families in those early days were unable to travel even to the nearest large center and hence were starved for culture, stimulation and good entertainment. The Chautauqua programs were of high caliber and filled a great need when there was no televison and radio was in its infancy and beyond the financial reach of most people in rural communities. Lecturers and entertainers from every part of the globe brought the world to the people's doorsteps. It offered food for thought in drama, opera, high-minded debate and lecture, music of all types, and sentimental corn for laughs, all served in a carnival atmosphere of wholesomeness and spangles that appealed to the entire family. Also, there were special programs, features and activities for the children which made it just that more attractive. Because the programs were held in a tent, the majority of people assumed it was something between a circus and a revival meeting and who could resist attending such an event.

The strange name of "Chautauqua" was derived from a town called Chautauqua in the state of New York, where popular summer concerts, lectures and university courses had been given since 1874. The idea of travelling Chautauqua was sparked by these performances, but there was no direct connection. The new version of Chautauqua became so popular that in 1926 alone, it is estimated that thirty million people attended in North America.

It thrived in the United States for some forty-three years before it saw the light of day in Canada in 1917. But once introduced it continued for nineteen years. J. M. Erickson came to Lethbridge, Alberta in 1916 to investigate the possibility of bringing Chautauqua to the Canadian prairies. The time was opportune, for S. S. Dunham, who was the vice-president of the Lethbridge United Farmers of Alberta at the time, immediately saw the value of Chautauqua for rural people and gave his support. He was the first man in Canada to sign a Chautauqua contract as a patron. In no time at all, with his encouragement and support, the Taber, Cayley, Nanton and Fort MacLeod districts were signed up. Such a show of interest was sufficient to obtain the necessary financial backing from the United States, and soon after Chautauqua became a reality in hundreds of prairie towns.

A 1912 Chautauqua magazine spelled out the aims of the organization as follows:

> Chautauqua presents the most wholesome entertainment, the greatest thinkers, the most satisfying artists and brings the best in the world right to your door.

The influence of Chautauqua was no doubt profound. A guest columnist of an article in the *Chautauqua Scout* of 1921 wrote:

> It seems to me that there is one feature of Chautauqua about which not enough has been said, and that is the 'getting together' feature. Under the Chautauqua tent we can all greet each other as brother and sister if we want to, and this is the part that appeals to me more than any other single thing.

One avid supporter said, "I feel that the Dominion Chautauqua is the chief factor in making life liveable in the rural areas and small towns of Western Canada."

The Chautauqua would not come to any center without a guarantee, so advance booking agents travelled the circuits, held meetings with the communities' influential people (businessmen, clergymen, school principals and farmers), generated enthusiasm for the show, and signed up the town or village for the coming season, In 1930, for instance, a $1500 contract provided for eleven performances of professional quality. A full week's admission cost $2.50 for adults and $1.50 for students, and the local committees worked hard to sell the advance tickets as they had to guarantee a minimum amount from the sale of them, or make up the balance from their own pockets. If there was any profit from the sale of season tickets it was split between the Chautauqua and the local committees. It was said that many fine community halls were built with the local committee's share of the profits.

Chautauqua was well advertised. All the rural schools in the area were visited, usually by a personable young lady who whetted the appetite of the youngsters by describing the treats in store for them at the Chautauqua. Attractive posters lured many to the gala week of entertainment. For instance, the advertising for the comedy play, "Daddy Long Legs" in 1914 carried the following catchy message: "If you take your pencil and write down in a vertical column the words delightful, sweet, beautiful, entertaining, and then draw a line and add them up, the answer will be, "Daddy Long Legs".

-- Mildred Affleck

Pictured (at left) is a cover design of the printed program prepared by the Canadian Chautauqua, advertising the daily program for each of the four or six days that they performed in a particular community.

-- Mildred Affleck

Comments and illustrations advertising the Elias Tamburitza Serenaders and Zellner, the protean artist, exemplify the type of information contained in a Chautauqua program.

The travelling promoters, who usually were talented women, got none of the glory, all the headaches and very little of the profits. An illustration of what they were up against is told in the following story:

"Seems to me," says the aged farmer, "that your show wouldn't go if you didn't send a lot of pretty girls to vamp men into buying tickets." The lady superintendent replied, "Well now, be honest! I'm asking you to buy a ticket and I'm not pretty, am I?" The old farmer scratched his head, thought for a while and commented, "Well yer can't say yer so durned scabby looking at that!"

The director arrived in town in plenty of time before the first show to see that the tickets were all sold, the hall or tent was in readiness, and that each group of artists arrived and left on time. This responsible individual also acted as master of ceremonies at each performance, announcing the various numbers and supplying enough introductory material to make each show just that more informative and interesting. He or she was the public relations officer for the troupe and the success of the Chautauqua at any particular center depended on his or her ability in this field.

Probably the director's most important function was to sell the contract for the following year. This meant obtaining enough sponsors to agree to sell tickets to make up the necessary guarantee. It wasn't always easy to achieve this, especially during times of economic recession. In fact, it was the depression of the thirties that spelled the end of Chautauqua on the prairies. The tragic death blow always took the same course, described by the following note from Byemoor, Alberta.

The last year, 1931, the guarantee was not raised as the sponsors could not sell enough tickets. The sponsors had to make up the deficit. It was impossible for the director to sell the contract for 1932. As a result Chautauqua ended in Byemoor.

On the day the big brown Chautauqua tent went up in a cow pasture, vacant lot or town square and the wooden benches and the stage were put into place, it was the signal for the start of a great week of educational entertainment and excitement for everyone in the district. There was always a big dress parade the morning of the opening day, and every forenoon at the Chautauqua grounds was the time for fun and games for all the children; the scheduled performances were held every afternoon and evening. People travelled miles to attend and often camped in town for the whole week and enjoyed wholesome entertainment, inspiring music and instructive lectures. It was an exciting time to say the least, and the following reminiscences, each from a different person, indicate just what the rural youngsters thought of Chautauqua.

Among my school memories was the day at Chautauqua when a ventriloquist astounded us with a conversation carried on with someone upstairs. We knew there was no one up there! Oh, we could be surprised, pleased and completely flabbergasted by things in those days! We were always ready to be wide-eyed and open-minded with the marvelous new world created for us.

The Chautauqua is coming! What an exciting day that was when I was a young lad. I can remember my father helping make benches and my mother often entertaining some of the interesting people who travelled with the troupe. A very efficient tent crew supervised the raising of the large brown tent but they needed plenty of local help. There were no amplifiers in those days and it was quite difficult for the performers to project their voices above the flapping of the tent if a wind happened to come up. However, in most cases the programs were very enjoyable indeed, consisting of humorous plays, musical numbers, solos and lectures. The topics of the lectures were usually on families and family life, other countries and science demonstrations. I recall particularly a science demonstration on liquid air and its properties. One man spoke on the Soviet Union and communism, warning all of the grave perils of world communism. In those days no one had even thought of such a thing.

We watched many performers, little knowing how famous some of them would become in later years. I especially remember Edgar Bergen and Charlie MacCarthy, and the kids were all invited backstage to meet him.

We were thrilled to attend the Chautauqua in Blackie. There were some fine musicians I think, and one or two humorists. I don't remember the musical numbers but I do remember the Kilted Scot who burst into tears each time he received a letter from his sweetheart. Then the young Greek speaker, who was leaning over the deck rail one evening during the crossing, violently ill so he told us, when someone came along and gaily remarked, "Oh, you are waiting for the moon to come up?" Almost collapsing he wailed, "Does the moon come up too?"

I enjoyed Chautauqua's varied and exciting programs. The man who swallowed the sword, and apparently suffered no ill effect, was indescribable, but wasn't someone going to stop that man from sawing the beautiful woman in half? Was father just going to sit there and let them do it? Mother whispered that it was just a trick, but I thought her tone of voice didn't sound too assuring.

Once a year Chautauqua would come to town. It would play all week. We would all go as soon as we could do the morning chores, spend the day there and go home and complete our evening chores. Most times mother washed and ironed our clothes so we could return to the evening show. But, my goodness, it was great fun and we looked forward to it each year.

Some of the Chautauqua artists spent their entire lives going from tent to tent, sometimes offering the same act or lecture for decades. It was such an exhilarating life that junior performers would often subsist on peanut butter-and-jam sandwiches and sleep in the cars for months, just to be part of the Chautauqua family. The show troupe, along with the necessary scenery and costumes, moved from town to town by car, boat, train, or any means of conveyance available at a given time and place. Once in a while the car broke down, was stranded in an unseasonal blizzard, stuck in a mudhole, or slid off the road into slough, but they got through somehow and the show went on. Even when the artists arrived safely and on time, that didn't mean their problems were at an end. On more than one occasion the tent blew down, sprung leaks during a heavy rainstorm, was ripped in places by hail, or became so thin and sheer from too much exposure to the drought-producing sun that it provided very little protection from the elements. In Calgary a deluge of rain flooded the Chautauqua site to such an extent that it was necessary to float boards in the aisles for the afternoon performance. The local hydro plant was often as unreliable as the weather, so it was not uncommon for the determined artists to perform in the dark. At one place the local committee illuminated the tent at night by soaking cattails in kerosene and lighting them.

In spite of such difficulties, the performers found comfort in the fact that the audiences were tremendously responsive, laughing, crying and applauding. By the final presentation, usually a play such as, "Uncle Tom's Cabin," "A Pair of Sixes," "Bought and Paid For," or "Skidding," worked the audience into a frenzy of excitement. The people seemed to love every minute of the various presentations and the artists could not have played before more appreciative audiences.

The Chautauqua booking agent, after looking over the prospects in any particular part of the country, set up a convenient circuit of towns. The first Chautauqua circuit was a six-day venture with performances in six different towns nightly. Later, it became a four-day event with afternoon and evening shows. A troop of entertainers would perform for one day and then move on to the next center, and so on for the four days of the Chautauqua.

The Chautauqua movement was very democratic and did not play one section of the country to the exclusion of some other part. Its main purpose was to bring culture to the masses, so it's no wonder it was familiar to people everywhere.

For weeks in advance of the big event, banners decorated the business section of the town; posters studded everything from store windows in the city to corner fence posts in the country; local committee members touted the talent at every opportunity and tried to sell tickets even to visitors and transients.

A typical Chautauqua was a potpourri and might begin with a rousing band, followed in succeeding programs by a magician, Hawaiian crooners, the Russian Cossack chorus, acrobats, marionettes, chamber music, opera divas, a dramatic play, and soar to a climax with an inspirational lecture on, "Education or Catastrophe." The following program was the one offered on the six-day circuit in Alberta and Saskatchewan in 1924:

DAILY PROGRAMME

. . . .

FIRST DAY   Evening   — McDonald Kiddies

. . . .

SECOND DAY Afternoon — A One-Act Play, "The Silent System".
                                 Lecture — Mrs. D. Pirie Beyea, "The
                                 Four Cornerstones of Citizenship".
                   Evening   — "The Mikado" — Gilbert and Sullivan
                                 Comic Opera.

. . . .

THIRD DAY   Afternoon — Howard Russell Revue — Musical
                                 Artists and Comedian
                   Evening   — Howard Russell Revue
                                 Lecture — Dr. George Henry Bradford,
                                 "This Way Up".

. . . .

FOURTH DAY Afternoon — The Tziganos — Character songs,
                                 monologue, Grand Opera Arias.
                                 Judge Fred G. Bale — "The Fiddler
                                 and the Fire".
                   Evening   — The Tziganos
                                 Judge Fred G. Bale — "The Fourth
                                 Line of Defence".

. . . .

FIFTH DAY   Afternoon — Boyd Concert Company — Concert
                                 Artists and Entertainers in Songs,
                                 Instrumental Music and Humorous
                                 Sketches.
                                 Dr. Homer B. Hulbert — "Where East
                                 Meets West".
                   Evening   — Play, "Daddy Long Legs".

. . . .

SIXTH DAY   Afternoon — Rainbow Novelty Company — Musical
                                 Company
                                 Dr. J. H. Rivers — "The Second
                                 Chance on Lessons from Life".
                   Evening   — Rainbow Novelty Company, with
                                 Eileen Hoff, dramatic soprano.

The program below is an example of a four-day Chautauqua presented in Camrose, Alberta, July 7, 8, 10, 11, 1932.

. . . .
DAILY PROGRAMME
. . . .

FIRST DAY	Evening —
	"Grand Concert" .... Deep River Plantation Singers

SECOND DAY	Afternoon —
	Lecture Recital —
	"Nuggets of Gold" .... Robert Hanscom
	Evening —
	Powerful Modern Drama —
	Sun-Up" .... Peerless Players

THIRD DAY	Afternoon —
	Musical —
	"A happy blending of the Classics and Musical Sketches" .... The Lombard Entertainers
	Evening —
	Prelude.............................. The Lombard Entertainers
	"On the Bottom of the Sea" —
	Lecture................................Robert M. Zimmerman

FOURTH DAY	Afternoon —
	Entertainment .... Sue Hasting's Marionetters
	Evening —
	"A Pair of Sixes" —
	Farce Comedy .... Canadian Players

SEASON TICKETS	Afternoon Programmes... 3.00 P.M.
Adults $2.00	Evening Programmes ...... 8.00 P.M.
Children..................................$1.00	

All programmes as above unless otherwise announced from the platform.

Mildred Affleck of the Esther S.D. (Oyen, Alberta) was in the habit of keeping notes in an old scribbler, and after attending the Chautauqua held in Camrose, Alberta in 1931, she jotted down the following comments:

> This year I bought a season ticket to the Chautauqua and went to every performance but one. I didn't attend the children's show as I gave my tickets to a little boy to use. I believe I enjoyed the programs more than I ever did anything else before. The plays were certainly good, especially *Skidding* in which the characters appeared very much true to life. The characters impersonated by Zellner, the Protean artist,

were beautifully done. He certainly could change quickly in costume, voice and manner. I thought the lectures would be boring, but I was mistaken, as they were all extremely interesting.

I think I enjoyed the Light Opera Company better than anything else on the Chautauqua program. They presented popular numbers from, *Rose Marie, The Student Prince, The Desert Song,* and *The Chocolate Soldier.* Each actor and actress seemed suited to the part he or she took in these operas. I liked *The Chocolate Soldier* the best. A George Mulvaney, the leading man in this particular opera, was slightly stout, but he was exceptionally good where he acted as the mechanical soldier. A girl would wind him up and he'd wobble forward a little, stop and remain as still as a real tin soldier. She would wind him up again with the same results time and again. I didn't think he was as good in the *Desert Song.*

The Elias Tamburitza Serenaders from Croatia of Jugo-Slavia were outstanding. Charles Elias told us the names of the strange instruments that they played, as well as the habits of the Jugo-Slavian people. His son and daughter gave several folk dances. Bert, the brother of Charles, who played the Berdo and several other instruments, was a sober-looking fellow, not nearly as jovial as the others.

The Chautauqua ended with Vierra's Hawaiians. For a background they had a beautifully colored scene of the bay at Waikiki, with the mountain rising in the background. The rippling waves, the moonlight, the erupting volcano, were faithfully reproduced by special lighting. Mrs. Albert Vierra also gave us an interesting talk on the island and the customs of its people.

The real spirit of Chautauqua is exemplified in the following story that has been told and retold by Marjorie McEnaney, a former Chautauqua superintendent during the years 1930 to 1934.

The memorable event occurred in a poverty-stricken Saskatchewan town during the depths of the depression, when Chautauqua had started to crumble. It happened to be the first show of the season and the morale of the town was as low as its cash. Notwithstanding, it was vitally important that Mrs. McEnaney get the whole show organized and the contract for the next year signed, or there would be unpleasant reverberations all along the line. She called a meeting of town officials to make plans and get the ticket sales going. No one turned up. The next day all refused to have anything to do with the troupe that had just arrived. Determined to have a show, Mrs. McEnaney found a ladder and hung the usual pennants across the street herself. A few hours later she found them torn down. On the day Chautauqua was to open, instead of setting up the stage and getting into their costumes, the artists had to go before a notary to demand that their contract be honored. No tickets had been sold locally. Just when the troupe had decided they might as well close up and move on, a little old lady turned up with a ticket she had bought down the line. It had to be honored. So for five performances she was the audience, at least officially, as she was the only one with a season pass. The good lady spread the word that the town didn't know what it was missing.

For the final performance the hall was packed, but again the old lady was the only person with a ticket. In the middle of the show the man who owned the local hydro plant demanded to be paid and threatened to turn off the electricity if cash wasn't produced promptly. Mrs. McEnaney insisted that supplying the electric power was the responsibility of the local committee. He stamped off indignantly and turned out the lights when Mrs. McEnaney was on the stage making an important speech. In desperation she groped her way backstage and paid him with the troupe's funds. When she told the head of the Chautauqua circuit about it later, he said it would have to come out of her own salary. It did! But she felt the boost the show gave the town's morale was worth every cent of it.

Laura (Hale) Farquharson of the Delia S.D. 3261 (Delia, Alberta) also remembers Chautauqua visiting her community during the drought and depression period of the thirties, but the morale booster came from an entirely different and unexpected source.

It had been a very hot, dry summer and few could exactly remember when we last had rain. The wheat fields were turning brown, and the farmers were saying that if rain didn't come within the week there would be no crop this year. It was a very anxious time. Chautauqua came to Delia that week. The big brown tent was set up and the entire countryside came. There wasn't much outside entertainment in those days and it was good to forget the burning crops for a while. The last night the highlight was a play which we had all been looking forward to with great expectations. The tent was filled! About halfway through the performance, suddenly there was a sharp flash of lightning, followed by a loud clap of thunder, then a moment of hushed silence as we listened. Yes, it was real rain and it started to come down in buckets. It was a real cloudburst and we felt it. That tent leaked like a sieve. Who would have thought it mattered to check a leaky tent in our part of the country! The lovely warm rain pelted through everywhere. We were so happy we embraced our neighbors, laughing and cheering. It became impossible for the play to go on, so the actors joined us as our rejoicing became louder. The play that night had a most happy if unexpected, ending.

Chautauqua was not the only event in the early days that provided some measure of entertainment and education for the rural children. Rodeos used to do the same thing. In addition to the usual events like roping competitions, horse, pony and harness racing, wild steer riding, bucking contests and horseback wrestling, historical pageants were presented. These might include, "Prairie Life," "The Gold Rush," "The Indian Massacre," "The Stage Coach Robbery," or "The Whiskey Trader."

The best-known rodeo in this respect was the Big Gap Roundup held annually in east-central Alberta between 1914 and 1919 near the Neutral Hills in a natural amphitheater. People travelled by horses and Model-Ts up to 200 miles to attend, and since there was no other accommodation, they came prepared to camp out in the hills. Some even brought their milk cows with them and stayed the two or three days. The Rawleigh man also came along and set up a tent from which to sell his products. It was estimated that the 1919 Roundup, the biggest held, was attended by 12,000 to 14,000 persons. By ten in the morning of that first day tents, covered wagons and all manner of make-shift camp shelters lined the valley for over a mile. Show tents, sleeping tents, eating tents, tents for almost every purpose imaginable, haphazardly dotted the area. The only space that was left clear was the arena grounds. In less than twenty-four hours a canvas city had sprung up and was inhabited by almost 15,000 people. Since there was no water supply on the grounds, several tanks of water had been hauled and spotted at convenient places.

The special attraction that was mainly responsible for the tremendous crowds that attended, was the staging of the Wild West shows and the re-enacting of many historical events from the lives of Louis Riel, Chief Sitting Bull, Billy the Kid, and other famous figures of the early West. The following summaries taken from several of the programs give a good example of the type and nature of historical events dramatized.

Prairie Life in the days of Louis Riel

A Prairie drama, put on by the O-8 Ranch.

A cabin on the prairie, where a man and wife appear, dragging wood to prepare dinner. As they drag in the wood an Indian scout is seen spying out the land for a raid.

A band of cowboys in search of stock ride up, and the man goes away with them to show them an obscure trail. While he is away the Indians attack; one of them jumps from the roof of the house and lands on the escaping woman; she is captured, the house is fired and the Indians ride away.

Attracted by the smoke of his burning house the settler returns; he pounds out the fire with a wet sack, finds the woman gone, and searching around finds "Indian signs" and starts upon the trail. He gathers up the cowboys, heads off the Indian, drives him back to the shelter of the cabin, where he is captured and dragged to death.

Overland Stage Robbery

A western play, by the Cowboys of Neutral Valley.

This is the drama that was staged last year, and is played this year by special request.

An old stage coach, with its guards, comes swinging down the trail; as they near the hill the outriders sight an ambush, pull their guns and fire, then fall back upon the stage; the stage turns and hits the back trail, pursued by a band of robbers. When the stage is disabled the driver pulls up, unhitches his leaders, and rides like the wind for help. The outlaws come, turn out the passengers, line them up and go through them for their money. Having robbed the passengers they blow up the safe, then the cowboy relief appears. The outlaws mount and ride with the cowboys in pursuit, and the act closes in a swirl of dust and a running pistol fight.

The local cowboys and would-be actors spent considerable time and effort in rigging up authentic props and costumes. Elaborate giant backdrops were designed and one time a town with false store fronts was erected. A number of other stage properties that had to be obtained included covered wagons, a stage coach and a portable cabin that could be pulled onto the grounds within minutes. In addition, there were more than twenty gaily decorated Indian costumes fashioned by the local amateur actors, complete with the tomahawks, bows and arrows, and the other appropriate accessories needed to play the Indian parts in the Wild-West dramas. Each year about 5,000 rounds of blank six-gun ammunition was used in the various acts or dress rehearsals. Some of the boys became very proficient at falling from a horse running at full speed, or using the bows and arrows. They even designed a protective armor of dried cowhide that was to be worn by any of the "victims" in a play, and permitted the heroes to shoot them in the back at close range. The arrows merely stuck in the sheet cork that was glued to the cowhide armor. This deceptive stunt, invented by Rolf Krohn, one of the local ranchers, added reality to the plays; every time a bow string was pulled and released with a loud twang, the spectators would cringe and gasp in horror. With such a cowhide armor, an actor could be dragged at the end of a lariat rope the full length of the arena without incurring any injury. The only precaution to be taken was in the matter of speed, because if the "victim" was pulled at full speed the dry cowhide became so hot from the friction between it and the ground that the actor's stomach was often scorched.

As these historical dramas were staged in the outdoors, dialogue was out of the question. So, C. S. Inman, the original promoter of the idea, equipped with a large horn, acted as narrator and gave the audience a running commentary as the plot unfolded.

These large outdoor pageants were not the only dramatic activities included in the Big Gap Roundup, for the Czar Dramatic Club presented a number of three-act plays in an open-air pavilion, including: "The New Schoolmarm," "The Big Show Under Canvas," and "At the Junction."

A press release of that day not only gave an eye-witness account of the play, but also provided some interesting incidental information about the

-- Robert Twa

This is a view of the large crowd attending the Big Gap Roundup, July 1-2, 1918.

actors. It is only through such accounts in *The Cattlemen* and the *Consort Enterprise* that much of the pioneer spirit displayed in re-enacting these historical events can be recaptured today.

Buffalo Bill to the Rescue was the story of an Indian attack on a settler's wagon. Rolf Krohn, the settler, came to trade ponies with the Indians. To facilitate his trading he gave the Indians some firewater. One of the Indians slipped behind Krohn and knifed him in the back, then tottered away to sleep it off. The other Indians rode off behind the hills. A settler's wagon, with Mr. MacAffee as the husband, Fred Burnham as his wife, and Bob Hargreaves as the little girl, drove into the valley. They discovered the murdered man and started to dig his grave, while the Monitor band played, "The Funeral March." The sleeping Indian awoke and inched his way through the long grass to safety. Over the hills swooped the Indians, horrible in their war paint and feathers. They carried off the little girl, tied the struggling man and woman to the wagon wheels and set fire to the covered wagon.

Up on a lookout point, Buffalo Bill (Ivan Inman) saw the spectacle and he raced to the scene with his bridle reins in his teeth and two six-guns blazing. The Indians fled and Buffalo Bill rescued the helpless pair. He quickly organized a posse of cowboys and pursued the Indians. A running fight ensued and the Indians and cowboys alike were shot from their horses at full speed. Of course, right triumphed, and the Indians were all killed, or dispersed. The little girl was returned to her grateful parents. The charred wagon was towed away behind a saddle horse while the applause was deafening.

These plays were so realistic and exciting that the audience was quite carried away. The wife (Fred Burnham) was tied to the wheel with a slip knot so that he might release himself and slump to the ground if

-- Robert Twa

The "Big Gap Roundup" (Neutral Hills, Alta.) was held in this natural amphitheatre.

-- Arthur Spencer

A cairn was erected in June, 1974, on the original site of the famous "Big Gap Roundup" to commemorate the event that proved to be so successful between 1916 and 1919.

the fire got too close. So anxious was he to play his part that the hair on the back of his neck became singed before Buffalo Bill rescued him.

The Indians and cowboys were superb riders. There were no Hollywood stunt men to take their falls for them. They had to fall at the gallop and that was no mean feat. Joe and Jack Richardson were some of the better Indians. In the heat of the battle Jack's horse stepped in a badger hole and fell heavily, catapulting its rider amongst the charging horses. That definitely was not part of the performance, but no doubt some of the spectators thought that he had a well-trained horse. Fortunately, none of the actors were injured.

After 1919 the importance of the Big Gap Roundup faded rapidly. There wasn't enough accommodation and water was a big problem as it had to be hauled several miles. Perhaps the very thing that brought the huge crowds, the Model-T Ford, was already starting to replace the cow pony.

Today, the Big Gap Roundup is nothing but a memory, and if it weren't for the commemorative cairn erected on the former location, through the noble efforts of Arthur E. Spencer, even these reminiscences would have disappeared some day. White-faced cattle graze in the vast amphitheater and up the silent slopes. Instead of the applause and outcry of excited crowds, there is only the mournful howl of the coyote or the melancholy hoots of an owl, to disturb the peaceful quietude of the hills today. However, the cairn, staunch and undaunted, tells the story of the Big Gap Roundup in the days when it not only provided entertainment, but enriched the lives of hundreds of children through its dramatic presentations of local history.

Children have a natural inclination to play, and their whole life is centered in play activities which they enter spontaneously as a means of expressing their physical and social interests. Country children seldom had opportunities to get together to play, except when they attended their local schools. A few rural districts did their best to promote some form of recreational and physical activities for the children and adults. One of the most interesting of these projects took place in the Excel S.D. 2593 (Excel, Alberta) in the late twenties. The Bishop brothers introduced curling to their fellow settlers, as well as building a straw rink that was just as unique as the game they were attempting to promote. The four brothers easily could be described as the pioneers of rural curling. Ruth, a daughter of C. A. Bishop, one of the brothers, gives an account of this singular historical and educational undertaking.

"Sweep! You're wide! Good Shot! Pshaw! You've missed the broom!" and various other expressions of exultation and consternation echoed above the crack of rocks from the straw curling rink on the Bishop farm, where families and neighbors gathered to enjoy the good old "roaring game". People used to travel for miles by team and sleigh to join in the fun, as this was the only entertainment available in this prairie community during the winter.

The above scene was repeated hundreds of times on my uncle's farm six miles north of the small hamlet called Excel, which is located on the Canadian National Goose Lake Railway Line, some twenty-seven miles west of the Saskatchewan border. Since the Bishop brothers were responsible for this rural curling rink I would like to tell you how the idea originated.

My father, C. A. Bishop, threw his first curling rock at Zelma, Saskatchewan, in February 1917. He wasn't too impressed, nor were his brothers when he told them about the experience. No doubt they thought it was ridiculous to try and throw chunks of granite with handles down a sheet of ice, and run beside them sweeping like your life depended on getting the object to the so-called house. At that time they didn't think that they would be responsible for building one of the first rural rinks in Alberta.

It all started back in the winter of 1922 when the Curling Club at Oyen, a village twelve miles from our home, invited the four Bishop brothers and several neighbors to a bonspiel. Right then the spark of enthusiasm for curling was kindled, but was not brought to life until five years later.

After the bonspiel in Oyen, the brothers thought of joining the village club, but the inclement winter weather and means of travel were against them. A twenty-four mile round trip by team in twenty to thirty degree below zero weather, through deep drifts or unexpected blizzards on the bald prairie was enough to dampen the idea. However, their enthusiasm for the game was not weakened, so in 1926 Uncle Horace jokingly suggested that they build a curling rink on the farm. The other three boys took him seriously and started the first sheet of ice. Once the news got around, there was much head shaking, many jeers and occasional sly winks from the surrounding neighbors, who thought it was all a preposterous joke. Apparently it was thought, at that time and still is in many places, that curling was a sport only for the urban dweller. However, despite the warnings and jeers, the boys went ahead with their plan.

They chose what they thought was a level piece of land by the windmill, and proceeded to make ice. This entailed a lot of hard work shovelling and packing snow, and eventually flooding. When the sheet was completed they put a level on it and found to their disappointment that one end was a foot lower than the other. Once again they shovelled and packed snow until the sheet appeared to be fairly level. Next the big problem was rocks. They tried to make them from cement but these creations proved disappointing. My father and Uncle

Floyd scouted around until they located four sets of "scrub" rocks that they were able to purchase for twenty dollars a set.

I can imagine there was great excitement that night around the open-air rink as the first rock was about to be thrown. They went away disappointed. The granite hemispheres resisted their best efforts to heave them the full length of the ice, so they decided to wait till daylight. The next morning they enthusiastically scraped the ice with scoop shovels, but still the rocks refused to slide very far on the ice. Suddenly they remembered that the ice had to be brushed, but having no brush they decided the next best thing to use was Uncle Horace. Dad took hold of his feet, Uncle Floyd his shoulders and proceeded to give the ice a good mopping. Uncle Horace must have made an excellent brush, for now the rocks sailed merrily down the ice.

The open-air rink worked well as long as the weather was clear, so in 1927 they constructed a covered rink on a slough north of the house. This didn't prove to be too successful as the ice heaved and cracked. In addition, they had to haul the water in barrels for the flooding and I imagine it was a discouraged group when they discovered the water running through the cracks into the slough. However, they persisted, and even bought four new sets of rocks that year.

It seemed something funny always happened, like the time the bull got a cement curling rock hooked in the ring in his nose. Guess that caused plenty of excitement and laughs as the poor animal capered around trying to get rid of his ball and chain.

In 1928 the Bishop boys had a new idea. They had posts and fox-wire shipped from Calgary and once more moved the rink back to the windmill. This time the building was erected of posts with net-wire nailed on both sides with the intervening space stuffed with straw. The roof was also constructed of straw but they found that it leaked too much. So the next year they put on a board roof which proved to be more successful.

The first club was formed in 1929 with eleven rinks. Members were of both sexes from the ages of ten to seventy years. It is also interesting to note that the rocks varied from thirty-six to forty-six pounds. Members even drove eight miles by team from Lanfine to participate in the regular crew.

The club also sponsored a bonspiel with two events and had eighteen entries. Bert Shantz and his rink drove all the way from Alsask, a round trip of some seventy miles, for the bonspiel. Future bonspiels had entries from all places along the Goose Lake Line. Dr. Cross, the minister of health for Alberta, entered several bonspiels held in our unique rural rink. I believe the curling club was a godsend to many rural people as it took their minds off trouble and worry during the hungry thirties.

The Bishop brothers were directly and indirectly responsible for numerous curling rinks that sprung up throughout Alberta. In 1930 Lafine built a rink where men from the neighboring town of Cereal came to curl, and eventually built a rink of their own. Joe Johnson moved from Lanfine to Acadia Valley and started a club there. T. O. Stevenson moved from Excel to Leslieville and was instrumental in building a rink at that point. Frank Morrell, who taught in the district, was a guiding light in forming a club at Irricana. L. H. Wiley, caretaker for the North Hill Curling Rink in Calgary, threw his first rock in the Bishop Rural Rink. Len Wiley won the first event in the Senior Bonspiel in Calgary in 1966 and again in 1971.

Down through the years the four Bishop brothers entered bonspiels all the way from Kindersley, Sask. to Hanna, Alta. On one occasion they travelled in four different conveyances to get to a bonspiel. The first bonspiel they entered the boys played according to age and still do most of the time.

Although the Bishop brothers eventually went their separate ways, once a year, Clint from Olds, Floyd from Excel, Horace from Edmonton, and Rob from Brandon, Manitoba, set all their work aside and gather in Calgary to enter that city's bonspiel. They must have set some sort of a record for they attended the Calgary Bonspiel for twenty-two consecutive years. The brothers don't profess to be curling experts, but thoroughly enjoy the "roarin' game" and take much satisfaction in looking back to the days of their straw curling rink, knowing that in a small way they had a part in encouraging hundreds of rural people both children and adults, in south-eastern Alberta in getting started in curling.

The history of rural schools indicates that many such institutions benefited in one way or another by outside organizations taking more than passing interests in their welfare. The Junior Red Cross Society and the Independent Order of the Daughters of the Empire were two such altruistic groups.

If a Junior Red Cross branch was organized in a rural school, the youngsters probably caught their first glimpse of democracy in action. The student members gained valuable training and experience in such activities as organizing the local branch, conducting their own meetings, holding elections, public speaking, recording minutes, budgeting, making financial statements, accepting individual responsibilities for carrying out the objectives of the society, sponsoring various projects in order to raise money, and where feasible, sending a delegate to the Junior Red Cross Rally often held in some nearby city. One of the most important objectives of the local branch was to promote the health and welfare of not only its members, but anyone who needed assistance, no matter where they lived. Hence the Junior Red Cross members in Canada were raising money for

The straw roof of the Excel Straw Curling Rink was replaced by a board roof in 1931 to prevent leaking.

— C. A. Bishop

children needing help around the world. Many times they helped local cases; they helped pay the hospital expenses of a girl with a fractured leg, paid twenty-five dollars to one boy for the removal of adenoids, and a similar amount to another boy who had pneumonia.

School Red Cross Societies made "friendship kits" for children abroad. The kits contained health supplies, a toy and pencils. The pupils also exchanged information and letters with children living in other lands. Children confined to special Red Cross Hospitals were not forgotten, for school members made up parcels of used and repaired toys to send to them as well as other small gifts that would be appreciated by long-term patients. Another common project was to prepare portfolios of information about their district to send to Junior Red Cross branches in other parts of the world. Such exchanges of portfolios brought a better understanding between children living in widely separated sections of the globe.

The Ganton S.D. 2058 (Vermilion, Alta.) compiled an excellent account of their district and sent it to Hawaii. The portfolio contained information about the geography, products and appearance of Alberta; it also described the activities of the people, both at work and play. They included pictures of Ganton School, the farm homes and buildings in the district, threshers at work, various kinds of farm machinery in action, and the wild plant life and native animals. The Ganton Red Cross Portfolio turned out to be of such a high caliber that the school received a letter from the national director of the Canadian Red Cross stating:

> This is one of the best portfolios we have received in a long time. We would appreciate having it for International Exhibit purposes. One will be held by the Norwegian Red Cross at Trondheim on June 29 and 30, 1951, and by the Irish Red Cross at Sligo, Ireland in July.

The children and teacher of this small rural school must have felt very proud to know that their work was seen by thousands of people in many parts of the world.

Most students took pride in being members of a Junior Red Cross Group. Ethel (Mitchell) Muddle, one such youngster, recalls rather proudly two activities of her Hillanvale Junior Red Cross Branch of the Hillanvale S.D. (Monitor, Alta.).

> We raised enough money to pay for an operation on a small baby in our district. Baby Willis was born with club-feet. Several years after the operation, we received a photograph of the child. He could walk! How rewarding it was for us all. The second was the yearly Red Cross Banner. Each year the Junior Red Cross Society gave out a banner to those groups achieving a one hundred percent membership. As it cost twenty-five cents to join, it took a lot of hard work and many gopher tails to pay for a membership. The students helped one another because it just wouldn't do to have a banner missing. Hillanvale

achieved an excellent record and I still remember the many banners strung up along the back of the schoolroom, one for each year.

Nisbet S.D. 961 (Innisfail, Alta.) boasted of a Junior Red Cross Society that operated successfully for so many years that they earned the "Five-Year Seal" and the "Ten-Year Seal". This group functioned for twelve consecutive years. To support it, the children held an annual spring tea and sold handicrafts, the work of the boys and girls themselves. It was not unusual in such sales for a youngster to act as auctioneer in selling the various items. In fact, more than one Junior Red Cross auction sale demonstrated the auctioneering ability of some boy and eventually encouraged him to become an auctioneer after leaving school.

The *Junior Red Cross Magazine* that each member received on a regular basis from headquarters was of considerable benefit to the children. It was probably the only up-to-date reading matter they had a chance to enjoy. The colorful publication contained the following: news of other Junior Red Cross Groups in their area of the province; awards presented to students, teachers, and branches for outstanding achievement, or for many years of service; pictures and articles that had especially appealed to children; many health stories; and news about the progress the Junior Red Cross Society was making in Canada and the provinces as a whole. The Junior Red Cross Society made the children health-conscious in schools which organized branches, as each member had a card which he or she checked off every morning; the student earned marks for such things as clean face, hands, teeth, fingernails, weekly bath, regular toilet habits and an unsullied handkerchief. At the end of the month merit certificates were presented to the youngsters who were able to maintain good records. Most members wore their distinctive Junior Red Cross buttons rather proudly, but usually by the end of the school term, some of them would have lost or misplaced them.

While the accomplishments of the rural school Junior Red Cross Society may seem small and trivial by today's standards, conditions were vastly different forty or fifty years ago, and such junior organizations were a boon in providing a real incentive for the rural students to learn about citizenship and health.

The Independent Order of the Daughters of the Empire had a policy of adopting some rural school, and then assisting the students and the teacher in any way they could. A good example was the Devonshire Independent Order of the Daughters of the Empire in Regina, Saskatchewan, who selected the Welby S.D. 1710 (Spy Hill, Sask.) as their special educational project. The teacher was very grateful for their encouragement and help.

They were very helpful in sending out books for the library, a dictionary, many workbooks, a big box of candy and nuts for a Christmas treat, also some money to be used as prizes for the races at our school picnic at the end of June. The ladies also sent large boxes of used clothing during the depression days to be divided among the needy families. It was usual for a car load of Devonshire ladies to come out each year for the afternoon of the school picnic and watch the pupils racing, jumping or playing ball.

Multiplying such examples of assistance to rural schools a hundred fold gives one an idea of the tremendous work done by Independent Order of the Daughters of the Empire on behalf of rural education. Even today this organization continues to support education by offering scholarships of all types in all regions of Canada. They still maintain their tradition of presenting a large colored picture of the reigning monarch to each school they adopt. This policy was of considerable value to the early rural schools as it helped to foster a feeling of Canadian patriotism.

12

A Few Miscellaneous Factors

There is a latent trichotomy in the society of man that occasionally surfaces and more or less affects educational conditions and progress. The trichotomy includes war, moot innovations, and racial, religious and economic diversity.

The dawning era of educational progress in rural Canada was rudely halted by two great calamities: the First World War (1914-1918) and the Second World War (1939-45). The war years proved to be hard on country schools. The accustomed trickle of trained teachers from Great Britain and the United States was practically cut off and that from inter-provincial sources greatly diminished. One after another of the male teachers enlisted for active service and replacements were most difficult to find. The married women who had been refused employment in peace time, were now begged to return to the classrooms. Some who had been away from teaching for fifteen years or more found the transition from home-making back to instructing in rural schools rather difficult. Many districts, unable to persuade housewives to resume their teaching careers, were forced to employ permit teachers. In Alberta, young high-school girls were given credentials as supervisors and placed in charge of rural schools to oversee the students working on correspondence lessons. All the children in the schools were registered for correspondence courses, no matter what grades they were in, and it was the duty of the supervisors to submit the complete lessons to the correspondence school branch in Edmonton for marking and grading. The supervisors also were responsible for keeping attendance and progress records. Usually they planned timetables for studies and tried to help the pupils with any problems they encountered in their correspondence lessons.

The enlistment of teachers was not limited to the males. A considerable number of female teachers left during World War I to work for the voluntary aid detachments in France and England. A few entered into nursing training in convalescent hospitals set up in various parts of Canada. In the Second World War more women teachers than ever left their classrooms. Some enlisted in one of the three women's divisions of the armed services, while others entered the essential war industries.

Many schemes were devised to ensure a teacher for every classroom in Canada, but this objective was never achieved. The normal school and university courses for teachers were shortened, entrance requirements reduced and the institutions geared for year-round operations. Unfortunately, these teacher-training schools were not able to compete favorably with the other professions and trades in attracting more or better students from the secondary schools. As a result, both the number and caliber of teachers graduating declined very noticeably during the war years. School boards resorted to operating schools during the summer when university students were available to staff them. Still others shortened their school terms by as much as two to three months to suit the convenience of some transient teachers.

Once a teacher was hired, it didn't mean that all the problems connected with the education of the children were solved. The pupils attended school very irregularly during the war years. It was difficult to secure hired help for the farm, so the children were kept out of school rather frequently to assist their parents with the work at home. Such instances of irregular attendance appeared entirely unavoidable and were leniently dealt with by the inspectors or truant officers. In the final analysis, it was the children's schooling that suffered.

Necessary repairs to schools, plans for replacement of buildings by more useful and comfortable structures, and the purchase of additional equipment and supplies were deferred during the war because of shortage of labor, materials and money. As a result, schools and their facilities became decrepit, thus losing some of their educational effectiveness.

War added to the difficulty of financing education in the rural areas. When landowners enlisted, their property was protected against any legal proceedings for the collection of taxes, while if they simply abandoned their homesteads the school districts could do nothing but wipe out the taxes outstanding against their property. This meant that the rest of the taxpayers in the district had to bear the entire burden of taxation if the school was to operate, and liabilities, such as debenture payments, met.

The manner in which the teaching profession responded to the call for military service afforded society grounds for solid satisfaction. The fine example set by the teacher who enlisted helped other members of the profession to teach the sacredness of duty and loyalty. Many educational leaders who could hardly be spared from the important work in which they were engaged felt the call of duty too strong to be denied. Hence universities, departments of education, normal schools, colleges and secondary schools suffered as a result of the absence of some of their key personnel.

The annual reports issued by the various provincial departments of education across Canada during the war years made special references to the important part that schools and teachers were playing in the country's war effort. Yet, in the same breath, they regretfully noted the gradual deterioration of the educational situation, due in part to the serious drain on qualified teachers; many young people were diverted from entering teaching as a career. A sampling of these reports follows:

> The number of teachers who have enlisted for active service has been large. Practically all the young men who were physically capable of service in war have enlisted. Many of those who remained behind have been very active in Red Cross work and in Patriotic Funds and Victory Bonds involvements. Our schools are doing their bit in the war.

> The general work of the schools is being retarded by the scarcity of trained teachers, which has necessitated the granting of provisional certificates to students without experience or knowledge of school organization, or methods of presenting the subjects taught. This defect will be remedied when the war terminates and a large number of the teachers who are at present serving their country in Flanders return with a wealth of experience which must have its influence on our educational system.

> Boards of trustees and teachers have attempted to keep up the standard of efficiency as it was before the war with reasonable success. It is a matter of congratulation that in the stress of war our young people have suffered so little educationally. The schools have been kept in operation and the best teachers available have been kept in charge.

> It is a source of pride and satisfaction to note the part the schools of the province (Saskatchewan, 1916) are taking in the war. Practically all the physically fit young male teachers have joined the colors. We are justly proud of the splendid contributions that have been made by the schools to the Canadian Patriotic Fund of $25,499.22 and the Belgian Children's Relief Fund of $56,047.16.

> We cannot fail to take an honorable pride in those of our teachers who have relinquished their professional ambitions in response to the call of duty. They will pass through experiences of self-denial and self-sacrifice and we hope will return to the profession improved in every way by a richness of service.

> It is a significant fact that practically all our male teachers of military age had enlisted for military service before the enactment of The Military Service Act of 1917, and that our schools are now in the hands of women and older men. Many of the teachers who enlisted have made the great sacrifice, others have returned wounded and

broken, while the remainder are valiantly fighting to make this world safe for all people. We have endeavored to keep a record of those who have joined the colors.

The occasional school official expressed some doubt about young male teachers who felt they could do more for Canada by remaining in their classrooms than by enlisting. Inspector J. Morgan of the Lethbridge Inspectorate included the following observation in his 1916 report to the Department of Education:

> During the year I lost a number of teachers through enlistment in the overseas forces of our country. I regret the necessity of their going, but I am pleased to see them respond to the call to higher service. Other able-bodied young men refuse to hear their country's call. I fear they will not be very successful in inculcating the true British spirit in their schools.

There was a general concern in educational circles that the absence of so many young male teachers from the classrooms would have an adverse effect on education. They felt that the ideal situation was to have young, middle-aged and older teachers of both sexes teach the children, as each such group could make its own unique and important contribution to the well-rounded education of any child. Wars result in a primarily female-oriented education for the youngsters, thus depriving them of some of personal qualities that only the influence of male teachers can provide. The thirteenth annual report of the Department of Education of Alberta included the following memorandum made by F. L. Aylesworth, inspector of the Olds Inspectorate, in respect to this problem.

> The almost complete absence of male teachers in our schools is to be deplored. In the broad training of boys and girls for citizenship, we need more men. Furthermore, I do not believe there will be much stability in the teaching profession itself, until conditions make it possible and even desirable for young men, who have an inclination for the work, to remain in it.

As the tide of patriotic fervor swept the country, even the usually sedate provincial departments of education paid tribute to the teachers who enlisted by including their names in the annual reports. A typical example was a list of such teachers compiled by P. H. Thibaudeau, inspector of the Stettler Inspectorate in 1918.

> The following teachers enlisted from this inspectorate and saw service overseas:
>
> A. M. Shook, Aunger S.D. 2008; D. T. Wright, Jakes Butte S.D. 3030; George Hardy, Big Valley S.D. 2545; John Lees, Stettler S.D. (killed in action); Meredith C. Griffith, Prairie Grove S.D. 836 (killed in action); Granton Griffith, Silver Prairie S.D. 1230; John Hollingsworth, Wild Rose S.D. 1129 (prisoner of war in Germany); Alex Ross,

Kindergarten S.D. 1694 (killed in action); Austin Holmes, Nebraska S.D. 586 (killed in action); R. L. Pretty, Morrin Consolidated S.D. 131; Hugh Blackmore, Jarvis Bay S.D. 856 (killed in action); C. R. Carman, Alix Consolidated S.D. 12 (killed in action); Wesley Irwin, M.M., Leo S.D. 2279; R. B. McGillivray, Zenith S.D. 1620; Findley Reid, Ranching S.D. 1877 (killed in action); Harold Riddell, Lake Bend S.D. 1511 (died overseas); Norman Scott, Science Mound S.D. 1417; Harold W. McAllister, Science Mound S.D. 1417; J. K. Mulloy, Liberal S.D. 1462; W. J. Smith, Imogen S.D. 1945; J. S. Hamilton, Ferry Point S.D. 790; J. B. Coupland, Spring Lake S.D. 1602; W. A. Henry, Docendo S.D. 2076; C.P. Garvey, Gadsby Consolidated S.D. 21.

Teachers and students alike participated in many kinds of patriotic activities. They sponsored concerts to raise money for various war relief funds and purchased gift packages for the servicemen and servicewomen from their particular districts. They wound bandages for the Red Cross; knitted socks, mitts, scarfs for the enlisted; and started school gardens as a war emergency measure. Even the recesses were given over to playing "war", although it was always difficult to get volunteers to be the enemy as the enemy invariably had to lose the battle. In the Herbert S.D. (Herbert, Sask.), for instance, the students found plenty of diversion by training with shields and wooden guns and then engaging in hostilities of one kind or another. One comical incident involved the general's white horse. One of the boys brought his white horse to school, and being the only equestrian owner present, he was quickly promoted to the rank of general. The battle was quickly over when the general's horse was "wounded" and very wisely took the bit in his teeth and headed for home.

War work was the order of the day for most rural schools, and pupils and teachers cooperated in activities they thought would help with the war effort. The youngsters, both younger and older, male and female, were taught how to sew, knit, wrap bandages and write letters of encouragement to service personnel they knew. They gathered prune pits, foil, rubber tires, old newspapers and anything else that could be recycled and used for war purposes. Lotta P. Thompson, a teacher in the Lillico S.D. 2208 (Delia, Alta.) in 1943, described the contribution to the war effort of this little rural school.

> I taught all the children, boys as well as girls, to knit. Once that was accomplished we gathered all the wool anyone had to spare and started to make an afghan of six-inch blocks. Some of the squares were on the large side others rather small, some were knit of heavy yarn others of a lighter skein, but when they were all finished and sewn together the blanket resembled Joseph's coat of many colors. We were very proud to send it to the Red Cross. About the same time we received a donation of a couple of little pigs to be raffled to raise funds

for the Red Cross. I think we raffled those unfortunate hogs three times before we drew a winner who could use them, or wanted to be bothered with them.

Inspector Walter Scott of the Hardisty Inspectorate in Alberta noted in 1920 that the spirit of patriotism generated by World War I persisted in many rural schools long after hostilities had ceased.

> Many of the schools have undertaken to perpetuate the memory of those who served in the Great War. Honor rolls of those who enlisted are found in many schools. Photos of those who fell often grace the front walls of numerous classrooms. Dalen S.D. 1822 (Hardisty, Alta.) has placed a beautiful tablet in its school to the memory of Grier Wilson, a popular teacher who was killed in action. The influence of the veterans returned from the war is seen in a much greater attention given to the British Union Jack and to the teaching of civics. Unfortunately, only a very few of the returned men entered the schools in this inspectorate.

There is no doubt that teachers who enlisted and eventually were posted to every part of the world, especially during the Second World War, gained valuable experience from their travels and sojourns in many lands. These teachers met each other in many parts of the world, as the following incident related by J. R. Robson, a former secretary-treasurer of the Vermilion School Division, indicates.

> The scene is an officers' mess located on an oasis in North Africa. A young Canadian airman just arriving at the stopover walked in, and among those already there, he noticed another airman from Canada, and the conversation went like this: "Where are you from in Canada?" "Alberta." "So am I." "What did you do before you joined up?" "I was a schoolteacher." "Gosh! So was I." "Where did you teach?" "In the Vermilion School Division." "No, in what school?" "North Home." "Then you're Stan Messum. I'm Henry Dickie and I followed you at North Home."
>
> I met them both again in the office, Stan when he was home on leave, and Henry after the war. Unfortunately, after surviving a bail out in the North Sea, Stan returned for another tour of operations and was shot down on a raid over Germany.

Educational authorities anticipated that with the end of the war, the increasing shortage of teaching staff would be ended and the returning teachers would have much to offer to the rural students. However, the contrary was true, because the veterans decided to follow other avenues of employment, or go back to university for additional training. The death knell of the rural one-teacher school was beginning to toll with the end of World War II; as enrollments were down and the schools were difficult to staff, the administrators turned to centralization to ease the problem. Yet there was no turning back when, a few years later, enrollment increased as the huge crop of war babies reached school age. Practically all the pupils from the rural areas were conveyed by buses to central schools.

The smallness of the investment which teachers had in professional training under the short-term system adopted by the normal schools, and the relatively small remuneration they received while teaching, made it possible for teachers to drop out easily as well as to drop in easily. During periods of war, prosperity and moral decadence, teachers found it to their advantage to leave the profession and felt no compunction whatsoever; however, during times of peace, economic depression and constraint, they considered the time ripe to re-enter the profession. Such sporadic service in the teaching profession was detrimental to education as a whole, for steady perseverance on the part of educators everywhere is required to provide the best education possible for all children, whether world conditions are favorable or not. In fact, in times of crisis the need for good teachers to remain in the classrooms is more urgent than ever.

War, the locomotive of history, has always left its mark on education. During World War I it was the idea of introducing consolidated schools that was going to remedy all the ills or difficulties of the one-room rural school. This concept of grouping school districts together was new to most early prairie settlers but was very familiar to those who had emigrated from the United States. School districts had been grouped in that country for a number of years. Proponents of the scheme promised many advantages; these included lower costs, because a single school and fewer teachers could serve several districts, and better instruction, because the children would be attending semi-graded schools. Also if one rural district could not provide a high-school education, certainly a consolidation of several should be able to do it. Finally, the parents would no longer be responsible for the onerous task of transporting children to and from school, as regular vans would be available. After a somewhat shaky start in 1913 and 1914, the consolidated school movement spread rapidly in the period 1915 to 1920, but within a decade had lost much of its appeal.

In general, the best consolidation occurred when a village district and four rural districts combined. The village with its business amenities was already the economic hub for the area, so it appeared logical to make it the educational center as well. Depending upon the wealth of the districts involved and the vision, enthusiasm and wisdom of the elected trustees, some consolidated schools were not only well-built but artistically built as well. A few contained libraries, science laboratories, lunch rooms, combination gymnasia-auditoria halls, modest manual training and home-economics workshops, commercial nooks equipped with two or three typewriters, and maybe an office for the principal. Many of the schools were steam-heated, boasted the latest in natural lighting, had passable ventilation systems, possessed sanitary drinking facilities, and had better equipped and more comfortable classrooms than their one-room counterparts. Such amenities of the consolidated schools as well as their central location in or near railway communities, not only attracted the better teachers but had a tendency to keep them there.

Then why did this type of central education, which was supposed to be the panacea of all rural-education ills, fail to measure up? The main reason was one of finances. The initial outlay for the project was larger than at first estimated; the over-all savings turned out to be merely nominal, especially in the smaller, or the two-district consolidations; a sixty percent drop in the price of wheat made money scarce in the rural areas; and finally, the biggest bugaboo of all, supplying conveyance services became too expensive for the hard-pressed farmers to support. Apparently the expense of providing transportation had been sadly underestimated in the first place. In addition, inherent in the scheme were many problems that came to light only after the plan had been in operation for several months. It was too late to backtrack then.

A former trustee of the Griffin Consolidated School (Griffin, Sask.) provided a good insight into the sad story of school vans with the following account.

> With consolidation came the necessity for school vans. It required seven horse-drawn vans to bring the children to school from a radius of some eight miles. These vehicles, which were built high to make them more comfortable for riding, bore a striking resemblance to the old-fashioned bakery wagons. They consisted of spring wagons with canvas tops and side curtains and a door and steps at the rear for entering and leaving. Two benches fixed along the sides provided the seating accommodation for the students. Needless to add the interior was drafty, dusky and claustrophobic. It was only in fine weather when the side curtains were rolled up that the children received some measure of relief. The front of the wagon which was recessed and protected from the weather by an overhanging roof, contained the seat for the driver. In very foul weather it was possible for him to withdraw into the interior and drive the horses from there through the open vestibule.

> The vans were colored yellow and black with each one bearing a number on its side to distinguish it from its like-appearing confreres. During summer they were on wheels but for winter driving they were placed on bobsleds. At first robes and footwarmers were supplied for each van, but eventually these items became lost or worn out and in the hard times could not be replaced. The children simply had to do without such conveniences and arrived at school shivering from the cold and suffering from chilblains.

> When the vans first went into operation, each driver was required to hand in a report each morning on arrival at the school. He had to state

his starting and arrival times, the state of the weather, number of children transported and their behavior enroute, any unusual incidents, and other such pertinent information. These reports were necessary as the transportation grant received by the district from the Department of Education was based in part on the information they contained. The practice was quickly discontinued when it was discovered that the secretary-treasurer or the school principal could complete the van-operation reports directly without the detailed and pointless eruditions from the drivers. Many a settler refused to drive a van because he lacked even the rudiments of an education to enable him to compile such reports.

During the thirties when finances hit an all-time low, the farmers sent in bids for the van routes, and supplied whatever conveyance they happened to have. There was a varied assortment of vehicles through the years, a sharp contrast to the neat and uniform ones that characterized the first vans.

Many stories could be told of the trials and experiences of the drivers; fears of the passengers; the long, cold trips; the storms; and the worried parents. No serious accidents ever occurred, although the odd upset on snow-drifted trails often created some excitement and inconvenience. The faithful drivers, in one way or another, managed to get their passengers safely delivered to school and back home. As the years went by, motorized vehicles came into general use. Drivers started using their cars only during the summertime at first, and these were certainly overflowing with children, two or three deep in the back and front seats. It would never have been allowed had there been safety standards and inspections as there are today.

A pupil of the Griffin Consolidated School who used to travel on a horse-drawn school van described above, recalled her experiences with conflicting feelings.

I remember the awful blizzards through which van travel was hazardous and often impossible. And those nights when all the rural students were "storm-bound" at the hotel. It was a hilarious time for us, but surely a harrowing one for the management. What excitement! Some were even homesick, but for most it was a lark. Then there was the beautiful spring day when everyone coaxed en masse and finally persuaded the van driver to roll up the side curtains.

The cost of operating the school vans might have been a heavy burden on the taxpayers in the consolidated school districts, but during the depression period it proved to be a blessing in disguise. It was the astute school board that saw how the transportation grants could be converted into much-needed cash and used to provide a high standard of education for the children. Many consolidated schools were able to operate during periods of

-- Allen Sharples

This is a typical horse-drawn school van that initially made the operation of consolidated schools possible. Ray Wilhite drove this one for Ruby S.D. (Claresholm, Alta.) in 1916; it took him one-and-a-half hours to cover his route, picking up seventeen pupils.

economic recession, while equivalent schools that did not provide van service floundered badly. Under this scheme, each landowner took turns in driving the school van for as many days as the remuneration from the job would equal the amount of his school taxes. No money actually changed hands, and this method of payment was appropriately called "driving out your taxes." When the transportation grant was eventually received by the school board from the Department of Education, instead of using it to pay the van drivers as would have been done normally, the ready-cash was used to pay the teachers' salaries, meet school-maintenance costs, purchase school supplies, and otherwise operate the school efficiently.

Since high school education through the medium of the consolidated district seemed to be beyond the financial means of some rural areas, they turned to other ways of solving the pressing problem.

One very unpopular method was to add grade nine and/or grade ten to the existing rural school, already overloaded with the primary and elementary grades. Parents with children in the lower grades complained bitterly, as they felt their youngsters were being deprived of some valuable instruction time. In certain years, due to small enrollment, several of the elementary grades would be non-existent, so under such circumstances the addition of a high school grade or two didn't seem to be too unfair. Conscientious teachers, not wishing to sacrifice any time allotted to the lower grades, arranged the timetables so that the grades nine and ten students were given instructions primarily after regular hours, and on

Saturdays and holidays. Teachers were willing to accept such extra work in those days as they had no security of tenure whatsoever, and could be replaced easily on the slightest provocation. Besides, there were at least fifty unemployed teachers ready and willing to take over any position no matter how much hard work it entailed.

Another scheme for providing high school education at a cost commensurate with the settlers' ability to pay, was to organize rural high school districts. This consisted of two or more districts combining to provide a school in which grades seven to twelve inclusive could be taught. The individual schools continued to operate as before, but the grade seven to twelve students had the opportunity of attending a small high school. Each district contributed to the cost of building and operating the central high school and appointed a trustee to act on its behalf on the high school district school board. Since the rural high school district was under no legal obligation to provide the expensive transportation for its students, it was felt that these small high schools could operate more economically than the consolidated districts which were committed to do so. Under this setup the youngsters were expected to devise their own ways of getting to school, no matter how far away they lived. In the end it turned out to be the parents of the high school students who had to assume the added responsibility and the expense of providing the transportation for their children. Sometimes this extra burden discouraged many students from taking advantage of a higher education.

The parents in the Gladmar area of Saskatchewan solved the problem of providing a secondary education for their children in a slightly different way. Mrs. John Anstad described their unique method.

It was impossible to send our youngsters to a high school, so we decided the school would have to come to us.

We didn't have much choice in a building, as the only one available was an old pool hall. Our first problem was to scrub it and I can assure you it was no small chore. Water wasn't too plentiful in those days, so chores such as this were usually taken care of on a Monday afternoon, with each lady saving the rinse water from her weekly wash. This recycled water was heated and carried to the dirty hall. We secured a stove, blackboard, chalk and erasers, a few essential books, and a table and chair for the teacher. All this was accomplished through a united community effort. Each student was responsible for his own desk or table and chair, and all his own books. The latter were all bought second-hand. The people of Gladmar accommodated by opening their homes to students from a distance who were desirous of furthering their education. Doors of our school opened in September, 1936, and after a period of four years students began graduating from our "Pool Hall High School"; they eventually became teachers, nurses, engineers and farmers.

Some towns and villages were already operating high schools of one, two, or three rooms, so many parents and rural school boards found a ready solution to their problem of higher education. They sent their youngsters to the "town school". The urban school boards were willing to accept these rural students; the tuition fees charged and the extra pupil grants received from the Department of Education were of considerable help in financing their own schools. Also, an increase in enrollment in the town high school made it more functional.

The main problem for the rural parents, as always, was how to get their children to school every day. Some secured boarding places for them in town, but the most promising solution seemed to be to provide dormitory accommodations. These could be housed in any one of a number of vacant buildings in the town and remodelled to suit their new calling. The dormitories usually were operated on cooperative plans which enabled them to be run very economically, never more than fifteen dollars per month for board and room. In addition, it was possible for the students to pay part of this cost in vegetables, meat, butter, eggs, milk or other farm produce.

School dormitories enabled thousands of rural boys and girls across Canada to avail themselves of a secondary-school education, but like the consolidated schools and the rural high schools, they disappeared from the scene with the coming of the rapid and reliable system of bus transportation. There were many reasons for the failure of dormitories. Rural parents didn't want to be deprived of the company or the help of their sons and daughters. Some feared that the town's ostentatiousness might prove to be too much of a temptation for their youngsters, especially without parental influence, example, and guidance. However, the real cause for the demise of dormitory accommodation was related to the effort to keep operating costs at a minimum. Under such a plan, supervisors were hired not for their ability, training or experience in running dormitories for adolescent boys and girls, but for their willingness to accept the lowest wages possible. The authorities felt that providing the students with the basic necessities of life was sufficient and that the social, recreational, spiritual and educational considerations of communal living could be justifiably overlooked. It was agreed that any scheme which necessitated the students living away from home in order to secure an education must, if it was to be successful, make provision for close supervision of the students' out-of-school activities. Unfortunately, no provision was made for organizing any social or recreational programs for the youngsters. The entire scheme bore a closer resemblance to a military camp than to a home away from home. For example, the Berry Creek and Sullivan Lake School Divisions adopted the following regulations to be observed by the students living in the school dormitory at Hanna, Alberta during the early thirties:

(1) Each student is responsible to the supervisor for good behavior and the proper performance of duty.

(2) Reveille, 7 a.m.

(3) Breakfast, 7:45 to 8:15.

(4) Dormitory duties, 8:15 to 8:45.

(5) Leave for school by 8:45 a.m.

(6) Noon hour, 12 to 1:30 p.m.

(7) Recreation, 4 to 6 p.m.

(8) Supper, 6 to 7 p.m.

(9) Study period, 7 to 10 p.m.

(10) Each student must devote two hours daily to studying out of school hours.

(11) There is to be no loitering down town at any time.

(12) Lights out each evening after the 10 o'clock news broadcast.

(13) There shall be washing and general house-cleaning every Saturday morning.

(14) On Saturday, Sundays and holidays, breakfast and dinner will be one hour later than on school days.

(15) When allowed special concessions by the supervisor, the students concerned must sign a record book setting forth the nature of the concession.

(16) Students will be expected to attend a religious service in Hanna once each Sunday.

(17) The supervisor shall have power to suspend from the dormitory any pupil guilty of open opposition to authority, habitual neglect of duty, the use of profane or improper language or other conduct injurious to the moral tone or well-being of the school. The supervisor shall forthwith report in writing with the complete statement of the circumstances, the fact of such suspension to the committee in charge of the dormitories which committee shall take such action as it may deem necessary with regard thereto.

While high school education for the rural child was passing through its metamorphosis via the consolidated school, rural high school, town high school, and finally the school-division centralization with its rapid bus transportation, an interesting development was taking place with the introduction of high school correspondence courses. If a child found it impossible to attend a regular secondary school for any reason whatsoever, such as living in an isolated part of the country or having some physical disability, he could carry on his education by mail. It also permitted the youngsters who were attending the smaller high schools to supplement their limited programs with correspondence courses. Even a few rural adults took advantage of the services offered by the correspondence branch of some Department of Education, to catch up on their general education, or study some specific subject.

Education by means of correspondence courses in those days was never equal to that provided by a good school, but it was better than no formal education at all, and was more effective than that found in a poor or mediocre school under an inferior teacher. The students taking correspondence lessons over a period of time developed habits of study, research and self-discipline that were beyond those attained by the majority of classroom students. In addition, the correspondence students did so much writing to complete their correspondence assignments that they just naturally learned to express themselves well, and wrote good, clear, thoughtful English. Hence, it was not surprising to find that their grammar, style and fluency of writing were well above average.

Education by mail must have worked well, for some of those who participated became Rhodes' scholars, Governor-General's medal winners, university gold-medalists, and better-than-average students while attending universities, technical institutions, agricultural colleges, commercial-training schools and normal schools. The students who took correspondence courses were well-aware of the advantages and disadvantages of such an education. Selected reactions from participants follow.

> I don't believe I could ever learn by going to school, and working with a lot of other young people. There would be too many distractions, and I am used to working my own way at my own pace.

> I like the correspondence method better than attending school. I can spend as much time as I like on one subject instead of breaking my time up into small periods. I can concentrate more deeply.

> The student who wishes to finish correspondence courses during the time allowed must be determined to succeed. He must have will-power and resourcefulness. He cannot do his work half-way.

> I'd rather go to a real high school any day. A correspondence course is no fun. Most of the correspondence teachers are very firm and make you toe the mark. If I mail lessons that have been carelessly or inaccurately done, they are invariably sent back to me to be repeated.

Obviously, learning by correspondence deprives the student of normal social development, personality growth, and he is at somewhat of a disadvantage in any language study, while in his science work, he is naturally limited to simple experiments. Then there were subjects, that, due to their very nature, could not be offered by correspondence. Nevertheless, correspondence courses provided an equality of educational opportunity for every rural child, no matter how poor, how crippled, how underprivileged, or how remote.

The real impetus to improve teaching methods came at the hands of the teachers, who after having served in the armed services in one capacity or another, returned to resume their peace-time duties in the classroom. Many such veterans, who were sincerely interested in education, recalled the techniques employed by the army, navy and air force in training the recruits quickly and successfully. Hence, it was only natural for the returnees to adopt some of these better teaching procedures in their own classrooms, or if they happened to be administrators, to recommend their use throughout the inspectorate. The postwar period found the schools making more effective use of such educational aids such as reference and library books, various types of visual education equipment, mock-up models, more and better laboratory facilities and equipment, and a variety of field trips. Teachers were attempting to dissipate the confining walls of the classroom and give the students a more comprehensive look at the world outside.

Many of the veterans, however, were not willing to go back to teaching and chose to enter other lines of work. They were fed up with the low salaries, the lack of tenure, the poor living and working conditions, and the lack of any future prospects in the teaching profession. Such ex-servicemen and women used their re-establishment credits to further their training and education in fields other than teaching.

This was a tragic period in the history of Canadian education. Here was the potential supply of experienced teachers who, through additional training and objectivity received in the war, could have become the best the country ever had, but instead they turned their backs on the prospects of returning to the classrooms. The scarcity of qualified teachers, just when it was expected that the veterans would fill all needs, resulted in thousands upon thousands of rural schools closing their doors forever and conveying their pupils to centralized institutions.

Early school districts showed considerable racial, religious and economic diversity; all, more or less, affected educational conditions and progress.

If the majority of the settlers in a particular district were from Eastern Canada, Ontario for instance, a good deal of interest was taken in their school; the attitude was usually serious and earnest, although at times it was closefisted and slightly skeptical of new developments. In communities where Americans settled in considerable numbers, there was perhaps more generous financial support, more enterprise and greater hospitality toward what was new in methods and equipment. These districts not only accepted change readily, but promoted it as well. The Russians and Germans were a sturdy race, hardworking and thrifty. Because of their increased prosperity they were ready to adopt the external comforts and conveniences of modern life; however, they were slow to change their traditional ideas. Girls frequently married at fourteen years and rarely attended school beyond that age. Little education was demanded for the boys and still less for the girls. The Ukrainian settlers were determined to make almost any sacrifice so their children would learn to read, write and understand English. Though they worked stubbornly to build their schools and used their hard-won tax money to finance these institutions, they resented the insistance that all instruction in school must be in English. They feared that, like their oppressors in the Ukraine, the Canadian officials would use the schools as a means of imposing a new language on the children and thus wipe out their Ukrainian mother tongue, their nationality and their culture. This worry, until time and a better understanding of democracy refuted it, resulted in passive resistance to education in their local school districts. A characteristic possessed by most settlers of Scandinavian descent seemed to be a driving energy for public good. With a historic esteem for education, cooperation and democracy, they were eager to do everything possible to provide good schools for their children. The French-Canadians understandably retained their language and their teachers in Quebec and this precedent led to the acceptance of the use of French in some prairie schools at the primary-grade level wherever conditions warranted. The School Act stated:

Section 385 — All schools shall be taught in the English Language.

Section 386 — Notwithstanding Section 385, the board of a district may cause a primary course to be taught in the French language.

Theirs was a way of life that made endless, grinding industry understandable and natural. The special mark of French culture was the priority it gave to language and to literary polish. Hence, things of the mind had automatic prestige and the purveyors of ideas were taken very seriously. No wonder the French settlers were eager to organize schools in their areas.

The early settlers who emigrated to Canada, regardless of their particular origins, were mainly peasants, adventurers, malcontents and the persecuted. They had either no schooling at all, or at best only enough to enable them to read and to write; they were ready to endure anything in their search for freedom and opportunity, not for themselves, but for their children. Their initial steps to organize school districts took time, for to those who had come from countries to escape oppression, the democratic way of life was strange. They were quick to grasp democracy's opportunities, but slow to accept its attending responsibilities. It didn't take them long to become aware that their lack of education and inability to speak English interfered with their ability to function efficiently under such a regime. Educational authorities realized that these ethnic groups, which had settled on the prairies and set up close-knit communities, needed more help than the average predominantly Anglo-Saxon, or American populated districts; they appointed school supervisors to provide this type of assistance. The general method followed in administering such schools was to make the management paternal to the point of having the necessary work or business done, but to decentralize as speedily as possible the exercise of authority, and have it devolve upon the trustees, so as to have them learn to do by doing what was necessary to carry on the work of the schools.

Rather conservative and set in their ideas and having in their church a sufficient guide and counsel, these new Canadians did not share the western world's feeling about the importance of the social part of school. In fact, the clergy of the Lutherans, Catholics, Mennonites and the Fundamentalists rather feared that this new western education for everyone might tend to cause their children to break away from their traditions. Hence, these groups, through their own education and strong discipline at home and in the church, attempted to instill in their young people much of the old-world conformity. Such a resolve on the part of the majority of the citizens in any school district often assisted local education, as in the matter of discipline and behavior, but at other times it seemed to oppose what was being attempted in the local school, when subjects and activities outside the "3 R's" were introduced.

Living next door to an innovative neighbor, Canada finds herself copying many of these changes. This is particularly true in the field of education. It is immaterial whether the new idea, method or device has proven to be successful or not; Canadian educational leaders feel they have to adopt whatever is new in order to keep up-to-date, as well as to keep up with the Joneses. So down through the years, for good or for bad, always lagging respectfully a year or two behind, Canada's educational system has mimicked the pattern set by the United States.

In the mid-thirties, Canadian educators were strongly influenced by the pragmatic philosophy of John Dewey and the progressive education movement which grew out of it. This "new deal" in education emphasized that the child, and not the contents of the textbook or the course of studies, was the all-important thing. Hence, the so-called "child-centered school" came into being in Canada, with its stress on an enterprise or activity program.

The 1936 program of studies for the elementary schools of Alberta explained "enterprise education" for the edification of the teachers in the following manner:

> The name "enterprise" has been chosen to designate the "doing or activity", rather than the familiar "project", because it has a somewhat stricter meaning. An enterprise is a definite undertaking; teacher and pupil agree upon it and tacitly promise to carry it through as agreed. An enterprise is an undertaking chosen, after consideration, for its interest and value; carefully planned in advance, carried out according to plan, and brought to a definite conclusion, after which some reckoning of gains is made. An enterprise is not only a carefully organized undertaking in itself, but it is also a part of the whole, a definite step in a course designed to cover three years of work. Each enterprise involves planning, the organization of ideas and of materials, and cooperation. Enterprises include both mental and manual work, the collection of information and the practice of skills. A well-chosen enterprise:

Is centered in the interests of the pupils.
Is within the range of their ability.
Suggests several kinds of information to be sought.
Offers several kinds of work to be done.
Provides different types of social experience.
Is capable of being completed within a reasonable length of
time.

Enterprise education was first introduced into Canadian schools on an experimental basis; since the participants, as in the majority of such educational experiments, were carefully chosen, the results were a foregone conclusion. In no time at all, every school in the country was struggling with the enterprise or activity system of education.

The innovation was not too successful in rural schools; teachers, confused and frustrated by what the new method was or demanded, gave only lip service to it. Besides, the very nature of the activity program made more, rather than less, demands of the already overworked rural teacher. If the new method was to succeed at all, it would require teachers of above-average intelligence, with good general education and well-directed professional training. Unfortunately, at that time most rural teachers had only eleven years of general education and one year of professional training, a far cry from what was needed to succeed with the enterprise system. In addition, the rapid growth of educational jargon perplexed these poorly qualified teachers no end. To complicate matters further, the new program required a wealth of resource material that was just not available in the average country school. As a consequence, rural education suffered for years as the fundamentals of every course were neglected in favor of activity for activity's sake. Children were spending their school days cutting, drawing, pressing, mounting, labelling, modelling, painting, collecting, building, hammering, pasting, tracing and visiting, completely oblivious to the ultimate objectives. Classrooms blossomed forth with imposing displays and exhibits of every sort, but the children were gradually losing their skills in reading, mathematical computations and writing. Enterprise education continued to fail miserably for years to come because planning was careless and specific outcomes were never considered seriously. At best, children received a hodgepodge education that was bereft of either the best of the traditional methods or those of the enterprise system.

It was just at this time that the publishers of educational materials saw their opportunities and flooded the market with teachers' aids, helps and manuals of all sorts. Enterprise projects on every topic were worked out in detail; all the teacher had to do was to purchase the commercially-produced sets that appealed to her, and then have the students follow the outline of suggestions and activities step-by-step. Some publishers even provided ready-made kits so there would be no need for the teacher or her pupils to improvise or do any research work whatsoever. Everything was at

-- W. H. Hay

The walls of the Elmer S.D. (Hanna, Alta.) display the efforts of the pupils and their teacher, Mrs. Joseph Haluschuk, to plan, initiate, and carry out cooperative projects.

hand, ready for the educational activity. Teachers' manuals were available in all subjects right through to grade twelve. In no time at all, teachers were religiously following these manuals word for word, and some even went so far as to require their students to purchase them. Suddenly the manuals became programs of studies, classroom correspondence courses, textbooks, testing devices and reference booklets, all rolled into one. As a result, the tyranny of teaching aids was evident in almost every classroom. This method of teaching and learning left little room for the development of individual interests, initiative, or special aptitudes; but it was a boon to the rural teacher who now had guidance and resource material for her enterprise projects. It wasn't until the teachers received a better insight into the philosophy and the methods of enterprise education, gained through experience and additional professional training, that the activity program began to attain some measure of success; however, it came too late for the rural schools. The idea of school centralization was catching on about this time, so thousands of these one-room schools were closing for the last time. Very few survived long enough to dissipate the defects of enterprise education; to the ones that did survive, progressive education was just another innovation that somehow didn't work too well. As always it was the children who suffered the most from those new educational practices introduced indiscriminately, before teachers were prepared and ready for them.

13

In a Whimsical Mood

Man differs from other earthly creatures in his ability to laugh. As this gift relaxes the mind and body and reduces tension, it is only natural to expect man to take advantage of this endowment and see humor, at least to some degree, in even his most trying situations. Any historical account of man that does not include some of his humorous moments is definitely anomalous. Yet it must be understood that his sense of humor, as well as his reasons for laughter, change from generation to generation. What was funny fifty years ago does not precipitate the same reactions today. After all, in the intervening years, man's pattern of living, working and playing has changed so dramatically that very few people are familiar with what life was like in the early days. Even words and expressions that once were a common part of our language, if used now, convey no more meaning than if they were uttered in Vedic.

The majority of people in the early days were born and raised, or partly raised, in the rural parts of the country, so a good deal of their humor was of a type peculiar to agrarian life. It was individualistic, remained intact and fresher much longer than those originating in the urban centers, and was by far the most easily found and enjoyed. Farm folks had kindly senses of humor and often allowed themselves to be the butts of jokes, even if the connotations were unkind. They didn't mind being laughed at but, to a degree, resented being taken as country dupes. A simple way of life bred a simple type of humor, and their witticism was often described as being "corny". Yet corny or not, their humor afforded them more enjoyment from life than that gained by many urban dwellers. Besides, people who possessed senses of humor could find laughter in most of their adversities; this was an asset that enabled them to meet the challenges of living under pioneer conditions. Maybe some of their humor was ribald in nature, but that was to be expected from inhabitants living in a rough and ready land. It was a time that most people are glad is past. Yet an important lesson in living was learned during that period for, by and large, a human being must retain a sense of humor if he wants to get the most out of life and meet its challenges successfully. Our prairie pioneers illustrated this stratagem most efficaciously.

The term "tenderfoot" is rarely used today, but not so long ago each newcomer to an agrarian community was tabbed by that name. It was only after participating in some unique initiating rites, of which he was blissfully ignorant, that he eventually found ready acceptance by his local peers. The snipe hunt and the badger fight were two of the commonest means of initiating the tenderfoot.

In the snipe hunt the unsuspecting tenderfoot is told of the delight of having a mess of snipe for breakfast, a feast for a king no less. Once the subject's interest in catching snipe is aroused, he is informed that it's not such a difficult task, because when the birds are disturbed at night they have a tendency to fly toward a light. Someone suggests that the clueless tenderfoot assumes the responsibility of holding the sack open, as all the other skills demand experience and training. Once the greenhorn agrees to participate, the hunt is on. He is taken to an isolated spot, given a lantern to hold or asked to keep a fire going, and instructed to hold a burlap bag wide open in front of the light. He is informed that the snipe will fly into the bag and all he has to do is wait until a dozen or so birds enter, snap the mouth of the sack shut, and call it a day. The others disappear, allegedly to carry out the intricate task of chasing the snipe off their roost. After a few minutes of earsplitting din somewhere in the distance, all becomes very quiet. The tenderfoot stands in great anticipation and carries out his duties to the letter. He waits, and waits, and waits, holding the sack open by the fire or light burning brightly. After an hour or so, depending on the patience of the victim, he becomes suspicious, gives up, and wends his way back to the farmhouse, where he is greeted with smirks and jeers from the perpetrators of the joke. It is from this classic snipe hunt that the western expression of "holding the bag" originated.

In the badger fight the tenderfoot is talked into volunteering to pull a cord which will open a box and release a badger to engage in a fight with a dog. He is selected, so he is told, because being a stranger, he is neither a supporter of the badger or dog and would not pull out the badger at a time that would be advantageous to either animal. The greenhorn is also told that when the two beasts clash, blood literally flies, so he is advised to roll up the legs of his trousers before performing his task, in order not to get them splattered with blood. Then the stage is set. A box with a rope dangling from one end of it is brought into the yard. This is supposed to contain the ferocious badger. A dog is also led in and held facing the box, about twenty feet from it. Dog, box and tenderfoot by this time are surrounded by a group of noisy spectators all making large bets on one animal or the other. Soon the great moment arrives! The signal is given and the tenderfoot yanks excitedly on the cord, expecting to see a hideous-looking badger come dashing out to hurl himself at the peaceful-looking dog.

Instead, out flies a chamber pot — and a full one at that. The result often was very embarrassing to the unfortunate victim.

These unique and jocular customs of welcoming newcomers were not limited to single people; newly-married couples were also given special recognition. The affair, known as a "charivari", involved more people and generally produced more fun and hubbub than the peer initiations.

Preparations for a charivari were secretive. If the young couple had a telephone, no calls were made on their party line, because it was so easy for someone to slip up and the newlyweds were apt to make plans of their own to circumvent the proceedings. Neighbors and friends would agree to meet at a designated spot near the young couple's home, where they would be safe from detection and yet could spy to see when the light went out. The objective was to catch the couple in their night attire as this added to the hilarity of the party.

At the rendezvous, everyone was warned about showing lights or making any noise, so there were no car lights, no lit lanterns, no cigarettes, no talking and no laughter. Everyone came prepared carrying all manner of noise-making gadgets, usually picked up from the nuisance ground or some garbage heap. These included such things as washtubs, plow shares, kettles, tin cans, pails, parts of machinery, horns, cowbells — anything that had the potential of making a loud racket.

The people might have travelled to the meeting place by wagon, buggy or car, but from there to the actual scene of revelry everyone went on foot. When all was in readiness, the leader gave the command; under cover of the darkness the crowd crept stealthily toward the unsuspecting couple's home and in short order surrounded the house. Then, at the firing of a shotgun or some other prearranged signal, everyone made as much noise as possible, marched around and around the house, and added to the din by shouting, screaming and laughing. This was kept up until the couple answered the banging on the door and invited the crowd inside to spend the evening. Any neighbor who hadn't heard of the charivari by moccasin telegraph was sure to hear the racket and hastened to join in the fun. In some rural areas the secret message was relayed to all and sundry by burning a specified strawstack or flying a flag in an unusual way.

The ladies who came to the charivari always brought ample lunch, so all the bewildered couple had to do was to provide the coffee. Such evenings were spent in singing, dancing, playing games, and just having a good time. It gave the residents of the district an opportunity to bid the couple welcome and extend their wishes for a long and happy married life. If the bride was new to the district, it provided her with a chance to become acquainted with her neighbors for miles around on the first night in her new home.

Not all charivaries turned out as planned, for since intrigue was part of their uniqueness, it was only natural that on some occasions plans would go awry.

When Edwin Miller and Annie Clayton were married on the first day
of June in 1912, they began their married life by driving out to the groom's
homestead in the Lid S.D. 1765 (Sundre, Alta.) with a load of lumber to fix
up the shack. They spent the better part of the day repairing the interior,
putting in a new floor, hanging curtains, and giving the place a general
cleanup. Since news of their wedding was common knowledge in the
district, and they had been seen driving out to the homestead, the
newlyweds were more than suspicious they would be charivaried that
evening. There is nothing like being prepared! They turned the coal-oil
lamp down, fixed their bed so it had the appearance of being occupied, and
then went over to their nearest neighbor who, as they had expected, had left
to take in their charivari. It wasn't long before they heard the banging of old
washtubs, the clatter of stove pipes and tin cans, the clanging of cowbells,
the shouts of many voices, and even the blare of an army bugle sounding
out the morning reveille. It was delightful! They waited for a discreet period
of time and then slipped across through the bush back to their own place.
Not being recognized in the dark, they joined in the fun. It wasn't until after
the merrymakers discovered that the sleeping occupants in the bed were
only rolls of building paper and the lights turned up that the couple was
recognized hiding in the crowd. The gathering had a wonderful evening, but
everyone kept wondering how the newlyweds managed to feed them with
such a fine lunch, when they had no idea anyone was coming. Yes! and how
about the rolls of building paper in their bed?

A similar intrigue occurred in the Buffalo Hills S.D. 1700 (Vulcan,
Alta.). A large crowd of neighbors and friends had gathered quietly near the
shack of a popular local cowboy who, according to his spying buddies, had
just returned from Calgary with his new bride. In fact they had seen them
riding together in his coupe along a little-used trail to his ranch in the hills
that very afternoon. However, after the usual outburst of serenading, there
was no response whatsoever from within the interior of the dwelling. The
crowd began to suspect a slip-up somewhere until an alert stake-out
discovered the cowboy's coupe in its usual place. It was taken for granted
that the newlyweds were still in the house, so the noisy parade was resumed
with new vigor. There still were no results! It was just at this moment that a
carload of noisy late comers drove into the yard with the horn blaring and
the lights blazing. A young couple, bearing a beat-up washtub between
them, made a dash to evade the beam of light. They were too late! A cry of
consternation burst from the revellers when they recognized the bride and
groom. The newlyweds had been marching around with the rest,
unrecognized in the darkness, and had been contributing their share to the
general bedlam of noise and confusion. The turn-around surprise was
accepted in good faith by the victimized crowd, especially when the newly
weds produced a washtub full of sandwiches and a boiler of coffee, ready
and waiting. Besides, the thoughtful couple had readied a nearby granary to

be used as an emergency dance hall. The building had been scrubbed clean and the floor sprinkled with cornmeal. Who could ask for more?

Peter Jacobsen of the Dalum S.D. 3969 (Drumheller, Alta.) had a childhood sweetheart in Denmark; however, he kept the secret so well that it was only after living in the district for some six years that the hush-hush matter was brought to light when, in April, 1924, he sent for Agnes Andersen to join him. When the people in the district heard of the forthcoming wedding they went ahead and organized a charivari for the couple. The only trouble was that they had the date wrong — one day too early. Fortunately, the leader peeked through a window just before giving the signal for starting the fanfare. He saw Peter, all alone in bed, reading a newspaper. The disappointed crowd sneaked away sheepishly, just as quietly as they had rendezvoused a few minutes before. The next evening, after securing the information that the wedding ceremony had been performed that day, the Dalum people gave the couple a real western charivari, including the firing of a shotgun. The new bride was terrified; she had no idea what all the shouting and racket was all about. She assumed that the Indians were attacking them. It was only after her husband explained the purpose of such a welcome that she felt reassured and stopped worrying. After that, everything settled down into a peaceful, happy party.

Probably the best example of intrigue connected with a charivari occurred in the Cayley S.D. (Cayley, Alta.) in March, 1905. Donald Sinclair, a popular bachelor in the district, made a trip to Eastern Canada and immediately the news was making the rounds that he would return with a bride. After some planning the neighbors decided to meet the train from Calgary, accompany the newlyweds to their farm with as much noise and hilarity as possible, and then spend the rest of the evening with a get-acquainted party for the new bride. Garfield Sloane, a recent bridegroom who had experienced a rather hectic charivari, decided to help his friend and throw a monkey-wrench into the proposed festive arrangements. He sent word, via the conductor of the local train, telling the Sinclairs in Calgary of the charivari and informing them that he had arranged with the conductor for the train to stop at a place some miles west of Cayley that evening; he would be waiting for them with a wagon and team.

Everything went like clockwork. The train made its unscheduled stop and Garfield was there to meet the couple and take them to his home. The people waiting at the station soon discovered that the newlyweds were not on the train, and, smelling a rat, all rushed out to the Sinclair house. With more enthusiasm and energy than ever, they serenaded the couple presuming they were inside. It wasn't until the greater part of their efforts had been exhausted that someone discovered the house was empty. It took several days for the community to learn how they had been duped, but by that time the newlyweds were settled comfortably in their new home and ready to meet their frustrated neighbors.

It was customary at a charivari in the early days to blow the stove pipe protruding through the roof of the newlywed's shack full of holes with a shotgun. A recently married young man in the North Star S.D. 577 (Clive, Alta.), aware of the custom, decided to do something about it. When the people assembled at his place to charivari him and his wife, they discovered there wasn't one stovepipe, but seven sticking out of the roof. The man delegated to do the riddling was confused as to which pipe was the real chimney outlet, so he ended up by giving each one a blast from his shotgun.

Some charivaries were anything but flippant. In the Brownlee S.D. (Brownlee, Alta.), if the bride and groom did not come out of their house within a reasonable time after being serenaded, someone would climb on top of the building and stuff an old sack in the stovepipe or chimney. It was a dangerous practice, but it always had the desired effect of "smoking out" the newlyweds from their hiding place.

In some districts the tricks played on newlyweds were downright embarrassing, indiscreet and vexatious, a far cry from the original intention of bidding welcome to a newly-married couple and extending the best wishes of the community to them. Rash tricks sometimes were played if the bridegroom boasted that they wouldn't dare to such a thing to him, or when someone had a score to settle because of some incident that occurred at his charivari. Gruff, unapproachable, defiant or conceited individuals were apt to receive such wanton treatment at their charivaries. Neighbors might lock the groom in a barn, put him down a well or even in the local jail; spirit his bride away for the night; fix their bed so it would collapse, or wire a cowbell to the springs underneath; take the groom a mile or two away from his home, remove his outer garments and let him wend his way back to his bride the best way he could, clothed only in his underwear.

The charivari was an early version of "trick or treat," but the routine was to trick as well as get treated afterwards. Usually after a noisy interlude the crowd left their noisemakers outside by the door and all went in, fully expecting a treat of some sort, notwithstanding that the newlyweds had no idea anyone was coming. Sometimes the new couples would make arrangements for lunch and refreshments, but somehow or other these goodies often had a strange way of reaching the wrong place. A good example of this occurred in the Langdon S.D. (Calgary, Alta.). A democrat that was headed towards the scene of a charivari contained two full kegs of beer and other refreshments, purchased by the groom to treat the guests at his charivari. Quick thinking on the part of some of the more avaricious celebrants present directed the vehicle down the road a couple of miles, where the refreshments were consumed. The conspirators then wound their way home, leaving the poor bridegroom without even a taste of his purchases.

Sometimes the pranks were of an absurd nature. In the Steep Rock S.D. (Steep Rock, Man.) for instance, a young man was in the habit of making periodic visits to Winnipeg to court his girlfriend. Everytime he returned, all his friends in the district would be waiting expectantly to see his bride. She never came! One time a local joker, fed up with Cupid's languor, had to go to Winnipeg on business the same time the local Romeo was in the city doing his courting. The business man couldn't resist the temptation of wiring his associate in Steep Rock the following terse message, "The unexpected has happened. Bride and groom arriving on the next train." In the meantime he borrowed a blue skirt, a big hat, some other accessories, and dressed as the supposed new bride. The town turned out to meet the train with the old ladies descending on the "bride" to welcome her with hugs, tears and kisses. One innocent bystander's only comment was, "The new bride sure has big feet!"

Through the ages, some of the activities and attitudes of the younger generation have been disconcerting elements in the lives of those in their years of discretion. The early days in Canada were no exception. The absence of any commercial or organized entertainment compelled the youngsters to make their own fun. Halloween, in particular, gave them as good an opportunity as any to put their diabolical potentials into high gear. Yet, to their credit, there was little damage to property and the majority of such escapades were unique in nature, waggish, and involved a considerable amount of work to perpetrate and an equal amount of effort to repair.

It was a common frolic on Halloween to take the buggies and wagons apart, carry them to the top of various buildings and reassemble them there. The roof of the local rural school seemed to be the ideal place for displaying the handiwork of the district's gagsters. If the perpetrators were less daring, the dismantled vehicle or machine was set up inside the school, after having first piled all the desks to one side. Inconsiderate jokers didn't even bother doing this; they rebuilt their monstrosity right on top of the desks.

W. B. Walrod of the Munson S.D. (Munson, Alta.) had a couple of late-model farm machines assembled on his lot, and the bigger boys couldn't resist the temptation of becoming mechanically minded that Halloween. Under cover of darkness they took the machines apart, borrowed a few long ladders, carried all the parts up on the roof of the implement shed, and then assembled them as best they could. Satisfied with their efforts, the boys came down only to find Mr. Walrod waiting for them. He persisted in staying there until the procedure was reversed and all the parts back on the ground and assembled to his satisfaction. After spending some five hours in carrying and handling the heavy parts, the boys were in no condition or mood or join in any other Halloween pranks that year.

Usually by the time Halloween rolled around, most homes had a good supply of split wood neatly piled somewhere near the house, all ready for winter. It was strange how such firewood seemed to grow legs and end up in a jumble against the back door, inside the biffy, on top of the house, or in some other unexpected location. Gasoline drums, and rain barrels also had such wandering tendencies on Halloween nights, and since it was much easier to roll them than to cart wood, they were found in doorways, neatly stacked in the middle of the street, strewn in the ditches along a well-travelled road, or precariously perched on a roof. Grain stooks had the habit of defecting from roadside fields and mysteriously taking up positions on the road allowances, trim and indomitable as ever. Halloween was certainly no time to leave a load of hay or sheaves around, for it frequently meant extra work the next day. The usual stunt was to move the loaded hayrack to some inconvenient location, unload it, lift the rack off the wagon, set it on the ground beside the pile of feed, reload the dismounted rack, and finally hide the running gear of the wagon. The next morning the unfortunate farmer would have to unload the disabled rack, locate the wagon and raise the hayrack back on it, reload the sheaves into the once-more mobile rack, and eventually haul the load to its intended destination. Work was the name of this Halloween stunt no matter from whose side it was considered.

Milk cows, being docile creatures and used to the idiosyncracies of man, proved to be excellent subjects for Halloween shenanigans. One trick was to push, squeeze and cajole such an animal into a chicken coop. No farmer in his right mind would ever think of looking for his lost cow in such a small place. Usually he searched near and far on horseback and even made inquiries of all his neighbors as to the whereabouts of his missing bovine. In the meantime, the cow would be discovered by whoever had the chore of feeding the chickens. The animal would be so well wedged in the diminutive quarters that it was often necessary to remove one of the walls of the shed to set her free. A cow was never left in a pasture near a schoolhouse on Halloween, for the owner was sure to find her inside surrounded by a stack of hay or straw.

Ainsley Young of the Chestermere S.D. (Calgary, Alta.) wasn't confronted by the problem of missing cows when he went to milk them on the morning following Halloween, but he was surprised to find his dairy herd all harnessed up and ready for work in the field. His horses, on the other hand, had been moved over to the cow's stall, apparently ready to be milked.

"Body painting" cannot be said to be a discovery of today's permissive society, for any oldtimer will vouchsafe for the fact that such art has been used for several generations. In the Sunny Alberta S.D. (Sunnynook, Alta.) it was John Ryan's practice to mix up a bucket of whitewash on Halloween and then travel around the district locating the schoolboys' saddle horses, whitewashing each one with an artistic design. The boys didn't find out who the artist was until many years later; by then it was too late to do anything about it. They should have had some inkling of the culprit's identity, for one Halloween night Mr. Ryan caught some of these youngsters in his chicken house. Every boy received a generous brush-stroke of whitewash across the seat of his pants, skillfully applied with a big brush by Mr. Ryan as they fled one by one out the door.

Submissive farm animals in particular suffered the indignity of having their bodies painted. On the morning after Halloween, cows, horses, pigs, and even poultry occasionally appeared so disguised under a coat of dye, paint or whitewash, that it took a wise owner to pick out his own livestock. A green-colored bird or animal might have had the protective coloration that nature denied it in the first place, but conversely, due to the artificial color barrier, the unfortunate was shunned by his own kind. If he tried to get near them they either scattered or turned on him with the full intentions of annihilating him on the spot.

Halloween or not, the young men in some rural districts were in the habit of putting on an annual "chicken feed" in the fall of the year. It was a clandestine affair from start to finish. No chicken house was free from raids, but in true western tradition no more than one bird was removed from any place, and none taken from farmers known to be in difficult financial straits. The foraging was so well apportioned that the scroungers rarely heard a word afterwards about anyone missing any chickens. The assortment of food collected was taken to the house of some bachelor whose culinary expertise was recognized and there the men worked together under his directions, killing, picking, cleaning and cooking the filched birds. Soon the young men sat down to what they always maintained was a sumptuous feast, no matter how badly it had been prepared. Stolen "sweets" were the best as far as they were concerned. Once in a while the women who tended the setting hens heard of these hush-hush feeds, but since they never knew for sure that the culprits weren't their own sons, they didn't complain too bitterly.

Many Halloween tricks were simple, harmless and full of surprises. Since ladders were in much more common use in the early days than they are today, one stunt was to paint the back of the upper rungs with red paint on the left and blue on the right, and then entice some unsuspecting individual to climb up the ladder.

"Prince Albert" was the name of a brand of tobacco, and it became a common joke on Halloween to ask the storekeeper if he had, "Prince Albert in the can." When the merchant said, "Yes!", the joker eagerly replied, especially if there was a good crowd of spectators around, "Well, why don't you let him out!"

Sounds in themselves are always interesting, but when produced spuriously to trick people into making wrong connotations they could become a very effective type of raillery to use on Halloween. Tick-tacking houses was one such stunt.

To tick-tack, the mischief-bent youngsters fastened a small lump of resin near the middle of a long piece of strong string or cord; then, two boys grasped the ends and dragged the resin back and forth very slowly across a corner of a house, just like a cross-cut saw, but made sure it was always in contact with the wooden siding. The resulting friction produced a sound like someone pulling nails. A bachelor in the Ferrodale S.D. 1909 (Vulcan, Alta.) was almost driven to distraction one Halloween night by such a trick. He took the trouble to light his coal-oil lantern and then got down on his hands and knees to examine the nails in the corner boards of his shack. The boys saw him shaking his head in disbelief as he went back inside.

A similar resin-on-a-piece-of-string device was used to tap on windows. Since it could be done from any distance, depending upon the length of string used, there was little danger of getting caught. Once people became aware of the source of such baffling sounds they didn't let it bother them but passed it off by mumbling, "Just a Halloween joke!"

Another Halloween intrigue came packaged in an envelope. The instigator bent a paper clip in the form of a horseshoe and fastened a rubber band across the open part with a button threaded on it. Then he wound up the button and placed it inside an envelope to hold it flat. The moment somebody opened the letter the button spun around crazily inside making a noise like a mouse trying to get out. Such a commotion often frightened the squeamish recipient half out of his or her wits.

The sound of cowbells emanating from a nearby field of wheat or oats was always interpreted as an alarm, for it usually meant that some stray cattle had broken through the fences and were damaging the crop. Walter Rosenau of the Bison S.D. (Chinook, Alta.) remembers one Halloween night when several young fellows, bent on some mischief, went into a field of oats that had been recently cut and ran hither and thither ringing cowbells among the green-feed stooks. George, a very conscientious farmer, upon hearing the bells, quickly pulled his denim coveralls over his night gown and chased around the field looking for the stray cattle. It took half-an-hour of pursuit before he discovered that there were no cattle, only some boys from town with cowbells.

The march of progress across this land has quietly and steadily erased the majority of the silent prairie sentinels which stood to the rear of many rural and urban homes, ever since they were first erected by the early settlers. Halloween will never be the same without these outhouses, for it was customary on that particular night to tip over as many of these so-called "conveniences" as possible, thus making life inconvenient for numerous families. It was such an accepted stunt that most people expected it and usually accepted it in good faith. In fact, one memorable night the boys discovered that the "parliament building" they had just overturned contained a "sitting member" of no gentle disposition. As the gang of youngsters had purposely planned to tip the building so it would fall forward onto the door, the unsuspecting meditator was well and truly trapped. As the boys fled at this unexpected turn of events they could hear, to their great glee, his infuriated calls for help through the twin portholes of his prison. They knew he was too stout even to contemplate making his escape through one of the openings and catch them.

A lad in the Rathwell S.D. (Rathwell, Man.) recalls the Halloween when they filled the two school outhouses with split wood and then pushed them over with the doors face-down. The next day, as it was impossible to restore the heavily laden biffies to their upright positions, the culprits were forced to crawl through the holes in the two buildings and retrieve wood until the privies became light enough to set up.

A few persons, knowing full well that their outhouses would be tipped, plotted ways and means of some form of retaliation. A common method was to move the outhouse slightly forward, backward, or sideways from its usual position. Hence, when the unwary mischief makers attempted to topple the little building in the dark, they usually stepped into the exposed opening expecting solid footing, and found themselves nose diving into a pit of excrement. What a horrible way to celebrate Halloween.

One Halloween, Bill of the Haynes S.D. (Clive, Alta.) decided it was time that different tactics be used in dealing with outhouses. He donated a generous supply of Black Beauty axle grease to the boys and asked them to smear the seats of every privy in the district. His henchmen carried out the instructions to the letter, for the next morning he discovered just how inconvenient and difficult it was to remove axle grease from his own anatomy.

The oldtimers of the Nobleford S.D. (Nobleford, Alta.) still chuckle about what happened to their outhouses one Halloween some thirty years ago. So many biffies had been upended that night that the Royal Canadian Mounted Police were called in the morning to check on the damage. They discovered that every outhouse, instead of being toppled over, had been lifted from its moorings, carried over to the Canadian Pacific Railway tracks, and loaded on some empty flat cars that had been left by a wayfreight that afternoon. However, during the night, the cars, privies and all were picked up by a through-freight and were eventually located at Blairmore in the Crow's Nest Pass, some ninety-miles away.

Langdon S.D. 220 (Langdon, Alta.) was another district that recorded an unusual Halloween stunt involving the Canadian Pacific Railway. It seemed that a few boys, well-read in science, collected a quantity of soap which they melted and spread on the railroad tracks. A little later in the evening the unsuspecting engineer drew the Medicine Hat train to a stop in front of the station at the very spot where the rails had been smeared. Perhaps he noticed the absence of the gang of young boys who usually came to meet the train, but on this special evening they had decided to watch proceedings from a safe distance. When the train was ready to leave, the wheels of the engine simply spun on the soapy track. The more steam the engineer turned on, the faster the wheels rotated; the rails got hotter, the soap softer, but the train stood still. Eventually, when the source of the trouble was discovered, a garage was contacted for some gasoline to remove the greasy film from the rails. It was only after the rails had been thoroughly scrubbed that the train was able to proceed on its way. The spinning wheels of the engine had worn some section of the track to such an extent that the next day it was necessary for the local section crew to put in several new rails.

The majority of the homesteaders, coming as they did from every walk of life, were anything but experienced farmers. In their attempts to wrestle a living from the soil, they were bound to make mistakes. Problems there were, in plenty, as well as all the worries accompanying them. Happily, the majority cultivated a sense of humor, a sort of safety valve that helped them to see themselves and others in true perspective.

Mr. Diefenbaker, an uncle of a former Canadian prime minister, proved to be a very capable and well-liked teacher in the Sunny Glenn S.D. (Vulcan, Alta.). He also farmed near the school, but never appeared to be as efficient a farmer as he was a schoolteacher. Once his neighbors observed him trotting his horses to the end of a field he was seeding. It was unusual to drive a span of six horses pulling a seed drill at such a fast clip, so the concerned farmer went over to find out the reason for the haste. He arrived there just in time to see Mr. Diefenbaker jump from the drill, open the lid, look inside and merrily shout, "I've made it! I've made it!"

"Made what?" enquired the curious neighbor.

"I had to hurry. I didn't think I had enough seed to finish this field," added the pleased teacher-farmer.

When Felix Corbiell arrived in Gleichen, Alberta from the United States in 1910, he went directly to the livery stable to hire a couple of rigs to take him and his family to a small farm he had bought in the Wheatfield S.D. (Cluny, Alta.). The proprietor who ran the barn didn't quite understand what the stranger meant by "rig" so he asked, "You mean a democrat?" Mr. Corbeill, now quite taken aback, retorted resentfully, "Do you have to declare your political affiliation before you can get a rig up here?" It was now the attendant's turn to be surprised. "Oh," he apologized, "You must be from the States!" Then he went on to explain, "In Canada, we call a two-seat rig a democrat." Mr. Corbeill, happy to learn that politics did not interfere with business transactions in the new land, quickly added, "Well, I'd like to hire two of them ... them, ... them, ... democrats."

A lumberjack from the province of Quebec took up a homestead in the Glen Afton S.D. 1725 (Semans, Sask.) and after "proving it up" decided to stay in this fine district. People liked him, for although he could neither read nor write, he was an interesting conversationalist and had a ready wit. One time he went into the bank at Semans and said to one of the clerks, "Give me one of those new calendars, kid. I've had the same one for five years!"

When the Canadian West was opened for settlement, there were signs throughout Ontario, Quebec and the Maritimes advertising the free land and the wonderful railway extending from coast to coast; the idea was to attract newcomers. One such sign read, "Come and make your fortune in this land flowing with milk and honey!" Such a promise of a halcyon life however took on a more sinister outlook when some wag pencilled in the words, "Yes, if you keep cows and bees!" directly underneath it.

Times change and taste changes with them. A few shenanigans that oldsters roared at in their youth would be described as uncouth today and draw sneers rather than laughter. Besides, it is doubtful whether the necessary environment and conditions, so common in the average early agrarian district for perpetrating such stunts, are even available in our present-day urban communities.

One such indelicate ruse was called, "Under the hat!" It was always good for at least one performance, but once an upstart had been fooled, there was no way he ever fell for it again. A cow pasture was the ideal place for pulling it off. While the boys were fooling around in such a field or just crossing it, one of the youngsters would let out a wild whoop to attract the attention of the scapegoat and then start dashing around a likely spot, as if he were trying to catch a gopher, a rabbit, a weasel, a field mouse, a bird, or even a butterfly. The instant the pursuer saw the gang head in his direction, he flipped his hat or cap forward as if trapping the imaginary prize; then he dove head first for the hat, placed his hands gently over it, and waited. In reality the hat was tossed over a pile of fresh cow dung. The "victim", who by now was almost dying from curiosity, was permitted to win the foot race to the hat, get down on his knees, and be ready to help capture the prize creature. After a few anxious moments to allow the rest of the boys to come up, he was rewarded for his burst of speed and curiosity, by being given the honor of slipping his hands under the hat and seizing the gopher, bird, or whatever had been conjured for the occasion. That's exactly what usually happened! Other than to say it worked well, there is no need for any further comment.

The hub of social life in any rural community was a schoolhouse, so it wasn't long before dances were held there on a regular basis. The whole family attended and every member was expected to participate in the activities, no matter how young or old they happened to be. Since mothers were their own baby sitters, even the infants were bundled up and taken along to the school. Here the babies were deposited on a bed in the teacherage or some adjoining room and left there for the evening. Every so often a mother would leave the dance, tip-toe over to the babies' room, look in on the sleeping tots, quiet any restless ones, and then return to her merrymaking. This custom of putting all the babies in one place often provided an opportunity for a person with a capricious turn of mind to play pranks. These pranks included switching the babies into different places, hiding them in another room or under the bed, or even exchanging their clothing and blankets. The confusion created was always overwhelming and nerve-wracking: mothers would scream upon discovering their baby girls had mysteriously become boys, or vice-versa. The dancers would rush into the room to see what all the commotion was about. Women with babies would awaken tots looking for their own; the tots would loudly protest against being handled by strange mothers. Other infants would cry in sympathy with their harassed colleagues. Husbands would look somewhat suspiciously at the offsprings their wives were holding; sometimes a father and mother would argue with other parents, or with each other, about the rightful ownership of an article of clothing, a blanket, or even the squalling infant himself. For days thereafter the people in the district would often speculate and ask, "Who would do such a thing?" Unless caught red-handed, the "baby mixers" were difficult to apprehend; as a result their identities remained as much of a mystery as whether some lad's surname after the embroilment should have been Prokopchak rather than Brown.

The most convenient way for a young fellow to escort his lady friend to church, to some social gathering, or for a Sunday-afternoon drive was to go by horse-and-buggy. Hence, it can be seen why practical jokers were always thinking up new ways of "fixing" the buggy in order to embarrass the swain and make his passenger's ride anything but pleasant. One stunt was to wire blocks of wood between the buggy springs. The young couple, no matter how preoccupied with other affairs, didn't have to travel very far before they began to wonder why the buggy rode as hard and uncomfortable as the farm wagon. Another trick was to exchange the front and back wheels just prior to the time the couple was scheduled to leave for some social engagement. The problem was quickly discovered, but the task of finding some sort of jack and a buggy wrench to return the wheels to their proper axles took a good deal of time. In addition, it was a messy job for anyone wearing his best clothes.

A young fellow would spend hours washing, polishing, greasing and preparing his buggy in anticipation of impressing his lady friend when he planned to take her for a drive, but things usually went awry, thanks to the skulduggery of some of his pals. The morning of the drive he was likely to find the buggy in anything but a serviceable condition. A wheel or the shafts would have mysteriously disappeared, or he would find the shafts thrust through a fence and securely wired to it, or the spit and polish splattered with mud and manure; occasionally, the vehicle itself would be nowhere to be found, or would have been dismantled part by part and reassembled in some inaccessible place like the top of the barn or at half-mast on the windmill. If the young lady happened to be the teacher, the logical place to put the buggy was on top of the schoolhouse or the schoolbarn.

Our pioneers might have decried much of the levity which they encountered, but at the same time they were most anxious to relate such humorous incidents to others. They had discovered that the best way to cheer themselves up was to cheer everybody else up. Many such stories of misadventure have withstood the test of time and today appear in increasing numbers in the community histories that are becoming so popular.

In a rural district near Major, Saskatchewan, Jim Colbourn and his brother Roy crawled into a tunnel in a straw stack to investigate the source of strange noises. They were well inside, crawling along on their stomachs like a couple of snakes, when the pigs that had taken shelter in the stack decided to come out. The boys were no match for the pigs in the football-like scrimmage that followed. When the lads reappeared some distance behind the last hog, they had skinned ears and heads, badly torn clothes, bruised backs, and no desire whatsoever to become detectives.

Jake Voisey of the Fireguard S.D. 3878 (Champion, Alta.) was preparing a roast chicken for Sunday dinner; the minister from Alston had been invited to attend. In the process of stuffing the chicken with dressing, Jake decided to add an egg, just as a prank. During the carving of the chicken at the table that evening, he pulled out the egg and casually remarked that he had forgotten to clean the chicken. The minister excused himself and left the room.

On another occasion, while sharpening a neighbor's plough shares, Jake was bragging that he could fix anything. "Can you fix this?" asked the innocent neighbor as he pulled out his one dollar pocket-Ben watch. Jake examined the timepiece carefully, shook it a few times, placed it on the anvil, and promptly smashed it with his blacksmith's hammer. Is it any wonder then that one pioneer philosophized when referring to the work of the old-time blacksmith, "He got a lot of our troubles to beat out!"

The men and boys in the Hillsgreen S.D. 2610 (Morrin, Alta.) hunted regularly for rabbits and partridges, and occasionally shot magpies when the opportunity presented itself. One winter day, Charlie Danielson shot a magpie and knowing that two of his friends would be along hunting, tied it in an upright position on the branch of a nearby tree. It soon froze solid. Just as Charles had anticipated, the boys came along, spotted the magpie, and although the feathers flew, the bird just sat there as if bullets had no effect. Upon a closer investigation of the magpie, they found out why and knew immediately who had played the trick on them. Sometime later, in order to turn the tables on Charlie, they shot and arranged a rabbit to look as lifelike as possible beside a fence post, just off the rail. The ruse succeeded. Charlie spotted the rabbit and shot it several times before he realized he had been duped. He was so disgusted at being taken in so readily that he gave the frozen bunny a whack with his gun and bent the barrel.

Charlie King was moving his cattle to another pasture in the Bounty S.D. (Bounty, Sask.). While the herd was being driven along the road to the new location one of the calves dropped dead. "Well, I declare!" exclaimed Charlie, "He never did that before."

A homesteader tried his best to make a favorable impression on the ladies in the Adanac S.D. (Adanac, Sask.). Since he was quite bald, he gladly followed the advice of a friend who told him how to grow hair. The treatment consisted of rubbing the head, especially the bald area, with coal oil, and then working out in the sun all day wearing an old hat with the crown cut out. The results, as anyone but a lovelorn swain could have guessed, were horrendous.

Another bachelor in the same district bought a beautiful box at a box social, thinking that only a very desireable young lady could have prepared such a work of art. The name of the owner was Miss Fortune, so he set out immediately to claim her as his supper-hour partner, as was the accepted custom. He spent the rest of the evening trying to find her. At last it dawned on him that it was all a hoax, and the "misfortune" was his own, as he had paid five dollars for the box.

Teunis Timmerman of the Hilbre S.D. (Steep Rock, Man.) had to learn the hard way of how to order from Eaton's mail-order catalogue. He had started raising hogs, and as feed was required he looked through the catalogue to find what he wanted. He experienced some difficulty in reading English so he concentrated on the accompanying illustrations. Yes, there it was, prepared in a condensed form and sold in kegs. It was just what he wanted! He sent in his order. No one could have been more surprised than Mr. Timmerman when he received his shipment and opened one of the kegs. It was pigs' feet, not pigs' feed! The Timmerman household took their mistake in stride and enjoy pickled pigs' feet for many meals during the next few months.

When Alice first arrived in the Cupar S.D. (Cupar, Sask.) from Glasgow, Scotland in August, 1912, her host, Mrs. Turner, sent her out to the garden one day to get some potatoes for dinner. The Scotch lassie described her experience as follows:

> I was really at a loss, because I had never seen potatoes except on a grocer's shelf at home, never growing. I guess I took so long, that finally, Mrs. Turner came to my rescue. "Hurry with the potatoes, Alice, for the men will soon be in for dinner," she said. "But I can't find them," I replied. "My dear, you are standing in them," she reproved, as she bent over and pulled up the green tops, and to my bewilderment, there were the potatoes at my feet. I never had to look for potatoes again.

In Canada, at one time, each owner of a radio receiving set was required by law to purchase a license on or before April the first of each year. Whether it was the ridiculously small license fee of one dollar for each radio, or the April Fools' deadline date, the tax was to say the least very unpopular. The federal government found it necessary to appoint radio license inspectors to seek out the evaders and have them appear in court and pay fines for breaking the law. As the issuers of radio licenses were the local postmasters, it was from them that the inspectors secured the names of those in the districts who had not bought licenses for the current year. During the time the officials were in the districts outside aerials were torn down, radios hidden, and the sound of music and song stilled in all the villages and surrounding countryside.

Rural education, as exemplified in the one-room rural schools, was not as austere and sullen as some critics have pictured it to be. Here are some typical incidents that must have spiced the hard work of learning, teaching and administration with a touch of pleasantry and humanity.

When Mr. H. R. Parker, an inspector of schools, visited the Morrison S.D. 1639 (Vermilion, Alta.) in 1913, he requested Sylvia Laughlin to teach a lesson about the abuses of tobacco. She thought she did it very well, but he told her later that some of the information she presented was not entirely correct. He said his father used tobacco all his life and lived to be ninety years of age. Miss Laughlin refuted this argument by pointing out that Mr. Parker's father might have lived to be one hundred years old if he hadn't smoked.

A young schoolteacher substituted for a friend who was taking a week's honeymoon. A month later, at a party in the school, someone started to introduce the groom to the understudy. "Oh," he answered brightly, "I know Miss Davis very well, indeed. She substituted for my wife on our honeymoon!"

When Frieda Lorch was the teacher in Deerhorn S.D. 3807 (Spy Hill, Sask.), she boarded with her uncle's family. This arrangement had many advantages, but as she discovered later, a disadvantage as well. It was her uncle's delight to intercept some of the children on their way to school and put them up to playing pranks. Later, when the teacher got home and began telling him about the mischief the children perpetrated that day, he always) shook his head sympathetically and said, "I wonder where they ever got the idea to do such a silly thing?"

One morning while Verna, the teacher in the Glen Afton S.D. (Glen Afton, Sask.), was putting some work on the blackboard, a number of pupils, with sheepish grins on their faces came up to her. Ronnie wanted to know if he could have permission to ask her a question. When she told him to go ahead, he asked, "Did you wash your eyes out this morning?" She replied, "Yes!" His eager comeback was, "Well, how did you get them back in?" With that he turned and walked out with a quiet chuckle.

Morris Kallevig, a grade-four pupil in the Hillsgreen S.D. 2610, (Morrin, Alta.), was trying to use the dictionary definition of the word "abdomen"; it was defined as "the lower part of the trunk." After a hard struggle, he wrote on the blackboard, "I packed my clothes in my abdomen."

In the same school, Miss Bickle, the teacher, after putting up with the disturbance created by a chirping cricket, asked Laura Stock to put it out in the shed. Not hearing correctly, Laura poured a cup of water on its head. The treatment, although not the one recommened by the teacher, worked well, for the cricket stopped singing there and then.

A student in the Monitor S.D. (Monitor, Alta.) always received full marks in the Junior Red Cross daily health and cleanliness checks. His mother was amazed, because on occasions she knew the lad's handkerchief was filthy. In explaining his remarkable achievement he assured his mother that for inspection he always took out the one from his other pocket, which he kept for looks, not use.

The beginning grade-one students in rural schools were always sincere and hence could not understand the unreal classroom situations often trumped up by their teachers. Irene Lumley attended the Ellsworth S.D. (Dewberry, Alta.) and took her brother, Gordon, who was just five years old. This was before the days the authorities required students to be at least six years old before starting school. One day the teacher, Herbert Parker, asked Gordon how many pencils he would have if he had six pencils and lost two. The youngster looked quizzically at him and eventually said, "I'd hunt them up!" Of course the rest of the students had a good laugh, but little did they appreciate the down-to-earth quality of Gordon's answer.

Most inspectors of schools in the early days also served as official trustees of several districts for varying periods of time. Such appointments arose from a variety of causes: not enough British subjects to form a school board, perpetual squabbling in a district, financial inefficiency, the abject poverty of a district, passive attitudes towards forming a school district, or a complete disregard for governmental regulations. Under such circumstances school boards resigned, disappeared, or were not even elected. For the most part, the official trustee had to act as his own secretary-treasurer. Although this work was often time-consuming, it occasionally had its lighter moments. Inspector W. H. Swift remembers the time he received two petitions; many of the signatures were duplicates. One petition called for the firing and the other called for the retention of the same teacher.

Many teachers had to share their teacherages with mice, but if a squeamish girl didn't like this idea, the only alternative was to exterminate the rodents. This wasn't always as easy as it appeared. When the teacher in Superba S.D. 284 (Oyen, Alta.) spotted the gopher traps that had been left behind in the cloakroom one day, she quickly made plans to put them to use. That evening she set a gopher trap to catch a mouse. In the middle of the night she was awakened by a strange noise; to her they sounded like spitting and scratching. She got up, lit a lantern, went to investigate and found a strange animal in her trap. Not knowing what it was and being scared of the slim ferocious-looking creature, she picked up a rock, hit the thing on the head, and left it there. In the morning, she called some of the boys over to her teacherage to identify the animal. They told her it was a weasel and that it probably was hunting for the mice in and around the teacherage. The teacher had never felt so dismayed in her life. She had destroyed the very thing that could have put an end to her mouse problem.

Mice and children had one thing in common: both could be troublesome to a rural schoolteacher. Stella, a former teacher in the Fife S.D. (Carnduff, Sask.), described an incident to lend credence to this contention.

One day one of my grade seven boys, aged thirteen, was caught fooling with something down under his desk. He was a nice lad, but full of mischief. "All right," I said, "What have you there?" "A poor, little, sick mouse!" he replied. Now it so happened that I was terribly afraid of mice, so I told him to put it outside. Everything was fine until the children trooped back into the school after recess, for the spoiler went into his sick-mouse routine again. This time I instructed him to throw the mouse into the stove, and made sure he did it. You should have seen the various nose dramas that the students put on for my benefit during the cremation.

In the Carn Ridge S.D. (Steep Rock, Man.) the girls had a game they called "pump". Two girls turned back to back, interlocked their arms, and then took turns pulling the other "up and over". When this happened the boys usually left their own games to look on. They saw many pairs of flour-sack "undies" still emblazoned with trademarks like "Robin Hood", "Ogilvie", "Eaton's Blue Seal", and "Quaker".

Then there is the classic story of the missing pants. A play was in progress in the Dauphin Plain S.D. (Dauphin, Man.) with a large crowd watching. A rebellious invalid on the stage rose in his hospital cot and reached into the clothes closet, but failed to find his pants. The property man had blundered again! Quick as a wink, the chairman, at the bidding of the teacher, shed his own trousers and thrust them into the frantically waving hand. The audience saw this byplay and knew how embarrassing it was for the benefactor to stand in the wings with a coat draped around his middle, waiting for the curtain to come down so he could retrieve his precious pants and restore his modesty. He received as much applause as the actors when, after an embarrassing delay, he appeared on stage to announce the next number on the program.

It was not always possible for a student to follow explicitly his teacher's instruction. This might sound like insubordination, but occasionally it was the teacher who was at fault. Take the time in the Bison S.D. (Chinook, Alta.) when Johnny Schmidt, with his feet sprawled out in the aisle, was sitting at his desk industriously chewing gum. The instant the teacher noticed the double breach of school discipline she called out, "Johnny, take your gum out of your mouth and put your feet in!"

The Dow S.D. (Pendant d'Oreille, Alta.) was named after Al Dow, and the reason was somewhat humorous. Al was a bachelor who was not interested in education and the schoolhouse was not even built on his land. Neither was he involved in its construction, nor did he serve on the school board. Then why was the school named after such an improbable person?

The answer given to inquisitive outsiders was simple enough, "He had the shortest name in the district!" However, the real unspoken reason was entirely different. Nearly all the other settlers in the area were related to each other and by choosing the name "Dow", the school committee figured it could avoid hard feelings and jealousy.

Martha Adair, a little girl in the Good Cheer S.D. 2531 (Bow Island, Alta.), ran into the schoolroom and excitedly told the teacher, "Earl and Otto are fighting behind the barn and I think Earl, the one on the bottom, wants to see you as quickly as possible! Please hurry, teacher, as Earl is really getting it."

Myra Stilborn, a former rural teacher in Saskatchewan during the thirties, reminisced about a couple of incidents that characterized her as being a nice little girl.

> I filled the honey-tin lids with mud-cake batter and set them to bake in the sun. It was going to be a layer cake, and it had real eggs in it, thanks to the sparrows that nested under the eaves of the shed. Suddenly Pearl looked down the road and said, "Here comes a man with a cow." Up we jumped and ran into the house, having been taught that nice little girls never stay outside when a neighbor comes with a cow. But Mother never said that we couldn't look out the upstairs window.

Then there was always the delicate matter of timing when the necessity arose of going to the outhouse.

> Pearl and I checked that the coast was clear,
> Then bounded like nimblefooted deer
>   Down the path in a jiffy.
> The men must never be allowed to suppose
> That any necessity ever arose
>   For us to go to the biffy.

14

The Way It Was

A philosophy of education is not something which stands apart in the experiences of the individual. If it is significant at all, it must give meaning to the methods of teaching and learning; it must throw light upon the goal of education; and it must suit the conditions prevailing at the time.

The philosophy of early rural education was very simple, as the unique needs of the new settlers dictated its objectives, its methods, its character and its direction. For example: the early settlers realized from their own experiences and inadequacies that their children should know how to communicate readily, so the early schools were committed to providing a thorough grounding in the basic skills of reading, writing and arithmetic, the so-called three R's; since horse-transportation was the only type available, the prairie pioneers build thousands upon thousands of one-room schools, so the students would be within walking or riding distance of educational centers; as all the students from grade-one up to and including grade-eight or nine had to be accommodated, rural schools were organized as one-teacher multi-grade institutions; apathy had no place in rural education as the people sacrificed for schooling and were so happy to have schools available; the children in turn were glad to have schools to attend, as there was little for them to do, and going to school was a change from everlastingly helping with the work on the homesteads.

Given good teachers, cooperative parents, and close-knit communities, the boys and girls grew up without many of the tensions of the present day, thus developing self-reliance and healthy outlooks on life. Because of the very nature of the one-room schools children were at home with their neighbors, received individual attention from their teachers, and for the most part found themselves in harmonious atmospheres.

When the students were in attendance at school, there was always expression of boredom and discontent with it. But just let time pass and without fail most of the memories were of happy schooldays. The musings about cranky teachers, strict discipline, hard work, the strap and lack of adequate equipment tended to disappear, replaced by positive mature opinions.

Our sons and daughters went to school to learn, teachers to teach and books were prized possessions.

Boys and girls yearned for an education that we, their parents, missed, or were denied in one way or another. The children accepted discipline as essential and the teacher, a good friend, brought them a picture of the outside world.

Regardless of what modern educators might say, many good citizens came out of the country school. A breed of men and women who pioneered the country, built schools, fought with distinction in two world wars and laid the foundation for a better Canada.

Into the mixing bowl of the school were dumped the children of the settlers, from different countries, religions and environments, and there we played and fought, hated and loved, cried and laughed and learned the philosophy of the new land, tolerance towards all.

It was noteworthy the way the children of the parents coming from foreign lands seemed to understand and appreciate the freedom that was the right of every Canadian. Perhaps it was some of the unpleasant experiences of these settlers in the old lands that helped them to appreciate their new country.

The teachers in our school were always popular. I remember sitting along the east wall with one long row of girls and the teacher sitting in the center, each girl trying to sit next to her.

An education was a pearl of great price and schooling a great tradition. In the early days people sacrificed for schooling, and children walked miles. But now that it comes painlessly and everybody can have it for nothing, with the children hauled to it by bus, perhaps it doesn't seem important.

The only way that the rural schools could function successfully with so many grades in one room was for the teachers to devise good timetables in keeping with local conditions. It wasn't an easy matter and the conscientious teachers spent a considerable amount of time and effort to produce workable schedules. One teacher reminiscing about the matter exclaimed, "Timetables! How we labored over them. We had to have them workable and they had to be detailed enough to satisfy the jaundiced eye of the school inspector."

Section 158 (3) of the School Ordinance stated that the following was the duty of every teacher.

To keep in a conspicuous place in the schoolroom a timetable which shall show the "classification" of the pupils, the "subjects taught" each day in the week, the "length of each recitation period" and the "seat work" given; and to submit each timetable to the inspector for his approval and signature on the occasion of his visit to the school.

Teachers soon discovered that timetables were influenced by their own values and ideas. If they allotted more time to spelling than to reading, or more to arithmetic than to history, or more to writing than to hygiene, this meant that they valued spelling, arithmetic and writing above reading, history and hygiene. The drafting of timetables forced the teachers to do one of three things: they could follow the recommendations contained in the program of studies as to the time to devote to each subject; they could accept the wishes of the school inspectors in the matter; or they could adopt a philosophy of education on their own and spend more time on the subjects they thought would prove to be of more benefit to their pupils.

Teachers could also see that the timetables were useful organizational instruments. They reminded teachers to do the things they had planned to do at the proper time, and in some cases this meant at the only time available. Timetables could be as rigid or as flexible as the teacher's own mind. They could either serve the teacher's needs and the needs of their classes, or dictate, and therefore cramp their educational practices. Most teachers did not reject either the rigid timetable or the open timetable entirely; instead, their philosophies prompted them to combine the two in a form of compromise that did not satisfy all the aims of either. The compromise allowed direction in some pursuits and flexibility and freedom in others.

The 1912 annual report to the Department of Education contained one observation by an Alberta school inspector that indicates just how common was the lack of suitable timetables in the schools.

> Few teachers have satisfactory timetables. About one-third have none at all, and scarcely one timetable in twenty fulfils the requirement of the school law by showing how long each class is taught.

The 1913 annual report showed that conditions had improved.

> In most schools fairly good timetables are in evidence and when these are faithfully adhered to, satisfactory work is usually done. Unfortunately, however, some teachers are not yet acquainted with the provisions of the School Act regarding timetables as they are with those clauses relating to salary, and consequently they neglect to make a timetable and their work is conducted in a more or less careless, slip-shod and haphazard manner. Whenever we find a teacher without a timetable, we give him a few suggestions as how to make one and then ask him to complete one out in full and forward a copy of it to the inspector concerned for evaluation.

The following copy of a letter sent by Mr. P. H. Thibaudeau, the inspector of schools, Stettler, Alberta, to Grace Guthrie, the teacher at Success S.D. (Leo, Alta.) in 1915, shows not only how important the topic of timetables was, but also the harmonious working relationship existing between a good teacher and her inspector. Under such conditions education was bound to make good progress.

MONDAY-WEDNESDAY-FRIDAY

Time	Min	I	II	III	IV	VII
9:00	5	OPENING EXERCISES				
9:05	15	Phonics	Word Building	Prepare	Study	
9:20	10	Word Tickets	Phonics	Arithmetic	Arithmetic	Study
9:30	20	Tiles	Transcription	Arith.		Arithmetic
9:55	15			Correct Arith	Arith.	
10:05	5	Story & Game		Supplementary	Correct Arith	
10:10	20	Drawing & Picture St.	Reading	Study Geog.	Arith.	
10:30	15	RECESS				
10:45	10	Reading	Study Read.	Prepare		Map Drawing of Geog. Ex.
10:55	10		Reading	Composition	Composition	
11:05	15	Transcription		Comp.	Exercises	Prepare
11:20	10	Physical Exercises				Composition
11:30	15	Dismissed	Papercutting	Drawing	Comp.	
11:45	15		or Drawing			Comp.
12:00	60	NOON INTERMISSION				
1:00		Music				
1:05	10	Arith.	Blackboard	Study	Study	
1:15	15	Writing	Arith.	Reading Lit.	Reading	Study
1:30	15	Numbers	Correct Arith	Read. & Lit.	Lit.	Reading
1:45	15	Stick laying	Supp.	Written	Read.& Lit.	& Lit.
2:00	15	Papercutting	Reading	Work	Geog. or Hist.	Read & Lit.
2:15	15		Writing			
2:30	15	RECESS				
2:45	10	Oral Composition	Study Spell	Study	Study	
2:55	5	Prepare for Dismissal	Arith. Drill	Spelling	Geography	Geography
3:00	15	Dismissed	Construction	Arith. Drill	Geog.	
3:15	15		Work	Const. Work	Const. Work	Geog.

Manual Training from 2:15 to 3:15 on Friday. Nature Study included in Composition.

TUESDAY-THURSDAY

Time	Min	I	II	III	IV	VII
9:00	5	OPENING EXERCISES				
9:05	15	Reading	Word Tickets	Prepare		Arithmetic
9:20	10	Written	Phonics	Arithmetic	Prepare	Review
9:30	20	Reading	Number Ex.	Arith.	Arithmetic	
9:50	05	Song & Game		Correct Arith		Study
9:55	20	Tiles	Written	Written	Arith.	Grammar
10:15	15	Word Tickets	Work	Work	Correct Arith	Grammar
10:30	15	RECESS				
10:45	15	Oral Composition		Study Read.	Study Hist.	
11:00	15	Paper Cutting	& Illustration	Reading		Study
11:15	15	Drawing			History	History
11:30	10	Dismissed	Physical Exercises			& Civics
11:40	20		Supp. Read.	Written Work	Written Work	Hist. & Civics
12:00	60	NOON INTERMISSION				
1:00	20	Music				
1:20	15	Arith.	Arith. Ex. (B.B.)	Prepare Lang	Study	Study Spell
1:35	10	Number	Arith.	Memory Gems	Grammar	Word Analysis
1:45	10	Cards	Correct	Language		etc.
1:55	15	Stick	Arith.	Supplementary		Spell. & Dict.
2:10	10	Laying	Study	Reading	Grammar	
2:10	10	Phonics	Reading			Supplementary Reading
2:20	10		Reading			
2:30	15	RECESS				
2:45	15	Drawing				
3:00	10	Dismissed	Construction	Arith. Drill	Spelling	Study Geog
3:10	20		Work	Const. Work	Const. Work	Geography

Grade VII — Geog. on Monday · Tuesday · Wednesday — Agri. on Thursday

-- T. G. Pattinson

This timetable was compiled by Grace Guthrie when she taught in the Success S.D. (Leo, Alta.) in 1914.

Stettler, Alberta,
February 10, 1915.

Miss Grace Guthrie,
Teacher Success, S.D.,
Leo, Alberta.

Dear Miss Guthrie:

Mr. S. W. Walters complains of the board of Success S.D. turning out a girl that was staying at his place and he was sending to school. He states there are three vacant seats so there is room. See Section 162 or Section 131 of the School Act. Mr. Miller says there is no room. Who is correct? As I cannot visit your school for some time yet I am appealing to you for information.

I congratulate you on getting the largest salary of any rural teacher I have ever had or heard of. My best last year was $900.00. Yours is the second largest in my inspectorate.

But really the board deserves more congratulations than you for the good sense they have in hiring you and practically appreciating your work and influence.

Although I am not paying you part of the $1200.00 salary, I am going to impose on you a task just as though I were. Miss Burnett and the teachers at the Hanna Convention were loud in their praise of that timetable you sent. All copied it as faithfully as though it was an annex of the Commandments. For which good sense I commend them. Now I have been asked to take "timetables" at the Provincial Convention at Easter, in Calgary. Kindly send me within two or three weeks, the same timetable, unless you are certain you can improve on it. Make it out for the first three grades. Grade I, (a), (b) and (c), divisions; Grade II, with (a) and (b) divisions; and Grade III not subdivided. Also send me your present timetable as you are actually using it.

I wish to express my appreciation of your tender and considerate note of sympathy last term on the loss of my little girl. Little did I think when I was talking to Mrs. Burriss about the terrible misfortune in the Grover family that my turn was to come the next month. Little did I realize how much the little one had bound herself up with my affections and life. For two months the craving to hear the little prattle did not leave me in the slightest. But time is a wonderful healer, or searer of wounds. But time did linger in easing the torture.

Yours very sincerely,

P. H. Thibaudeau,
Inspector of Schools.

Mr. Thibaudeau gave a few guiding principles in compiling a timetable at the 1915 provincial convention at Easter in Calgary. He presented the following ideas:

Have a timetable.

Show the length of time you take each class.

Show what each class is doing as seatwork.

The best form by which the above can be achieved is to rule a fairly large sheet of paper with horizontal and vertical lines, place in the grades along the top and the divisions of time down the left side, write in the spaces the subject the class is taking, then by underlining, in different colored ink, or otherwise, show the periods in which classes are being taught.

The subjects that each grade should be taking, and which should appear on the timetable, are listed in the Program of Studies.

Each class should be taken at least once each quarter day.

The teacher should not overlook the just claims of the primary classes to her time.

The busy work following a lesson should be based on what was taught in that lesson.

Busy work should have educational value.

The length of school time before each recess should be about a quarter of-an-hour longer than that after recess.

A temporary timetable must be used by the teacher when she takes charge of a new school, until such time as she has learned the relative standing of her classes and of the individual pupils.

Before the timetable is made, the teacher, knowing her classes should distribute her time to the various grades and various subjects in these grades in certain relative proportions, based on this knowledge.

It is necessary to choose the proper time in the day for carrying on of work in any subject. For example, the morning is a better time than the afternoon to teach arithmetic, while reading for the primary grades is preferable during the first lesson in the afternoon.

Primary classes should have the first teaching lesson, both in the morning and the afternoon, and also after each recess.

Mental arithmetic should have a place on the timetable.

The same class should not be taken in two successive teaching lessons.

Multi-classes under the direction of one teacher created many problems, but at the same time much could be said in favor of such instruction. Many, perhaps all, students profited by listening to the lessons of the lower grades; sometimes such instruction improved their knowledge of something that had been forgotten or never fully mastered. With as many as nine grades in the same room it was generally accepted that the higher grades should learn to work independently. An additional benefit occurred during class instruction of the higher grades, in that the lower grades were able to listen in and learn. Thus new vistas were opened up for the younger students, providing them with incentives to make greater efforts. While the system may not have been ideal, it did work and enabled many who left school to have the equivalent of much more schooling than their final grade officially completed.

Many rural teachers tried to help the older students whose chances for education had been slim because of no schools, lack of teachers, or lack of funds to provide them. The true pedagogue knew that the older girls and boys would soon leave school, so attempts were made to give them as much general knowledge as could be crammed into them in the short time available.

In the Elbow S.D. difficulties were compounded as there were forty children attending, coming from several different provinces and states, together with a few from overseas, who did not speak English. It was difficult for the teacher to draft a workable timetable and do justice to such a heterogeneous group.

Multi-grade one-room schools enabled the students to enjoy the pleasures of being lumped into cliques ranging in age from six to sixteen; because of this they learned tolerance for the older brother, sister, or friend. In addition, those schools taught students to protect the shy and slow from the older thoughtless pupils and to be fiercely loyal to their teams in games, even if the makeup changed from recess to recess. Each group of students from a particular school was a tight little community when their team played another school. Somehow, being thrown into the mixed-age group of the rural school was in itself a very thorough education in the art of making friends, which is something each person must learn if he is to succeed in life.

A teacher had to be a master in her own right to follow the exacting timetable that she designed for the school, for it meant daily preparations beforehand, no waste of time or effort, and a thorough knowledge of the students, the subject matter, the minimum requirements for each grade, and a good sense of timing.

An efficient teacher in action in a rural school was like a five or eight-ring circus. She would start with her shining-eyed grade-ones, teaching them that under the picture of the red-haired boy and his dog on the first page of the *Canadian Reader,* Book I, the story read: "Tom Tinker had a dog. It said bow-wow." And on page two, it said "Jack Sprat had a cat. It said meow, meow!" Then telling them "A" says "aye" as in "aim", she would leave them to read and reread page one and two, then write "a-a-a-a-apple", and perhaps draw or model one from the plasticine. She would go on to grade two and start them reading. After ten minutes with them she would go to some other grade while her second graders worked by themselves with spelling, number cards and writing. This hectic pace continued all day long, and the teacher literally flew from grade to grade spending five minutes here, ten minutes there and maybe fifteen minutes with one of the senior grades who were experiencing some difficulty with compound interest.

With so many grades to teach, the teacher would remind the other grades not to pay attention to the class up front, but of course this was not always possible. It was difficult to concentrate when the primary class was being told an interesting story, while a funny answer always brought an immediate response from the rest of the school. It often happened that someone would become so engrossed in a book that he didn't prepare his lessons properly. When his recitation period arrived he would be far away in a land of make-believe. He may have been waiting eagerly to find out whether Horatius succeeded in holding the foe at bay while the bridge was being torn down. The voice that rudely jolted him back to reality was not what he expected for it was, "Grade six, attention, please!"

The recitation of one class or another meant that those doing seat work were forbidden to do anything that might disturb the group in session. Whispering was probably the worst of these outlawed activities, but the students eventually found an alternative. They wrote notes to each other and passed them back and forth when the teacher was not looking in their direction.

True, the students did not have modern visual aids, or access to good libraries or laboratories, but they did learn to use their textbooks to the fullest extent, and to dig out information from such reference materials as were available in the school. There was little time for spoon feeding in the multi-grade set-up, so a pupil had to develop self-reliance and an ability to study for himself from grade-one up.

Children in the rural areas that were mentally retarded, physically handicapped, or afflicted with some other disability had no place to go except to the one-room schools in their districts. In fact, it was the practice of the parents to attempt to hide or downgrade disabilities. As a result, many rural schools had a handicapped student or two attending along with the non-handicapped youngsters. The arrangement was certainly not fair to the teacher concerned, for in a multi-graded classroom an undue proportion of her time was often spent with such pupils; in addition, there were extra problems created by these children. Besides, the teacher was not qualified to provide any type of skilled professional help to these unfortunate students. However, there was an advantage for the handicapped child; instead of being segregated at home, he had the behavior of normal children to imitate, and as a result achieved some progress. It has been proved time and again that when the handicapped youngster was integrated with normal children, he didn't need as much help as most authorities considered necessary. In fact, most of today's progressive educational systems are adopting the method that once was used by rural schools in dealing with handicapped children. Such boys and girls are now being integrated into the regular classrooms as well as being provided with specialized instruction.

The multi-graded classroom was ideal for the gifted, talented or advanced youngsters. By cultivating the habit of listening in to the other grades, they received an enriched curriculum, which presumably is the best educational formula for talented students by today's standards. Besides, such youngsters learned to tolerate other less intelligent, less creative, or less talented classmates and there was no snobbery or elitist stigma attached to their own status.

Schools were competitive, unrelentingly and overtly. Report cards indicated the student's rank in class, his marks in each subject, and finally his attendance and behavior records. In addition, all these monthly returns were sent to the weekly newspaper in town and published for all to see. Examinations were emphasized throughout the school term, while the final examinations in June determined if the student moved on to the next grade or, embarrassingly, kept his place as a repeater. There was no such thing as social promotion; the pupil was promoted only when he demonstrated through examinations that he was ready for the next grade, and not before. It was also necessary to pass every subject in his grade, whether or not he had excelled in them the previous term. Departmental examinations under the direction of the Department of Education were held annually in June for grades eight and up, while in the lower grades, teacher-set examinations were held.

Such a strict policy of promotion was based upon the philosophy that a child received more benefit if he was held back in the same grade until he achieved a certain level of mastery, than if he was permitted to go on to the next grade to attempt a challenge he was not prepared to meet.

Everyone wrote the final examinations and there were no exceptions, so incidents such as the following one from the Penhold S.D. (Penhold, Alta.) were common.

During an experiment in class an explosion burned and temporarily blinded Mary Dixon, so that it was impossible for her to write the final examinations. The Department of Education required her to write these subjects the following year along with the examinations for the next grade. This was quite a task, but Mary succeeded on both counts.

Margaret Shaw, an Ontario student, described a personal involvement in failing one subject on a departmental examination and having to repeat her grade the next term.

> Just before the final Department of Education examinations were held in June, tragedy struck, and I failed for the first time. There was a boy I knew quite well, in fact I had been talking to him the day before, and just as I was about to go into the classroom to write a final examination, I was told that this boy had drowned the previous evening. It was not a personal tragedy. It could have been just the same had it been any other person I knew, but it was a shock. I could not concentrate and I failed that paper by less than five marks. Ironically, it was my very best subject, Composition. But the Department of Education refused to make any allowance whatsoever. If you failed, you failed and there was no writing off just the subject in which you failed. If you wanted to keep on in school you took the whole year all over again. So on I went.
>
> In those days in Ontario, the final Department of Educationexaminations were set by school inspectors throughout the province. There was one individual, Inspector Ball by name, who seemed to delight in seeing how nasty he could be. Whenever we saw his name at the top of a paper a groan would go up among the students about to write the paper, for he could set the meanest, trickiest paper one could imagine.

Competition highlighted every school activity, whether it was in the drill to gain skill in the use of the addition or multiplication tables, the spelling or geography matches, the discovery of the first crocus in the spring, the memorization of a literary gem, or some oratorical or reading contest.

The pupils in the rural school had a certain amount of fun, but they never imagined that school was a place where a person went to enjoy himself. School was serious business and learning was primarily associated with books. Hard discipline was the keynote to successful learning so drill, drill, and more drill was used to get the facts across to the students, whether it involved the multiplication tables, the names of the provinces of Canada along with their capitals, dates of famous battles in history, the digestive juices, the rivers of the world in order of length, rules for using the comma, parts of a flower, or the components that had to be included in parsing the words of a sentence. It was the era of memorization, resulting in respect for facts. The pupils spent a good deal of their time copying notes from the blackboard, committing them to memory and giving them back on tests or final examinations. In literature it was memorization of literary gems, not just a few significant passages but hundreds upon hundreds of lines. Many adults today who are products of one-room rural schools can still recite many poems as well as recall numerous classical sayings, mottoes, declarations and opinions that they learned years and years ago. These literary selections not only became a part of their mental set-up but ultimately a yardstick for life values.

The pupils did not do very interesting or profitable things with the facts that they had so laboriously memorized, outside of making lists and charts with them during seatwork periods, answering questions that had been put on the blackboard for them, satisfying the inspector with their fund of factual knowledge when he visited the school, and probably most important of all, passing their final examinations.

All the notes that the students received from their teachers, from their textbooks, or from any suggested reference books, were entered into special notebooks. There were separate scribblers for each subject and they were kept as neat and complete as was possible within the capabilities of the youngsters. Headings were made, then underlined in red, and the best penmanship used in compiling the precious notes. Those notebooks, models of neatness and elegance, were for the teacher to check and to grade at regular intervals, for friends and parents to admire, and for the school inspector to judge. In fact some middle age people today often proudly bring forth such notebooks just to show their friends how good they used to be in school.

The teaching approach to most subjects in those days was somewhat mechanical as the students were taught to respect rules rather than principles. As a result the youngsters learned to perform whatever they were assigned to do automatically, but not to grasp the underlying meaning of the process involved. The area of a rectangle was the magical expression of "length times the width", but there was no rhyme or reason connected with it.

Since books were scarce and made up the hub about which the learning and teaching revolved, they were considered prized possessions and given special care. A good example was the readers. Everyone from the officials in the Department of Education down to the child that used them, considered such books of considerable value and not to be handled indiscriminately. The regulations governing the distribution, the use and the care of readers bears out this point very well.

The *Alexandra Readers,* which were especially compiled and produced for the provinces of Alberta and Saskatchewan with a view to free distribution to school children, were published early in the summer 1908 and the first distribution took place at midsummer of that year. The regulations for their use follow.

(1) Upon receipt of the requisition form signed by the teacher and secretary of each school, the necessary readers are forwarded to be distributed to the pupils as required. Each pupil in actual attendance receives a reader upon admission to the school and subsequently upon being promoted to a higher standard. And the reader so received becomes the absolute property of the pupil. He is thus privileged to retain his set of readers as a souvenir of his schooldays; while at the same time the objections frequently urged from a sanitary standpoint are eliminated.

(2) Should the pupil however, lose or destroy his reader, the department does not supply him with another until he has been regularly promoted to the standard in which the next reader is used.

(3) Half-yearly statements are made to the department, showing the disposition made of book supplies, together with the number still held for distribution.

In addition, the Department of Education was very strict as to which books could or could not be used in the classroom, as the following regulations would indicate. Strict censorship was maintained throughout.

(1) The textbooks used by the pupils in any school shall be those authorized by the minister of education. No teacher shall require his pupils to purchase any other books.

(2) All reference books purchased by school boards for the use of pupils and teachers shall be selected from the list authorized by the minister of education. In case any board desires to provide its school with books other than those contained in the authorized list, it may do so only upon receiving the approval of the minister.

(3) All books purchased for school libraries shall be selected from the list authorized by the minister of education.

(4) The librarian shall not issue to any pupils more than one volume at a time, nor shall any pupil be allowed to retain a book for more than two weeks.

Such an appreciation by the Department of Education of the importance of books had a marked effect on the attitude of the general public. For instance, good books came to be considered the most appropriate and most cherished type of gift. Hence, it became a common practice in the schools in those days to give books as prizes to deserving students. The recipients were very pleased to receive the books and took extra good care of them. A book came to be recognized as the best prize a person could get.

The extensive drill, the repetition, the practice and the endless demonstrations required strict discipline, not only in the actual learning process, but in the way the students behaved as a whole. In the latter case it was very rigorous and involved with the administration of corporal punishment. The home usually cooperated with the school in this regard and if the youngster received a strapping at school, he got another one when he arrived home. The school board could require the parent or guardian of any pupil to replace or pay for any school property destroyed, broken or damaged by such pupils and could suspend such pupils until the property was replaced or paid for. In addition, all pupils were responsible to the teacher for their conduct on the school premises and also for their behavior on the way to and from school unless accompanied by one of their parents or guardians or some person appointed by them. The pupils also had to conform to the rules of the school and submit to such discipline as would be exercised by a kind, firm and judicious parent.

Extra, or even necessary school equipment, was hard to come by, so if the students or teacher desired some special item for the school the trustees expected them to assist in its purchase. Since the students had sacrificed in one way or another to obtain it, they were disciplined enough to take good care of it.

Incidents such as the following might appear rather harsh and unreal to people today, but in the days of the little white schoolhouse they were common occurrences:

Tilley Schneidmiller remembers her first day at the Elkton S.D. She couldn't come the first day school started in the fall, so she came the second day, and a little late. For this the teacher gave her the strap.

A well-liked teacher in the Tindastoll S.D. 483 from 1906 to 1908 was A. P. McMillan. He was a good organizer of games at recess and during the noon hour. Some of his pupils living today remember him washing students' mouths out with soap and water for use of profane language.

Discipline could involve mental anguish rather than physical pain. The following is such an example.

In reading lessons in rural schools it was the common practice for the teacher to call on a pupil to stand up either at the front of the room or at the side of his desk and read from the day's lesson. Quite often a poor reader, or one ill-prepared, would stumble and hesitate over every third word. Some teachers lost patience and prescribed a punishment similar to the following.

They informed the pupil, "Don't stumble. If you come to a word you don't know, just use your own name and keep going." The teacher would insist on this type of penalty and the youngster had to go through with it. Sometimes, instead of permitting him to insert his own name, he was required to use such words as, Orlando, Columbus, Moses, or another word that would be sure to mock the unfortunate reader. He received no sympathy whatsoever, for the rest of the children in the classroom would giggle and have a merry time at his expense. Nevertheless, it must have been cruel to hold any child, no matter what his faults, up to such ridicule.

The discipline and standards of value became engraved on the minds of the students to such an extent that sometimes they made their presence felt at important times. Grace (Wilkinson) Flately of the Burnside S.D. described one such occurrence.

> Mr. McNab, the minister, travelled by horse and buggy, stopping in regularly to read the Bible and to hold prayers at the various homes. One incident I remember well. Dad and my older brothers were skinning and dressing jack rabbits for winter storage in a deep-freeze box, which was located on brackets outside an upstairs north window. The rabbits had to be chopped out with a hatchet when needed, as they would be frozen solid. When the minister came, I was both horrified and worried as to what he would think of them working on a Sunday. Young as I was, I had already grasped the idea, that work on the Sabbath was taboo.

Although the majority of teachers considered their main objective in teaching as the hammering out of as many facts as possible, there were some worthy teachers who went one step beyond the accumulation of facts. They thought all the school subjects should help the teacher to accomplish one simple objective; that was to teach the pupils to think, to reason clearly, to proceed by a logical process from a set of facts to a sound demonstrably true conclusion. True, a trained, disciplined mind was required to accomplish this objective, but the conscientious teacher was constantly trying to achieve this, and some did.

In the Riverston S.D. 2128 an animal connected with the education of the children was a little black ox called Darky. The ox used to haul the Mathison twins to school on a stoneboat. Mrs. Graham the teacher, believed in practical teaching; she used the little ox and a piece of chalk to draw lines on him to show the pupils how to cut up a beef into the most suitable sizes and shapes. Fortunately, the little ox was not ticklish! This was a most useful lesson in those days of butchering one's own animals.

A pupil of the Glenmore S.D. 2314 (Viking, Alta.) described how her teacher taught effective lessons in reading.

> Mrs. I. Rowson, taught us how to read with expression, which was new to us at that time. When reading a poem written by Pauline Johnston, we had to imitate the sounds of the wilds so that the listeners could

experience the feel of the winds; we had to tune our voices to the lull of the quiet stream, but quickly change the tone when coming to the verse about the rapids. When reading about Marmion and Douglas we had to create the atmosphere of hostility. She told us to bring out the action because we sure knew how to fight when playing ball.

The students of the little white schoolhouse studied many more subjects than their counterparts today. Instead of lumping related subjects into one as is the practice now, the various courses were separated and taught as different entities. Instead of one subject called English, they took seven different ones: namely, oral reading, silent reading, spelling, grammar, composition, literature and the so-called penmanship or writing. In place of the single subject of social studies, they wrestled with history, geography and civics. Mathematics was made up of arithmetic, rapid calculation, algebra, geometry and trigonometry.

The objectives and methods underlying the teaching and learning of such an array of subjects have changed drastically over the years, so it is interesting from a historical and educational point of view to recall what these were.

Spelling consisted of comprehensive lists of words, dictation, rules, sentences using the words from the spelling lists, meanings of the words looked up in the dictionary, and daily tests. The correct spelling of any word was fixed by drill and still more drill. It was not unusual for students to be compelled to rewrite misspelled words up to one hundred times. However, it must be admitted that the voracious readers unconsciously absorbed more correct spelling from reading than they did through drill.

Grammar was taught formally with a considerable amount of drill and memorization involved. Students spent most of their time in such exacting work as analyzing sentences, parsing the words in a sentence, picking out phrases, doing clausal analysis, distinguishing infinitives, gerunds and participles, and giving the principal parts of verbs. The work was endless. Yet, if the students came from homes where the people said "ain't" and misused "done", they kept right on saying "ain't" and misusing "done" in spite of all the grammar lessons and exercises they had assimilated.

The teaching of literature followed a set pattern. First, the students studied the life of the author of the particular selection; then, the notes were put on the blackboard or dictated by the teacher and the students copied this material into their notebooks; next the poem or prose selection was read aloud to the class; and finally this was followed by a detailed analysis, discussing noble thoughts, beautiful descriptions, wise sayings, interpretations of the meanings of some of the lines and paraphrasing the difficult portions. If it was a poem that was being studied, most of it was committed to memory.

Every literary gem selected from the reader for study communicated some value in life for the child to follow. The value could have been kindness to others, gentleness, politeness, cleanliness and neatness, kindness to animals, truthfulness, fidelity in duty, obedience, nobility, love, respect, reverence, gratitude, thankfulness, forgiveness, confession, honesty, honor, courage, humility, self-respect, self-control, prudence, good name, good manners, temperance, patriotism, industry or economy, and the list could go on and on. The majority of the selections contained in the readers dealt with the unfamiliar, the strange and the mysterious. Every field of human endeavor was covered. A sense of the importance of man as an individual was stressed; the emphasis was that any man, no matter who he was, could become great.

The students were in the habit of reading and rereading the various selections from their readers as they were so novel and interesting. Besides, there was nothing better to read or to do. There were no libraries, no magazine stands, no paperbacks, few newspapers, and books were expensive and difficult to obtain. Radios were just coming into being and television was a long way off. In the process of reading and rereading the literary gems, the pupils adopted values for living that had been subtly concealed in the poem or prose selected for detailed study. The readers also contained the magic of many fine writers, and the memory work gave the pupils a storehouse of lovely quotations they would not have acquired except by such compulsion.

Reading, whether oral or silent, was considered of great importance. After all, reading efficiency influenced the progress of pupils in all other subjects and this made it the most influential subject on the curriculum. Teaching the beginners to read was quite a task in the early days as the teachers had to wrestle with the folly of teaching the two forms, script and print, at practically the same time, and using phonics as the only key to new words. Oral reading was continued right up through the high school grades, a practice that was dismal and monotonous for the good readers but helpful to those who needed the incentive and the opportunity to perform before an audience.

Composition in the little white schoolhouse consisted of memorizing long lists of rules and writing paragraphs or essays on lifeless and uninteresting topics. Supposedly the students were applying the laws that they had learned, like those pertaining to the topic sentence, unity, coherence and emphasis. Usually the students wrote their composition on topics based on stories contained in readers, or on the contents of lessons taught in the other subject areas.

In writing, the students used the whole arm or muscular movement system, making use of the larger muscles of the arm and shoulder rather than the small muscles of the fingers. The up-and-down strokes of the letters were supposed to have a slant of from twenty-five to thirty-five degrees from the perpendicular. The students used copybooks from which they literally copied the perfectly-formed script as faithfully as possible, maybe more faithfully on the first line than on the last line at the bottom of the page. Thus, writing lessons consisted primarily of coordination of muscular control with the careful study and production of the correct letter form. There was a correct writing position that the pupils were commanded to assume time and again throughout the writing lesson as they laboriously made their practice ovals, the up-and-down strokes, or whatever happened to be the contour of the letter they were studying. Left-handed writing was not permitted and stringent methods, even involving corporal punishment, were employed to convert left-handed youngsters into right-handed writers.

History consisted of dry-as-dust dates, battles, causes of wars, kings, queens, explorers, terms of acts and treaties, all of which had to be committed to memory. All these facts were remembered until after the final examinations and then promptly forgotten. Fortunately the students studied both English and Canadian history, and consequently had some inkling of life in parts of the world other than just Canada.

The study of geography included some outlandish names to learn, to spell, and dreary lists of products to be memorized. Most teachers really drilled in this subject as so many facts were available, like the capitals of every country in the world, mountain ranges, rivers, lakes, oceans, continents, and various types of climate. The students drew their own outline maps and painstakingly marked the geographical features on them, as well as anything else the resourceful teacher could think up, which in most cases was plenty.

Civics was another subject taught by rote. The textbook in this subject was ideal for this purpose as the information was neatly tabulated in a definite order. Hence, civics which could have included local adaptations was learned as a subject far removed from actual experience. As a result, some students who secured high marks in this subject, knew very little civics, and did not even know how the local school district or municipality operated.

The teaching and learning approach to arithmetic and algebra was for the most part very mechanical. The pupils memorized rules like: to divide by a fraction invert the divisor and multiply; to find the area of a triangle use the formula $A = \frac{1}{2} ab$; to subtract in algebra change the sign of the subtrahend and proceed as in addition; to change percents to decimals drop the per cent sign and move the decimal point two places to the left; after multiplying one decimal number by another, point off as many decimal places in the product as there are decimal places in the numbers being multiplied and count from the right; interest = principal x rate x time in years. Thus, the youngsters learned to perform operations, but failed to attach any meaning to these operations. It was like performing feats of magic. The boys and girls who knew the mystic key words came up with the correct solutions; the rest failed. Geometry, which could have been the best subject for teaching logic and reasoning, turned out to be a course in pure memory work. The pupils managed to memorize a sufficient number of

-- Emerson Robinson

The pupil's position at his desk was of paramount importance during the writing lessons. The teacher usually walked around checking the position of each child.

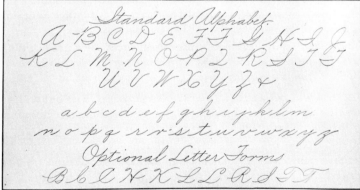

-- Emerson Robinson

The writing examples above indicate the type of exercises the students were required to do. Finger movements were forbidden and all writing had to be done with free-hand movements.

-- Emerson Robinson

The samples of good writing, illustrated above, were kept constantly before the students so they could copy the proper form of each letter of the alphabet.

propositions to pass the final examination and did not need to know how to apply the theory in solving the deductions or the exercises.

School inspectors were keen observers of how well the various subjects were being taught and their annual reports to the Department of Education contained much pertinent information about the topic.

The greatest fault in reading is a lack of emphasis and expression, which may account for the fact that in most cases the child does not thoroughly understand the subject matter of his reading lesson.

Grammar is undoubtedly one of the most poorly taught subjects on the curriculum, and the essence of the trouble lies in the formal way in which it is handled. Pupils spend years learning definitions, picking out clauses and parsing words, with scarcely an idea as to the real purpose of it all.

Spelling is still tested, not taught. The reading is characterized by quantity rather than quality. Literature is neglected. Arithmetic should be made more mental and practical. Pupils in ungraded schools below the eighth grade know very little history. Many teachers are neglecting the teaching of writing. Oral composition should receive more attention, and the language of the pupils at recess, especially on the playground should be watched as carefully for bad grammar and faulty English as is his written work.

In a very considerable number of schools composition does not receive the attention which it deserves, the training in the subject being confined to the reproduction of stories contained in the reading lessons. This is a useful and important practice in composition but it does not take the place of the formal teaching of the subject. The result is very mechanical work and no originality of thought or expression!

In writing, the influence of good lessons in the subject is often obliterated by a careless habit allowed in all other written work. Position and movement do not receive enough attention. The vertical writing lacks individuality, and even in the higher grades, the results are childish in character. It is worth noting that most of the teachers who write well use slant script.

Patriotism was not a subject on the program of studies but it received as much attention as if it were. The schools were something like human mixing bowls in the early days. The children of the settlers attending school were from different countries, of different religious faiths, and from different environments; hence, with such a cosmopolitan population, there was a definite need to have them adopt the Canadian way of life, the Canadian language and the Canadian customs, even if in some cases their parents failed to do so. It was understandable why the Union Jack flag was displayed in the schoolroom at all times and the pupils were taught what it stood for. Some schools had the flag flying from a flagpole in the schoolyard and formal ceremonies of raising and lowering it were conducted daily, while others had exercises in which the flag was saluted by all the pupils every morning whether it was outside or inside.A ratepayer, for instance, could not serve as a school-board member unless he was a British subject, could read and write, was at least twenty-one years of age, and owned property in the district. In 1918 the Alberta Department of Education, in a flash of patriotism, demanded that all teachers should take the Oath of Allegiance, whether citizens or not. Victoria Day was supposed to be appropriately celebrated as a patriotic school holiday. The 1913 regulations from the department in this regard were as follows:

> Victoria Day (May 24) has been fixed as a school holiday to commemorate the anniversary of the birthday of Queen Victoria, to familiarize pupils with the growth and development of the Empire, and to encourage and foster patriotic and imperial sentiments. In order that the observance of this holiday may serve the purpose for which it is intended, it is very desirable that exercises appropriate to the occasion should be arranged for. These may be held on the afternoon of May 23 and should include short addresses, suitable recitations, the singing of the patriotic songs, and the raising of the national flag.

At one time so much school time had been lost in the Penhold S.D. (Penhold, Alta.) because of illness that it was decided to hold school on Victoria Day. Hugh Field, a very patriotic Englishman, became so incensed at the idea of showing disrespect for the beloved Queen's birthday that he threatened to picket the school. As a result of his ire no school was held on that day, and a flag-raising ceremony was conducted instead.

Since the majority of youngsters were newcomers to Canada they were unbelievably race conscious, and often carried on schoolyard feuds between students that hailed from the Empire and those from the United States or from European countries. It was a good thing that the denunciation "dammed Yankee" wasn't in vogue at the time, or the teachers would have been busy not only quelling the fights but attempting to thwart the swearing.

The school children were quick to react to patriotic sentiments and even their games portrayed these feelings. In the Cassell Hill S.D. the pupils devised a game of war between the English and non-English armies, although it was always difficult to obtain recruits for the foreign side. The two armies would line up on either side of the center of the schoolyard. They guarded a couple of flags posted at either end of the field of battle. The idea was to capture the opposing side's flag and return it to home base without the enemy touching anyone from the raiding forces. Then it was up to the other side to come down and recapture it. If a "soldier" was touched after crossing the middle line, he became a prisoner and was forced to remain beside the enemy flag until someone from his side released him. The game was over when the flag and the entire army of one side or the other was captured.

Doreen (Winning) Solberg of the Winning S.D. described a patriotic skirmish that took place at her school.

> There was a good fist fight between Norman Henshaw, the United States flag defender, and Gordon Batrum, the supporter of the Canadian flag. After they had struck each other a sufficient number of times to get bloody noses, Mr. Bough, the teacher, had them make up and shake hands. It was real exciting for the rest of us onlookers.

In geography, the pupils whose parents were of British extraction always showed great pride in the red splashes on the world map that marked the encircling British Empire, on which the sun never set.

Youngsters can be decidedly cruel to those who have unusual accents in their speech. In the Verdant Valley S.D. (Drumheller, Alta.) since gophers were entirely new to her family, Rose, a mere infant at the time, used to call them "Gokies". She continued this habit for several years, until one day a neighbor, with a decided English accent heard her. He reprimanded her, saying, "You're too big a girl to talk like that. You know better than to say Gokie." "Well," she retorted, "It's no worse than saying 'Gophaw'." She gave a very good imitation of his own pronunciation, and he didn't like it a bit.

Early in World War I the schools planted victory gardens. Each child was assigned a small plot of ground and given vegetable seeds. Plans were carefully made, seeds were planted and the youngsters awaited the results with keen anticipation. The rains came but so did the weeds, the grasshoppers and the summer holidays. The victory garden projects were not productive war efforts, for what the gophers didn't nibble in the daytime, the stray cattle munched at night. Nevertheless the victory gardens have been among the memories of those distant days; they reflected people's desire to do something to prove their patriotism.

Teachers fostered the idea of patriotism in many ways.

Miss A. V. Milloy of the Gleichen S.D. (Gleichen, Alta.) was of the old school and believed every boy and girl should have a thorough knowledge of British history as well as Canadian history. She made the pupils feel proud of their ancestry, whether Irish, French, United Empire Loyalist, and especially Scottish. She was a most enthusiastic song leader and patriotic songs such as "Men of Harlech," "The Maple Leaf Forever," and "Rule Britannia" were her favorites; they soon were at the top of the hit parade for her pupils as well.

Sheilagh Jameson of the Ballyhamage S.D. (Midnapore, Alta.) recalls the patriotic sentiments shown by the youngsters in her district in those early days.

Many rural schools had a cosmopolitan population. The Ballyhamage School District, for instance, had pupils of Russian, Czecho-Slovakian, Polish, Dutch, Norwegian, American and British origin. In their relationship with each other nationality was not a factor. It was the individual that counted. If left to themselves, it is a characteristic of children to accept others as they found them — a tendency which most adults have, unfortunately, outgrown.

I remember one Czecho-Slovakian father telling me, "My boy, he tell me all the time at home to spik Anglese!" He seemed quite pleased about this reprimand from his son.

It was noteworthy the way these children seemed to understand and appreciate the freedom that is the right of every Canadian. Perhaps it is some of the unpleasant experiences of their parents in the old lands that helped them to appreciate their new homes.

I will always remember these children's faces as they stood proudly together and sang, "O Canada", "The Maple Leaf Forever" or "God Save the King."

Margaret Graham, a one-time teacher in the Tobacco Plains S.D. in the southern part of British Columbia, described an interesting and unique patriotic experience she had while teaching there in 1907.

Although Tobacco Plains was a Canadian school, the provincial Department of Education in Victoria, British Columbia, had made an agreement with the Department of Education in the United States which would allow the American children to enroll as pupils in a Canadian school if they lived closer to a Canadian school than an American one. Consequently I had ten to twelve pupils from the wrong side of the road attending. They had never studied Canadian history, never heard of Wolfe or Montcalm, but could rattle off the names of all the presidents of the United States, while my Canadian pupils could seldom get farther along than Abraham Lincoln or George Washington. This discrepancy in knowledge was a good thing for both sides, and helped to establish the "Good Neighbor" policy, although they did sometimes quarrel about which country was best to live in. They never did settle the question satisfactorily.

As far as any organized recreational activities and entertainment in the rural schools were concerned, the children didn't expect them. They knew how to amuse themselves and were better for it. The youngsters depended on each other, they helped each other and the things shared welded a link between them stronger and finer than blood relationship.

No story of the rural school would be complete without mention of the individual attention that the students received. Children thrive in an atmosphere of harmony and of being wanted. A loving understanding of the child and his problems is necessary if best results are to be achieved by the teacher. When individual attention exists, troubles vanish and the child is secure in the feeling of unanimity between his school, his home and himself, and all is well. To be perfectly in tune with school life, any physical handicap or minor worries which are clouding the child's mind must be coped with before the child is in the ideal receptive mood for his studies.

A parent discussing the matter of individual attention in the large modern school said, "I feel my daughter is lost in a large crowd of children; in spite of the disadvantages of the one-room school she would be happier and receive more personal attention there if such schools existed today."

What a wealth of fond memories must be recalled from the fifty years or more of the little white schoolhouse. What a contrast between the small white schoolhouse basking in the prairie sunshine and the modern brick giant. No longer is the barn, which provided shelter for the faithful horses the children rode to school, an essential building in the schoolyard. No longer is needed the oatbundle, the sack of oats or chop, slung on the back of the horse or tucked discreetly in the back of the buggy. Instead, a yellow bus travelling from farmyard to farmyard is now a common sight throughout rural Canada. Lunches, formerly wrapped in cloth or newspapers and packed in syrup, jam or lard pails, now are carried to school in specially designed lunch kits; the contents are protected in waxed paper and foil. No longer do the pupils gather around the pot-bellied stove to keep warm, for air-conditioning keeps the large central school at a uniform temperature winter or summer; the youngsters gather around the lockers instead. No longer is the drinking water brought to school in cream cans, for drinking fountains are located in every part of the modern school, with hot water available in the washrooms. No longer do the older pupils vie for the job of sweeping the floor at fifteen cents per day, or lighting the fire at twenty-five cents per day. That's a full time job for adults now.

However, this is progress. As Lord Tennyson so aptly put it in *The Idylls of the King*, "The old order changeth, yielding place to new, and God fulfills himself in many ways, lest one good custom should corrupt the world."

For better or for worse, the rural school is gone. It served its purpose. It was expendable, but the memories it left behind will be a long time dying — the memories of those bittersweet schooldays.

Index